THE OXFORD
ILLUSTRATED HISTORY
OF
IRELAND

Roy Foster is Professor of Modern British History at Birkbeck College, University of London. His previous books include *Charles Stewart Parnell: The Man and his Family* (1976), *Lord Randolph Churchill: A Political Life* (1981), and *Modern Ireland, 1600-1972* (1988). He is currently working on the authorized biography of W. B. Yeats, to be published by Oxford University Press.

The six scholars who have contributed to *The Oxford Illustrated History of Ireland* are all distinguished authorities in their field. They are:

Donnchadh Ó Corráin, Professor of Irish History, University College, Cork: *Prehistoric and Early Christian Ireland*

Katharine Simms, Lecturer in Medieval History, Trinity College, Dublin: *The Norman Invasion and the Gaelic Recovery*

Nicholas Canny, Professor of Modern History, University College, Galway: *Early Modern Ireland c. 1500–1700*

R. F. Foster, Professor of Modern British History, Birkbeck College, University of London: *Ascendancy and Union*

David Fitzpatrick, Fellow and Lecturer in Modern History, Trinity College, Dublin: *Ireland Since 1870*

Declan Kiberd, Lecturer in English, University College, Dublin: *Irish Literature and Irish History*

THE OXFORD

ILLUSTRATED

HISTORY OF

IRELAND

EDITED BY
R. F. FOSTER

Oxford   New York
OXFORD UNIVERSITY PRESS

Oxford University Press, Walton Street, Oxford OX2 6DP
Oxford New York
Athens Auckland Bangkok Bombay
Calcutta Cape Town Dar es Salaam Delhi
Florence Hong Kong Istanbul Karachi
Kuala Lumpur Madras Madrid Melbourne
Mexico City Nairobi Paris Singapore
Taipei Tokyo Toronto
and associated companies in
Berlin Ibadan

Oxford is a trade mark of Oxford University Press

First published 1989
First issued as an Oxford University Press paperback 1991
Reprinted 1991, 1992, 1993, 1994 (three times), 1995

British Library Cataloguing in Publication Data
The Oxford illustrated history of Ireland.
1. Ireland, history
I. Foster, R. F. (Robert Fitzroy) 1949-
941.5
ISBN 0-19-285245-0 pbk

Library of Congress Cataloging in Publication Data
The Oxford illustrated history of Ireland.
Includes bibliographical references.
1. Ireland—History.   2. Ireland—History—Pictorial
works.   I. Foster, R. F. (Robert Fitzroy), 1949-
DA910.094   1989   941.5   89-16168
ISBN 0-19-285245-0 pbk

Printed in Great Britain
on acid-free paper by
Butler & Tanner Ltd
Frome, Somerset

EDITOR'S FOREWORD

ONE of the marks of maturity in Irish historical studies has been a growing interest in pinpointing discontinuities rather than ironing out elisions. The oddly Anglocentric view that stressed simple and continuous opposition of Norman and Irish, planter and Gael, landlord and tenant, appears less convincing than a perspective focusing on breaks, paradoxes, contradictions, and ambiguities. Nor do Irish historians conceive their function as the imposition of a seamless and retrospective view over the centuries. Thus a compendium approach to a general history of Ireland is well suited to reflecting recent historiographical developments; and it also highlights certain uncomfortable fragmentations in the evolution of modern Ireland. The jagged edges are coming back into focus.

At the same time, chronology cannot be denied, and some dominant themes inevitably assert themselves. Waves of settlement impose patterns and frontiers, social and cultural as well as physical. Religion retains its political importance. Violence, both imposed and reactive, remains a chilling inheritance. All these elements contribute to the contested question of Irish identity, and the concept of long-term 'colonialism' in the very special Irish case. And in considering these themes, there is a constant preoccupation with the uses of language—adaptations of English as well as survivals of Irish. In its way, the development of language, and therefore of literature, preserves a record of Irish history in itself.

These preoccupations spin connecting threads through this book; though this is by no means to say that a neatly unified 'approach' is discernible overall. The scholars who contribute to it have all marked out new paths in their chosen territories—not necessarily by automatically repudiating traditional views, but by redefining preoccupations and casting a cold eye on ruling pieties. All are specialists in their fields, but all are highly conscious that their findings must be made as accessible to the general reader as the ancient, popular versions.

Given the form of the book, it is dangerous to generalize about the results; but it is worth trying. What emerges is a treatment which stresses an ancient and rooted culture, but also charts the mobility and shifting of Ireland's constituent peoples into fractured and sometimes unexpected patterns. Early Ireland, in Donnchadh Ó Corráin's treatment, is not the communalist paradise conjured up by turn-of-the-century pietists: it is characterized by slavery, famine, epidemics, and pagan backslidings as well as by the Christian mission and the

vi   *Editor's Foreword*

high culture of monastic cities. New emphases show not only an unexpected element of Roman influence, but also incursors like the Vikings becoming more integrated than previously supposed. The confused overlaps of early Irish settlement and cultural exchange are demonstrated. Land, language, and communal identity form battlegrounds from the time of the earliest records. International connections establish themselves early on. The same might be said of Katharine Simms's view of the Norman invasion of Ireland and the Gaelic reaction. Not only is the country integrated into a larger picture; an alteration is traced in the nature of the divisions within Ireland, social, political, national, and eventually religious.

Equally striking is the realism of Irish political leaders, faced with the inexorable shift of emphasis in English intervention 'from acquiring lordship over men to colonizing land'. The word 'colonial' impinges at an early stage; the language itself, in naming people and things, reflects it. At the same time Irish forms, practices, and power-structures continue beneath colonial impositions, and sometimes turn those impositions to native advantage. Here too the political use of language, highlighted by Declan Kiberd, is a dominant theme.

Nicholas Canny's view of early modern Ireland also indicates as much; it is marked by the movement and disruption entailed by new waves of colonization in the sixteenth and seventeenth centuries, and the alterations of every kind of frontier within the island. He also emphasizes the European parallels with Irish society and Irish history—too often seen, to its detriment, as an offshore island falling short of imposed British standards. Most striking of all is the dissonance between the government's perception of how Ireland should be administered, and the intractable realities on the ground, where the law meant different things to different people.

The ensuing chapters sustain these preoccupations. The gap between what the theorists of the Union, or mid-nineteenth-century modernizers, expected Ireland to become, and what actually happened, is delineated by David Fitzpatrick, in terms of implicitly revolutionary legislation as well as allegedly revolutionary organizations. He also follows through yet another kind of demographic alteration, the establishment of an Ireland overseas through emigration— perhaps the fundamental social fact of modern Irish history.

Culturally and in a sense politically, the strongest pattern is also one laid down initially in the early modern period and repeatedly demonstrated in the following era: the creation of a confessional identity (or more accurately, several confessional identities). Ulster Presbyterianism from the eighteenth century, no less than the established church in its day of 'Ascendancy', and *a fortiori* O'Connell's Catholic nation mobilized in the early nineteenth century, embody powerful and competing political cultures. The final chapters chart the conflicts between them. They also carry through an injunction which repeatedly occurs from the beginning of the book: the necessity to observe an astringent approach to consciously self-validating 'records', and the whole highly politicized edifice of Irish historiography through the ages.

From a very early period, a powerful idea of national culture and identity has been marketed by one interest or another—often defined, at least implicitly, against another element within the fragmented Irish polity, and asserting a rival and superior legitimacy. These impositions distract from some of the fruitful ambiguities and paradoxes pointed out in this book, such as, for instance, the strange prevalence of nineteenth-century Victorian norms in several areas of twentieth-century Irish life. Such interpretations have often evaded the uncomfortable fact of the legitimization, and even sanctification, of violence in Irish history. And they ignore the intense variations in agriculture, prosperity, political affiliation, and much else, over a very small area. As a French observer in the early nineteenth century noted, 'the Irish themselves, from different parts of the kingdom, are very different. It is difficult to account for this surprising localization. One would think, on so small an island, an Irishman would be an Irishman: yet it is not so.'

In demonstrating these kind of differences as well as the persistence of certain themes in an island whose terrain is nearly as complex as its historical inheritance, visual illustration is essential. Maps of one kind or another are a beginning. What this book has attempted to assemble is far more ambitious. An illumination in the margin of a charter, the achievements of medieval artists or Georgian architects, the panoply of a seventeenth-century countess's funeral procession, the iconography of 'No Surrender' or 'Erin Go Brágh', the romantic portraits of national heroes and heroines on a banner or a banknote, provide a vivid synthesis of rich traditions. Most of all, perhaps, the landscape itself is evidence of a historical palimpsest, whether viewed from the air or the ground. The shape of fields, the positioning of ringforts, castles, and cottages, the style of architecture, the planning of estate villages, the archaeological excavations in Dublin's threatened centre, the landscape of the west with its omnipresent rocks and scattered cabins, provide powerful validation of the points made throughout. Such evidence also brings sharply home the encompassing context of the conflicts, settlements, discontinuities, and unities which are brought together in this book. Irish history, as illustrated here, may not be as neatly encapsulated as in P. S. O'Hegarty's classic account of *Ireland Under the Union*: 'the story of a people coming out of captivity, out of the underground, finding every artery of national life in the possession of the enemy, recovering them one by one, and coming out at last into the full blaze of the sun.' But in many ways it appears both more challenging and a great deal more interesting for that.

R. F. FOSTER

Dublin, June 1988

ACKNOWLEDGEMENTS

THE publishers and editor are grateful to Sandra Assersohn, the picture researcher, and Susan le Roux, for their great assistance with the design and selection of the illustrations; to Edwin Pritchard who copy-edited the text; and to John Vickers, who compiled the index.

CONTENTS

LIST OF COLOUR PLATES

LIST OF MAPS

THE OXFORD

ILLUSTRATED

HISTORY OF

IRELAND

1

Prehistoric and Early Christian Ireland

DONNCHADH Ó CORRÁIN

Celtic Ireland: The Earliest Accounts

THE fitful dawn of Irish history is illuminated by the works of the classical writers. Festus Rufus Avienus, in his *Ora maritima*, based on a Greek original of the early sixth century BC, calls Ireland *Insula sacra*, 'holy island': its inhabitants are *gens hiernorum*, which may mean 'the race of the Érainn'. The name of the island in Greek is *Ierne*, and it is likely that Avienus' record means that Ireland was then known as *Ériu* (modern Irish *Éire*) in one form or another. If we were certain that *Ériu* was Celtic (and we are not), this would be good evidence for dominant Celts in Ireland at this period. In fact, scholars are not at all sure when Ireland was conquered by the Celts, but many would agree that the Celtic conquest or conquests (for there may have been a number of them) took place during the second half of the first millennium BC. Pytheas, writing in the late fourth century BC, refers to the British Isles as 'the Pretanic islands'—and this term is certainly Celtic (it comes from *Priteni*, and gives Welsh *Prydain* 'Britain'). The name is likely to have reached Pytheas from the Gauls.

Poseidonios, the Stoic philosopher and historian, writing before 70 BC (his original is lost but substantial passages survive in the works of Diodorus Siculus, Strabo, Athenaeus, and, somewhat edited, in Caesar), has a detailed account of the continental Celts, and historians have been all too ready to apply what he says to the early Celtic inhabitants of Ireland. True enough, the threefold division of society, and the institutions of druids, bardic praise-poetry, and clientship (described by Polybius for the Continental Celts) are known in early Ireland and such Celtic customs as head-hunting, fighting with two-horse chariots, and honouring the greatest warrior present with the 'hero's portion' (the best joint) at feasts occur in early Irish literature. However, much else of what Polybius says applies only to the Celts of Gaul—their preference for oligarchy rather than kingship, for example. It must be remembered, too, that Ireland had highly developed and impressive cultures in the Neolithic and Bronze Age, and the incoming Celts, who were never more than a dominant minority amongst a

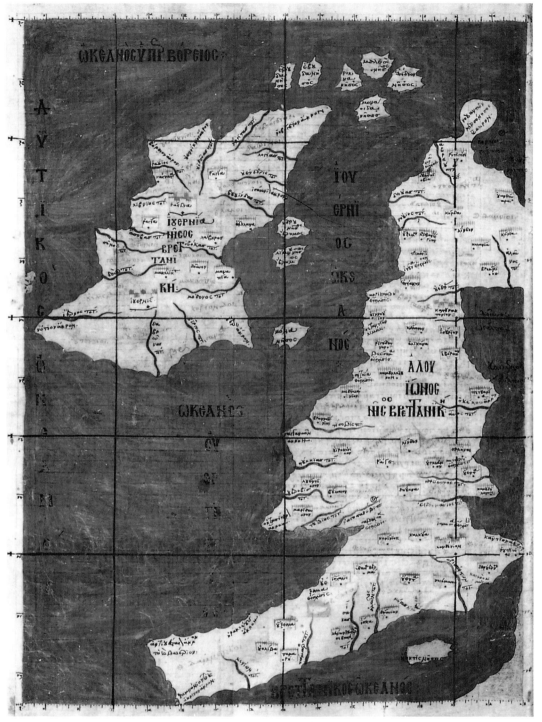

PTOLEMY'S MAP OF IRELAND. Ptolemy's information may derive from Philemon the Geographer (*fl. c.* AD 5–60), through Marinus of Tyre. His knowledge of the north may come ultimately from Agricola's activity in northern Britain.

non-Celtic and non-Indo-European majority, were heavily influenced by the societies which they found before them in Ireland. This is clear in a number of ways. The Irish language is an indigenous realization of Celtic, heavily influenced by the pre-Celtic languages spoken in Ireland and containing an unknown number of words (personal and population names among them) borrowed from these languages. And it may be useful to note here that Brittonic (or the British form of Celtic) was spoken in early Ireland as well as Goidelic, the ordinary Irish form of Celtic. We do not know what other languages were spoken in prehistoric Ireland, though some scholars attempt to make educated guesses.

Early Irish mythological writings link the great Neolithic and Bronze Age sites with the ancient gods and regard them as cult centres of great importance—displaying a continuity of cult as well as of occupation. The best example is Tara, symbolic site of the overkingship of Ireland, which was a major cult centre long before the coming of the Celts. And it is probable that much of what is regarded as Indo-European myth and cult (for example, the sacred marriage of king and goddess, and the linking of fertility with the reign of the good king) is in reality a much older inheritance from the Neolithic agriculturalists and their metal-using successors.

The Roman occupation of Britain stopped short at the Scottish Highlands, and did not extend to Ireland. In the course of his campaign in southern Scotland, when he established forts along the Forth–Clyde isthmus, Agricola looked at the clearly visible coast of Ireland, but postponed any ambition he may have had to conquer it. Tacitus tells us that Agricola 'saw that Ireland . . . conveniently situated for the ports of Gaul might prove a valuable acquisition'. He also relates how an Irish petty king, expelled in the course of a dynastic struggle, was received by Agricola in the hope of making some use of him in the future. Tacitus says: 'I have often heard Agricola declare that a single legion, with a moderate band of auxiliaries, would be enough to finish the conquest of Ireland'—perhaps the understated estimate of the Irish kinglet. But the projected Roman conquest of Ireland went no further.

The most detailed account of pre-Christian Ireland is that of Ptolemy, an Alexandrian Greek geographer who wrote in the middle of the second century AD and who based his account on a lost work of Marinus of Tyre. T. F. O'Rahilly has argued vigorously that Ptolemy's account of Ireland is much earlier than that of Britain and is based on a lost work of the Greek traveller, Pytheas, dated to *c*.325 BC, but his arguments are not convincing and it seems wiser to treat Ptolemy's account as referring to AD 100 or thereabouts. O'Rahilly noted that there were no traces of Goidelic in the names listed by Ptolemy, but this is not surprising: the most likely source of information (and that indirectly) is British sailors working into Irish ports—and these would have spoken Brittonic and reported peoples and places in their own dialect. Because Ireland lay outside the Roman empire, and was far less familiar than Britain, information was harder to get and the chances of inaccuracy and corruption were much greater. In these circumstances, it is pleasantly surprising that quite a number of rivers, kingdoms, and royal centres can be identified with certainty, and a number of others with probability. Of the fifteen river-names, the Boyne (*Buvinda*), the Lee estuary (*Sabrona*, emended from *Dabrona*), and the Shannon (*Senos*) are certain. Ptolemy's *Oboka* seems to be the Liffey estuary and his *Birgos* the Barrow. Howth, Rathlin, Man, and to the north-east of Ireland, the Hebrides, are clearly marked. The west and north-west coasts are poorly recorded. The kingdoms of the east coast, from Antrim to Wexford, are well represented. Ptolemy's *Robogdii* may be a corruption of *Redodii*, in which case they would be identical with the Dál Réti or Dál Riata who later colonized Scotland. The *Darini* must represent a people claiming descent from an ancestor or ancestor-god Dáire, and the Dál Riata, and Dál Fiatach of Down, are amongst the historical dynasties of the area that claimed descent from Dáire. The Voluntii are the Ulaid, still the dominant dynasty in northern Ireland in the very early Christian period. They had their cult centre (but evidently not their capital) at Emain, near Armagh, and Ptolemy's *Isamnion* and Emain are identical. The north-east of Ireland appears conservative: the kingdoms of *c.* AD 100 can be fairly confidently identified in Early Christian records.

Not so the east midlands and the south-east. The Ebdani and the Kauki may have left their traces but their dynasties had disappeared by the Early Christian period. The Manapii (a variant of Gaulish *Menapii*) are identical with the Monaig. Two small communities of Monaig survive into the Early Christian period, one in Co. Down and one near Lough Erne (who eventually gave their name to Fermanagh, *Fir Manach*), and the early Irish genealogists claim that these emigrated from the south of Leinster. The Koriondi (who may be related to the Corionototae of Britain, known from an inscription at Hexham) have left no trace in south Leinster, but are probably identical with the Coraind of the Sligo area. The name also survives in the tribal names Cuirenrige and Dál Cuirind. The Brigantes of Wexford must be identical with Brigantes who occupied a great deal of the north of Britain in the Roman period. Their dynasty seems to have collapsed at an early date (O'Rahilly thought the later Uí Bairrche were their successors), but there are clear memories in the Early Christian records of British peoples in south Leinster. The Iverni, whom Ptolemy shows to be dominant in Munster, are identical with the Érainn, a large group of dynasties which included the Corcu Loígde and which ruled Munster until the rise of the Eóganacht dynasty well into the Early Christian period. Of the remaining dynasties, only the Auteini can be confidently identified. These are the Uaithne of Limerick and Tipperary, who were probably of significance because they dominated the waterway of the Shannon, and Early Christian genealogies record that they occupied lands, too, to the west of the Shannon and stretching northwards.

A sailors' chart and not an ethnographical survey which attempts to be complete, Ptolemy's map gives us an interesting glimpse of Ireland at a very early period—an Ireland where the Connachta (and Uí Néill, from which the later Ó Néill (O'Neill) dynasty derived), Laigin, and Eóganacht have not yet risen to power and where some important later dynasties (the Ulaid and the Érainn, in particular) are seen to be rulers of great kingdoms. Given the rise and fall of dynasties in the Early Christian period, and what may have been a period of considerable changes between the third and the late fifth centuries, the continuity between the Ireland of Ptolemy and that of the early native records is remarkable. What is interesting, too, is the mixed racial and linguistic background of the rulers of Ireland—Britain and Ireland share languages, dominant aristocracies, and whole local populations such as the Cruithin of Ireland and Scotland (where they are known to Latin writers as Picti). This racial mixture is well borne out by later Irish records. For example, the Dumnonii (who were settled in Devon and Cornwall, and in Scotland about Dumbarton) occur in Ireland in the Irish form *Domnainn*. Their name survives in Inber Domnann (Malahide Bay, Co. Dublin). Early genealogical tradition locates them in Leinster, and later in Connacht where their name survives in Tírechán's seventh-century *campus Domnon* 'plain of the Dumnonii', to the west of Killala Bay, Co. Mayo, and *Irrus Domnann*, Erris, in the west of Co. Mayo.

Ireland and Roman Britain

Ireland lay outside the Roman Empire but was soon to be heavily influenced by it. This was inevitable, and came notably in the wake of the decline of Roman power in Britain in the fourth and especially in the fifth century. Roman material found in Ireland falls into two groups: an early one in the first and second centuries, and a late one in the fourth century and after. The objects of the first period reached Ireland in different ways, including a Roman trading base at Stoneyford on the Nore, but may not (in the view of some scholars) indicate well-established trading or raiding. The evidence of the fourth and fifth centuries points to close contact.

As the Roman grip on Britain weakened, the Irish in the west and the Picts in the north (who had long been a threat as raiders) began to attack the province with growing success. Each had fleets and each ravaged the coastline. Britain was devastated in 367 by a simultaneous attack of Irish, Picts, and Saxons, from the west, north, and east. Ammianus Marcellinus, a contemporary, calls it 'a barbarian conspiracy'. It marked one of the many stages of Roman collapse, and Roman imperial rule effectively ended in the very early fifth century.

Concurrently, Irish settlement in Britain began. It has been suggested that some of these settlements may have been formed with Roman encouragement or at least connivance, in the hope of setting up small buffer-states against further raiders. But this is uncertain.

In the fourth and fifth centuries, a large Irish colony, originating from south-east Ireland, was established in south-west Wales (Pembrokeshire, Carmarthenshire, and Cardiganshire (now Dyfed)). The rulers were of the Déisi, the ruling class spoke Irish, and the kingdom was apparently bilingual in the fifth century. There was another, less important, Irish colony in north Wales in Anglesea, Carnarvonshire, and Denbighshire. Here some of the colonists (for we do not know whether others were involved) left their name on the Lleyn peninsula, which derives its name from Laigin, the ruling dynasty of Leinster in the Early Christian period. Their name also survives in that of a village on Nevin Bay, Porth Dinllaen, 'the harbour of the fort of the Leinstermen'. A third colony was established in south-west Britain, in the Cornish peninsula, by colonists called Uí Liatháin. These were probably Érainn and were settled in historic times in the east of Co. Cork. The learned scholar-bishop and king of Cashel, Cormac (d. 908), preserves in his *Glossary* an account of Irish colonization in western Britain: 'The power of the Irish over the Britons was great, and they had divided Britain between them into estates; . . . and the Irish lived as much east of the sea as they did in Ireland, and their dwellings and royal fortresses were made there. Hence is Dind Traduí, . . . that is, the triple rampart of Crimthann, king of Ireland and Britain as far as the English Channel. From this division originated the fort of the sons of Liathán in the land of the Britons of Cornwall. . . . And they were in that control for a long time, even after the coming of St Patrick to Ireland.' Cormac's source is not known, but his account is broadly confirmed elsewhere. As Professor Jackson says, 'it seems a certain fact that, at some time in the late Roman period, Irish colonies from East Munster settled in South Wales, Cornwall and Devon, and from one of them there sprang a line of kings of south-west Wales who were still ruling there in the tenth century'. Less is known of the colony in north Wales: there is no information in Irish sources, but Nennius records how Cunedda and his eight sons drove the Irish out of north Wales in what may have been the middle of the fifth century, though there may have been further struggles before the Irish were finally conquered in this area.

By far the most successful Irish colony in Britain was that of Dál Riata in Scotland: it lasted, and finally laid the basis for the kingdom of Scotland. As we have seen, the Dál Riata or at least the group of dynasties to which they belong are located by Ptolemy in the extreme north-east of Ireland. When and why they crossed over to Scotland is uncertain. Medieval Irish legends which tell that this began in the third or fourth century—or indeed before—are most unlikely to be historical. Other traditions state that Fergus Mór mac Eirc and his brothers established Dál Riata in Scotland and scholars have argued (on the basis of very flimsy evidence, mainly genealogy which is no earlier than the seventh century) that this event took place about the middle or late fifth century. Whatever its beginnings, the Scottish kingdom of Dál Riata was a great success and by the time Columba came on his mission to Iona in 563 the king of Dál Riata was extending his authority over the Picts to the east. In the middle of the ninth century, Dál Riata took control of all Pictland, and Scotland became a united kingdom under Kenneth mac Alpine.

Close relations with Britain, with Roman and latterly Christian culture, brought about dramatic changes in Ireland. It is likely that the products of successful plundering expeditions changed the balance of power amongst dynasties within Ireland, and colonies abroad may have provided the resources for dynastic expansion at home. It has, for example, been suggested (perhaps with some plausibility) that the Eóganacht, who were to take the kingship of Munster from the early Érainn, were colonists returned from Britain. The earliest origin-tales of the Laigin convey an impression of extensive overseas raiding, and a poem on their early kings contains Latin borrowings (*legión* < legio, *trebun* < tribunus, *long* < (navis) longa, *Mercúir* < (dies) Mercurii, *Saturn* < (dies) Saturni) which suggest close and extended contact with a Roman area. Is this the

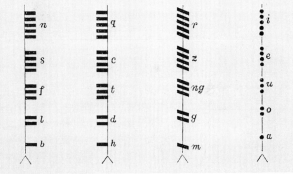

OGHAM STONE from Coolmagort, Co. Kerry. Ogham (scholars do not agree about its origins) is the earliest written Irish, used especially for inscriptions. The sounds which lie behind the Ogham inscriptions shade gradually into those of early manuscript Irish. The 'alphabet' indicates the significance of the range of markings.

underpinning of their powerful kingdom which stretched from the Boyne to the south coast?

Recently, archaeologists have become increasingly aware of the romanization of the material culture of Ireland. This is dated to the fifth century, though the process may have begun in the fourth, and the most obvious source is the late Romano-British culture of western Britain, that of the areas of concentrated Irish raiding and settlement. In this general context, too, we must look for the origins of *Ogham*, the earliest form of written Irish. It is an alphabet of lines and notches cut on the edge of a stone, and it is clearly based on the Latin alphabet. Its origin lies in the contact of Irish and Roman, in Britain or in southern Ireland under Roman influence. Ogham inscriptions written in a very early form of the Irish are found throughout Ireland, but most densely in the south and south-west. Quite a number of them are also found where the Irish settled in Britain: Cornwall, Devon, south Wales, north Wales, and Man. They belong to the fifth, sixth, and seventh centuries and provide solid evidence for the extent and continued Irish character of the colonies in Britain. In Britain, too, the Irish encountered Christianity, and the most famous missionary to the Irish, St Patrick, first saw Ireland as a boy from a comfortable background in western Britain, enslaved by Irish raiders. He was to be one of the many missionaries who brought Ireland more fully into the Roman world and, in consequence of the literacy in Latin introduced by them, into the clearer light of written history.

Christianization

We do not know when the first Christian missionaries began work in Ireland, and it is reasonable to assume that a fairly long time elapsed before Ireland as a whole began to leave evidence of Christian culture. Very likely, Christian missionaries arrived in Ireland first in the late fourth and early fifth centuries— and probably from Gaul where, after the Arian crisis was over, the church was fairly thoroughly organized in the end of the fourth century. Britain and Ireland lay within the prefecture of the Gauls, and the Gaulish church took responsibility for the insular one. The first exact date in the history of the Irish church occurs in the *Chronicle* of the anti-Pelagian, Prosper Tiro, who records under AD 431 the sending of Palladius, probably deacon at Auxerre, as bishop to 'the Irish who believe in Christ'. The context of this mission is the mission of Germanus and some Gaulish clergy to Britain to oppose the Pelagian heresy which had taken root there, and probably in Ireland. Indeed, the phrase 'the Irish who believe in Christ' may mean the orthodox, as opposed to those who had fallen into the Pelagian heresy. In another work, *Contra Collatorem*, which may date to 433 or 434, Prosper remarks about Pope Celestine that he ordained a bishop for the Irish, kept the Roman island (i.e. Britain) orthodox, and made the barbarian island (i.e. Ireland) Christian.

This, of course, is just fine talk: the conversion of the whole of Ireland was a much slower and more complex business. The concentration of historians on the life and writings of St Patrick—not to mention the successful cultivation of his legend from the seventh century, and the central place it has won for itself in the Irish consciousness through the centuries—has tended to distort the story of the conversion and draw away attention from the other missionaries. Yet, in the seventh-century dossier of Patrick, some evidence of other missionaries is preserved, though these are represented as submitting to the claims of Patrick: Sachellus, Cetiacus, Iarnascus, Camelacus (who is associated with Rahan), Auxilius, Iserninus, and others. There are some traces of an older order. The champions of Armagh and its Patrician claims were aware in the early seventh century that churches with the element *domnach* (the Latin *dominicum*) were early and important. And they were right, for this term was going out of use on the Continent from the fifth century. These are the sites of early missionaries in well-settled areas, the equivalent of local parish churches, and appear well represented in the east and south of the country. The *dominicati rhetorici* who held Patrick in low regard, as he himself says in his *Confession*, may have been beneficed, learned, upper-class, and worldly clergy, already well established in the Christian areas.

Ireland is indebted overwhelmingly to Britain for its Christianity, and the most famous of British missionaries is St Patrick. He is generally regarded as the greatest of Ireland's missionaries, but his history presents difficulties at every turn. He left behind two works, his *Confession* and his *Letter to the soldiers of Coroticus*. The first is spiritual biography and justification of his mission, the second a letter of protest against the enslavement of some of his new Irish converts. Neither is intended to provide a life-story or a history of the conversion. We know only a few facts about him and these do not include the date of his birth, that of his mission to Ireland, or that of his death, though it seems reasonable to place his mission in the first half and middle of the fifth century. He was born in western Britain and was the son of a deacon and minor official who had a country estate; he was captured at the age of 16 by Irish raiders and shipped as a slave to Ireland, where he remained, probably in north Connacht, for six years; he escaped, travelled 200 miles, and shipped out of Ireland with a pagan crew; the Irish continued to haunt his thoughts, and he returned to them (perhaps as a bishop, though probably not part of any official mission) to preach the gospel; he worked hard, experienced danger and hardship, and suffered the bitter criticism of his own countrymen, who questioned his fitness for his mission; he won many converts and penetrated into parts of the country where no Christian missionary had gone before; and he asserted, with some considerable emphasis, that he was a bishop. So much is clear from his own writings. All the rest is uncertain, at best. It seems likely that Patrick's memory was cherished in the north-east, particularly in Armagh and its neighbourhood. The expansion of his cult (a carefully crafted undertaking of the clergy of Armagh) took place later when Armagh claimed apostolic precedence and primacy, and it had spread widely, even into Munster, by the late seventh century.

We know little about the organization of the missionary church. It is often said that the early church was ruled by bishops, and some have held that there was a metropolitan structure, but these views rest on doubtful evidence, or none. Christianity in Ireland underwent a long period of complex development, during which the churches came of age in a relatively stable society, undisturbed by barbarian invasions or major conquests. Nor can we be sure when the country as a whole had become Christian. It has, for example, been argued that Diarmait mac Cerbaill, king of Tara in the mid-sixth century, was still a pagan—or at least, a reluctant Christian. And, naturally, a great deal of pagan belief survived into the Middle Ages, and beyond.

Monasticism (and monastic ideas are very much present in St Patrick's writings) made rapid strides in the Irish church of the sixth century, but the great monasteries which sprang up in this period do not claim Patrick or his disciples as their founders. They looked rather to the British church—to Ninian who is the reputed teacher of Finian of Moville, Tigernach of Clones, Enda of Aran; and to St David who is regarded as the teacher of Máedóc of Ferns, Scuithín of Slievemargy, and others. Columba, Ciarán of Clonmacnoise, Brendan of Clonfert, Comgall of Bangor, and Finian of Clonard are amongst the great leaders of the monastic movement. Some southern monastic founders are traditionally considered pre-Patrician, or at least independent of the Patrician mission, but the evidence which supports this claim is dubious: Ailbe, founder of Emly and patron of the Eóganacht; Declan, founder of Ardmore and patron of the Déisi; and Ciarán the Elder, founder of Seirkieran. Originally retreats from the world, places of asceticism, and stricter discipline, the monasteries soon attracted the patronage of the rich and powerful, and themselves became influential institutions on many levels. These great self-governing monastic churches, each with its own rule, its own organization, and its own estates, became in time the bearers of a rich and varied literary and artistic culture, and provided the patronage and the economic support necessary for the cultivation of high art.

Law, Church, and Society

The extensive writings, especially the law tracts in Latin and the vernacular, of the seventh and the early eighth centuries, allow us to form a detailed picture of Irish society and, in particular, of the Irish churches.

The churchmen brought with them into Ireland much of the learning of late antiquity, and the Irish schools of the late sixth and seventh centuries achieved a

CRUCIFIXION PLAQUE, St John's, Rinnangan, Co. Roscommon. This fine gilt-bronze crucifixion plaque, which dates from the late seventh century and may have originally decorated a book-cover, makes the clothed crucified Christ the dominant figure, between the lance-bearer and the sponge-bearer on the lower plane and the angels on the upper. The whole is heavily decorated in the ultimate La Tène style.

high level of scholarship. The church scholars, grammarians (of Latin and Irish), poets, canonists, lawyers, and historians formed a single mandarin caste whose writings, in Latin and in Irish, are the products of a single, if broad-based and broad-minded, ecclesiastical culture. That is not to say that all poets and lawyers became clerics, but rather that these disciplines were fitted into the ecclesiastical order of things and literate ecclesiastics became the masters of the professions. These scholars were well equipped. They had an extensive library of the church Fathers. For example, the text known as *De mirabilibus sacrae scripturae* ('Of the wonders of Holy Scripture'), written in Ireland in 655, draws on Ambrose, Augustine, Basil of Caesarea, Eugippius, Gregory the Great, Jerome, John Cassian, Orosius, Philippus Presbyter, Rufinus, Tertullian, and Victorius of Aquitaine. To take another example, Cummian, in his Paschal Letter, quotes Cyprian, Origen, Jerome, Augustine, Ambrosiaster, Dionysius Exiguus, Ps.-Anatolius of Laodicea, Ps.-Cyril of Alexandria and it is clear that he has a good computistics library. They also possessed a great deal of legal and para-legal material: decisions of councils and synods, papal rulings, and such texts as *Statuta ecclesiae antiqua*—many of them reflecting the legal vocabulary and concepts of late Antiquity. Above all, they had the Bible and a rich library of biblical commentary, to which they added significantly and which they used as a primary source for law and legal ideas. Armed with this formidable learning, they set about compiling law, in Latin and the vernacular, for church and secular society.

In Latin, the principal surviving witness to their work is the *Collectio canonum hibernensis* (of *c.* AD 700–50). This wide-ranging systematic treatise deals with the orders of the church, jurisdictions, legal procedures, property (and especially church property), inheritance and bequests, government, sanctuary, theft, deposits, marriage, and many other topics. This is a very considerable achievement, and it had a great deal of influence in Ireland and outside it, for the text was soon disseminated widely in western Europe.

When they turned to consider the law governing secular society in general they faced an even more complex problem: they knew well that some of the customs of secular society were inherited from the non-Christian past, yet the Bible and its exposition by the church authorities was the law of the Christian. How was this paradox to be resolved? By regarding their pre-Christian past as the Old Testament of their race in which their ancestors were governed by the law of nature in St Paul's sense of the term, and by developing the teaching that St Patrick had thoroughly cleansed their inherited law:

There are many things in the law of nature which the law of the letter did not reach . . . What did not conflict with the Word of God in the law of the letter or with the conscience of the faithful has been fastened in the canon of the judges by the church and the poets. The whole of the law of nature was right save for the Faith and its entitlement, and the harmony of church and secular community, and the entitlement of each from the other and the due of each to the other, for the secular community has an entitlement in the church, and the church in the secular community.

They leave us in no doubt, however, of the superiority of church law. An Old Irish legal poem states:

The law of the church is as a sea compared with streams, the law of the church is most wonderful law . . . It is known that *fénechas* [inherited native law] is vain in comparison with the words of God, where neither man is defrauded nor God neglected, as a result of which prosperity increases . . . the law of the church is founded on rocks of truth . . ., it speaks for all conditions of persons . . . every grade, every kind . . . It binds, it is not bound; it restrains, it is not restrained; it is appealed to, it does not appeal; it overswears all, it is not oversworn; each one is ignoble compared to it, it is noble compared to all; it is a sea compared with streams.

There is evidence that the compilers of the vernacular laws drew heavily on the Old Testament in regard to the foundations of law and for rules governing theft, deposits, guilt by association, and tithes. In regard to the theft of livestock, for example, they use Exodus 22: 1–4, but they modified the biblical rule to include economically important animals like the horse and pig, which the Bible omits. And this kind of adaptation is typical of their methods. The vernacular laws are not, then, ancient custom written down by a backward-looking secular legal caste which eventually became Christian and literate, but the carefully considered product of learned Christian jurists, drawing on native and foreign legal materials in order to set out the law for a Christian society. These legal sources are our best guide to the organization of the churches and secular society in the seventh and eighth centuries.

The older view was that a church ruled by bishops, whose dioceses corresponded to the local petty kingdoms (*túatha*), was established by the missionaries, and that this church was overwhelmed by the monastic movement, which established great federations of monastic churches, took over the earlier organization, and put the abbot in the place of the bishop as ruler of the church.

In reality, church organization and government were a good deal more complex. The monastic movement led to the establishment of great monasteries (Kildare, Cork, Clonard, Emly, Clonmacnoise, etc.), but one should think of these as great ecclesiastical centres, *civitates* or 'cities' (as they called themselves). These were well integrated into the upper ranks of society, ruled mostly by aristocrats, rich and politically influential, and important centres of economic activity. Here there were a variety of clerics and churches, and a bishop and priests as well as monks (who were not usually in orders), nuns, virgins, holy widows, the devout married laity, monastic tenants, artisans, and hangers-on of all kinds (including some very nasty ones).

Some of the greatest monastic centres (for example, Kildare, Emly) were the

TWO FILIGREE PANELS FROM THE DERRYNAFLAN PATEN. The Derrynaflan hoard—a silver chalice, silver paten, paten-stand, and bronze strainer ladle—was discovered in 1980 at an early church site to the north of Cashel, Co. Tipperary. The paten displays most of the techniques of fine Irish metal-working of the eighth century. Amongst the best work are twenty-four delicate filigree panels executed with beaded wire. The designs are mainly anthropomorphic and zoomorphic, such as the two kneeling beasts, and four snakes—their heads in the corners—shown here.

regular residences of the provincial king. In the case of Kildare, in the early ninth century, the king of Leinster lived there when his brother was abbot and his sister abbess. The king of the northern Uí Néill had a house in Armagh, though he did not usually live there. These kings must have brought in a more motley bunch of officers and soldiers, king's officials, courtiers, royal mistresses, dependent nobles, and favourites. Several of these greater monastic establishments had vast estates in land, some at a very great distance. Clonard was a landlord in Munster, Armagh in Meath and Munster, and Kildare (which declared that it was the seat of a metropolitan) evidently had extensive and distant estates for it claimed the right of sanctuary for 'all its church lands throughout the whole of Ireland' in the seventh century. Some of these towns were ruled by worldly and wealthy abbots, who married wives from the upper aristocracy, led the lives of princes, and were the friends and confidants of the greatest men in the land. In the arts—and above all, in metal-work, illumination, and calligraphy—the seventh, eighth, and ninth centuries were periods of great flowering. These monastic towns had the resources to maintain workshops and craftsmen of a high order, had a taste for opulence that was probably part of their worldliness, and were the patrons of an art distinguished by its taste and delicacy. In the rather high-flown words of Dr Françoise Henry:

The sumptuous appearance of metal objects must have contributed a great deal to brighten eighth-century churches. Chalices and book-covers on the altar glittered with silver and gold ornament; everywhere shone the crisp gilding and studs on croziers, shrines and censers. The lamps were resplendent with multi-coloured enamels. On the vestments of the priests and probably on the cloaks of the laity penannular brooches sparkled in the light. Seldom has the art of the goldsmith and the bronzer attained such dazzling brilliance and such technical virtuosity.

Iona and Armagh were the two greatest ecclesiastical power-centres in the Irish world. Iona, the foundation of Columba, had dependent churches in Ireland and in Scotland. Evidently, Iona kept its Scottish foundations on a tight rein. Its Irish monasteries included such major foundations as Durrow, Derry, and (from 807) Kells, together with very many lesser monastic properties. Adomnán (d. 704), its ninth abbot, was the greatest Insular churchman of his age, the friend and cousin of the most powerful rulers in Northumbria and Ireland. He was a scholarly hagiographer who wrote the Life of his founder, and a very able church politician who did much to add to the influence of Iona. In 697—on the centenary of the death of Columba—he held a great synod of bishops, abbots, and kings at Birr and promulgated his 'Law of the innocents', a law excluding women and children from battle, and protecting women from violence. Later, Adomnán was regarded as a saint, second only to Columba in the devotions of the Iona community.

Armagh claimed Patrick as its founder. It linked itself to the rising dynasty of Uí Néill and came into great prominence in the seventh century when its clergy—

THE EMLY SHRINE. This house-shaped reliquary, of yew with applied silver, gold cloisonné, gilt-bronze, and enamel, dates probably from the late eighth century.

notably in the *Liber angeli*, bishop Tírechán's *Collectanea*, and Muirchú's *Vita Patricii*—claimed that as Patrick's church it was the primatial church of all Ireland with appellate jurisdiction over the whole island. It was not a monastic church. In the seventh century, it was ruled by a bishop who claimed to be metropolitan of a province. Armagh claimed jurisdiction of a very large number of churches in northern Ireland and elsewhere, and was able to enforce its claims very effectively. Its primacy was generally admitted everywhere by the end of the seventh century, and its head took precedence over all the clergy of Ireland.

Despite Armagh's primacy, there is no evidence that the Irish church was subject to a hierarchy or a canonically recognized metropolitan. Jurisdiction was distributed and complicated. The individual churches or federations of churches enjoyed a high degree of independence. The monastic movement had very great

BEGINNING OF ST PATRICK'S *CONFESSION*. Book of Armagh, folio 22ʳ. The Book of Armagh, which contains the dossier of St Patrick (as well as New Testament texts and a copy of the Life of St Martin), was commissioned by Torbach, abbot of Armagh in 807, and executed by Fermdomnach, master of the Armagh scriptorium, and two other scribes.

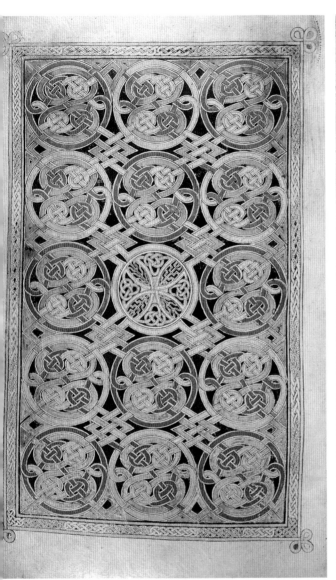

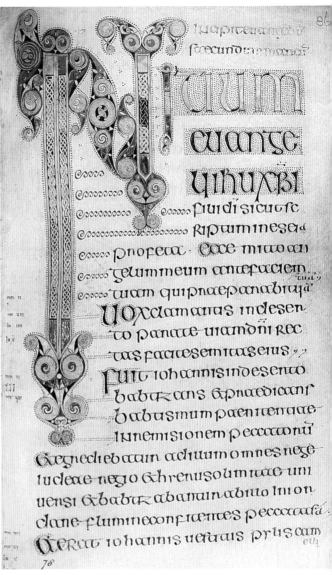

THE BOOK OF DURROW, folios 85ᵛ and 86ʳ. Generally dated to the second half of the seventh century, this Gospel manuscript contains 248 folios in Irish majuscule. The illuminations—spirals, trumpet-patterns, ribbon and animal interlace—draw on a wide repertoire from La Tène, the Mediterranean, and the Germanic world.

THE ARDAGH CHALICE, a large chalice made of silver and bronze, ornamented with gold filigree, blue and red glass studs, and rock crystal, found at Ardagh, Co. Limerick, with other church treasure in 1868. It is the finest piece of Irish metalwork of the eighth century.

influence, but it did not displace the secular bishops. The bishops, often operating from a monastic base, controlled a very significant part of church life in the seventh, eighth, and later centuries. And in the laws, a celibate bishop held the highest status of all clerics.

One must distinguish between economic control and episcopal jurisdiction. There were many kinds of churches: some were free, that is, not attached to a monastery or bound by any obligations to the original owner or donor of the land, whether king or noble; others were unfree, that is, under royal control and taxation, owned by another powerful church and owing its owner taxes, or held in ordinary hereditary control by an aristocratic family (founder, donor, or landlord). Very many churches and their estates were owned by great hereditary church families, who were the cadet branches of royal families. On occasion, we can trace their continuous occupation of a church over several centuries. This was true of Armagh, Cork, Trim, Killaloe, and very many other churches, and the medieval genealogies record the names of hundreds of church families. The offices of owner and abbot were sometimes combined, and more frequently in the ninth century and later.

Small churches, free and unfree, were common, perhaps roughly as numerous as parish churches are today. At the bottom end of the scale, a church could simply be a family estate, with a church-building and little graveyard, and the services of a priest, when available; at the top, it could be a great monastery with a large number of dependent estate churches, and great revenues from land, stock, monastic tenants, and church offerings and alms. Over these different kinds of churches the bishop ruled as pastor. As the *Riaghail Phátraic* (probably eighth century) states: 'There shall be a chief bishop of each *túath* to ordain their clergy, to consecrate their churches, to be confessor to rulers and superiors, and to sanctify and bless their children after baptism.' The bishop oversaw the work of the clergy, and ensured that churches, altars, and burial-grounds were kept in proper order, and he could inflict penalties on those church superiors who did not carry out his instructions.

The Irish clergy thought of the relationship between church and people as a contract, and each side had obligations. The church provided religious rites and services—preaching, baptism, communion, requiems, mass on Sundays and on the chief festival days. In return, the people paid the church its dues and maintained the clergy. These dues included first fruits, firstlings, tithes, and burial payments, but it is doubtful whether the clergy always received these payments. And frequently, there were shortages of priests.

The law tracts show that Irish society was divided into classes: kings, lords, and commons. Our sources are intensely aristocratic in attitude—not surprisingly, because the clerical scholars who produced them came mostly from noble backgrounds themselves. The distinction between lords and commons, at least at the

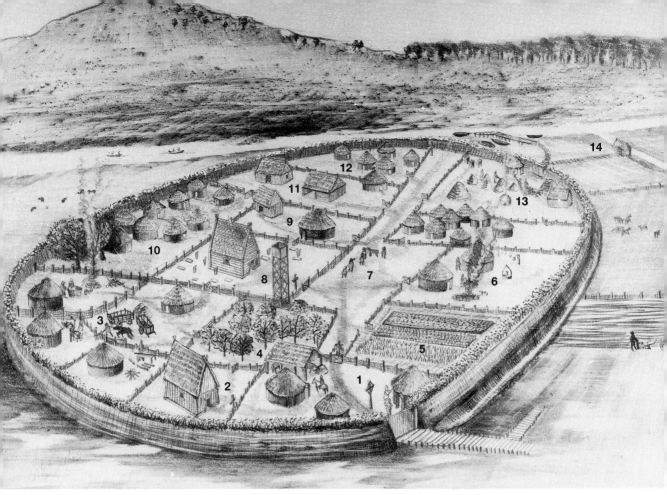

A LARGE EIGHTH-CENTURY MONASTERY. Hypothetical reconstruction drawing (by Robin Carson) with numbered guide to the key. The enclosure is a ditch and bank, topped with a thorn hedge. 1. Porter's house, guest-houses, and stable. 2. The north church, used by visitors. 3. Craft-area: workshops for carpenter, smith, and bronze-worker. 4. Orchard (screens off guests from the main church). 5. Vegetable garden. 6. Kitchen and refectory, with well and *fulacht fiadh* for heating water and boiling food. 7. Open space in front of church (*plateia*). 8. Principal church with graveyard and wooden belfry/look-out tower. 9. Abbot's house and writing hut. 10. Monks' houses. 11. Communal building for monks' use: *magna domus*, open-sided building for good light, and another *domus*. 12. More houses for monks, or monastic tenants (*manaig*). 13. Agricultural area with barn, corn-drying kiln, bee-hives, and 'back door' to mill. 14. Water-mill. Bog in the foreground, arable and pasture land to sides, and beyond the river rough ground, woodland, and mountain. In the ninth and tenth centuries, some monasteries became much more extensive.

borderline between the two classes, was not watertight: it was possible for a family to become noble over three generations by amassing wealth and dependents—to become squireens, in fact—but the traffic was usually the other way. What really distinguished the lord from the commoner, apart from wealth, was having clients, men bound to him by well-defined relationships of dependence.

The commoners (called by the lawyers *grád Fhéne*) were freemen, usually owners of their own land and having full rights at law. One of their typical representatives was the *bóaire*, 'cowman', who was roughly the equivalent of the Anglo-Saxon churl, a comfortable and independent farmer. The law tract *Críth Gablach* (of about AD 700) has a classic description of the better-off man of this class:

There are always two vessels in his house, a vessel of milk and a vessel of ale. He is a man of three snouts: the snout of a rooting hog which banishes shame at all times, the snout of a bacon pig on the hook, and the snout of plough under the sod, so that he is able to receive king or bishop or scholar or judge from the road, against the arrival of every party of guests. He is a man who has three sacks in his house always for each season: a sack of malt, a sack of sea-salt for the salting up of one of his beasts, and a sack of charcoal for iron-working. He has seven houses: a corn-kiln, a barn (his share in a mill so that it grinds for him), a dwelling-house of 27 feet, a lean-to of 17 feet, a pigsty, a calf-fold and a sheep-fold. He has twenty cows, two bulls, six oxen, twenty pigs, twenty sheep, four farmyard hogs, two sows, a riding horse with enamelled bridle, and sixteen sacks of seed-corn in the ground. He has a bronze caldron into which a hog fits. He has parkland in which there are always sheep, without need to change ground. He and his wife have four outfits. His wife is the daughter of his equal, wedded in lawful matrimony.

Lower down there were others, still freemen but with lesser assets. And beneath them again were the cottiers and landless men (*bothach, fuidir*), and lastly the hereditary serfs (*senchléithe*), bound to the soil, part of their lord's estate. The lawyers subdivided these classes, and display a very fine awareness of differences in status, precisely because status was of vital importance in the legal system. A man's legal rights and powers, and the compensations to which he was entitled for wrongs done him, were measured in terms of his status. Kicking a bishop was a good deal more expensive than kicking a peasant, as an early Latin law tract explains, and outraging a king was an offence for which few commoners could hope to be able to pay the compensation.

Clientship (*célsine*) was the institution which bound together lord and man in a relationship which had benefits for both, but was more favourable to the lord. The lord granted the client (*céle*, literally 'companion') a fief (very often of cattle but sometimes of other goods, including land) and, in return, the client bound himself to make specific payments to the lord. The lord undertook to defend the client and his rights against the aggression of others.

There were two types of clientship, free or noble clientship (*sóerrath*) and base clientship (*gíallnae*). Both, of course, were contracts entered into with nobles by freemen. They differed in origin and purpose. Free clientship was established by formal homage, and the client bound himself to the service of his lord, and this included military service. Clients of this kind were often noblemen themselves. This was originally the institution by which ambitious lords (and often royals) built up a military following of young aristocrats and freemen, and set out on military adventuring and raiding—on occasion, to prove that they were fit to succeed to the kingship. And the clients took a share in the lord's plunder. The payments made by this kind of client are very heavy, and when we meet this type of clientship in the law tracts, it has already become a way of advancing loans of stock at very high rates of interest.

Base clientship was like the medieval manor—it provided the economic basis of lordship and kept the aristocrats in style. First, the lord made the client a payment equal to his status at law (a substantial sum); then he advanced to the client a fief, usually milking cows but it could also be land, other stock, oxen, or farm implements. In theory, at least, the size of the fief corresponded to the status of the client: poor men could not handle big fiefs and the payments that went with them. The advantages for the client were that his lord protected him and in the case of wrongs done him (for example, personal injury and theft) helped him to pursue his rights, but he took a share of the compensation. The fief, which was really a way of leasing stock and profit-sharing on the produce,

THE TROUBLES OF CLIENTSHIP, from the Book of Kells, folio 253ᵛ (detail). This lively cartoon-like drawing of two men pulling each other's beards whilst another crouches beneath them in hiding, illustrates the gospel text (Luke 16: 13): *Nemo seruus potest duobus dominis seruire* ('No man can serve two masters'). In Irish law, a base client (who was probably often short of cattle) could take a second, or even a third lord—and this led to conflicting loyalties and duties. Here the Kells painter may be illustrating the gospel from his everyday experience of clientship.

provided the client, who was always short of stock (due to his own consumption, natural wastage, renders, debt payments, and, frequently, theft) with milking cows, at a fairly reasonable rate of interest. And the lord came much better out of the deal. Clients gained him status and he was guaranteed a supply of food and certain other services. For example, the annual return on a fief of twenty-four dairy cows, the normal fief of the *bóaire*, is:

one dairy cow, a calf valued at a sack of wheat for summer roasting, a calf valued at four sacks suitable for cooking in summer, half the dripping of a year-old bull calf, a caldron of new milk for cooking as sweet cheese with butter, a vessel of ripe cream, 20 loaves of bread, a slab of butter eight inches wide and four inches thick, two fistfuls of Welsh onions and two of leeks as summer render, a bacon flitch thirty-six inches long and with two fingers of lean as winter render, and a calf valued at two sacks, for roasting.

Besides, the lord, accompanied by four or so companions, was entitled to one night's feasting in the house of his client, at some date between New Year and Shrove, and this was a major expense for the client. The lord was entitled to labour services as well: for building, and in spring and autumn for sowing and harvesting.

Slavery was fairly extensive in early Ireland and it became common again when Viking traders of the ninth, tenth, and eleventh centuries provided a new supply of slaves. Some were prisoners of war, others were the children of the poor sold into slavery in times of famine, while yet others were brought in from abroad. Unwanted children dumped on the church, prisoners condemned to death but released to the church, and perhaps other wretches, provided a servile population within the great monasteries.

The family rather than the individual was the legal unit. This was the case in regard to the ownership of property, inheritance, and liabilities. The legal family was not the conjugal family (father, mother, and children) but an extended family or kinship group called the *derbfhine*, 'certain family'. The *derbfhine* consisted of the descendants in the male line only of a common great-grandfather. If one looks outwards and backwards from one's own place in the group, it extends (in the male line only) out to one's second cousins, and backwards to one's great-grandfather.

Marriage was unstable. Divorce and remarriage were common, and polygamy was practised by the upper classes. This was not so much the survival of pagan customs—though there was an element of that—as the continuation in Ireland of practices which went back to early missionary days, to Vulgar Roman law, and to pre-Augustinian attitudes to marriage. The churchmen made strenuous efforts to regularize marriage practices, but without much effect, amongst nobility and commoners. Polygamy, which assured heirs and provided the great lineages with plenty of manpower, remained until the end of the Middle Ages, to shock reformers and outside observers alike.

In a sense, the Irish were doing formally what other aristocracies did inform-ally, but there were major social effects: the families of royals and great nobles multiplied rapidly, slipped gradually downwards in society, and ultimately dis-placed the commoner freeholders. As Mac Firbhisigh put it: 'It is a usual thing in the case of great princes, when their children and their families multiply, that their clients and followers are squeezed out, wither away and are wasted.'

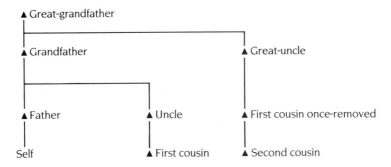

THE *DERBFHINE* AND *GELFHINE*. The triangles represent males. The children of females of the family belong to her husband's kindred. For legal purposes the *derbfhine* is one's family. It came into play only on very major occasions, such as the division of an inheritance, the repartition of the family's assets, or the payment of a major liability incurred by the group. Normally, however, one lived one's life with a narrower family group, the *gelfhine*, the descendants in the male line of a common grandfather.

There was a slow, steady turnover in the ownership of the land, and a constant replacement of the lower orders of society from above.

Early Ireland had a population of between half a million and a million people—it fluctuated because of recurrent plagues and famines—and these were sup-ported by a mixed farming economy. Large expanses of deciduous forest dom-inated the landscape and great bogs covered large areas of the country, especially in the midlands and in the western uplands. Against these, the impact of man must have appeared small, and in very many areas marginal. The borders of many kingdoms were wilderness, mountains, moorland, and forest—the place of the outlaw, the refuge of the hermit fleeing society. In the rich lowlands and river valleys, there were large monastic towns like Trim and Lismore, and dense farming settlement. The remains of some 60,000 ringforts dot the landscape (or did so until recently) and many more have been destroyed by centuries of land use. These were the farmsteads of the well-to-do in Early Christian Ireland: the undefended huts of the cottier and the serf have left little trace.

CASHEL AND EARLY FIELDS, near Corrofin, Co. Clare. These stone cashels (or ring-enclosures), set among irregularly shaped large fields walled with stone, occur on a limestone hillside. The foundations of houses are visible within the three cashels, and there are some isolated hut sites (probably of herdsmen) among the fields. These remains probably date from the Early Christian period.

The ring-enclosure, whether dry stone wall or earthen ditch-and-dyke, protected the farm-house and farm-buildings, with the exception of mills (which only the rich had) and corn-kilns, which were a fire-hazard. The milking yard also lay outside, and in some cases houses, which may have been for servants. Farmers' houses were between 19 and 27 feet in diameter, and more than one conjugal family frequently lived within one enclosure. The land which was tilled lay in fenced fields near the farmyard. In many cases, land was farmed in strips (divided by shallow ditches) by groups of kinsmen. Beyond lay the fenced pastures, some of which were reserved for winter grazing because the Irish made no hay. Very often, farmers had commonage in bog, upland, and woodland. Cows were grazed in summer on mountain and moorland, tended by women, and stores of dairy products were laid up for the winter. Milk and dairy products were very important and milk kept its primacy in the Irish diet until after the end of the Middle Ages. The summer plenty was preserved as heavily salted butter and cheese of many different kinds. As excavation shows, the upper classes ate a great deal of meat—mostly beef (and veal), but between 10 per cent and 20 per cent of the meat eaten was pork and bacon. Carcasses of pork and sides of bacon formed a normal part of the client's payment to his lord. Sheep were raised principally for their wool, but also for meat and milk—sheep provided a good deal of the milk and butter of the poorer classes.

Though dairying was very important, grain-growing was vital, too. Ploughing was done in March with yokes of four or six oxen drawing a heavy unwheeled plough, but only the well-off owned a full plough and ploughing-team. (The spade, a wooden implement with an iron sheath, was used over large areas, and by the poor everywhere.) Corn was grown on narrow ridges, and cut with a reaping-hook. In order of importance, the grains grown were oats, barley, wheat, and rye. Oats were eaten as porridge and gruel, and provided the bread of the masses in Ireland down to the nineteenth century. Barley was malted for ale-making and also used to make coarse bread. Wheaten bread was a luxury: the food of kings and nobles, as we learn from the sagas. Corn was threshed with the flail or beating-stick and artificially dried in kilns before milling because of Ireland's high rainfall. Grain was stored in straw-rope granaries, pits, and, perhaps in troubled times, in souterrains with other valuables—burning corn in the ear or in storage was a common act of war. Corn was ground by quern or in horizontal water-mills, which were commonly the property of monasteries and noblemen. Vegetables were grown on a small scale—some members of the onion family (Welsh onions, leeks, chives, and probably garlic), parsley, some tap-roots (probably including parsnips), and kale. Of the fruit, only apples were widely cultivated but wild fruit and nuts, especially hazel nuts, formed an important part of the diet.

Survival depended on the success of grain-growing and animal husbandry:

there was no significant trade in food, and little surplus to cushion the population against shortfalls. The failure of the one brought very great hardship; the failure of both meant famine, disease, and social disorder including internal migration (which tended to spread disease) and a rise of violence against the church. For most people life was 'nasty, brutish, and short'. Major epidemics struck every generation of the Irish population in the second half of the seventh century, throughout the eighth, and in the first quarter of the ninth—so much the annals report, and we can be sure that the record is incomplete. They record what may have been bacillary dysentery, influenzal pneumonia, plague, small-pox, famine fever, and rabies. The only orthodox remedy was an appeal to God and his saints: the churches, in response to the needs of the people, went on circuit with the relics of the saints and, in close association with the secular rulers, promulgated various laws to restore social order (including respect for the church and its personnel). On occasion, the poor and the ignorant (and perhaps others) turned to the old gods.

Kingship and the Royal Dynasties

Kingship was an important institution, and kings were much more powerful than some scholars have thought: the annals are full of their doings, the genealogies of their noble descents. The sagas preserve the ideology of kingship: the qualities of the good king, the benefits of his rule, his heroic actions, courage, and nobility are set out in story form in Old and Middle Irish literature, for instruction as well as for literary enjoyment. In the literature, the king has much of the aura of the sacral: his inauguration is the 'holy marriage' of the king and the goddess of the land, and makes land and people fertile. These conceits and metaphors of kingship have attracted scholars a great deal more than the much more mundane accounts of the theory and practice of kingship in the Latin canon laws and the annals. The vernacular law tracts describe three grades of king: the *rí túaithe*, king of a local petty kingdom; the *ruiri* 'great king', who was overlord of a number of petty kings; and the *rí ruirech* 'king of overkings', who was king of a province and a ruler of considerable power and significance.

Some have thought that there were between 80 and 100 local petty kingdoms in Ireland, but we simply do not know how many there were at any given time. It has been argued that the *rí túaithe* was the essential king (any higher grade of king was merely a glorified *rí túaithe* who had managed to obtain the submission of a number of other kings), and some scholars have seen in him many of the features of the primitive Indo-European tribal king. It has been claimed, too, that, whatever may be true about the remote past, the king was neither supreme judge nor lawgiver: he was the representative and leader of his people in war and in relations with other tribes. Much of this—especially the primitivism and the tribalism—is very doubtful indeed as far as the Early Christian period is concerned. In fact, the petty kings, *rí* and *ruiri*, were on the way down and out in the eighth century or earlier; some of them are called by lesser titles (*dux* 'duke', *toísech* 'leader', and *tigern* 'lord') in contemporary records, and the annals have examples in the eighth century of the conquest of their petty kingdoms. These kings were becoming dependent local noblemen, if indeed they were ever much more.

The five or six who were kings of provinces were the real makers and movers. These are the kings who exercised real powers, and the annals are full of their battles and dynastic struggles. The churches backed their pretensions and expected to profit from their protection. Canon law lays down that if an offence has been committed against the church, and if no one can be found to offpay it, the final appeal is to the king of the province. And this is what the annals record. In 809, for example, Áed Oirnide, king of the northern Uí Néill, within whose overkingdom Armagh lay, invaded the Ulaid because they had attacked a church belonging to Armagh and killed its superior. In Munster, we find Artrí mac Cathail of the Eóganacht being ordained king of Munster in 793 and, in return, he allowed Emly, the ordaining church, to levy its church-tax on the province. Two or three of the abbots of Emly were kings of Munster in the ninth century. The Uí Briúin kings of Connacht courted the blessing of Armagh: they allowed the 'Law of Patrick', essentially an Armagh church-tax, to be proclaimed in Connacht frequently between 783 and 836. But they also cultivated the friendship of Clonmacnoise: the 'Law of Ciarán' (Clonmacnoise's church-tax) was proclaimed on a number of occasions in Connacht, and in 814 the king of Connacht joined with the abbot of Clonmacnoise in avenging an outrage against the monastery.

The churchmen were very much the theorists of kingship. Drawing on the Old Testament and specifically on 1 Samuel 10, they developed the idea of the ordained and consecrated king. This occurs in Adomnán's *Life of Columba* (written *c.*700): he refers to two of the kings of the Uí Néill and to Oswald of Northumbria as monarchs 'ordained by God'. The same term occurs in contemporary Armagh documents and in *Collectio canonum hibernensis* (of *c.* AD 700–50), where the text from Samuel is placed at the very beginning of the book on kingship—and it is likely that the early medieval consecration of kings as a regular ritual began with the Irish. The canonists' book on kingship is strongly pro-royal and based firmly on Scripture (especially the Old Testament) and the early Fathers. They were interested in promoting effective kingship and they stress the coercive powers of the king: 'The word of a king is a sword for beheading, a rope for hanging, it casts into prison, it condemns to exile . . . fear the word of a king: it punishes the enemy, it honours the friend.' (The clerics were strong advocates of capital punishment.) Those who disobeyed the king's law were to be punished (by death, exile, confiscation of property, or imprisonment) and those who did not guard the 'Lord's anointed' were doomed to die. The king's taxes must be paid: 'Render unto Caesar the things that are Caesar's and to God the things that are God's'—and they take St Jerome's definition of what belongs to Caesar: 'the coin, the tribute, the reverence, and the respect'. However, the church must not be taxed at all, kings must not overtax their subjects or plunder them (in the words of Orosius, shear the sheep, not skin them), and they must rule justly and fairly. It is likely that these ideas and their clerical advisers had a powerful influence on the power-hungry provincial kings of the eighth, ninth, and later centuries who were now carving out and consolidating the kingdoms which were to dominate Irish politics down to the twelfth century.

There has been much discussion amongst historians of the 'high-kingship of Ireland', the claim that there existed a king who exercised authority (of one kind or another) over the whole of Ireland. This implies a certain consciousness of unity. It is clear that from a very early period the Irish learned men had begun to work out a prehistory of their race. This was being done in the seventh century and out of it grew eventually *An lebor gabála*, 'Book of the taking of Ireland', which united all their dynasties and peoples by descent from a single set of ancestors. This proved to be a powerful and all-pervasive myth which used race, language, land, and landscape as the basis of national unity. The awareness of language is particularly keen: Irish is constructed from the best elements of language available at the Tower of Babel and, according to an eleventh-century scholar, is 'the speech which is melodious and sweet in the mouth'. The sense of unity is present in the vernacular laws: the lawyers speak of the custom and law of the 'island of Ireland'. This, of course, spilled over into politics. The clerical propagandists of the Uí Néill dynasty had a well-developed concept of the kingship of Ireland as early as the last quarter of the seventh century. Muirchú calls Lóegaire (St Patrick's alleged contemporary) 'a great king, fierce and pagan, and emperor of non-Romans, with his royal seat at Tara, which was then the capital of the realm of the Irish' and Niall (the ancestor of the Uí Néill) is 'the ancestor of the family that rules almost the entire island'. Adomnán calls another early Uí Néill overking 'ruler of the whole of Ireland ordained by God'. A vernacular law tract defines *tríath* (a title for a great king) as a king 'who goes through the kingdoms of Ireland from sea to sea . . . The five provinces of Ireland, he goes through all their submissions, as has been sung of Conchobar'—and there is a good deal more evidence that the lawyers were familiar with the idea of the high-kingship. In fact, there was no monarch of Ireland—a king whose rule was effective over the whole island—but the Uí Néill, the most powerful dynasty in the country, claimed to be overkings of Ireland, and were able to make that claim effective over very large areas, and from time to time compel many, if not most, of the provincial kings to submit to them. In the middle of the ninth century, their king, Mael Sechnaill, made very formidable efforts to declare himself king of Ireland.

The remote origins of the Uí Néill are far from clear: they dominated the midlands and the north-west in the seventh century, but claimed in their legends and genealogies to be kings of Tara since the time of St Patrick and before. Nobody quite knows what the kingship of Tara was: its glory lay in the past, it was claimed by a number of early dynasties, it was cursed by the Christian saints. Whatever it was, the Uí Néill grabbed the title 'king of Tara' for themselves: it meant overking of the whole Uí Néill, and later, 'high-king of Ireland'. Their origin-legends are clearly fictions, some of relatively late date, and historians have believed far too many of them. At some unknown time, they split along geographical lines into two branches, the southern and northern Uí Néill. The southern Uí Néill were divided into two major rival branches (there were others of less importance), called Síl nAeda Sláine and Clann Cholmáin, and dominated the rich lands of Meath, Westmeath, and parts of the surrounding counties. Síl nAeda Sláine were very powerful in the seventh century. Clann Cholmáin first managed to take the overkingship of the Uí Néill in 743, and after that (with one exception) they kept their rivals out and expanded their overlordship. In the mid-ninth century their king claimed to be king of Ireland. The northern Uí Néill, located in Donegal and Derry, were also divided into two main branches: Cenél Conaill and Cenél nEógain. Cenél Conaill were the more powerful from the late sixth to the middle of the seventh century. Columba and Adomnán both belonged to this dynasty, and they gave their kinsmen a good press in the early version of the annals that was edited at Iona. The last of their kings to hold the overkingship of the Uí Néill was Flaithbertach mac Loingsig, who abdicated in 734. Cenél nEógain did everything they could to exclude their rivals and, after a long series of dynastic struggles, they succeeded in doing so in the late eighth century. At the same time, they expanded southwards and eastwards from Inishowen and Derry across the mid-Ulster plain and slowly brought the scatter of minor kingdoms ruled by the Airgialla under their control in the eighth and ninth centuries. Armagh, now the most important church in Ireland, was in Airgialla territory, and between 750 and 850 it came under Uí Néill control. Though it continued to be ruled by Airgialla families, these were dependents of the Uí Néill. In 804 the king of Cenél nEógain and overking of the Uí Néill, Aed Oirnide, apparently was ordained king by the abbot of Armagh and began to act as protector of the interests of Armagh. East of the Bann, in Antrim and Down, the ancient Ulaid recognized their supremacy only in the middle of the ninth century. The Ulaid in the east and Cenél Conaill in the west remained bitterly hostile to the dominant Cenél nEógain.

Originally, Leinster stretched northwards to the Boyne but the land between

HIGH CROSS AT KILLAMERY IN OSSORY. CROSS OF THE SCRIPTURES, CLONMACNOISE. The high crosses of the ninth and early tenth centuries are the products of royal patronage and devotion, but they also express the claims and ambitions of kings. That at Killamery bears the name of Mael Sechnaill (d. 862) and may mark his success in getting the submission of Munster (854-9). The Cross of the Scriptures at Clonmacnoise (dating probably to the first decade of the tenth century) was commissioned by his son, Flann mac Mael Sechnaill (d. 916). He is called 'king of Ireland' in an inscription on the cross.

it and the Liffey was lost to the advancing Uí Néill. The heartland of historic Leinster was the vale of the Liffey, and the valleys of the Barrow and the Slaney. The great dynasties, the winners, were in the plains and river valleys; the losers were on the eastern coastal strip, the Wicklow highlands, and the north-western boglands. In the eighth century Leinster was ruled by the Uí Dúnlainge, a group of dynasties settled in the vale of the Liffey and in the plains of Kildare. They were new men: the annals and genealogies show that other groups—whom they had pushed out into the badlands—had held the kingship before them. The Uí Dúnlainge allied themselves closely with the great church of Kildare in a mutual profit venture. They had other rivals to the south of them: Uí Chennselaig, who had threatened the vale of the Liffey in the seventh century—but they were foiled and pushed south, where they carved out an important kingdom for themselves in association with Ferns and a number of other monasteries. The Uí Néill pursued a long struggle with the Laigin; by 800 they had come to dominate north Leinster, and in the first half of the ninth century they were appointing kings of Leinster, who seemed to have ruled Leinster for them as provincial governors.

The Eóganacht ruled Munster in the period from the seventh to the mid-tenth century—a long-tailed group of dynasties with powerful local kingdoms in east, south, and west Munster. They traced their rule of Munster back to the fifth century: angels pointed out the site of Cashel to their founding ancestor and Oengus, their king, was baptized and blessed by St Patrick. This is typical propaganda, and it is clear that the Érainn or their descendants (Corcu Loígde) ruled the province before them, and well into the historic period. The eastern branches of the Eóganacht, located about Cashel and Glanworth, began to dominate from about AD 700. Their most famous eighth-century king was Cathal mac Finguine (721–42), who waged successful war against the Uí Néill and was thought (at least by Munstermen) to have been king of Ireland. The Eóganacht maintained close clerical connections, especially with the monastery of Emly, and claimed to be the most Christian kings in Ireland. Ironically, Feidlimid mac Crimthainn (d. 847), scribe, anchorite, bishop, and king of Munster, one of the ablest of all the Eóganacht kings, was a ruthless politician in church and state and a plunderer of monasteries—he attacked Kildare, Durrow, Fore, and Gallen, foisted his own candidate on Clonmacnoise, and played politics with Armagh. He saw clearly the political and economic power of the monastic towns. He campaigned successfully against the Uí Néill, raided their territory—and their monasteries—and forced the king of the Uí Néill to meet him for peace talks on the border at Birr. Eóganacht power crumbled in the late ninth and early tenth centuries and their place was taken by Dál Cais, who rose to power in north Munster in the mid-tenth century as the Eóganacht kingship collapsed in disorder.

The two dominant Connacht dynasties were Uí Fiachrach and Uí Briúin, and both claimed to be cousins of the Uí Néill. Uí Fiachrach had two main branches: one in the north in the valley of the Moy, the other in the south, about Gort. The southern branch dominated Connacht and much of north Munster in the seventh century. Their most famous king (in life as in literature) was Guaire Aidni (d. 663), a model of generosity and goodness in Irish tradition. Uí Briúin emerged in the seventh century, obscure in origin, but later fitted out with a fine pedigree and prehistory. Their expansion in the eighth century was fast, Uí Fiachrach lost ground rapidly, and by about 725 Uí Briúin were the dominant dynasty in Connacht. They threw out branches on all sides and these gave

Connacht a new and aggressive aristocracy. A branch of Uí Briúin pushed north-eastwards and established the new kingdom of Uí Briúin Bréifne on the frontiers of the Uí Néill, eventually driving a wedge between their two great branches. Uí Briúin succeeded in confining the kingship to a fairly narrow royal group and built up a powerful kingdom in central Connacht, which dominated the whole province, and which they made a springboard for the domination of Ireland in the twelfth century.

The Viking Wars

The Scandinavian background in the pre-Viking period is obscure, and the cause of the Viking raids is debated. Baltic piracy, feeding off trade, seems to have spread outwards at the end of the eighth century. The Vikings were bands of warriors, led by royals and aristocrats—pirates, looking for plunder in the first place and whatever they could get after that. The development of excellent sailing ships made them exceptionally mobile and brought western Europe (including the British Isles) within easy reach. The first raids in Ireland, Britain, and France came almost at the same time. Lindisfarne was attacked in 793; in 794 the annals report 'the plundering of all the islands of Britain by the pagans'; in 795 Rathlin was burned, and Iona, Inishmurray, and Inishbofin were attacked. In 798 the monastery of St Patrick's Island (near Skerries, Co. Dublin) was burned by the pagans; they levied a cattle tribute on the surrounding territories, smashed the shrine of the monastery's patron Dochonna, 'and they made great raids besides in Ireland and in Scotland'. Alcuin, in his letter to the community of Lindisfarne, consoling them after the raid, is put in mind of the lamentations of the prophet Isaiah and writes:

. . . when the pagans desecrated the sanctuaries of God, and poured out the blood of saints about the altar, laid waste the house of our hope, trampled on the bodies of saints in the temple of God, like dung in the street. What can we say except lament in our soul with you before Christ's altar, and say: 'Spare, O Lord, spare thy people and give not thine inheritance to the gentiles, lest the pagans say, "Where is the God of the christians?" '

In 802 Iona was burned by the Vikings; they returned in 806 and killed 68 members of the community—enough to persuade the great federation of Columba to start building the 'new city of Columba', at Kells (in Co. Meath), in the lands of the southern Uí Néill, and over twenty miles inland. In 807 they burned Inishmurray and attacked Roscam on Galway Bay. By 823 they had rounded the whole of the Irish coastline, and in 824 they attacked the island-monastery of Sceilg, eight miles off the Kerry coast (its superior died of hunger and thirst as their prisoner).

The Vikings who attacked Ireland were mainly Norwegians. For the first forty years or so the raids were hit-and-run incidents by small, fast-moving, sea-borne forces that appeared and disappeared quickly. They were difficult to catch up with, but the Irish hit back with some success: in 811 the Ulaid slaughtered a band of raiders; in 812 the men of Umall (Co. Mayo) defeated their attackers and, in the south-west, the king of Eóganacht Locha Léin slaughtered a Viking band.

In the 830s the raids became much more intense: the main onslaught came at about the same time in Ireland, England, and France. In 836 came the first recorded extensive inland raid: on the lands of the southern Uí Néill, where they killed many and took a large number of captives. In the same year, the annals record 'a most cruel devastation of all the lands of Connacht by the heathens'. Next year a fleet of sixty ships appeared on the Boyne and another of sixty ships of the Liffey. These fleets plundered the vale of the Liffey and the plain of Brega (Co. Meath), churches, fortresses, and farms. And the southern Uí Néill were heavily defeated in battle. Already, the Vikings had made their way up the Shannon, the Boyne, the Liffey, and the Erne; in 839 they put a fleet on Lough Neagh and plundered the neighbouring monasteries and the surrounding countryside, and from this base they attacked Louth (where they took 'bishops and superiors and scholars prisoner and killed others') and Armagh. They overwintered on Lough Neagh in 840–1. They set up defended positions at Annagassan (Co. Louth) and Dublin which they used as bases to plunder widely in Leinster and in southern Uí Néill lands. They wintered for the first time in Dublin in 841–2—a ninth-century cemetery with well-furnished warriors' graves uncovered at Kilmainham to the west of the city marks their presence. Now the attacks grew very intense and it seemed that the country was about to be conquered. The Vikings had made the Shannon waterways their own and Clonmacnoise, Seir, Birr, and Clonfert were plundered. In 845, Forannán, abbot of Armagh, on circuit in Munster with his retinue and with the insignia of his office, was captured and carried off to the ships in the Shannon estuary.

Some of the heads of the great monasteries took the field: the abbot of Terryglass and Clonenagh and the deputy-abbot of Kildare were killed fighting the Vikings at the fortress of Dunamase in 845. The Irish kings began to counterattack with growing success—and their success is reported in the Frankish annals for 848, where we have the views of an Irish mission to Charles the Bald. Though further fleets arrived in 849 and 851, the great raids of the ninth century were now over and in the 860s and 870s the Vikings seemed to have turned to England.

They had been involved in Ireland for over half a century and, once settled,

THE ARREST OF CHRIST, Book of Kells, folio 114ʳ. In this highly stylized illustration, the soldiers look powerless compared to the dominating figure of Christ, with blue eyes, golden hair, and reddish beard, depicted with tragic formality—perhaps emphasizing the voluntary nature of his sacrifice for mankind.

they were as vulnerable as any Irish petty kingdom and soon played an increasingly active part in local dynastic warfare. The first Viking–Irish alliance is recorded in 842—they killed the abbot of Linn Duachail—and such alliances, with major kings and minor, became very common in a decade or two. Some plunderings of monasteries took place, but not on a large scale, though there were occasional outrages. Dublin was the most significant Viking settlement but there were others: at Waterford, which attacked Ossory in 860; at Youghal, which suffered defeat in 866; at Wexford and up river at St Mullins (a monastic site on the Barrow); at Cork; in the Shannon estuary and, very probably, on Lough Ree. In 866, Áed Finnliath, king of the northern Uí Néill, cleared the north coast of Viking bases. Some survived or returned: Vikings from Lough Foyle attacked Armagh in 898 and there was a fleet on Lough Neagh in 900. Others, based on Carlingford Lough, attacked Armagh in 879.

The second Viking period in Ireland began in the second decade of the tenth century and lasted until the 930s. It began when a great sea-fleet arrived in Waterford harbour in 914; more Vikings arrived there in 915, and they began to attack Munster and, later, Leinster—they plundered the monasteries of Cork, Lismore, and Aghaboe, and met with little resistance. Niall Glúndub, now overking of the Uí Néill, led the Irish counter-attack on the Vikings. He marched into Munster in 917 with the combined forces of the Uí Néill, but he had no decisive success, and the Leinstermen, whom he had ordered against the Vikings, were heavily defeated. In 919 he himself was defeated and killed by the Vikings at the battle of Dublin, and the cream of the Uí Néill fell with him. For the next two decades the Vikings of Dublin were rather powerful, but they devoted much of their time and resources to establishing themselves in the kingdom of York and attempting to control the other Viking settlements in Limerick and Waterford. By about 950 the second period of Viking raiding was virtually over.

There has been a lively debate on the impact of the Viking wars on Irish society and the Irish church in particular. Professor Binchy believes that the 'the Norsemen had a profound—one might say shattering—effect upon native Irish institutions' and he attributes the changes which took place in Irish society in the tenth and eleventh century to the Vikings, who caused the passing of the old order, of the structure of early Irish society as depicted in the law tracts. However, Ireland did not have the deep disruption that Francia suffered between 840 and 870. Neither did the Vikings take over whole kingdoms, as they did in England where they conquered all north of a line from the Thames estuary to Chester (the Danelaw) and settled intensively. Within the Danelaw, Hexham, Leicester, and other sees and most monasteries—and their records—simply disappeared. Nothing like this happened in Ireland. No major Irish monastery went under. Dublin was ringed with monasteries: Tallaght, Clondalkin, Swords, Crumlin, Shankill, Kilmainham, Glasnevin—to name but some—and they all survived the Viking wars. Swords and Lusk, in fact, lay within Fine Gall, the land settled by the Vikings of Dublin. The great monastery of Cork lay within a few minutes' walk of the Viking city; it was raided perhaps half a dozen times, but it survived so well that there is no break in the succession of its abbots. A few small local kingdoms disappeared near the Viking settlements. The Vikings may have contributed to the collapse of the already shaky kingship of the Eóganacht in Munster in the ninth and early tenth centuries: if they did, this made way for the much more effective Dál Cais (subsequently O'Brien) kings. The argument that the Vikings caused the passing of the old order does not hold water: the 'old order', if ever there was one, had passed away long before the Viking wars.

The Viking wars have been blamed for a number of 'abuses' in the Irish church: lay abbots, married clergy, hereditary succession to church offices, pluralism, and growing violence towards the church. Recent research has shown that all these existed long before the Viking wars, and continued long after them. Hereditary succession goes back to the seventh century and was the rule rather than the exception in the eighth. If families owned churches, pluralism was a natural extension of that. Some of the greater churches were rich and powerful, great landowners, in a sense kingdoms within kingdoms, and ruled by aristocrats closely related to the royal houses; it was inevitable that they were drawn into the wars of the kings, and raiding monastic towns became a normal part of Irish warfare. And the great Irish monasteries engaged in pitched battles against each other and, on occasion, against local kings. The great churches were well used to violence and the Vikings had little to teach such kings as Donnchad Midi, the overking of the Uí Néill, who attacked the Leinstermen and 'devastated and burned their territories and their churches', as the monastic annals relate. The wealth of the churches, and their ability to build up surpluses in a largely subsistence economy, made them the targets of attack in time of famine, and this is documented before, during, and after the Viking wars. The Vikings were after plunder, captives (who could be ransomed or enslaved), and food: they found the Irish monastic towns, the areas of concentrated wealth and greater economic development, good for all three. They did a great deal of damage, killed a number of clerics and frightened a lot more. A ninth-century scribe, taking comfort from the storm outside which made the sea impassable, wrote in the margin of his manuscript:

> The wind is fierce to-night
> It tosses the sea's white hair
> I fear no wild Vikings
> sailing the quiet main.

But church life went on. The Irish monastic annalists report the attacks factually—they keep a stiff upper lip, and do not whine like Alcuin and their

continental contemporaries. Had they less to suffer or did they, as realists and administrators of great institutions, see the Vikings as just another bunch of nasties in a nasty world?

From the mid-tenth century, the Ostmen—for that is what they called themselves—made a great impact on Ireland as traders. They introduced more sophisticated ships and boats, for trade as well as for war. The northern rulers developed great sea-going fleets in the tenth century, and the kings of the eleventh and twelfth centuries made a lot of use of navies. The Ostmen took the trade of Ireland in hand, including the slave trade which was extensive and profitable down to the twelfth century. As sailors and traders, they left their

THE HIGH CROSS AT MOONE, CO. KILDARE (*left*). Details show Daniel in the lions' den, the flight into Egypt, and the miracle of the loaves and fishes. This striking and elegant monument, carved from granite and 17 feet high, is the masterpiece of a talented sculptor. Its extensive carvings illustrate the Old and New Testaments (Adam and Eve, the sacrifice of Isaac, and portraits of the twelve apostles) and represent the eremitical life, especially scenes from the lives of SS Paul and Anthony.

WOOD QUAY. The excavation of Viking Dublin has illuminated the history, material culture, and trading relations of the city from the tenth to the twelfth centuries and has brought out the remarkable continuity of urban settlement. The finds provide evidence for extensive trade: Dublin became one of the richest ports in western Europe.

marks on the landscape, islands, bays, and headlands: Smerwick, Blaskets, Dursey, Fota, Helvick, Saltees, Selskar—all on the south coast—are Old Norse names which passed directly into English. Naturally, they left Old Norse names on some of their cities and settlements: Waterford, Wexford, Wicklow, Strangford, Carlingford, Howth, Dalkey, and Leixlip, for example; but apart from the remarkable fact that the names of three of the four provinces of Ireland (Ulster, Leinster, and Munster) are made up of elements compounded as in Old Norse, they left few names on the landscape. The Irish borrowed a small number of words, most of them connected with sailing, fishing, and trading: *ancaire* 'an anchor', *bád* 'a boat', *scód* 'a sheet', *stiúir* 'a rudder', *dorgha* 'a fishing-line', *langa* 'ling', *trosc* 'cod', *margad* 'a market', *pinginn* 'a penny', *scilling* 'a shilling'; but there were hardly fifty borrowings of this kind.

In contrast with Scotland, where the incomers became farmers and fishermen, the Ostmen in Ireland became merchants and seamen, who hugged the coastline. In Scotland there were no Ostman cities, no real evidence for what was the flourishing trade of Ireland, and no local coinage. The Ostmen of Ireland were rich in silver and gold—some of the silver they put into circulation reached the Irish metal-workers and made possible new styles—and that wealth mainly came from the trade of their prosperous towns, especially Dublin. Here excavation has uncovered the evidence of the far-flung trade that made Dublin one of the great cities of the Viking world. An early twelfth-century Irish writer describes the treasure found by the Irish in Limerick: 'They carried away their jewels and their best property, their saddles beautiful and foreign, their gold and their silver; their beautifully woven cloth of all colours and of all kinds; their satins and their silken cloths, pleasing and variegated, both scarlet and green and all sorts of cloth in like manner'—a shopping-list of luxuries for kings and nobles. As Dublin declined politically in the late tenth and early eleventh centuries, it boomed economically as a great European trading city, and the kings of the twelfth century vied with one another for control of it and its hinterland, its trade, its taxes, and its mercenary fleet.

The Uí Néill and the Dál Cais

The Eóganacht of Munster were pushed aside in the tenth century by the Dál Cais of north Munster. These were helped by the attacks of the Uí Néill on the Eóganacht, by the dynastic wars which soon kept the Uí Néill busy, and by the fact that they straddled the strategic waterway of the Shannon, which had become even more important in the Viking period. On his death-notice in 951 Cennétig, king of Dál Cais, is called 'king of North Munster'; his son Brian Bóruma, or Brian Boru (ancestor of the O'Briens), who succeeded in 976, was to make himself king of Ireland and rival of the Uí Néill.

From the 940s to the 960s, the leading branches of the Uí Néill were engaged in a vicious power-struggle amongst themselves—a united Uí Néill kingdom was in the making, and the struggle was to determine who was to be ruler of it. Domnall ua Néill, overking of the Uí Néill (956–80) and king also of the northern Uí Néill, brought a new ruthlessness to the game: despite violent opposition, he attempted to govern southern Uí Néill directly and put a garrison in Meath. His

BRIAN BORU'S ENTRY IN THE BOOK OF ARMAGH. This recites the claim that St Patrick ordered that the whole fruit of his labours be due to his apostolic church of Armagh. 'So I have found in the libraries of the Irish. Signed Caluus Perennis [i.e. Mael Suthain], in the presence of Brian, emperor of the Irish. And what I have written, he has determined for all the kings of Munster.'

A CHARACTERISTIC VIKING MOTIF. This drawing incised on a ship's plank was found in a wooden house excavated in Christchurch Place, Dublin. It depicts the look-out man on a ship's rigging.

successor was Mael Sechnaill II (of the southern Uí Néill), the last of the Uí Néill kings of Tara in the old style.

The rise to power of Brian Boru was swift. He succeeded his assassinated brother and rounded on his killers, among them the Ostmen of Limerick. Their king Ímar and his sons, all Christians, took refuge in the monastery of Scattery Island. Brian desecrated the church and killed them in the sanctuary. In three years, Limerick and Munster were in his hands, and he came into conflict with the Uí Néill when he tried to conquer Ossory in 980. Allied with the Ostmen of Waterford (he needed their fleet), and holding the petty kingdoms and the monastic towns of Munster in a tight grip, he pushed his armies into Connacht and Leinster. Mael Sechnaill's attempts to contain him did not succeed, and in 997 Brian and Mael Sechnaill met at Clonfert and divided Ireland between them. This made Brian master of Dublin and Leinster. Late in 999 the Leinstermen and the Dubliners revolted against Brian; but he marched north and inflicted a crushing defeat on them at Glenn Máma, and took the king of Leinster prisoner. He followed this up with a winter war against Dublin; he plundered the city, burned the fortress, and eventually forced Sitric Silkenbeard, king of Dublin, into submission. Now Brian set out, with caution and determination, to dominate the whole country—and in this attempt he was consistently supported by his new subjects, the Ostmen of Dublin. This was done by 1011. And he sought the blessing of the church: in 1005 he spent a week in Armagh, formally recognized it as the apostolic city of Ireland, placed twenty ounces of gold as his offering on the high altar, and had himself described in the Book of Armagh as 'Emperor of the Irish'. His success changed the rules of the game entirely. He had shattered the Uí Néill monopoly and had made the kingship of Ireland a prize to be fought for by the greatest of the provincial kings.

Brian Boru was killed at the battle of Clontarf on Good Friday 1014. About 1012, relations between Brian and Leinster became strained, and there was a general reaction in Ireland to his rule. Late in 1013, Brian's son was sent to attack Leinster, which he spoiled as far as Glendalough, and he camped at Kilmainham within view of Dublin. He was joined by Brian and together they blockaded the city from September to Christmas, but without success. The Leinstermen and the Ostmen knew they would be back and attempted to put together a large force of Vikings from the Western Isles and Man to help them. The battle which followed was unusually bloody: Brian won, but he himself was killed, as were many of the leaders on both sides. Clontarf became a great battle of saga and literature—for the Ostmen as well as the Irish. It was not a struggle between the Irish and the Vikings for the sovereignty of Ireland as people have often thought. Nor was it a great national victory which broke the power of the Vikings forever—that did not need to be done. In fact, Clontarf was an important event in the struggle for dominance between the great provincial rulers: Brian was

DONORE DOOR-FURNITURE. A highly ornamented set of door-furniture, executed with great skill and precision, found at Donore, Co Meath, 4 km north of Kells. It probably belonged to a major monastery. It is decorated in the developed Ultimate La Tène style, comparable with the Lindisfarne Gospels and the Tara Brooch, and in the style of the late eighth and early ninth centuries.

stopped short just when he seemed to be about to make the kingship of Ireland a reality, and the possession of his dynasty.

The Reorganization of the Church

The Irish church of the eleventh and early twelfth centuries was very old-fashioned, especially in the eyes of the Gregorian reformers who were transforming church organization in western Europe. Historians, mostly clerics, have been eager to describe its vices, not its virtues. There were still saintly bishops, and the monastic schools conducted a lively intellectual life—their masters were in touch with the new European learning and were respected in the schools of France and the Rhineland. The archbishops of Canterbury, Lanfranc (1070–89) and Anselm (1093–1109), busied themselves with the reorganization and established dependent sees in the Ostman cities, especially Dublin. There was no shortage of native reformers, particularly in Munster. The principal problem was that abbots (now usually laymen) had too much power, and bishops too little, and the church was not organized into territorial dioceses outside the

THE HIGH CROSS AT DYSERT O'DEA, which graphically represents the attitudes of the twelfth-century reformers. This cross belongs to a north Munster series which may reflect the munificence of the O'Brien kings of Munster, who were also highly influential in reforming circles. It is a striking example of the later crucifix-cross. It is dominated by the high-relief figures but the back and sides of the cross are covered in low-relief animal and floral ornament in the Hiberno-Viking style.

Ostman towns. As in most of northern Europe, there were no parishes. Quite apart from that, the church was heavily laicized, as elsewhere in Europe: laymen had power and income in the church, churches were under lay control and subject to taxation, sanctuary was abused, and clerics were charged with simony and concubinage. The morals of the laity also came under fire, especially in regard to marriage—an area where the church was now busily making new rules. Besides, there was a new surge of monasticism: European religious orders were being imported, and Irish houses brought under the Augustinian rule.

The organization of the church was revolutionized by three major national synods: Cashel (1101), Ráth Breasail (1111), and Kells–Mellifont (1152). Essentially, these gave the Irish church the diocesan organization it has today, and the last-named absorbed Dublin into the system and created a national church

ELEVENTH- TO TWELFTH-CENTURY FIGURE PANELS from the Breac Maedhóc, a house-shrine associated with Drumlane, Co. Cavan. These are in bronze, originally gilt, and comprise eleven figures. The female figures are demurely draped in long cloaks and wear their hair in long ringlets. The male figures are highly individualized in dress and expression. Lucas thought them 'the most powerful and realistic representations of the human figure in Irish art'.

under the primacy of Armagh—a development that did not please Canterbury. The provincial kings had a major influence in the shaping of dioceses: kings chaired the first two synods and their political interference stretched as far as Rome. Killaloe, Limerick, and Cashel, for example, are the dioceses of O'Brien—and the same occurred elsewhere. Not all royal influence was bad: the kings patronized the great Irish Romanesque church-building, notably Cormac's Chapel at Cashel, and endowed schools and churches.

The monasteries were clearly separated from the dioceses and were taken over by foreign rules and orders—the most influential were the Cistercians, introduced by St Malachy in 1142. Hereditary succession was officially abolished, and clerical celibacy insisted upon, but it was easier to make rules than enforce them. The bishops took over much monastic land and, in time, formerly powerful monasteries were to sink to the level of parish churches.

On the whole, the reform was a triumph for the administrators and a disaster for Irish literature and general culture. The reformers destroyed the social, economic, and cultural base of Irish learning. Nothing replaced the greater monasteries with their schools and learned cadres, now robbed of their resources and their status. The monastic scholars moved out and joined with the praise poets to form the class of bardic poets of the later Middle Ages. The clerical lawyers, too, became secularized and most of what survives of vernacular law is due to late medieval secular legal families. Even the Irish script practically

THE CROZIER OF THE ABBOTS OF CLONMACNOISE belongs to the first half of the twelfth century and is in a Hiberno-Viking style. The crozier is in two parts, the curved crook and the staff, both of bronze decorated in subtle adaptation of the Ringerike and Urnes styles, as shown by detail of the staff illustrated.

CORMAC'S CHAPEL, named after its patron, Cormac MacCarthy, king of Munster from 1127 to 1134 and friend of St Malachy and supporter of church reform. Cormac had close connections with Lismore and with its bishop, Malchus, a former Benedictine of Winchester. Cormac's Chapel is heavily influenced by English Romanesque. Its context is the twelfth-century reform of the Irish church and the growing closeness between Ireland and Anglo-Norman England.

AERIAL PHOTOGRAPH OF THE MODERN CITY OF ARMAGH. The extensive circular outlines of the early medieval town are clearly visible. Armagh was then divided into demarcated sections, with streets; the annals record a series of disastrous fires in 1112, 1121, 1150, and 1166. Twelfth-century Armagh appears to have been a large town with wooden houses, arranged in streets, and some stone churches (and perhaps other buildings) roofed with slates.

disappears in the thirteenth century. The disruption which followed the Norman invasion was, of course, responsible for much of this, but the reformers had laid the groundwork.

The Politics of the Eleventh and Twelfth Centuries

The death of Brian and the subsequent weakness of his dynasty allowed Mael Sechnaill II to be 'high-king' of Ireland until his death in 1022, but the world of the Irish kings had changed. That change may have been coming about slowly, but it becomes very evident in the eleventh century and later. Provincial kings now began to exercise very wide powers and we find their officers of government

THE ANNALS OF INISFALLEN (*left*), now preserved in the Bodleian Library in Oxford, is the earliest surviving manuscript of Irish annals. It now consists of 57 vellum folios. From the beginning to folio 29^c (AD 1092) the manuscript is in a single hand, and it continues in some 38 different hands, with some very large breaks, down to AD 1321. The illustration shows folio 32^v, columns a–b.

A TYPICAL LEGAL MANUSCRIPT (*right*) produced by a hereditary legal family. The vernacular law tracts throw light on material culture, canon law, cultural organization, and many other aspects of early Irish life. At the foot of the page the scribe dates his work: 'AD 1350 and that is the second year after the coming of the plague to Ireland.' Note the interlinear glosses and the marginal commentary.

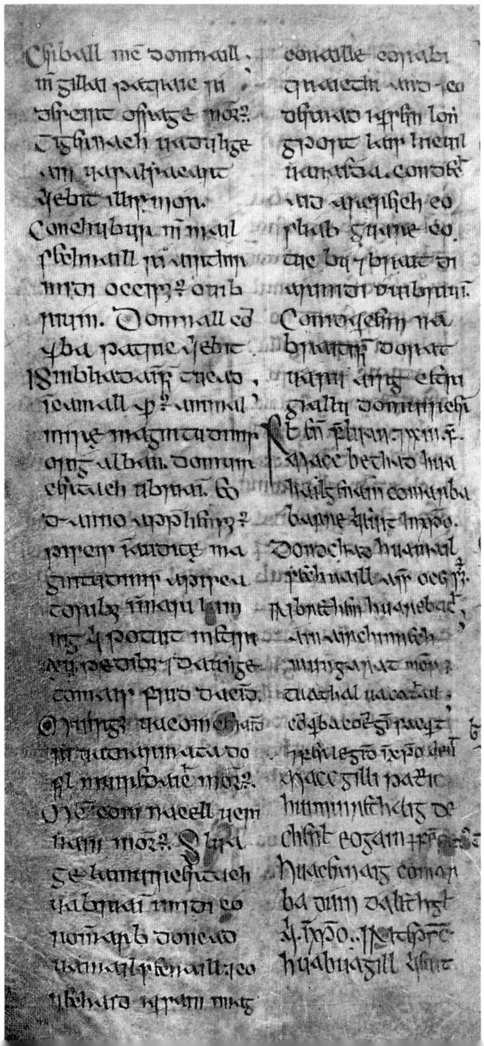

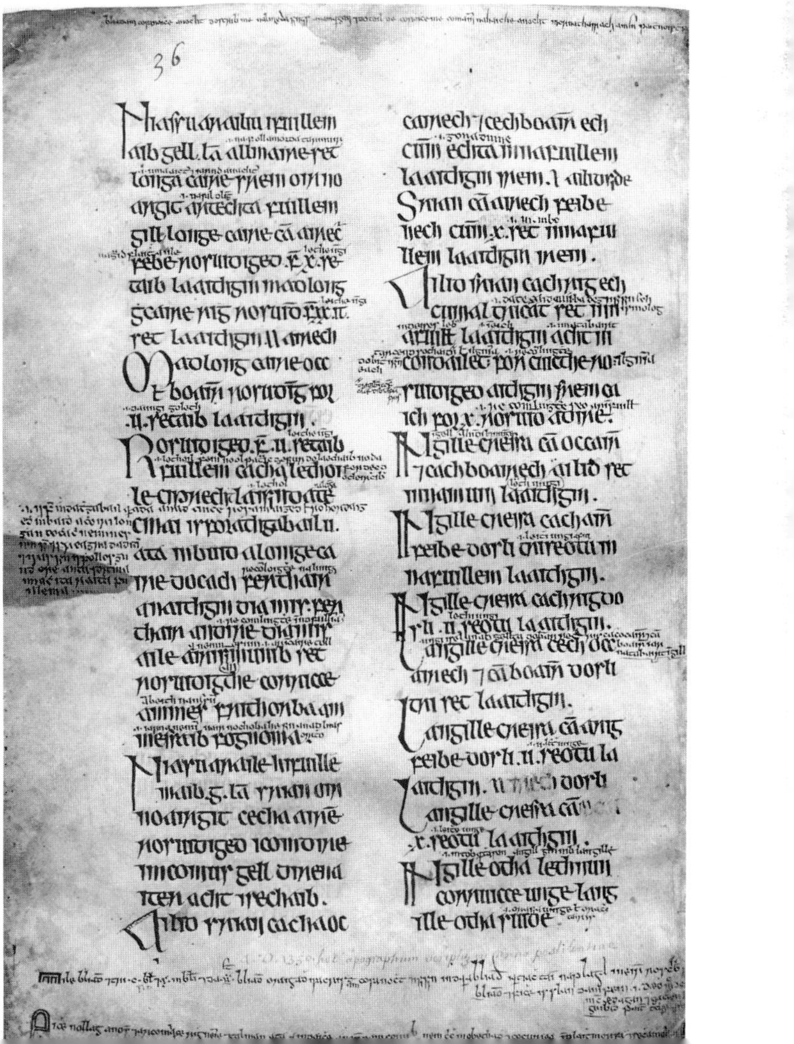

mentioned in the annals and elsewhere. As the pace of change quickened, wars became more frequent and more lengthy. Kings remained in the field for long periods and needed royal officers to govern their territories when they were away. And as these territories became more extensive, the need for administrators increased. Toirrdelbach Ó Conchobair or Turlough O'Connor, king of Connacht, was frequently on campaign for months on end; in 1111 Muirchertach O'Brien spent from 29 September to Christmas in his city of Dublin. One of the most important of these officers was the *airrí*, the king's deputy or governor. Ua Fáilbe, who was killed in battle in 1103, was king of Corcu Duibne (a petty kingdom in Co. Kerry); but he held high office under Muirchertach O'Brien, king of Munster and would-be king of Ireland—he was O'Brien's governor of Leinster. The king's *rechtaire*, in earlier times his steward or bailiff, had now become the castellan of a royal fortress or governor of a city such as Limerick. The annals refer also to the office of head of the royal household, a nobleman who was commander of the king's household troops. The increased use of cavalry and of fleets in war led to other new offices: commander of the king's cavalry and admiral of the fleet. These positions were held by the leading nobility, powerful persons but not powerful enough to be a threat to the king's authority.

These kings acted as owners of the land. We find them granting land to the church, often by charter. The most spectacular of these was when Muirchertach O'Brien granted the fortress of Cashel to the church in 1101 as a seat for an archbishop. A generous gesture, but it also deprived his rivals of their royal centre. On the broader political level, kings granted away large territories and carved up whole kingdoms among their supporters. Turlough O'Connor first tried to make his son king of Meath, and when this failed he divided it up repeatedly among his allies. Muirchertach O'Brien expelled the Connacht dynasty in 1095, lopped off three territories for himself, and granted the rest away. He failed to make this stick, but his intentions are clear. Others followed his example and had more success. The political map of Ireland was changing quickly.

The kings made laws and imposed taxes. In 1040 we find the king of Munster, Donnchad mac Briain, legislating against theft, military activity, and manual labour on Sundays. In 1050, in the course of a famine when there was great disorder and attacks on the churches, he summoned a council of the Munster rulers and clergy to his royal residence of Killaloe and promulgated laws forbidding injustices of all kinds. Royal government is expensive: kings levy taxes,

THE BOOK OF KELLS, folio 34ʳ. Written in a Columban monastery (probably Iona) in the late eighth century, this sumptuous and brilliantly illuminated copy of the gospels in Irish majuscule (a mixed Old Latin and Vulgate text of the Irish family) is the work of three scribes and perhaps four painters. In the complexity of its design, the delicacy of its intricate ornament, and artistic mastery, it surpasses all Irish illuminated manuscripts. In folio 34ʳ the Greek monogram of Christ's name, the Chi-Rho, fills almost the entire page. Outlined in mauve, the letters are filled with circles, spirals, animals, birds, and human figures—a wealth of early medieval religious symbolism, much of which still escapes us.

34

hゴenerario

FIGURE OF A HARPER from the triangular end-panel of the Breac Maedhóc house-shrine, which is also illustrated on p. 42. The harper is executed in cast bronze openwork, and depicts David playing the harp, but with a realism drawn from the harpers of contemporary eleventh- and twelfth-century Irish society: musicians favoured and accorded high status by the upper classes. The bird perched on the harp symbolizes music and song.

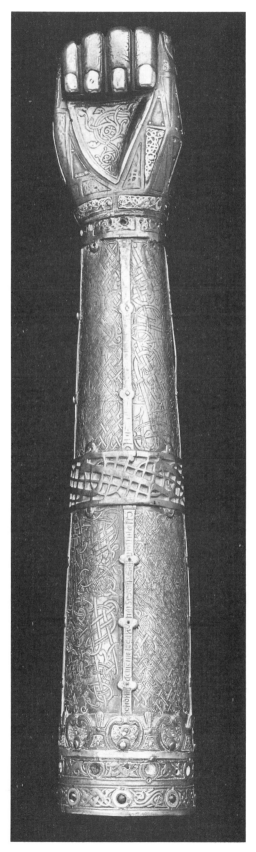

THE STOWE MISSAL (*above*) is a vellum manuscript of 57 leaves dating from about AD 800 and is associated with St Maelruain of Tallaght. Between 1045 and 1052 it was enshrined in an oak box covered with silver plates. Figures on the sides include a man with a sword and a seated man with a musical instrument. Amongst the inscriptions two kings are named as patrons: here again royal status-seeking and devotion appear side by side.

THE SHRINE OF ST LACHTIN'S ARM (*left*) is the only surviving Irish arm-reliquary. It has a bronze covering inlaid with silver overlaying a wooden cylinder which held the relic. The bronze sheets which form the covering are highly ornamented in the Irish version of the Urnes style and the hand and fingers are wreathed in silver filigree or cast interlace. The nails are covered with silver plating. It dates from 1118 to 1121: inscriptions on the shrine betray Munster royal powerbroking and prestige-seeking. Cormac MacCarthy, whose name appears, became king of Munster and a famous patron of the church and of church art.

to maintain their style and their armies. In 1007 Mael Sechnaill II bought front panels for the high-altar at Clonmacnoise, and then levied a tax of a hide on every farmer in Meath to pay for it. But this is small change. In 1166, Rory O'Connor (Ruaidhri Ó Conchobhair) held a great royal council at Athlone and levied a tax of 4000 cows on Ireland: over 2.5 million pounds at current prices. He needed it to buy the loyalty of the Ostmen of Dublin, and he got it. The sources do not tell us about the taxes which kept up the large armies and fleets of the twelfth-century kings and paid for their warfare: we can guess that they were heavy. A poem of about 1150 reflects this: 'iniquitous law and great arrogance in kings . . . wicked lords likewise . . . the needy transitory king will subdue the miserable husbandman'.

Kings granted land in return for homage and military service, very much like the feudal kings of contemporary Europe, and those who were once minor kings in their own right were now becoming a feudal aristocracy. Royalist propaganda texts of the twelfth century give us a model of the relations between a king and his nobles: they are loyal to their lord, brave and disciplined in battle, prepared to follow him to the ends of the earth, and ready to lay down their lives for him. The most important literary text of the century, *Acallam na senórach*, describes a

THE SHRINE OF ST PATRICK'S BELL is a reliquary made between 1094 and 1105, probably at Armagh, to house an iron bell traditionally held to belong to St Patrick. The shrine is made of thick sheets of bronze. The sides are decorated with openwork zoomorphic panels.

world of chivalry: brave young lords, fair ladies, fine clothes, feasting, adventures, beauty, honour, and fidelity—the recreational literature of a noble class. The bloody realities of twelfth-century political life—war, conquest, violence, treachery, and assassination—were quite different.

The struggles of the twelfth-century kings were long and complicated, and the details need not hold us here. From 1086 to 1114 the most powerful king in Ireland was Muirchertach O'Brien. He had dealings with the Anglo-Normans and the Norwegian king, dominated most of the country, and played politics in church as well. However, Domnall Mac Lochlainn, king of the Uí Néill, was able to hold him in check until the dynamic Turlough O'Connor, king of Connacht (1106–56) came on the scene.

O'Connor was the greatest Irish warrior king of the twelfth century. He built a ring of fortresses (some of them called 'castles' by the annalist) about Connacht, threw strategic bridges over the Shannon, and maintained a large army and navy. Between 1115 and 1131 he destroyed the power of Munster, and from 1140 threw all his energies into making himself king of Ireland. With his death in 1156, supreme power passed to the king of the Uí Néill, Muirchertach Mac Lochlainn. He allied himself with Dermot MacMurrough (Diarmait Mac-

THE CROSS OF CONG is a magnificent processional cross in the Hiberno-Viking style at its best. It was commissioned by Turlough O'Connor, king of Connacht, to enshrine a relic of the True Cross; the work was done in Roscommon between 1123 and 1127. The inscription clearly expresses the ambition of Turlough O'Connor and his close relations with the leading clergy of Connacht.

THE NUNS' CHURCH AT CLONMACNOISE is a good example of Phase II Irish Romanesque. The bene-factress of the Nuns' Church was Dervorgilla (Dearbhfhorgaill), daughter of Muirchertach Mac Loch-lainn, king of Meath, and wife of Tighearnán O'Rourke, king of Bréifne. She eloped with Dermot MacMurrough, king of Leinster, in 1152. She completed the Nuns' Church in 1167 and died in religious retirement in Drogheda in 1193 at the age of 84.

Murchadha), king of Leinster. His main opponent was Rory O'Connor, king of Connacht. Mac Lochlainn held the upper hand in Ireland until his sudden fall in 1166 due to his own treachery. In common with all the greater kings of the twelfth century, he realized that Dublin was the capital of Ireland—the power-base from which to control the land was the city and its hinterland within a radius of 40 miles. He and MacMurrough did their best to hold it. When Mac Lochlainn fell, the Dubliners did their bit in unhorsing MacMurrough, and they and O'Connor's allies drove him out. He appealed for help to Henry II and changed the course of Irish history by doing so. The invitation inevitably became an invasion. Like most great changes in history, it was an accident, unforeseen and unplanned, which opened up Ireland politically to expansive Anglo-French feudalism—as England and Scotland had been. Ireland would have been drawn into that feudal world eventually, closer to its neighbour and trading partner, and would have received feudal colonists, but no doubt in a different way. Ironically, the emerging Irish political unity destroyed itself just when it appeared to be successful.

2

The Norman Invasion and
the Gaelic Recovery

KATHARINE SIMMS

Ireland in Europe

WITH the Norman invasion, Ireland could be said to have 'joined the club'. This implies not only that she shared the experience of many other countries in Europe and the Middle East who were peacefully infiltrated or militarily conquered by Normans between the eleventh and the thirteenth centuries, including of course England, Scotland, and Wales, but also that she entered a world of shared ideology, custom, law, and culture which gave most of western Europe in the high Middle Ages a sense of community, inaccurately expressed from time to time as the unity of Christendom under the pope, or the alliance of feudal kingdoms led by the Holy Roman Emperor. Exactly who was in and who was out of this magic circle very much depended on one's point of view. Thirteenth-century Icelandic saga-writers and Irish bardic poets saw themselves as educated members of the European cultural community. Courtiers from Westminster or

IRISH TYMPANIST. A marginal illustration to the Topography of Ireland by Gerald of Wales. Gerald's enthusiastic praise of Irish music contrasts with his generally critical attitude to the manners and morals of the native Irish and Welsh.

Paris regarded them as outsiders. Gerald of Wales, a royal clerk in the service of Henry II, and kinsman to a number of the Cambro-Norman barons who first invaded Ireland, argued with devastating eloquence and erudition that the frontier of European civilization included the marcher lords of Ireland and Wales but excluded the barbarous societies of the native Irish and Welsh. One fascinating aspect of Ireland's history during the later Middle Ages is the gradual blurring of this deeply felt division, until in the sixteenth century fresh lines were drawn on the basis of religious affiliation, lines which barred many families of Anglo-Norman descent from participation in the new Protestant establishment and accentuated their recently acquired sympathy with the native Irish.

The invasion itself was partly the outcome of underlying economic and social trends at this time, partly provoked by a particular train of events, ecclesiastical and secular. In view of the fragmentation of the Irish political scene, it is helpful to begin by examining the central role played by the city of Dublin.

Dublin and the Invasion

Twelfth-century Dublin, with its stone fortifications, its densely packed rows of houses, its locally minted coins, and its overseas trade, above all with its Ostmen inhabitants of Norse descent, might appear something of an anomaly, an alien implant on Irish soil. Like the other Norse seaports, it had become the administrative centre of a territorially defined diocese subject to Canterbury while the rest of the Irish church was still dominated by hereditary lay abbots. When the ecclesiastical reformers developed a new episcopal hierarchy for Ireland and pressurized Dublin to join, the Dubliners resisted. In 1121 the burghers and clergy wrote to the archbishop of Canterbury: 'The bishops of Ireland are very jealous of us, and especially that bishop who lives in Armagh, because we are unwilling to be subject to their rule, but wish always to be under your authority.' In its church organization as in its urban form of settlement Dublin was a prototype for changes taking place in the rest of Irish society.

It is of some interest, therefore, to note that the recent archaeological excavations in Dublin's city centre have produced evidence to suggest a shift in the pattern of its overseas trade occurred as early as the late eleventh century. Instead of dispersed contacts along the Viking sea-routes of northern and north-western Europe, finds for this period indicate a new concentration on the Anglo-Norman world of Britain and the coasts of France, and especially south-west England. This evidence is supported by written sources. A charter of 1175–6 states the townsmen of Chester had enjoyed a steady trade with Dublin during the reign of King Henry I (1100–30), though they were subsequently overtaken by the port of Bristol, whose connection with Dublin also antedated the Norman invasion. Once again the lead given by Dublin was soon followed by Ireland as a whole. In the mid-twelfth century the chronicler William of Malmesbury exclaimed contemptuously: 'Of what value could Ireland be, if deprived of the merchandise of England?' This economic dependence, he commented, explained why the High-King Muirchertach O'Brien and his less celebrated successors were almost invariably careful to maintain a show of devotion, even subservience, to Henry I.

Dublin's function, however, was not simply that of a half-way house between two cultures, drawing Gaelic Ireland into increasingly close contact with the religious, economic, and political concerns of the nascent Angevin Empire. It had a central role in the fierce competition for supreme power within the island. Together with the little Ostman kingdom that formed its hinterland it was a recruiting-ground for Norse fighting-men and warships that served any master for pay, and its urban fortifications and concentration of wealth made it an essential acquisition for successive kings asserting a claim to rule all Ireland. When Rory O'Connor advanced on Dublin and had himself inaugurated as king there in 1166, the Four Masters, who compiled their annals in the seventeenth century with a liberal dose of historical hindsight, viewed the ceremony as a formal induction not to the kingship of Dublin alone, but to the high-kingship of all Ireland.

Herein lay the nub of the dispute that resulted in the Cambro-Norman barons being invited to intervene. For Dublin, with its central position, its agriculturally rich hinterland and commercially successful port, was suited to act as capital not only for Ireland as a whole, but for the provincial kingdom of Leinster, then ruled by Dermot MacMurrough. Indeed we find the contemporary chronicler, Roger Howden, calling MacMurrough king of Dublin, just as the O'Brien and MacCarthy kings of north and south Munster were then known as the kings of Limerick and of Cork respectively. It was consonant with Dublin's position as political centre for the province of Leinster that in 1152 its see was finally incorporated into the Irish hierarchy as a metropolitan archbishopric, with all the bishops of Leinster as its suffragans, and that the next archbishop appointed in 1161 should be King Dermot's brother-in-law, the bishop-abbot of Glendalough, Laurence O'Toole (Lorcán Ó Tuathail).

The Dubliners themselves, who had killed Dermot's father and, so we are told, buried his corpse along with that of a dead dog under the floor of their assembly-hall, apparently preferred the prestige and comparative independence of association with a distant national ruler to the domination of a local tyrant. A conflict of interests had been avoided in earlier years when the northern high-king, Muirchertach Mac Lochlainn (d. 1166), repeatedly allied with Dermot MacMurrough to subject Dublin to their joint authority. However, no such compromise was available to the new high-king, Rory O'Connor. Based as he was in the province of Connacht, Rory's most strategically placed ally was the one-eyed king of Bréifne, Tighearnán O'Rourke (Ó Ruairc), an implacable enemy of Mac-Murrough. In 1152 the rivalry between these two kings for overlordship of the agriculturally rich but politically weak province of Meath had found expression in Dermot's abduction of O'Rourke's wife, the Meath princess Dervorgilla (Dearbh-fhorgaill). When O'Connor came to power in 1166, O'Rourke ensured that Mac-Murrough was not merely forced to submit and give hostages to the high-king, but was subsequently dethroned. Since the Dubliners were fighting for O'Rourke and O'Connor on this occasion, Dermot was forced to travel overseas in search of mercenary troops to retrieve his position.

The idea of invading Ireland had been discussed from time to time at the English court during the reigns of William the Conqueror and Henry I, and most recently in 1154–5, immediately after the accession of the young Henry II. In this instance the subject may have been raised as a result of Canterbury's outrage at losing all metropolitan rights over the see of Dublin, when it opted to become an Irish archbishopric in 1152. Certainly the only action taken was in the ecclesiastical sphere. The archbishop of Canterbury's secretary, John of Salisbury, was sent as an envoy of Henry II to the English pope, Adrian IV. As a result of his negotiations, the pope invested Henry and his successors with the right to rule Ireland, sending the king a gold ring set with a large emerald as a symbol of his investiture, since by virtue of a clause in the Donation of Constantine the pope was held to be lord of all the islands of the sea. It was a colourful episode, but Henry II would have been mad to divert his forces towards Ireland at the outset of his career when his hold on England itself was still insecure. He is said

CAMBRO-NORMAN KNIGHT AND FOOT-SOLDIER from the seal of Richard de Clare ('Strongbow'), earl of Pembroke, leader of the first generation of invaders. (This is a nineteenth-century drawing, as the seal is now in too poor a condition to reproduce.)

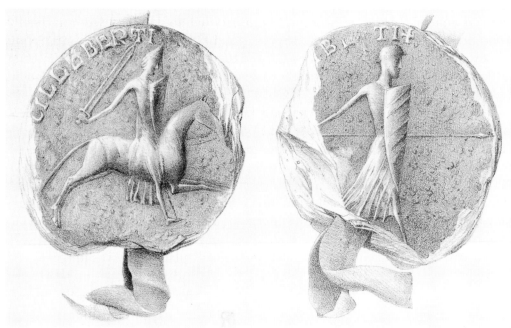

to have been dissuaded by his mother, the dowager-Empress Matilda. When King Dermot approached him for help in 1166, Henry was not prepared to become actively involved. He accepted homage and fealty from the Irish ruler and authorized his own subjects to come to MacMurrough's aid.

Using Bristol as his base, where he had been given a civic reception, Dermot initially recruited Richard fitz Gilbert de Clare, earl of Pembroke, and a group of Cambro-Norman barons including the half-brothers Maurice FitzGerald and Robert FitzStephen, both sons of the Welsh princess Nesta. These latter were promised Wexford and two adjoining cantreds for their services, while de Clare, better known to tradition as 'Strongbow', was offered Dermot's daughter Aoife in marriage and promised the whole province of Leinster on Dermot's death. Between 1169 and 1171 the Cambro-Normans not only reconquered all Leinster including Dublin for Dermot, but invaded the neighbouring province of Meath and harried Tighearnán O'Rourke's kingdom of Bréifne.

As soon as the scale of their activities became apparent, Henry II withdrew his consent, belatedly forbidding Strongbow to embark for Ireland and placing an embargo on exports to that country to cut off the invaders' supplies. Dermot died in May 1171, and Strongbow succeeded in crushing a general revolt of the Leinster Irish and establishing himself as lord of the province. The threat of an independent Norman kingdom on his western seaboard and, we are told, appeals for help from the Irish themselves, brought over the king of England at the head of a large army, landing near Waterford on 17 October 1171.

As things turned out, the army was hardly needed. Even before he embarked Henry had been intercepted *en route* by Strongbow, begging forgiveness for his disobedience and offering to hold the kingdom of Leinster as a fief. A delegation from the Ostmen of Wexford, who had defeated and captured Robert Fitz-Stephen, volunteered to deliver him into the king's hands for punishment. Once he arrived at Waterford, Henry made Strongbow a formal grant of Leinster in return for homage, fealty, and the service of 100 knights, reserving to himself the city and kingdom of Dublin and all seaports and fortresses. Thereafter in Munster, and on his leisurely journey to Dublin, the English king received submission and hostages, with the promise of tribute, from Dermot MacCarthy, (Diarmait MacCarthaigh), king of Cork, Donal Mór O'Brien (Domhnall Mór Ó Briain), king of Limerick, the chiefs of Leinster, Murchadh O'Carroll (Ó Cearbhaill), king of Airgialla, Tighearnán O'Rourke, king of Bréifne, and Donn Sléibhe MacDunleavy (MacDuinnshléibhe), king of Ulaid.

The Crown and Ireland

Arriving, as he did, fresh from the murder of Archbishop Thomas à Becket, the time was not opportune for Henry to publish his papal grant of dominion over

Ireland from the deceased Adrian IV, still less to champion the metropolitan claims of Canterbury. Nevertheless, he was careful to establish his image as the instigator of church reform. His own clerics, the abbot of Buildwas and the archdeacon of Llandaff, arranged for a great national synod of the Irish church to be held at Cashel in the winter of 1171/2, whose legislation on tithes facilitated the development of territorial parishes to complement the diocesan organization already set up, and whose general trend was designed to bring the Irish church into step with that of England in matters of liturgy and discipline. After Henry's penance and reconciliation with the church in May 1172 the reforming Pope Alexander III was confronted with a shoal of letters from the Irish prelates and an oral report by the archdeacon of Llandaff on the parlous state of Irish morals before the invasion, the improvement brought about by Henry and the voluntary submission of the Irish chiefs. Not surprisingly the pope gave his blessing to the *fait accompli* in three letters urging Henry to continue to uphold the church's rights, the Irish chieftains to abide by their oaths of fealty, and the bishops to excommunicate those who did not.

Romantic nationalists of the nineteenth and twentieth centuries have writhed with shame at the instantaneous submission of the Irish kings and bishops to Henry II, but in the circumstances the Irish had nothing to lose and something for which to hope: protection. They had repeatedly offered military resistance to the territorial aggression of the barons without much success, and they were shrewd enough to realize the English king was unhappy about the unbridled extension of Strongbow's power. For these chiefs submission entailed no loss of sovereignty; they merely exchanged the rule of the high-king of Ireland for that of the more prestigious 'son of the Empress'. By contrast the high-king himself, Rory O'Connor, was understandably reluctant to come to terms, and no overtures were received from his nearest rivals, the northern Uí Néill of western Ulster.

Once in Dublin, Henry granted the city by charter to his men of Bristol (who had played a large part in supporting his own accession to the throne as well as in forwarding the Irish campaign) with all the rights and liberties Bristol itself enjoyed. Since Meath had already been invaded in Dermot MacMurrough's lifetime, Strongbow had a claim to overlordship there. Instead Henry granted the whole province from the Shannon to the sea to his own follower, Hugh de Lacy, whom he subsequently appointed constable of Dublin, with the right to enfeoff tenants on the king's lands there, and justiciar, or representative of the royal government in Ireland as a whole. Having placed garrisons in the other seaports, including Cork and Limerick, Henry was compelled by crises elsewhere in his dominions to embark from Wexford on 17 April 1172.

Within a few months de Lacy had killed O'Rourke, *soi-disant* 'king of Meath', in the course of a parley, but it was not until 1175 that he and Strongbow finally controlled Irish resistance within their vast liberties, allowing the land to be shared out among their chief vassals. Often the new baronies were territorially defined in terms of an earlier Irish sub-kingdom, particularly in Meath. The year 1175 also saw the Treaty of Windsor drawn up between Rory O'Connor and Henry II, through the mediation of Archbishop Laurence O'Toole. By its terms Rory was recognized as high-king of all Ireland outside Leinster, Meath, and the environs of Waterford; he was to enforce and collect from the other kings the tribute Henry demanded of every tenth merchantable hide from beasts slaughtered in Ireland, and he was to compel any Irishmen who had fled from the conquered areas to return and pay tribute or perform their customary labour services for their lands—a hint that the conquerors were not finding their holdings as profitable as they might have been, for lack of tenants.

Rory's followers vaunted this treaty as a diplomatic triumph, but its significance swiftly dwindled to a guarantee of immunity for Connacht itself, as long as the tribute was paid. Neither side could control their subjects. In 1176, after repeated rebellions against both O'Connor and the English, O'Brien burnt Limerick to prevent its being garrisoned. South Munster was rent by dynastic strife. In 1177 the newly arrived John de Courcy exceeded instructions by mounting a free-lance expedition into Ulaid, and having conquered the area with breath-taking rapidity, ruled for a while as an independent 'Prince of Ulster'. A halfpenny struck at Downpatrick, in or before 1185, bears St Patrick's name on one side and De Courcy's on the other, with no explicit acknowledgement of the authority of Prince John as Lord of Ireland, though this was rectified on subsequent issues of coinage in that area. On the other hand, the death of Strongbow himself in June 1176, leaving only a short-lived boy and a baby daughter as heirs, temporarily transferred the whole province of Leinster into the king's wardship. Rather than remaining a neutral arbitrator between the invading barons and the Irish, the Crown was acquiring a greater financial stake in the success of the conquest. At a council held in Oxford in May 1177 Henry transferred all his rights as Lord of Ireland to his youngest son, Prince John. De Lacy's charter for Meath was renewed on stricter terms, and the two Irish kingdoms in Munster, considered to be in rebellion, were speculatively granted away: Cork to Robert FitzStephen and Miles de Cogan, who took possession of seven cantreds and exacted tribute from MacCarthy for the remaining twenty-four, and Limerick to Philip de Braose and others, who failed to conquer any land at all from O'Brien.

When Rory O'Connor retired to the abbey of Cong in 1183, Henry unsuccessfully petitioned Pope Lucius III to have John crowned king of all Ireland. The prospect thus raised of two allied but independent Plantagenet kingdoms in the British Isles was ultimately prevented by John's succession to the throne of England on the death of his brother Richard in 1199, but the concept had already died when the young prince was knighted and sent to Ireland on a first visit in 1185. The Irish were becoming increasingly disenchanted with Plantagenet lordship. It is noteworthy that Gerald of Wales, not usually accused of pro-Irish prejudice, felt that in confiscating the kingdoms of Meath, Cork, and Limerick the English had broken the terms of their original agreement, and by 1185 John de Courcy, self-made lord of Ulster, had been accepted as a tenant-in-chief of Prince John. The prince and his advisers made no effort to be conciliatory. We are told that some of his courtiers pulled the beards of Irish chieftains coming to greet his arrival in Waterford, and he received no submissions thereafter from the provincial kings. Even the first generation of invaders were alienated, finding themselves superseded by new men. Maurice FitzGerald had died in the same year as Strongbow, and when Hugh de Lacy was assassinated by an Irish subject in 1186, leaving under-age heirs, the vast territory of Meath, like that of Leinster, passed into the hands of administrators: 'men who . . . spent all their time in the greedy pursuit of wealth . . . who had the temperament of Mercury rather than Mars, who had more experience of civil life than of soldiering . . . neither loyal to their subjects nor formidable to their enemies', as Gerald of Wales fumed.

The Pattern of Colonization

The truth is, the purpose of English involvement in Ireland was beginning to change from acquiring lordship over men to colonizing land. The end of the twelfth and the beginning of the thirteenth centuries saw the last decades of a medieval population explosion in Europe which caused not only land-hunger and migration, but high food-prices and low labour costs. The sudden acquisition of large areas of underpopulated agricultural land in Ireland meant wealth for those who could develop its full potential. There was no overall blueprint, but the initiative of countless private individuals resulted in a surprisingly consistent and effective pattern of colonization. The original feudal grants were made on a military basis, in terms of baronies and knights' fees, and the conquerors defended the larger holdings by building mottes, high earthen mounds topped by a wooden tower (*bretesche*), or ringwork castles, such as de Lacy built at Trim or John de Courcy at Downpatrick, consisting of a circular bank surmounted by a strong wooden palisade and gate-tower. Even these early examples, however, show the characteristic choice of location—not on some high rocky crag for maximum defensibility, but at a pre-existing population centre with economic potential, normally one of the larger ecclesiastical settlements of pre-Norman Ireland.

When their hold on the land was sufficiently secure for them to subinfeudate and import tenants, it is noticeable that lords of every degree reserved large areas as demesne, to be directly farmed by their own labourers, and many set aside an even larger portion to found a borough town, where they hoped to market their agricultural surplus, endowing each burgage plot with anything from three to ten acres of arable land in the town fields. Since the original tenants-in-chief had first choice of location, it was usually towns founded by the great lords of the liberties, such as Kilkenny, Trim, and New Ross, which flourished into the modern period. Many less strategically placed foundations were fated to remain 'rural boroughs', where no urban commerce or manufacture developed, and the rent-paying burgesses supported themselves solely by farming the town fields.

The degree to which planning entered into the colonizing process is shown by the street patterns of towns newly founded in this period. Whereas the streets in earlier Norse or monastic settlements tended to wind along the natural contours of the site, Anglo-Norman foundations are typically laid out in a grid of intersecting straight lines, each street bordered by long narrow burgage plots, designed to allow the maximum number of substantial premises to enjoy the benefits of a street frontage. A roll giving the names of members of the Dublin merchant guild in the years immediately before and after 1200 indicates the new citizens were immigrating not only from the privileged town of Bristol, but from all over England and Wales, with some from France and Flanders. Similarly, the

THE NORMAN MOTTE AT CLONARD was located beside a celebrated Early Christian monastic settlement (the modern parish church and cemetery marking the site lie here behind the belt of trees in the background). At Kells, Kilkenny, Kildare, and Trim this combination of old and new foundations gave rise to medieval towns. Clonard was to prove an exception.

THE DUBLIN ROLL OF NAMES. A register of members of the Dublin Guild Merchant, beginning just before 1200 and continuing into the later thirteenth century.

surnames of tenants in rentals and manorial extents from the thirteenth and fourteenth centuries show that the great estates imported from England, Wales, and Flanders not only their knights, hereditary free tenants, and burgesses, but artisans and peasant farmers, cottiers, and gavillers, some of whose holdings were too small for subsistence, so that they earned their living labouring on their lord's demesne. All the colonists, however humble, were personally free, but living side by side with them were the native Irish tenantry, who were termed 'betaghs' and considered as serfs, bound to the soil like the villeins of England. In many cases they seem to have been organized as self-contained communities, paying their collective rent as a single lump sum. Where such families descended from the serfs or *daor-bhiataigh* of pre-Norman Ireland, their conditions may not have been greatly changed, but it seems likely that, as with the Norman conquest of Anglo-Saxon England, many of the poorer free landowners found their status redefined as serfdom. Only one Irish family is recorded as having been assimilated into the colony's feudal aristocracy, the FitzDermots of Rathdown, descended from Dermot (Diarmait) MacGiollamocholmóg, son of Domhnall the last king of the Vale of Dublin, a wavering supporter of Strongbow in the early days. The other Irish nobles within the lordships found themselves confined to the uncolonized districts, in practice the woods, bogs, and uplands, with a rather better tract being reserved in north Wexford for the descendants of Dermot MacMurrough himself, as cousins to Strongbow's heirs. The chieftains did not enjoy the security of hereditary feudal tenure, but held their shrunken territories as tenants-at-will, paying an annual rent or tribute to their Anglo-Norman overlord and joining his hosting with all their forces when he summoned them to war.

Throughout the lowlands of eastern Ireland, from Cork to Coleraine, the changes involved far more than a simple transfer of landownership. The English language took root in the towns and among the peasantry. Norman-French became so well established as a literary language among the upper classes that we have from the early thirteenth century a *chanson de geste* on the invasion of Ireland, christened by its twentieth-century editor, G. H. Orpen, 'The Song of Dermot and the Earl'. Domestic architecture in Dublin changed from the wattlework of the Norse period to heavier, timber-framed buildings, with an increased use of stonework. The churches and cathedrals of the colony were built in Early English Gothic style instead of Irish Romanesque, using not only imported decorative motifs but imported stone from English quarries. Most fundamentally, as long as the agricultural boom lasted, eastern Ireland changed from a subsistence to a market economy. The colonial manors, with their large demesne lands and English-style rotation of crops, produced a surplus which was effectively collected and marketed through the network of little borough towns linked by trade to the provincial centres and ultimately through the seaports to

DECORATED CAPITAL from Christchurch cathedral, Dublin, late twelfth-century. The design shows affinities with Wells cathedral, and some of the stone for this period of construction was imported from a quarry near Bristol.

TRIM CASTLE (*facing*), Co. Meath, the largest stone fortress in Ireland, was erected in the early thirteenth century by Walter de Lacy, lord of Meath, on the site of the twelfth-century earthwork of his father, Hugh de Lacy the elder, conqueror of Meath. After Meath was partitioned between Walter's two heiresses and their husbands, the castle served as the administrative centre for the liberty of Trim. The drawing by D. Newman Johnson reconstructs its extent about 1250.

England and the Continent. The wealth thus generated can be seen in the great stone castles of the thirteenth century, normally built not as outposts but as centres for the major Anglo-Norman lordships, housing not only the military garrison, but the administration of finance and justice.

King John and the Administration of Irish Government

John, lord of Ireland and later also king of England (1199–1216), was curiously fitted to impose a framework of unity and central control on this creative ferment. He was even more suspicious than his father of the power of men like Hugh de Lacy, who was not only lord of Meath on his death, but overlord of Bréifne and Airgialla and son-in-law to Rory O'Connor. John's rudeness as a young prince to the Irish chieftains may have arisen from his perceiving them also as rivals to his authority, though after he became king he learned to treat them as a separate element in society, like the towns or the church, who might be wooed for support in his constant struggle to control the great feudal barons.

Under John, the territorial expansion of the colony continued, but speculative grants were normally divided into smaller shares among a greater number of

tenants-in-chief. In 1185, during his first visit to Ireland, John granted the north-eastern portion of O'Brien's kingdom of Limerick (in and around the modern county of Tipperary) to Theobald Walter, whom he created first hereditary Butler of Ireland, to Philip of Worcester, and to William de Burgh. Both the Butler and William 'the Conqueror' de Burgh were to found important Anglo-Irish dynasties thereafter. They immediately took up arms to possess their allotted districts, but it was not until 1193 that occupation of the area became effective, when de Burgh married King Donal Mór O'Brien's daughter and undertook to support his father-in-law against MacCarthy. Tempted by the succession struggle raging in Connacht, de Burgh followed up his initial progress by obtaining a speculative grant of the whole Connacht kingdom, but almost immediately Prince John temporized. A peace was made between his justiciar and the late King Rory's brother, Cathal Croibhdhearg O'Connor (Ó Conchobhair), and the grant to de Burgh was eventually allowed to lapse. In 1201 John revived the Braose title to the whole kingdom of Limerick in favour of Philip's nephew, William de Braose, an absentee who thus became overlord of all the north Munster colony except for the lands of de Burgh, the church, and the city of Limerick. Meanwhile the O'Carroll (Ó Cearbhaill) kingdom of Airgialla was divided between Gilbert Pipard and Bertram de Verdon on the death of King Murchadh in 1189. The coastal plain between Drogheda and Dundalk, which became known as Louth or Uriel, was rapidly colonized, a process that may have begun even before O'Carroll died, while the settlement of Meath and Leinster took on a new impetus with the coming-of-age of Hugh de Lacy's son, Walter, in 1194 and the arrival in Ireland of William Marshal, husband of Strongbow's daughter, Isabel de Clare, in 1207.

To the north John de Courcy began to expand west of the River Bann. By marrying the daughter of the King of Man in 1180, he became distantly connected to the Mac Lochlainn dynasty, and appears to have supported their candidates against the new king of Tír Eoghain, Aodh Méith O'Neill. Subsequently, de Courcy began to play kingmaker in Connacht. With a typical combination of jealousy and economy, King John destroyed him, using as his tool Hugh de Lacy the younger, brother to the lord of Meath. This warlike and ambitious young man already held much of the de Verdon lands in Louth by right of marriage. In 1204 he invaded Ulster and defeated and imprisoned de Courcy. In 1205 the king created Hugh palatine earl of Ulster, with all the lands de Courcy held on the day of his capture. Finally in 1209 the former favourite, William de Braose, quarrelled with his royal master and fled to Ireland, where he was sheltered by William Marshal and the powerful de Lacy brothers in defiance of the king's justiciar. King John came to Ireland a second time with an avenging army in 1210. William Marshal, lord of Leinster, succeeded in making his peace, but the honor of Limerick, the lordship of Meath, and the earldom of Ulster were all

CASTLEROCHE, CO. LOUTH, begun c.1236 by the lady Rohesia de Verdon to defend her lands in Co. Louth. The Roche, or rocky precipice on which the castle stands, continued to mark the border between the Anglo-Irish settlements and the territory of the Great O'Neill for the rest of the Middle Ages. It was held by the Bellew family during the fifteenth century when it served as an important outpost of the Pale.

declared forfeit to the king. (An honor was a seigniory of several manors held under one baron or lord.)

Not surprisingly the Irish were more appreciative of the king's role on this occasion. Twenty Irish kings are said to have done homage to John at Dublin, and Cathal Croibhdhearg O'Connor, king of Connacht, and Muirchertach O'Brien, king of Limerick, joined his expedition to Ulster against Hugh de Lacy. It could be argued that by his stop-go policy towards the marcher barons King John bears some responsibility for slowing down the tide of conquest, and thus perpetuating the frontier between English and Irish-held areas which was to bedevil society in Ireland for the rest of the Middle Ages. On the other hand, it is hardly unduly speculative to assume that in the absence of royal control the struggle for the high-kingship of Ireland would have recommenced with Anglo-Norman candidates, and there is no guarantee that it would have been rapidly decided in favour of a single ruler.

As well as undermining the feudal nobility, John laid the foundations of royal government in medieval Ireland. Under Henry II the justiciar was already expected to act with the counsel of the feudal tenants-in-chief, but as the administration expanded in later reigns, the King's Council in Ireland included more and more permanent salaried officials. The Great Councils, when the king's officers were joined by the barons in general, gradually evolved in the course of the thirteenth century into parliamentary sessions, as in England. With so much of the conquered land held as liberties, royal revenue was confined at first to feudal dues and the rents and profits of justice from the king's lands round Dublin and Waterford. Under John this income was received and accounted for by a team of exchequer clerks working under the justiciar. A chamberlain of the exchequer is mentioned in 1215 and the head clerk was promoted to become the first Treasurer of Ireland in 1217. An *ad hoc* Court of the Exchequer sat to decide financial disputes in Henry III's reign, though there were no salaried barons of the exchequer before 1277. In the king's absence the justiciar was originally accustomed to issue writs under his own seal, and it was only under Henry III that a separate royal seal was made for Ireland, with a chancellor as its custodian, and sometimes only one or two chancery clerks under him to keep the rolls. More importantly the machinery of sheriffs and shires, county courts, and itinerant justices was first instituted under John, with the subsequent establishment of a permanent King's Bench in Dublin in 1248. Before he left Ireland in 1210 John exacted the barons' consent to a decree that the laws and customs of England should be observed in Ireland also.

The more the liberties were phased out, the further the king's writ ran. Dublin had a shire court in the 1190s. Waterford and Cork were under the care of a single sheriff in 1207–8. The forfeited lands of de Braose became the county of Munster, though separate shire courts were established for Limerick and Tipperary by 1235. Louth and the forfeited earldom of Ulster were jointly administered by royal officials until Hugh de Lacy was restored to his title in 1227, after which Louth was shired. Walter de Lacy had regained his liberty of Meath as early as 1215, but in 1241 he died and his lands were partitioned between his two granddaughters and their husbands, of whom only Geoffrey de Geneville (or de Joinville) acquired the full rights of a liberty with the lordship of Trim, while the de Verdon share of Meath was eventually shired, with a county court at Kells after 1297. Similarly in 1245 the last of William Marshal's five sons died childless, leaving the whole lordship of Leinster to be partitioned among his five daughters or their heirs. Four liberties emerged, centred on Wexford, Kilkenny, Carlow, and Kildare, Kildare becoming a shire in 1297 and Carlow in 1306. Since the westward expansion of the mid-thirteenth century had produced three further counties, Kerry, Connacht, and Roscommon, by the end of Edward I's reign there were twelve counties in Ireland directly under the Crown and only four remaining liberties (map, p. 70).

This increasingly elaborate system of government created an imperative need

THE IRISH EXCHEQUER IN ACTION, late fourteenth to fifteenth century. A drawing from the Red Book of the Exchequer. The chequered cloth acted as an abacus to assist calculations.

KILDARE   county
TRIM   liberty
O'NEILL   Irish chief
(Ulster)   lordship claiming chief's
          obedience
-------   approximate division between
          Meath and the liberty of Trim

O'DONNELL
(Ulster)

ULSTER

O'NEILL
(Ulster)

MACCARTAN
(Ulster)

MAGUIRE
(Ulster)

O'HANLON
(De Verdon)
(Ulster)

O'ROURKE
(Connacht)

MACMAHON
(De Verdon)
(Ulster)

O'CONNOR OF SLIGO
(Connacht)

O'REILLY
(Ulster)

LOUTH

O'CONNOR
(Crown)

MEATH

CONNACHT

O'FARRELL
(Trim)
(De Verdon)

(M)

TRIM

ROSCOMMON

MEATH

TRIM

KILDARE

DUBLIN

O'BRIEN
(Thomond)

KILDARE

CARLOW

TIPPERARY

KILKENNY

WEXFORD

LIMERICK

KERRY

WATERFORD

CORK

MACCARTHY (Crown)

0   20   40   60   80 km
0   10   20   30   40   50 miles

IRELAND IN 1307

for trained clerks. The Plantagenet kings by insisting on their rights as feudal overlords of the church's temporalities, and on the need for chapters to obtain the royal *congé d'élire* or 'licence to elect' a new bishop or abbot, had succeeded in using the English church not only as a recruiting-ground for their administrators, but as a lucrative source of benefices to maintain and reward these 'civil' servants. The system was extended to all colonized parts of Ireland. After the death of St Laurence O'Toole in 1180 there were no further native Irish archbishops of Dublin, and the successful candidates were normally royal appointees, not infrequently combining their archiepiscopal office with that of chancellor, treasurer, or even justiciar of Ireland. St Patrick's, Dublin, was founded as a collegiate church and elevated to the position of a second cathedral

ARCHBISHOP JOHN DE SANDFORD, tomb effigy in St Patrick's cathedral, Dublin. A nephew of Archbishop Fulk de Sandford, John (d. 1294) served the royal administration in Ireland as escheator, justice itinerant, and after his promotion to the archbishopric, as justiciar, deputy-justiciar, and keeper of the Great Seal.

largely to provide prebends which would support clerks for the royal and archi-episcopal administrations, since the existing chapter of Christchurch was monastic. During the reign of King John there was a systematic campaign to ensure that all dioceses under royal control should have Anglo-Norman bishops, and to this same end a royal mandate was issued soon after his death in 1217, that no Irishman should be promoted to a cathedral chapter in future. The pope refused to tolerate such discrimination and also repeatedly intervened to preserve the neutrality of the primatial see of Armagh, since during the thirteenth century the colonized county of Louth formed the southern end of the diocese, but the cathedral city itself was under native Irish rule. Only after the death of Arch-bishop Nicholas MacMaoilíosa in 1303 did the Armagh succession pass to an almost unbroken series of Anglo-Irish prelates, permanently resident in Co. Louth.

Royal control was not the only source of contrast, however, between the church in colonized territory and outside it. Since the territorial definition of parishes was taking place in the very years of the invasion, along the east coast their boundaries coincided in many cases with that of the manor, the basic unit of colonization, whereas in the west of Ireland the practice varied from kingdom to kingdom, parishes often being of a larger size, based on the boundaries of an ancient population-group, or the area attached to a particular shrine. There were marked regional differences in the allotment of tithes and glebe-lands. The generous endowment of Early Christian sites had resulted by the twelfth century in large areas of church land throughout Ireland, from whose hereditary tenants the ecclesiastical hierarchy was normally recruited. At the time of the invasion a portion of these lands had already been set aside to endow bishoprics and monastic communities who followed the newly introduced Cistercian, August-inian, and Benedictine rules. More was to be used for parish glebe-lands, and in areas of Norman rule the remaining estates were disposed of either by endowing the new communities founded by the barons—daughter-houses of monasteries in England and France—or simply by annexing them to the secular fiefs. Outside the colony, however, large tracts of church-land continued to exist over and above the property of diocesan clergy and monasteries, the tenants claiming benefit of clergy, and paying rents to the local bishop through their hereditary headmen or erenaghs (*airchinnigh*). Most of the native Irish clergy were still drawn from these intensely conservative communities, and their vested interests perpetuated many pre-reform traits, clerical marriage and concubinage, her-

ABBEY OF HOLYCROSS, Co. Tipperary. Founded as a Cistercian house in the twelfth century by king Donal Mór O'Brien, and endowed with a fragment of the True Cross, the abbey became a centre of devotion for both the Irish and the Butler house of Ormond and was largely rebuilt in the comparative stability of the fifteenth century. A bardic poem of that period probably celebrates its restoration: 'A sanctuary inviolable hung with gold variegated tapestry, a bright castle with carved doorways, a house full of books and light and music of psalms.'

editary office-holding, patronage of the bardic classes, and a tendency for Irish monks, though nominally Cistercian or Augustinian, to abandon dormitories and refectories and live in separate houses with their families, parcelling out the community lands between them.

Of course such regrettable lapses lent credibility to colonial legislation against the promotion of Irish clergy. It seems possible that the more remote areas now remaining under Irish rule had never been greatly affected by the pre-Norman reform movement. As late as 1256 the Dominican bishop of Raphoe complained of laymen in his diocese who worshipped idols. Franciscan and Dominican friars, by avoiding the trap of hereditary land-tenure, succeeded in maintaining their ideals relatively untarnished, and it was they who shouldered the burden of preaching and pastoral work in Gaelic Ireland. True to their founder's interest in vernacular song, the Franciscans formed an early and enduring alliance with the bardic poets, and were accused by the late thirteenth century of preaching insurrection to the Irish chiefs.

The Irish Reaction

From the beginning popular opinion in Ireland had reacted to the invasion more sharply than might appear from the actions of the chieftains, intent on salvaging their personal positions by diplomacy. Through Gerald of Wales we know that by 1185 retrospective 'prophecies' in the names of various early Irish saints were circulating, in which traditional fulminations against the Viking hordes were adapted to the Normans, and a Messianic deliverer was foretold. In 1214 a brief sensation occurred when a false 'Aodh, the Deliverer' claimed to be the fulfilment of such prophecies. We have the text of one poem from thirteenth-century Bréifne which alludes bitterly to de Lacy's murder of Tighearnán O'Rourke:

> Numerous will be their powerful wiles,
> Their fetters and their manacles.
> Numerous their lies, and executions,
> And their secure stone houses . . .
>
> Though great you deem the success of the Foreigners,
> You noble men of Ireland;
> The glorious Angel tells me
> That the Brefnians will avenge Tighernán.

Sooner or later the ruthless pressure of the barons towards expansion of the colony was bound to precipitate a crisis, but this was postponed to the mid-thirteenth century by the surprisingly long reigns of the provincial kings, Cathal Croibhdhearg O'Connor of Connacht (*fl.* 1195–1224), Aodh Méith O'Neill of Tír Eoghain (1198–1230), Donough Cairbreach O'Brien (Donnchadh Cairbreach

Ó Briain) of Thomond, or north Munster (1210–42), and Dermot MacCarthy (Diarmait MacCarthaigh) (1209–29) and his brother Cormac Fionn (1230–47) of Desmond or south Munster. Each of these rulers paid rent or tribute for his lands, was responsive to the mandates of the English king and his justiciar, and normally resorted to arms only to preserve the *status quo*. By so doing they avoided the confiscation of their kingdoms at the height of the colonizing period. During this breathing-space, continuity of Irish culture and a modest prosperity in the kingdom of Connacht is suggested by the fine late Romanesque or Transitional-style church of Boyle Abbey, Co. Roscommon, consecrated *c*.1220. On the shore of nearby Lough Key, O'Connor's chief vassal, Cormac MacDermot (MacDiarmata), founded a market town after the Norman manner in 1231. However, the English refused to grant such kings security of succession, though Cathal Croibhdhearg in the year of his death wrote twice to Henry III contrasting his own steadfast loyalty with the rebellions of the de Lacy brothers, and re-questing a renewal of King John's charter in favour of his son, Aodh.

Instead, since the government of England during Henry's minority was in the hands of Hubert de Burgh, brother to the late William 'the Conqueror', the whole kingdom of Connacht was declared forfeit in 1226, and granted to William's son Richard de Burgh, with five cantreds near the royal castle of Athlone being reserved for the king's use. A prolonged war broke out which ended in 1235 with de Burgh in possession of twenty-five cantreds of Connacht while Cathal Croibhdhearg's surviving son Feidhlim, still clinging to the title 'King of Connacht', held the five 'royal cantreds' near Athlone as a tenant-in-chief of Henry III, at a rent of £400 a year.

There is a detailed narrative of the conquest of Connacht in the annals, describing not only the Norman siege-machines and fire-ships, but a new element in Irish warfare, first noted in Munster at the end of the twelfth century, the 'kerns', bands of native Irish mercenary soldiers. Barefooted, bare-headed, and lightly-armed, they roamed the countryside in groups of twenty or so, hiring themselves out to Norman or native Irish leaders for the duration of a campaign, and remaining organized in bands in the brief intervals of peace, resorting like the *routiers* of fourteenth-century France to brigandage to support themselves. They were a natural product of the prolonged, piecemeal invasion, and were mirrored on the Anglo-Norman side by *routes*, larger bands of heavy-armed footsoldiers, known to the Irish as *seirseanaigh* (=*sergents*?), who also took service wherever they found an employer, whether baron or Irish king. This free interchange of personnel meant that the armies of either side were fast becoming indistinguishable, the more so as the barons began to follow Gerald of Wales's advice to wear lighter armour when fighting on the rough Irish terrain, and chieftains by the end of the thirteenth century had taken to wearing tunics and pisanes of chain-mail. With the polarization of attitudes that took place during the fourteenth century, and the insistence that there should be one war and one peace in the king's land of Ireland, the supply of Cambro-Norman *seirseanaigh* ran out, but in Connacht and Ulster they were already being replaced by troops from the Western Isles of Scotland. Feidhlim O'Connor's son and heir, Aodh *na nGall* ('of the Foreigners'), was so called not because of any close association with the Anglo-Normans, but because in 1259 he married the daughter of Dougal MacRory (Dubhgall MacRuaidhri), king of the Hebrides, who brought 160 warriors to Connacht with her, under the leadership of her uncle, Ailín MacRory. This is the earliest formal record of the importation of Scottish galloglass (*gall-ó-glaigh*, 'foreign warriors'), though we hear that a king of Argyle died fighting in O'Donnell's army in 1247.

The overall effect of these developments was twofold. In the first place the English no longer had a clear military superiority. Whereas in the twelfth and early thirteenth centuries Dermot MacMurrough, Cathal Croibhdhearg O'Connor, and their like gave land and money for the fighting services of the Norman barons, by the late thirteenth and early fourteenth centuries justiciars often contracted with Irish chiefs and their forces to aid the king's army. Secondly, within the Gaelic territories power began to centre on every minor chief who could command a war-band. The military role of the ordinary freeholder was reduced, and the overlordship claimed by the descendants of former provincial kings could only be asserted with the backing of an even larger war-band. Elsewhere in Europe the trend towards mercenary armies during the thirteenth century led to increased taxation and an elaboration of the administration necessary to collect, receive, and account for the money. In Ireland, by an extension of the royal billeting-rights of pre-Norman times, mercenary bands were simply authorized to collect their own wages from the husbandmen in both Irish and Anglo-Norman lordships. This was a custom (known as 'coign and livery') that encouraged anarchy and a subsistence economy by enabling every substantial landlord to maintain a little army, while dissipating the agricultural surplus on which the prosperity of the colony was based. From at least 1297 onwards, colonial legislation in Ireland attempted to confine the practice to the march lands or frontier, 'the land of war', where it was regarded as necessary for defence.

Another change in the mid-thirteenth century which was to have long-lasting consequences was the rise of the Geraldines. Maurice FitzGerald the invader had not played a very prominent role. Two of his sons, William, baron of Naas, and Gerald, baron of Offaly, were tenants of the lords of Leinster. Together with

CISTERCIAN ABBEY AT BOYLE, Co. Roscommon. Consecrated in the reign of Cathal Croibhdhearg O'Connor, king of Connacht, the abbey church was probably in part the work of 'Donnsléibhe Ó hIonmhainéin, a holy monk and chief master of the masons of the monastery of Boyle' (d. 1230). The decorative carvings were more ornate than the official Cistercian ideal required.

GALLOGLASSES, fifteenth century, from a tomb-front in Roscommon Abbey. These heavily-armed professional soldiers of Scottish extraction first came to the north and west of Ireland in the late thirteenth century. By the late fifteenth their descendants were finding employment in all parts of the country with chief and baron alike, as bodyguards, police, or élite corps among the army.

a third son, Thomas of Shanid, they received lands in Limerick during the occupation of north Munster. The free hand the barons of England and Ireland enjoyed for some time after the issue of Magna Carta and the death of King John resulted not only in the confiscation and conquest of Connacht but a certain expansion of the colony in Munster under Thomas fitz Anthony, royal *custos* of Cork and Waterford 1215–23. As a ward and son-in-law of fitz Anthony, John fitz Thomas of Shanid acquired lands in North Kerry and Waterford to add to his Limerick estates, laying the foundations of the power his descendants wielded as earls of Desmond. Further north Maurice FitzGerald, baron of Offaly, held the justiciarship 1232–45 and during that period deliberately used the forces of the Crown to support and extend the territorial power of the magnates, and was duly rewarded with the greater part of the modern county Sligo and further estates in Mayo and Galway after the conquest of Connacht, together with a speculative grant of Tír Conaill from Hugh de Lacy, earl of Ulster. Subsequently Maurice was to claim the whole kingdom of Fir Manach (Fermanagh), where he built a castle at Belleek in 1252, but with the news of his death in 1257 his town at Sligo and the castle at Belleek were destroyed by the king of Tír Conaill, Godfrey O'Donnell (Gofraidh Ó Domhnaill).

By this date there was widespread revolt in the Irish kingdoms. In Thomond, where old speculative grants were being revived, and some colonization had begun, King Conor *na Siudaine* O'Brien's young son Tadhg defeated and plundered the new settlers in 1257. In Desmond, having stirred Finghin Mac-Carthy into war by supporting the kingship of his cousin Donal Rua (Domhnall Ruadh), son of Cormac Fionn MacCarthy, John fitz Thomas obtained custody of the Decies and Desmond in 1259, becoming Finghin's immediate overlord. Finghin raided fitz Thomas's lands and burnt the frontier castles that had been erected around his shrunken kingdom. In 1261 he defeated the avenging army of Munster colonists and killed both John fitz Thomas and his heir Maurice at the battle of Callan. Although Finghin himself was slain the same year, and the co-operative Donal Rua MacCarthy (Domhnall Ruadh MacCarthaigh) eventually succeeded to the kingship, the long minority (1261–82) of the Geraldine heir, Thomas fitz Maurice of Desmond, put a stop to colonization in the south-west.

In Connacht King Feidhlim O'Connor was deprived of the 'royal cantred' of Omany (Uí Mhaine) after his son Aodh *na nGall* attacked the colonists in 1249. In 1255 Aodh formed an alliance with Brian O'Neill, king of Tír Eoghain, who was taking advantage of the lax administration of the earldom of Ulster after Hugh de Lacy's death not only to refuse all payment of rent for his lands, but to raid across the River Bann into Ulaid and destroy the towns and castles of the colony there. With Brian's help, Aodh *na nGall* doubled his territory by conquering the neighbouring kingdom of Bréifne in 1256, and then in 1258 Brian O'Neill, Aodh O'Connor, and Tadhg O'Brien met near the ruined Geraldine castle at Belleek, or Caol-Uisce, on the Erne. Aodh's overlordship of Bréifne was confirmed, and Brian O'Neill was accepted as high-king of Ireland, a claim immediately disputed by his near neighbour, O'Donnell. As it happened, Tadhg O'Brien died the following year, and the combined armies of Brian O'Neill and Aodh *na nGall* O'Connor were defeated by a local muster of the colonists near Downpatrick in 1260. Brian's head was cut off and sent to London to King Henry III, with much rejoicing at the downfall of one who presumptuously bore himself as 'King of the kings of Ireland'.

This sequence of revolts in the mid-thirteenth century has sometimes been seen as the beginning of the Gaelic recovery, but although Aodh *na nGall* lived on until 1274, to ravage the Geraldine lordship of Sligo in co-operation with King Donal Óg O'Donnell (Domhnall Óg Ó Domhnaill), the colony as a whole was still expanding, and in some ways this period of upheaval should be seen as the end of an era. Never again did a native Irishman attempt to make himself high-king. Seldom thereafter would the English Crown look to an Irish ruler for support against an Anglo-Norman baron. In fact few native rulers were left directly subject to the king or his justiciar. In 1263 the vacant earldom of Ulster was bestowed on Walter son of Richard de Burgh, who was already lord of Connacht. In 1276 the whole of Thomond was granted to Thomas de Clare, younger brother of the earl of Gloucester, and son-in-law to the FitzGerald lord of Sligo; then in 1292 Thomas fitz Maurice of Desmond was granted custody of the homages, rents, and services of all the king's tenants, English and Irish, in the Decies (Co. Waterford) and in Desmond.

Now Irish kings who wished to retain their lands had to co-operate, not with the royal administration, but with the barons themselves, and their political obligations of hostages, rent, and hosting-service were reinforced by close personal bonds. Earl Walter de Burgh gave his cousin, Eleanor de Nangle, in marriage to Aodh Buidhe O'Neill, the new king of Tír Eoghain. Thomas de Clare is said to have undergone a rite of blood-brotherhood with Brian Rua O'Brien, king of Thomond, though he subsequently had him executed in 1277. Gossipred, a relationship forged by standing godparent at a baptism, was common and may lie behind the sudden wave of Anglo-Norman names for Irish rulers, as 'Henry' O'Neill, 'Ralph' MacMahon (MacMathghamhna), and 'Thomas' Magauran (MagShamhradhain).

In 1276–7 the Irish bishops in Munster petitioned to have all native Irish outside the palatine earldom of Ulster granted the same access to common law as the colonists enjoyed. This was a step that would have promoted the integration of the two nations in Ireland, and weakened the power of the native rulers, but it would also have undermined the jurisdiction of the barons, and no such grant was elicited from Edward I, who pointed out that any free Irishman could apply for an individual grant of English law.

ARCHAEOLOGICAL FINDS illustrate the continuity of Dublin's trade links with south and west England between the eleventh and thirteenth centuries. Knight jug (left) and Ham Green pitcher (Bristol, 13th century). In foreground fragments of eleventh-century cooking-pots from Bristol and Cheshire.

ÉAMONN ALBANACH, the Gaelicized head of the Mayo Burkes, who dominated all Connacht in the mid-fourteenth century in defiance of both Irish chieftains and the English Crown. He is here shown in an imaginary portrait drawn for his sixteenth-century descendant.

CHIEFTAIN AND EARL. On the left the tomb effigy of a lay notable in Corcumroe Abbey, traditionally identified as Conor *na Siudaine* O'Brien, king of Thomond (d. 1268). Geographical location suggests the deceased was indeed a Gaelic chieftain, but the sculptural style belongs to *c*.1300, when the political and cultural influence of the barons over their vassal chiefs had reached its fullest extent. On the right a tomb effigy of a lay noble at Athassel Priory, perhaps either Walter de Burgh, earl of Ulster and lord of Connacht (d. 1271), or his son Richard de Burgh, 'the Red Earl' (d. 1326), who were both buried here.

Controlling the Irish kings was not the only means whereby the magnates of the colony consolidated their holdings. After a feud between the de Burghs and the Geraldines that lasted from 1264 to 1296, John fitz Thomas, baron of Offaly, consented to hand over the Geraldine lordship of Sligo to Richard de Burgh, earl of Ulster, in exchange for lands elsewhere in Ireland, leaving de Burgh supreme throughout Connacht and Ulster. Meanwhile fitz Thomas embarked on a quarrel with his immediate overlord, William de Vescy, lord of the liberty of Kildare and justiciar 1290–4, which resulted in Kildare being shired, and fitz Thomas being emancipated in consequence from de Vescy's jurisdiction. Quarrelling magnates drew support from their kinsmen and adherents. At a time when Irish rulers still considered themselves territorial kings, Anglo-Irishmen like John fitz Thomas and the earl of Ulster were becoming known as 'chieftains of their surname' (*cheueteyn de lynage, capitaneus de natione sua*). Each lord's following of blood-relations was reinforced by adherents, lesser nobles bound to their service for life by written agreements ('indentures of retinue'), and of course there were the ubiquitous bands of hired mercenaries. Acts of the Anglo-Irish parliament from 1310 to 1366 gave the heads of aristocratic lineages such as the Geraldines, de Burghs, Butlers, Berminghams, and so forth the authority and duty to arrest criminals among their kinsmen and adherents wherever they found them, to be tried and punished by the king's courts in the 'land of peace' or by the kin-head himself in the 'land of war', a strange jurisdiction over certain individuals rather than over specified territories which underlines the contrast between conditions in England and the colony.

Decentralization and Decline after 1300

By the opening of the fourteenth century the territorial extent of the Irish lordship was at its height. Every native ruler, even Maguire (Mag Uidhir) and O'Donnell in the extreme north-west, was legally the tenant of some earl or baron, or of the English king directly. In the north Richard de Burgh, 'the Red Earl' of Ulster, was colonizing the peninsula of Inishowen, and had wrested the little port of Derry from the control of the church with a view to developing it. In the west the ambitious circuit of the walls built for the medieval town of Athenry far exceed the area occupied by the twentieth-century town, while the Red Earl celebrated his acquisition of the Sligo lordship from the Geraldines by commencing work on the fine castle of Ballymote in 1300.

However, this colonization of the west in the second half of the thirteenth century did not stem from England directly, but from the recently established lordships of eastern Ireland, where there was little in the way of surplus population to draw on. The west was encastellated, and divided into baronies and knights' fees among a military aristocracy, burgesses were attracted to the newly founded towns, but there was no influx of peasant cultivators to bring the English language and customs to the countryside. Where the land was divided into manors, the tenantry seem to have been overwhelmingly Irish, and large areas were left under native rulers, subject merely to tribute and services. Here the character and organization of society was not greatly changed. The tributary kings could bring some profit and a considerable military following to a lord who was permanently resident, and had the energy and experience to keep them bound to his authority. The Red Earl of Ulster seems to have delegated this role to his cousins the de Burghs or Burkes of Mayo in Connacht, and to the de Mandeville family in Ulster. It was not a relationship that could be exploited by absentees, and the de Clares were less successful in managing Thomond. Similarly the justiciars who succeeded one another in office at Dublin lacked the continuity to establish any stable relationship with the O'Byrne (Ó Broin) and O'Toole chiefs of the Leinster mountains, and a constant guerrilla war on their own doorstep forced them to seek aid at times from the barons and their more docile Irishmen of Connacht, Meath, and Ulster to contain the threat.

It may well be asked why the reign of Edward I, a time of centralization in England, should see so much delegation of power in Ireland? Responsibility for the lordship of Ireland had first been granted to Edward in 1254 when he was still a prince, heir-apparent to the throne of England. From that date until his death in 1307, his chief interest in Ireland was as a source of money, men, and food to provision his campaigns in Scotland, Wales, and France. The constant drain this imposed on Irish revenues was continued under his son, Edward II. It brought the exchequer there to a state of near bankruptcy, and was accompanied by a stream of accusations about the incompetence and corruption of the Dublin administration. Local government by the magnates was cheap and effective, and for most of the Middle Ages the king's representative did not have the resources to do much more than arbitrate between them. The magnates' interests, however, were not identical with those of the colony as a whole. Private wars between the lordships disrupted trade and devastated agricultural land. Barons did not merely bring their Irish vassals on hosting with them against Anglo-Irish enemies, they might actually support and encourage another man's Irish vassals to revolt against him, as the de Burghs of Connacht urged O'Brien of Thomond to war against de Clare in 1311. The population expansion in Europe and the related boom in agricultural prices was now levelling off, and the falling profits from Irish estates led to disinterest among many of the colony's landowners who also possessed more desirable estates in England. By the end of Edward II's reign (1327), almost half the colonized land in Ireland belonged to absentees. The resident Anglo-Irish nobility accused these absentees of draining off the land's wealth, instead of investing it in the defence of their holdings, their derelict castles and unmanned frontiers encouraging the Irish to encroach and making their neighbours' military problems doubly difficult.

To make matters worse the Scottish war spilled into Ireland. Robert Bruce had been intriguing for support in Ulster for some time, reminding the native rulers of the common Celtic origin of both Irish and Scots, but also approaching the colonial nobility with whom he had many personal ties, having become the Red Earl's son-in-law in 1302. However, when his brother, Edward Bruce, landed at Larne, Co. Antrim, with an army of Scots in May 1315, it was as the ally of Donal O'Neill (Domhnall Ó Néill), king of Tír Eoghain and son of that arch-rebel, Brian of the Battle of Down. This association probably doomed the Scots' expedition from the start, because it alienated the overwhelming majority of the colonists, who were still the dominant force in Ireland. This political failure was already evident before Edward Bruce, who took the title 'King of Ireland', was finally defeated and killed in October 1318 at Faughart, Co. Louth. Nevertheless, his three-year campaign had devastated much land in the colony, an effect

COMMON SEAL OF THE TOWN OF
ATHENRY, fourteenth century. The
severed heads of Irishmen over the
gateway commemorate the Anglo-Irish
victory at the Battle of Athenry (1316)
over a federation of chieftains from
Connacht, Thomond, and Westmeath.
The heads may represent Feidhlim Ó
Connor king of Connacht, 'from whom
the Irish had expected more than from
any other Gael then living', and Tadhg Ó
Ceallaigh, king of Uí Mhaine (East
Galway).

magnified by the coincidental North European famine of 1315–17. He exposed
the impotence of the royal administration in Ireland and weakened the grip of
the magnates themselves. The Red Earl was defeated by Edward Bruce at the
battle of Connor in 1315, after which he not only lost Ulster for a time, but
the Irish of Connacht revolted, and were only brought back under control by the
savage battle of Athenry in 1316 in which five Irish kings were slain, with many
chieftains from Connacht, Thomond, and Westmeath. In Thomond Muirchertach
O'Brien supported Lord Richard de Clare and the other barons in 1317, blocking
the southward march of Edward and Robert Bruce, who were allied to a rival
branch of the O'Brien family, but when de Clare attempted to reduce Muirchertach's territory war broke out, and at the battle of Dysert O'Dea in May
1318 Richard de Clare was killed. Since his heir died without issue in 1321, claims
to the lordship of Thomond were divided among absentees and O'Brien chiefs
enjoyed *de facto* independence for the rest of the Middle Ages.

In 1316 responsibility for organizing Anglo-Irish resistance to Bruce had passed
to Roger Mortimer as king's lieutenant. In addition to his lands on the Welsh
marches, Mortimer held the lordship of Trim in Meath in right of his wife, and
his periods of influence in England (1316–21, 1327–30), like the justiciarship of
Hubert de Burgh in the thirteenth century, saw an upsurge in grants of privileges
to the Anglo-Irish magnates. The head of the Leinster Geraldines, John fitz
Thomas of Offaly, was created earl of Kildare in 1316, and the liberty of Kildare
was revived in 1317 for his son, Thomas fitz John, who succeeded him as second
earl. John de Bermingham, the victor at the Battle of Faughart, was created earl

of Louth in 1319, with a life-grant of liberty jurisdiction there. In 1328 James Butler was created earl of Ormond, with jurisdiction over the new liberty of Tipperary, and in 1329 the head of the Munster Geraldines, Maurice fitz Thomas, was made earl of Desmond with jurisdiction over the new liberty of Kerry.

With the fall of Mortimer in England a reaction took place. In 1331 the young Edward III announced he would shortly visit Ireland in person (a promise that was to remain unfulfilled), all grants made by the hated Mortimer were resumed, the administration was to be purged, magnates were not to quarter their private armies on the countryside, Irish hostages were to be held by the government rather than the nobility. Besides the new justiciar, Sir Anthony Lucy, the young king's interests in Ireland were forwarded by his friend and contemporary, Earl William de Burgh, grandson and successor to the Red Earl of Ulster. On his first arrival in Ireland the English-reared 'Brown Earl' found himself a leader in the age-old de Burgh–FitzGerald feud, and attempted to make peace, but a series of inquisitions on the turbulent conduct of the first earl of Desmond suggested that Maurice fitz Thomas had been in treasonable conspiracy with Walter MacWilliam Burke of Mayo and Henry de Mandeville, seneschal of Ulster. Earl William promptly attacked these two mainstays of de Burgh control in Connacht and Ulster. Henry de Mandeville fled to Dublin where he was imprisoned, and the death of Walter MacWilliam in the earl's own castle of Northburgh provoked widespread revolt among his vassals. Earl William was murdered by the de Mandevilles in 1333, leaving a baby daughter as heiress to his vast estates. In Ulster the royal administrators released Henry de Mandeville and recovered control of the colonized area, but lost the homages and services of all the Irish chiefs west of the River Bann, together with outlying settlements in that area. In Connacht the rebellious Irish chiefs were eventually subjected by Walter's brother, Éamonn Albanach ('Edmond the Scotsman') MacWilliam Burke of Mayo, who violently established himself as head of all the de Burghs or Burkes in Connacht and reigned in independence of both the earldom and the English king.

These momentous events, coming just fifteen years after the O'Brien chief's reconquest of Thomond, seemed to halve the colony overnight. The baby heiress of the de Burghs was later married to the king's son, Lionel of Clarence, and the subsequent union of their daughter Philippa and Edmund Mortimer meant that the earldom of Ulster, the lordship of Connacht, and the liberty of Trim in Meath were vested in a single absentee owner, the titles eventually passing to the house of York and thence to the English Crown. For the rest of the fourteenth century messages sent to England from the Anglo-Irish parliament complain insistently of decaying defences and incompetent administration in the lands of the great absentees, and prophesy the imminent ruin of the colony through reconquest by the Irish chiefs and rebellion by 'degenerate' or Gaelicized Englishmen.

Political problems were compounded by economic ones. The inclement weather and famine which accompanied the Bruce invasion ushered in a series of bad harvests followed in 1348-9 by the Black Death. Shrinking population levels and an agricultural depression led to the abandonment of marginal land in many parts of Europe, and in Ireland this was reflected in the migration of colonists from all classes back to England. Lands wasted by the Scots in 1315-18 remained derelict for decades. Athenry was never to fulfil its early promise and excavations in Drogheda, though too restricted to be conclusive, indicate an area of the quayside was abandoned in the early fourteenth century and not brought back into use before the seventeenth. The revenues of the Irish exchequer ceased to be a source of profit to the English Crown.

Attempts at Restoration

This last consideration spurred Edward III and eventually Richard II into a series of attempts at restoring the colony's prosperity. An initial policy of blaming the financial decline on the corruption and incompetence of Irish-born administrators, and replacing them with 'Englishmen from England', combined with a Draconian decree of resumption to raise a storm of protest between 1341 and 1342, and drove the townspeople and lesser landowners into an incongruous semblance of alliance with magnates like Maurice fitz Thomas, first earl of Desmond, who had been repeatedly accused in the course of his career of plotting to seize power as an independent king of Ireland. In the face of this united opposition, wiser counsels prevailed. The king decided that in order to make the colony profitable, a preliminary investment of men and money was necessary, to re-establish royal control over English rebels and Irish enemies by military force. If possible the districts that lay waste were to be replanted, and the absentees compelled to return to Ireland or provide for the defence of their lands there. The colonists in these years seem to have genuinely feared the eventual extinction of their community. They begged the king not only for armies and money, but that he should come himself or send some great noble of England who could wield unquestioned authority over the Anglo-Irish magnates.

This community of interest between the ruler and the ruled prompted the organization of a series of major expeditions from England to relieve the plight of the colony in the later fourteenth century: first (1361-6) under Edward III's son, Prince Lionel of Clarence, now earl of Ulster and lord of Connacht in right of his wife; then (1369-72, 1373-6) under William of Windsor, husband of the old king's mistress, Alice Perrers. Two planned expeditions under Robert de Vere, earl of Oxford, in 1386 and Prince Thomas of Woodstock, duke of Gloucester, in 1392 were aborted by the instability of English politics in the reign of Richard II.

ART MACMURROUGH KAVANAGH, lord of the Irish of Leinster, riding to meet the earl of Gloucester during Richard II's second expedition to Ireland in 1399. Jean Creton, from whose verse chronicle the above illustration is taken, says that Art 'was calling himself King of Ireland, where he owns many a wood and little arable land'.

RICHARD II'S FLEET returning to England in 1399. The force at the king's disposal on his first expedition of 1394-5 had numbered some eight to ten thousand men, an army on the scale of those used against France during the Hundred Years War. However, financial difficulties considerably reduced the size of his ineffective second expedition.

Finally, the king himself came to Ireland leading an army of eight to ten thousand men in 1394–5, and again with a smaller force in the summer of 1399, just before his deposition.

   These repeated efforts to solve what was already beginning to be seen as an 'Irish problem' ended in disillusionment for both sides. The subsidies and soldiers certainly strengthened royal government in Ireland against the decentralizing tendencies of the magnates. The second and third earls of Desmond were by no means as turbulent as their father had been; but the Hundred Years War was taking up most of England's attention and energy in these years. The interventions in Ireland's affairs came sporadically, with government reverting to unsubsidized rule by the earls of Kildare, Ormond, and Desmond in the intervals. No military conquest could repopulate the colony or solve the economic depression, and consequently it began to emerge that no amount of investment in the lordship of Ireland was likely to bring the king a financial return. In particular the device of warding, or surrounding areas under native Irish rule with a string of small, strategically placed garrisons, though effective in containing the threat, was a constant drain on the exchequer without reconquering a foot of land. The statutes passed in Kilkenny in 1366 at a parliament summoned by Lionel of Clarence had shown that the English government was now converted to the Anglo-Irish commons' own view of themselves as a beleaguered outpost of civilization. The statutes codified over fifty years of colonial legislation against magnates quartering their armies in 'the land of peace', waging private wars, and making private peaces with rebels, against the use of March or Brehon law instead of English common law, against degenerate English who wore Irish costume and spoke Irish, against intermarriage and fosterage with the Irish enemies, selling them food or horses in time of war or weapons in time of peace. Englishmen from England were forbidden to abuse the colonists, faithful lieges of the lord king, by calling them 'Irish dogs' or the like. However, in spite of this moral, financial, and military support from England, it emerged during William of Windsor's term of office that the colonists were unwilling to contribute largely themselves towards the cost of reconquest. Efforts to force absentees to return or pay for their lands' defence led many to sell off their estates to residents in Ireland, and this reduced the interest in Irish affairs felt in English court circles. Eventually, these considerations combined with the chronic financial difficulties of the Lancastrian kings to bring about a much less interventionist policy towards Ireland in the fifteenth century.

The Gaelic Resurgence

Meanwhile, the native Irish rulers had been nourishing high hopes. In 1364 the inauguration ode for Niall Mór O'Neill, king of Tír Eoghain, began:

Ireland is a woman risen again
from the horrors of reproach . . .
she was owned for a while by foreigners,
she belongs to Irishmen after that.

The son and successor of this king, Niall Óg O'Neill, was described on his death
in 1403 as 'a man who the [learned] companies and pilgrims of Ireland thought
would take the kingship of Ireland on account of the prowess of his hands and
the nobility of his blood'. In 1374 the King's Council in Ireland wrote that O'Brien
of Thomond 'falsely and without title claims to have the lordship of Ireland'. The
ambitions of the Irish and the fears of the Anglo-Irish were both exaggerated.
Some land previously colonized was indeed reoccupied: as the peninsula of
Inishowen, the town and lordship of Sligo, the coastline of Clare from Ennis to
Limerick, the barony of Farney in Monaghan, arable lands bordering the bogs
and mountains of Leinster. Irishmen entered into possession of castles built by
Anglo-Norman magnates, as at Sligo, Ballymote, Cloughoughter, and Don-
aghmoyne, sometimes as a result of conquest, more often perhaps by a tenancy
agreement with their former owners, after the disappearance of the settlement
that the castle was originally built to defend.

As the peasants and artisans of English descent migrated out of the border
areas, landlords became increasingly dependent on Irish tenants if they wished
their lands to return a profit. Such colonists as remained often alleged that their
Irish neighbours, and more especially the troops of Irish kern the landlords
billeted on householders to defend the border, were spying out the land and
prompting their wild Irish kinsmen to attack the district—or at the very least
that Irish husbandmen were inhibited by fear or favour from taking up arms to
resist such attacks.

The greatest change between the fourteenth century and earlier times was
this assumption that areas not actually colonized were in the hands of 'wild Irish
enemies' rather than rent-paying vassals. The most significant gain for native
rulers was thus liberty, not territory. In Ulster and Thomond this liberty was
almost absolute, in Connacht and Desmond the O'Connor and MacCarthy chiefs
were restrained by the presence of the Burkes and the earls of Desmond, and in
Leinster the chieftains had most freedom of action in the late thirteenth and
fourteenth centuries as the royal government inadequately attempted to fill the
gap left by the former lords of Leinster. As time wore on this role was to be more
effectively undertaken by the earls of Ormond and Kildare.

Since the magnates at the height of their power had followed the policy of
'divide and rule', treating every petty king in the territories subject to them on
an equal footing, some of the most savage fighting in this period of Gaelic
recovery took place between the Irish themselves, when the descendants of the
provincial dynasts strove to reassert their authority as overkings in a society

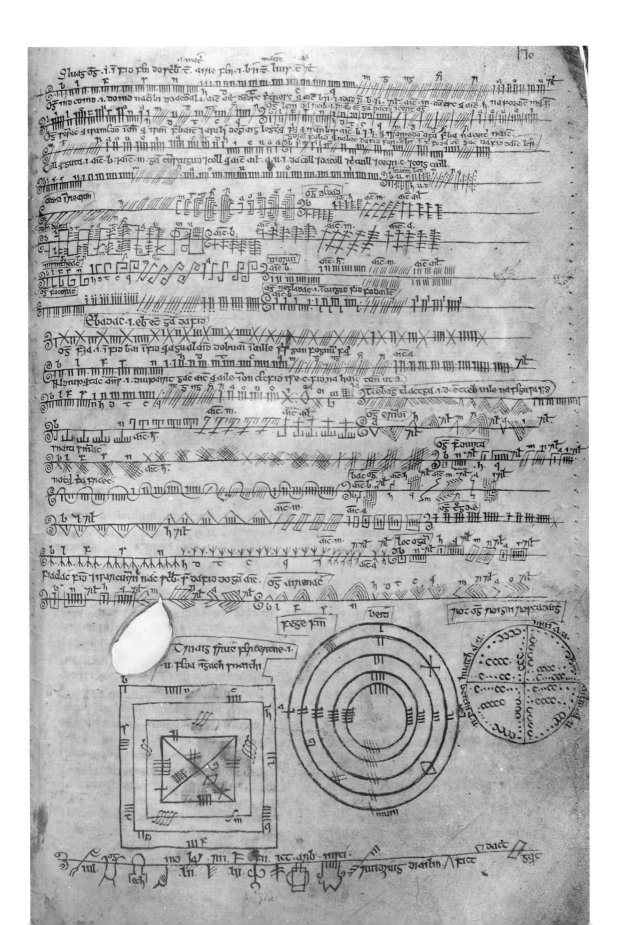

where every chief and noble maintained his own force of professional soldiery. Side by side with the military effort came a cultural revival. Bardic praise-poets had been experiencing competition in the mid-fourteenth century from less educated and consequently less expensive balladeers; their art had been condemned as a form of extortion by the more Anglicized Irish churchmen, an attitude possibly connected with the legislation against Irish minstrels at the Kilkenny parliament of 1366. Now the bards' ornate, elaborate verse, wholly directed towards increasing the prestige and legitimizing the authority of their patrons, towards celebrating their victories and recalling their illustrious ancestry, came back into fashion, and flourished until the seventeenth century and the final conquest of Ireland under James I. Similarly the scribes and *seanchaidhe* or traditional historians enjoyed enthusiastic patronage. Great manuscript compilations, like the Book of Ballymote, written *c.*1383–97, preserved the lore of the pre-Norman monastic schools, tracing the ancestry of contemporary chieftains back to the pre-invasion kings, and stating the original boundaries of their territories with their customs and tributes. Even the styles of manuscript illumination, leatherwork, and wood-carving looked back for inspiration to the twelfth century.

Only by re-creating the provincial kingships could the Irish hope to accumulate sufficient power to challenge the great earls, and this question of overlordship was a burning issue when King Richard II attempted to reconcile the chiefs to his authority in 1395. There was some amusement in the English army when, having narrowly failed to capture the Leinster leader, Art MacMurrough Kavanagh (MacMurchadha Caomhánach), they discovered his personal seal, on which he styled himself 'by the grace of God, King of Leinster', a title comparable to that on the inscription he had inserted into the shrine of the Book of Mulling, restored by his orders in 1402: 'King Arthur, Lord of Leinster'. However, when the minor Leinster chieftains had submitted one by one to Richard II, some of them with a rope about their necks, the articles of Art MacMurrough's own submission recognized his authority over the others, and his responsibility to ensure that they abode by the terms set. Similarly the submission of O'Brien of Thomond in 1395 recognized his authority over a long list of chieftains ruling in the area of the modern Co. Clare. The Great O'Neill father and son, Niall Mór and Niall Óg, were styling themselves at this time not merely kings of Tír Eoghain, but respectively 'Prince' and 'Governor of the Irish of Ulster'. In their

PAGE FROM THE BOOK OF BALLYMOTE. Compiled *c.*1400 for Tomaltach MacDonagh, lord of Tír Oilealla in the modern Co. Sligo, the Book preserves sagas and historical tracts from the pre-Norman period, together with genealogies of the late fourteenth-century Irish chieftains. Some sections are explicitly stated to be copied from a twelfth-century monastic manuscript, the Book of Leinster. Looking still further back, the oghams on the page above are a series of arcane alphabets based on the script once employed on monumental standing stones of the pre-Christian and Early Christian period. (*See above*, p. 7.)

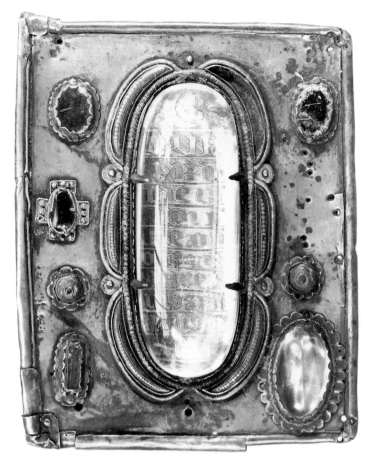

SHRINE OF THE BOOK OF MULLING, constructed to house a small gospel book of the seventh to eighth century belonging to the monastery of St Mullins, Co. Carlow, and claimed to have been written by St Moling himself. The restoration of this book-shrine by the lord of the area, Art MacMurrough, in 1402 is typical of the general revival of pre-Norman art and learning which accompanied the political resurgence of the Gaelic Irish at this time. Under the central crystal a partially legible inscription styles MacMurrough 'King Arthur, lord of Leinster, baron of...'

case the claim was understandably challenged by Roger Mortimer, earl of March and Ulster and heir apparent to the English throne. King Richard, whose policy at this time was to restore the Crown's original role in Ireland as lord of Irish and English alike, offered to arbitrate between his cousin Mortimer and the Great O'Neill, but in practice his appointment of Mortimer to govern Ireland after his departure made war inevitable. Mortimer won a military victory in Ulster with the help of the earls of Kildare and Ormond, but died in battle against the Irish of Leinster in 1398. Any possibility that Richard II could restore the position by his second expedition in 1399 was cut short by his deposition at the hands of the Lancastrians.

Ultimately, the winners in later medieval Ireland were to be neither the Crown nor the native Irish rulers, but the Anglo-Irish magnates. The area controlled by the royal administration shrank during the fifteenth century to the four eastern counties of Louth, Meath, Dublin, and Kildare. In order to protect the lives and property of the remaining 'faithful lieges of the lord king' in this district, a fortified earthen rampart known as the Pale was built to enclose it in the later fifteenth century, leaving half Meath and half Kildare on the outer side. (Map, p. 93.)

The Scots
of the Glens

MacQuillan
of the Route

O'Cahan

O'Donnell

O'Neill of
Clandeboye

Carrickfergus

The Great
O'Neill

L. Neagh

Maguire

O'Neill
of the
Fews

Magennis

O'Connor
of Sligo

O'Rourke

Magauran

MacMahon

The English of Ulster

MacWilliam
Burke of
Mayo

MacDermot

MacRannell

O'Reilly

CO.
LOUTH

O'Malley

O'Conor
Don and O'Conor
Rua

O'Ferrall

CO. MEATH

O'Flaherty

O'Kelly

English of
Westmeath

Clanricard Burke

Irish of
Westmeath

Connor
Faly

CO. KILDARE

CO. DUBLIN

O'Madden

O'More
of Leix

O'Toole

O'Brien

The Irish
of Ormond

CARLOW

Ormond

O'Byrne

O'Connor Kerry

Clanwilliam Burke

Earldom and
Supremacy
of Ormond

MacMurrough

Earldom and Supremacy
of Desmond

CO.
WEXFORD

O'Morchoe

Poers

MacCarthy

MacCarthy

O'Sullivan Mór

O'Sullivan Beare

| 0 | | 20 | | 40 | | 60 | | 80 km |
| 0 | 10 | 20 | 30 | 40 | 50 miles |

IRELAND IN THE LATER FIFTEENTH CENTURY SHOWING BOUNDARIES OF LORDSHIPS

The independent Irish lordships had been strong enough in the first part of the century to attempt interprovincial federations. A succession dispute in the O'Neill family after the death of Niall Óg in 1403 allowed the lord of Tír Conaill, Niall Garbh O'Donnell (d. 1439), to rise to power; he welded the whole province of Ulster into a sworn confederation against its absentee earls, and led the allied hosts on an alarming series of attacks on counties Louth and Meath. For the first time Louth undertook in 1423 to make regular payments of 'biack-rent', or protection-money, to the Ulster chiefs. About this date O'Donnell formed a marriage-alliance with the daughter of Calvagh O'Connor (Calbhach Ó Conchobhair) Failghe, lord of Offaly, who was waging a successful campaign against the colonists on the southern borders of Meath. Similarly, when Conn, son to this Calvagh, defeated and captured the Great Earl of Desmond, then Lord Deputy, in 1466, Tadhg O'Brien, lord of Thomond, invaded Desmond and exacted a promise of perpetual black-rent from the city of Limerick. It was said that O'Brien had bribed the Irish of Leinster 'so that they were working his coming to Tara' (the legendary seat of the high-kingship).

All such schemes foundered, partly because of the inability of the Irish to achieve long-term co-operation, but more essentially because of the power of the Anglo-Irish lordships, occupying the more agriculturally profitable and well-populated parts of Ireland. Just as O'Donnell and O'Neill had become paramount over the other northern chiefs, so in the fourteenth century the earls of Desmond had brought tenants-in-chief of the king in Munster, such as the Roches and the Barrys, under their own authority, and by the fifteenth century were closely intermarried with the MacCarthy chiefs and counted the corporate towns of Munster among their clients, since royal rule was now virtually extinguished in the area. Similarly the fourth (or 'White') earl of Ormond (d. 1452) had effectively annexed the royal county of Kilkenny to his own liberty of Tipperary, including towns and church-lands, summoning local assemblies of the inhabitants which legislated and granted taxation like miniature parliaments. In addition the White Earl in the course of his career enjoyed the alliance of MacMurrough Kavanagh, the Great O'Neill, and the Clanricard or Galway branch of the MacWilliam Burkes. The earls of Kildare had since the fourteenth century exercised a degree of lordship over the Irish chiefs in Meath, apparently with the consent of those chiefs' nominal landlords, the Mortimer family. From 1459 onwards they are found wielding increasing influence over the O'Neill chiefs of Tír Eoghain, in return for military support against O'Neill's rivals. They could only offer such support on an effective scale, however, when occupying the office of Lord Deputy, or chief governor of the colony.

The privatization of the royal administration itself had first been attempted by the White Earl of Ormond *c.*1420–44, by building up a supporting faction among government officials and, according to his enemies, packing the Anglo-Irish

House of Commons with his own grooms and household servants, even with Irishmen, and inciting Irish chiefs and rebel English to rise in war whenever his political opponents held the supreme office. The object was to ensure perpetual reappointment as chief governor of the colony, but Ormond was thwarted at every turn by an 'Englishman from England', Sir John Talbot, earl of Shrewsbury,

ARCHBISHOP RICHARD TALBOT, a brass effigy in St Patrick's cathedral, Dublin. Like his brother John Talbot, earl of Shrewsbury, the archbishop served repeatedly as chief governor of Ireland between 1419 and 1449 and headed a strong faction hostile to the White Earl of Ormond, which split the Anglo-Irish colony in two for a generation.

and his formidable brother, Richard Talbot, archbishop of Dublin, who fought him with his own weapons.

Ormond's sons became involved in the losing Lancastrian side of England's Wars of the Roses, and the Butler earldom fell for a time into abeyance. The Geraldines of Desmond and Kildare were associated with the victorious Yorkists, and at first tended to alternate in the office of Lord Deputy. However, an ill-judged attempt by Edward IV to recover control through the appointment of Tiptoft, earl of Worcester, in 1467–70 resulted in the attainder and execution of the Great Earl of Desmond in 1468 and the outright rebellion of the Munster Geraldines. This was to leave the earls of Kildare, Thomas fitz Maurice (1456–78), Gerald Mór (1478–1513), and Gerald Óg (1513–34), as the only surviving Anglo-Irish magnates of the first rank still eligible for high office.

Hitherto Kildare had not been the most powerful of the Anglo-Irish lordships, but it was strategically placed to annex the Pale, and to the horror of some of the more Anglicized inhabitants, society there began to be organized like a marcher lordship, with troops of galloglass billeted on the husbandmen, and unpaid hospitality or coign and livery exacted for the maintenance of the earl and his retinue as they passed about their business. Through the ostensibly independent Guild of St George the Palesmen were at last manœuvred into maintaining a standing army for their own defence, while disaffection could be punished by the deliberate incitement of border raids from the earl's Irish allies. In general, however, control of the Anglo-Irish parliament and the members of the King's Council in Ireland made the earls' continuous hold on supreme office virtually unshakeable, even in the face of occasional attempts at intervention by Edward IV and Henry VII.

Growth of a New Order

However much English officials and some Palesmen might disapprove, the Geraldine supremacy confirmed the trend towards relative stability in fifteenth-century Ireland. That this hard-won political stability was only relative is demonstrated by the mushrooming of little stone tower-houses throughout the Gaelic and Anglo-Irish lordships in this century, even within the walled towns, every substantial property-holder fortifying himself against riot and robbery. On the other hand, this new rage for castle-building contrasts with the absence of such undertakings during the depressed and war-torn fourteenth century, and argues for a degree of economic recovery. A new pattern of trade developed, depending not on the little market-towns, many of which continued to decline, but on the purchase of monopoly-rights from Gaelic chiefs and Anglo-Irish magnates. Trading-houses in the bigger cities would pay a local lord for licence to send their 'grey merchants' or 'forestallers' from house to house among his

SIEGE OF GLIN CASTLE. The slender tower-house, surrounded by the stone walls or in some cases the bank and palisade of the 'bawn' (Ir. *badhún*, 'cattle-fort'), became the typical fortified residence of Gaelic and Anglo-Irish lords alike during the fifteenth and sixteenth centuries. This contemporary illustration shows also the rectangular hall inside the bawn, which seldom survives to the present day, since it was normally constructed of wattle-and-daub and roofed with thatch or shingles. The Dubliner Richard Stanihurst wrote in 1584 that the Irish feasted in these halls but slept in the stone castles 'seeing that enemies can very easily set burning brands to the roofs of the halls, since that material catches fire very speedily'. Even the tower-house, he adds, had night-watchmen posted on the roof calling aloud to warn nocturnal marauders that the head of the household slept lightly, alert to repel attack.

subjects, buying up goods before they reached the public markets, and thus increasing their profits by cutting out the middleman. Similarly Spanish fishermen and wine-merchants frequenting the west coast negotiated directly with the chieftains.

More evidence for growing prosperity is supplied by the widespread erection of new religious houses in this period, mainly for the Franciscan Observants. Spiritually, Gaelic Ireland was influenced by the *Devotio moderna* of the Continent of Europe, though institutionally old-established church settlements like that on Devenish Island in Lough Erne had hardly changed since the early twelfth century. The fact that almost all the new houses were founded by Gaelic

HEAD OF A BURGESS from the carved misericords in St Mary's cathedral, Limerick. The ornate tombs and sidechapels in this cathedral bear eloquent testimony to the prosperity of the city's merchants in the fifteenth century.

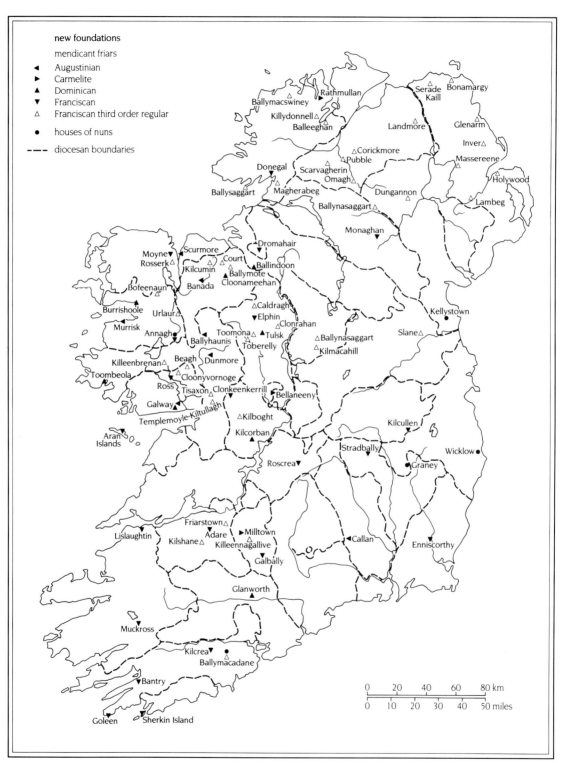

new foundations

mendicant friars
◀ Augustinian
▶ Carmelite
▲ Dominican
▼ Franciscan
△ Franciscan third order regular

● houses of nuns

--- diocesan boundaries

Ballymacswiney
Rathmullan
Serade Kaill
Bonamargy
Killydonnell
Balleeghan
Landmore
Glenarm
Inver
Masereene
Corickmore
Pubble
Donegal
Scarvagherin
Omagh
Dungannon
Holywood
Ballysaggart
Magherabeg
Ballynasaggart
Lambeg
Monaghan
Dromahair
Scurmore
Moyne
Rosserk
Court
Kilcumin
Ballindoon
Ballymote
Banada
Cloonameehan
Bofeenaun
Caldragh
Burrishoole
Urlaur
Elphin
Clonrahan
Kellystown
Murrisk
Annagh
Toomona
Tulsk
Slane
Ballyhaunis
Toberelly
Ballynasaggart
Killeenbrenan
Beagh
Dunmore
Kilmacahill
Toombeola
Cloonyvornoge
Ross
Tisaxon
Clonkeenkerrill
Bellaneeny
Galway
Templemoyle-Kiltullagh
Kilboght
Kilcullen
Aran
Islands
Kilcorban
Stradbally
Wicklow
Roscrea
Graney
Friarstown
Milltown
Lislaughtin
Adare
Killeennagallive
Callan
Enniscorthy
Kilshane
Galbally
Glanworth
Muckross
Kilcrea
Ballymacadane
Bantry
Goleen
Sherkin Island

0 20 40 60 80 km
0 10 20 30 40 50 miles

THE SPREAD OF RELIGIOUS ORDERS, 1420–1530

KILCREA FRIARY, founded *c*.1465 for the Franciscan Observants by Cormac son of Tadhg MacCarthy, lord of Muskerry. The Observantines were widely patronized among the Gaelic chieftains during the fifteenth century.

rather than Anglo-Irish patrons (map, p. 98) does not seem to spring from a cultural contrast between the two aristocracies. For instance, a list of books in the Great Earl of Kildare's library *c*.1500 contains besides twenty-one books in Latin, eleven in French, and seven in English, twenty Irish titles, the bulk of them concerned with religion and piety. Rather it would seem that the administrator-bishops, whom English kings continued to appoint to all dioceses that were even partially colonized, could not tolerate the challenge to the pastoral work of ordinary parish clergy posed by the Observantines. In Gaelic areas chieftains led their people in assaults on the persons and property of clerical concubines, which sometimes resulted in the alienation of church property also. Although the cause of the contrast was thus largely administrative, the decay of monastic houses in the Pale, and the more dynamic spirituality abroad in Gaelic Ireland, emanating from the Continent rather than England, had some part in moulding reactions to the Protestant Reformation when it came.

In general the cultural uniformity prevailing across Ireland was becoming

CANOPIED TOMB OF AN IRISH MERCHANT of the Ó Croidhin family (*left*), 1506, in Sligo Abbey. The Ó Croidhin merchants of Sligo town became so prosperous in the late fifteenth century that they intermarried with the local chieftains and extended their activities to Donegal where a trading settlement seems to have developed beside the O'Donnell castle and Franciscan abbey there.

CULTURAL INTERCHANGE (*facing*). On the left a page from the Saltair of MacRichard Butler, a miscellany of historical tracts and genealogies from pre-Norman Ireland compiled 1453–4 for Edmund MacRichard Butler, nephew of the White Earl of Ormond, the most prestigious of a number of Gaelic manuscripts written for Anglo-Irish patrons in the fifteenth and sixteenth centuries. On the right the intensively researched Life of Columba compiled for the early sixteenth-century chief Magnus O'Donnell shows influence from the Observantine Franciscans and the European Renaissance. Note that the saint's portrait is bordered with acanthus leaves rather than Celtic interlace.

more striking than the contrasts. The Gaelic chiefs lived in stone tower-houses with hired troops of kern and galloglass like their Anglo-Irish counterparts, and some, like O'Connor of Sligo or O'Reilly (Ó Raighilligh) of Cavan, centred their lordship on a town. The Anglo-Irish magnates had employed Irish bards and harpers at their courts from at least the beginning of the fourteenth century, and now began to lavish patronage on the scribes and *seanchaidhe*, the traditional historians, who reassured them about their place in Ireland's destiny as the latest in a long series of invaders, no more alien to the soil than the first Celts. A tendency among poets to stress the Irish blood flowing through the barons' veins as a result of frequent intermarriage with the native dynasties was to become even more pronounced in the sixteenth and early seventeenth centuries. Much

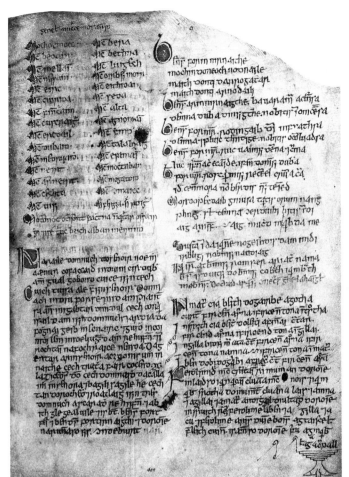

fifteenth-century Irish literature consists of translations and adaptations of English and Continental texts, saints' lives and homilies, Arthurian romances, medical and astronomical hand-books, the Travels of Sir John Maundeville and Marco Polo, the tales of Guy of Warwick and Bevis of Hampton, the Life of Hercules, and so forth. Scribal comments in the manuscripts refer to patronage from both Gaelic and Anglo-Irish magnates.

In November 1459 Richard, duke of York, officially lost his title of lieutenant of Ireland when convicted of treason against the Lancastrian king, Henry VI, and attainted by an English parliament. Nevertheless, in 1460 the duke summoned the Anglo-Irish parliament to meet before him in Drogheda. Its members confirmed him in office and made it high treason to compass his death or provoke rebellion against him, declaring 'the land of Ireland is and at all times hath been corporate of itself by the ancient laws and customs used of the same, freed of the burthen of any special law of the realm of England' unless such law had subsequently been accepted by the Anglo-Irish parliament. The political advantage for the duke of York in having this statute passed is obvious, but the wording makes it clear that he was drawing on pre-existing sentiments of separatism, already voiced during the fourteenth-century tension between the 'English of England' and the 'English of Ireland', and the resistance to taxation under William of Windsor. The historian Edmund Curtis hailed this statute as a move towards 'Anglo-Irish home rule', but it is premature to think in terms of nationalism in this context, even colonial nationalism. The desire for self-rule was more obvious among the magnates than the commons, and was frequently realized in the form of regional autonomy. It was only when a single aristocratic faction controlled or hoped to control the machinery of the royal administration that the whole lordship of Ireland was treated in practice as a separate entity from the kingdom of England, entitled to make an independent choice as to which candidate for the English Crown should command its allegiance.

PIERS BUTLER AND WIFE, St Canice's cathedral, Kilkenny. After the accession of Henry VII to the throne of England in 1485, the Great Earl of Kildare, who had supported the defeated Yorkists, found it expedient to marry his daughter Margaret to Piers Ruadh, son of James son of Edmund MacRichard Butler, the leading member of his family still residing in Ireland and thus the country's most prominent Lancastrian. In the event 'Maigín' or Lady Margaret FitzGerald became a virulent supporter of her husband's family in their feuds with the Geraldines, and Piers Butler himself eventually rose to power as earl of Ossory and Ormond.

By opting for the duke of York in 1460, the Geraldines and their friends had chosen the winning side, but they were less prudent in supporting Lambert Simnel in 1487 and Perkin Warbeck in 1491–6. The limited threat these incidents posed to the new Tudor dynasty was first and foremost countered by administrative changes which restricted the Great Earl of Kildare's control of central government. An English Lord Deputy, Sir Edward Poynings, was sent over in 1494, and the parliament he summoned to Drogheda forbade the holding of any future parliaments in Ireland without the king's licence, and his prior approval for all intended legislation. The Irish chancellor, treasurer, and other chief officers were no longer to be life appointments, as had been enacted in 1485, nor were they to have the power of electing a new justiciar of Ireland in the case of an unforeseen vacancy. The Guild of St George was dissolved. However, Kildare's dismissal, attainder, and imprisonment on this occasion was the signal for widespread border raids by his Irish allies, and it became obvious that he could be effectively replaced only by a continuing large-scale commitment of English financial and military resources. He was returned to office in 1496, and ruled until his death in 1513, when he was succeeded as Lord Deputy by his son.

In the changing political climate of the sixteenth century, this compromise could not last. There was a particular significance attaching to Poynings' Law which took away the Lord Deputy's control of parliament, since in England the success of the Tudors was based to a large extent on an alliance of the knights and burgesses in parliament with the Crown against the disruption caused by aristocratic factions. The gentry and burgesses of the Pale began to seek a return to that community of purpose between Crown and colony that had characterized the later fourteenth century, bitterly contrasting their present plight with the security enjoyed by the commons in England. It may not have been fully realized at first that the plotted downfall of the Geraldines would not only free the Pale, but leave the rest of Ireland ungoverned and ungovernable, unless the Crown was prepared to undertake a complete reconquest.

3

Early Modern Ireland
*c.*1500–1700

NICHOLAS CANNY

Irish Society, 1500 and 1700

THE most striking contrast between Irish social conditions in 1500 and in 1700 relates to the authority enjoyed by the Dublin government. Where in 1700 this authority seemed all-embracing and extended to all parts of the country, it was in 1500 feeble and confined to the river-valleys in the east and south-east of the country. Practically all the landowners and principal tenants in these areas were descendants of the Anglo-Norman settlers who had occupied those fertile valleys during the twelfth and thirteenth centuries and who then had brought much of Ireland beyond these areas under their effective political control. These sixteenth-century descendants of the Anglo-Normans, who are known to historians as the Old English in Ireland, spoke English; they were firmly attached to English legal procedures; and they owed unquestioning loyalty to the English Crown which they regarded as their ultimate protector.

To this extent, they could always be counted on to provide support to the king's lieutenant in Ireland in the matter of defending the English interest against Gaelic assault. Such assault was always a possibility. The settler population had originally been established in Ireland in the wake of a partial military conquest of Ireland, and memories of the original conflict were still vividly remembered on both sides. Recollections of lost greatness had encouraged successive generations of Gaelic chieftains to launch attacks upon the settler community, while in turn these attacks further convinced the Old English that they were the upholders of civil standards in Ireland against the ever-threatening barbarism that surrounded them.

But while it served to intensify their smug self-righteousness, the ever-present fear of attack also led to a high level of militarization within the Old English community. As a consequence, the primary allegiance of subjects was to their immediate lords rather than to remote monarchs or their lieutenants, and these lords took it upon themselves to provide for defence of their followers in return for specified payments or exactions. Such arrangements resulted in the formation

KERN OR CEATHARNAIGH were professional foot-soldiers in Gaelic Ireland. They were customarily represented by English and Old English observers alike as the essential disturbers of the peace. Those depicted here are revealed as bloodthirsty savages attired in Irish mantles, sporting *glibs* of hair and brandishing Irish swords and the Irish *scian*, or dagger.

of strong bonds of loyalty between man and man, and the more powerful lords tended to make manifest their greatness by maintaining bands of armed retainers and by constructing strong, defensible castles and towers.

The most overbearing of these lords were the FitzGerald earls of Kildare and the Butler earls of Ormond. Each of these families fostered the ambition to become the sole protector of English interests in the country, and their rivalry in this matter became so intense that its pursuit became of more concern to them than the suppression of their Gaelic neighbours. It had become evident by the end of the fifteenth century that the FitzGerald faction was the more powerful of the two, and it was out of a recognition of this fact that Henry VII and Henry VIII each successively appointed the ruling earls of Kildare to be their representatives in Ireland. Long tenure in this office further consolidated the power of the FitzGerald family, whose base was Maynooth Castle, and provided them with the pretext to enter into compacts with Gaelic chieftains who were far removed from the more Anglicized parts of Ireland.

These developments were allowed to proceed with scant interruption down to 1534—either because English monarchs were insecure on their thrones, or because they attached more importance to the pursuit of a Continental policy than to recovering their power in Ireland. The effective delegation of royal authority to the earls of Kildare for a sustained period demonstrates the low level of English interest in Ireland during the half-century previous to 1534. These earls, however, never succeeded in winning general acceptance of their authority among the Anglicized community in Ireland. While their long tenure in office did provide them with the opportunity to extend their influence, it also provoked their opponents into mobilizing themselves for defence against any possible assault.

This prolonged delegation of royal authority in Ireland to Anglicized Irish aristocrats led to the formation of political factions, and increased militarization of what had previously been the most pacific parts of the country. Critics of these developments alleged that the Anglicized parts of the country were succumbing to Gaelic influence. This was rendered plausible by reference to the developments in those parts of the country where Anglo-Norman control had previously been established but where settlement had been less intense: particularly southern Connacht where, it was alleged, the ruling de Burgh families had so far deviated from English civil standards as to be indistinguishable from Gaelic chieftains. It was also argued that the fertile lands of south Munster ruled over by the FitzGerald earls of Desmond were following the same course. Specific reference was made to the impoverishment of the farming population in Munster, because of the military exactions imposed on them by the earl and his supporters. These exactions and billeting practices, known collectively as coign and livery, were likened to the Gaelic practice known as *buannacht* and their application in previously Anglicized areas was taken as evidence that these areas were degenerating from their previous civility.

As a consequence of this criticism the term 'degeneracy' assumed a political meaning, and we now know that the extent to which English habits had been abandoned by the Anglicized population in favour of Gaelic ones was greatly exaggerated by contemporaries. Moreover, by constantly seeking evidence of the alleged degeneracy of Old English lords, the critics failed to recognize that the social trend which they were really witnessing was the fragmentation of Ireland into a sequence of political lordships, each governed over by a particular lord. Some of these lords were of Anglo-Norman descent, and others were of Gaelic origin; but the features which they shared in common were a desire to maximize their control over the residents of their territories and a wish to extend their jurisdictions by forcing previously independent noblemen to owe allegiance to them. The maximizing of authority was manifested by an increase in military spending and by an effort to establish control over the administration of justice within the lordship. There was little difficulty about effecting this within the Gaelic lordships, because the *breitheamh* or judge was always a member of a learned family who enjoyed a privileged status within a particular lordship and

A CIVIL WOMAN FROM THE PALE AND A GAELIC IRISHMAN, illustrated by Lucas de Heere, c.1575. Their juxtaposition was intended to represent the essential cleavage that was thought to exist in Irish society between the Old English and Gaelic populations. Later English observers tended to look with less favour on the Old English.

under the patronage of the ruling lord. Something similar could be achieved within an Old English lordship through the negotiation of a palatinate status from the Crown, and the three principal Old English lords—the earls of Kildare, Ormond, and Desmond—each enjoyed palatinate jurisdiction over a portion of the lordships over which they ruled.

This increased monopolization of power by the great lords meant an erosion of whatever independence had previously been enjoyed by their inferiors, as well as a reduction in the authority of Crown government. This reality was partly disguised as long as the earls of Kildare held office as Lord-Lieutenant because they worked diligently to raise revenue for a government that was under their personal control. But though they were willing to do so while they were in power, the earls of Kildare made it clear on several occasions that they would do everything possible to obstruct Crown government if ever they were dismissed from office. And whenever they were dismissed they lived up to their promise to render the country ungovernable.

Such episodes reveal both the fragility of whatever authority still remained with the Crown in Ireland and the extent to which political 'balkanization' had occurred. The balkanization in itself did not make Ireland unique, because several feudalized societies in Europe became dismembered into small segments during the later Middle Ages. In most of these, however, efforts were underway to have one nobleman or monarch establish political dominance over the warring factions. The reverse was happening in Ireland at the beginning of the sixteenth century. While the political boundaries of the several lordships were constantly shifting, the overall pattern remained constant.

The Sixteenth-century Economy

The most visible result of these trends was the construction of ever more elaborate towers and castles in the more Anglicized parts of the country, and the spread into Gaelic areas of defensible towers such as had previously been characteristic of the parts of Ireland subjected to Anglo-Norman settlement. Rival lords also increased the number of soldiers at their command; they extended the range of impositions that were placed upon the occupiers of the land for the maintenance of these men; and, as the sixteenth century progressed, lords in Ulster made increasing use of Scots mercenary soldiers who were notorious for the high payments they demanded of the farming population. The weapons of war also became more sophisticated, and hence more expensive, with the passage of time.

The object of this internecine warfare was the extension of dominion, and the aggressors hoped to achieve this through raiding and the destruction of property rather than through the imposition of heavy casualties. None the less, civilian life was affected—both as a consequence of the disruption that is inevitably associated with war and of the detrimental effect that the accumulation of exactions had upon the general standard of living. Contemporary accounts and pictorial illustrations of the farming population in the Gaelic parts of Ireland make it clear that their housing was of the most primitive and transitory kind. Clothing was also very basic, and the heavy wool mantles and linen shirts that were universally worn in the Gaelic areas were the product of domestic manufacturing. Some grain was produced and consumed in the Gaelic areas, but oats seems to have been the most common cereal crop, used for the production of oat meal which was sometimes made into cakes or else mixed with butter or other milk products. The systematic production of green vegetables seems to have been unknown in the Irish rural economy, and people supplemented their diet with watercress and other wild herbs, mixed with the ubiquitous butter. The one portrayal that exists of a Gaelic feast suggests that meat was eaten in profusion; but this probably applied to the upper social levels rather than the population at large. The enormous herds that populated the countryside were valued principally for their wool and skins rather than for their meat. Their contribution to the diet of the population lay in providing plentiful milk, which was then converted into butter or other milk products, and also blood which was taken from the live animals and mixed with oatmeal to make some kind of blood pudding.

These factors serve to illustrate both the importance of pastoral farming in the

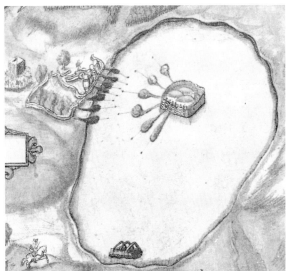

RUDIMENTARY FARMERS' HOUSES (*left*) were the norm throughout Gaelic Ireland. Their primitive condition indicates that the principal profits of agriculture were consumed by those at the upper reaches of society. Low investment in housing did, however, leave tenants free to abandon an oppressive lord.

A CRANNÓG (*right*). Artificial lake island dwellings where grain and valuables were stored at moments of danger. These proved serviceable throughout Gaelic Ireland until the late sixteenth century. Then the sophisticated weaponry of the English army rendered them obsolete.

Irish rural economy and the rudimentary nature of the pastoralism that was practised. Pastoralism continued to dominate because the technology of arable farming remained backward and was still primarily dependent upon the spade, but it is also true that semi-nomadic pastoral farming on unenclosed countryside was particularly suited to unsettled political conditions. Herds of cattle were eminently movable, and whenever danger threatened they could be removed to places of security in woody and mountainous areas. On the other hand pastoral farming—and particularly that on unenclosed countryside—was extremely wasteful of resources. Wherever it prevailed, there were strict limits placed on possible population levels.

Agricultural practice appears to have been more advanced and tillage more prevalent in those parts of the country where the Old English population was predominant. Familiarity with the agricultural economy in the more southerly parts of England was one reason; but another was the fact the most of the better farming land in the country was included within these Old English areas. The full range of cereal crops was grown on this fertile ground, the plough was in general use for tilling the soil, and the farming population lived in permanent village communities. But the fact that this population was more settled than that in the Gaelic areas meant that it was also more subject to disruption whenever political disturbance happened, and there are some indications that it was the Old English areas of Munster which suffered the greater population loss over the course of the sixteenth century.

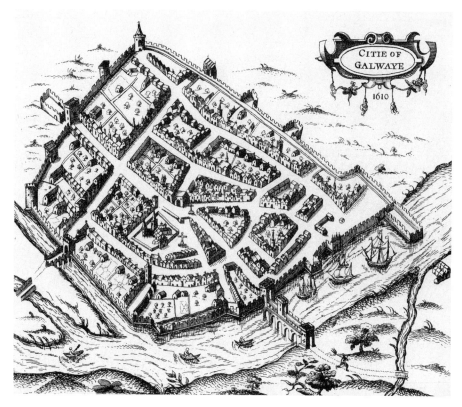

THE TOWN OF GALWAY, 1610. Speed's map provides an accurate depiction of the town. Its small size reveals the relative insignificance of urban settlement in Ireland previous to the seventeenth century. The presence of gardens within the walls of the town also suggests that there was no great pressure on space.

The reference to population loss reveals a fundamental difference between Irish social conditions in the late fifteenth and in the late seventeenth century. The trend at the end of the seventeenth century was for the population to move upwards, increasing except when periodically pulled back by high mortality rates during years of bad harvests or poor market conditions. We can take it that birth-rates in the late fifteenth century were also high, but the resulting underlying trend towards population increase was constantly halted by the recurrent political disruption that characterized the history of Ireland throughout the sixteenth century. This means that the Irish demographic experience was then completely at variance with that of western Europe. Where the population of Europe almost doubled in size over the sixteenth century, that of Ireland at best remained constant and may have stood at little more than 750,000 people at the close of the century. Even this figure, which is no more than a crude estimate, conceals as much as it reveals. The population was not evenly distributed, and we know from literary evidence that the more fertile areas of Munster and Ulster were left almost entirely denuded of people in the aftermath of the wars that had been fought over these territories during the 1580s and 1590s.

While it is thus possible to attribute population loss over the course of the

The freres
KRAGFARGUS TOWNE
KRAGFARGUS CASTELL

THE OLD ENGLISH OUTPOST OF CARRICKFERGUS was the only sizeable town in Ulster down to the end of the sixteenth century. This depiction of the town about 1570 shows that it was not very extensive. Of particular interest are the castellated houses of the principal merchants, which were a feature of all Irish provincial towns at this period. The haphazard location of Gaelic huts suggests that there was but a dim concept of town planning and the boats in the harbour indicate that trade was on a modest scale.

sixteenth century to war and political dislocation, the original low population base has to be attributed to a generally backward technology. The contrast with the late seventeenth century is most apparent when we look at human habitat. By the close of the seventeenth century almost all land that could be put to profitable use had been converted into farms, and the members of scientific societies devoted themselves to the question of how bogs and other marginal land could be rendered suitable for agriculture. No such concerns were manifest in the late fifteenth century when dense settlement occurred in only the most fertile and the most secure parts of the country. The remainder was left under natural forest or had become scrubby marshland, exploited for agricultural purposes only in providing grazing land for the huge herds of cattle, sheep, and goats that constituted most of Ireland's movable wealth at the close of the medieval period.

Trade had little prospect of flourishing in such conditions, and what little overseas trade did exist was concerned with the exchange of such raw materials as hides, tallow, and linen yarn for wine, salt, and manufactured goods. This trade was handled by Old English merchants of the port towns; they and their subordinates extended commercial activity into the Irish countryside, which they traversed with their small horses. Even this trade was only possible when safe conducts had been negotiated from the lord of each territory through which they passed, and abundant complaints are recorded over the lords' having defaulted on these promises. What these complaints amounted to was the charge that Old English lords were attempting to concentrate the profits of trade in their own hands, and in this they were imitating the practices of Gaelic Irish lords. These latter, through their exactions, had made it impossible for towns to survive in their lordships; and Old English merchants faced a grim future as efforts to forestall their trade become ever more frequent.

Religion and Authority

Such activity serves to illustrate what little respect was accorded to the privileges and immunities which these towns were supposed to enjoy. A similar disregard was displayed towards the liberties of the church in Ireland, and its immunities had been so intruded upon by the late fifteenth century that it had become almost entirely absorbed into secular society. This was immediately evident in the Gaelic lordships, where the priestly office had become to all intents and purposes a hereditary one; special provision was made for the maintenance of priestly families as it was for the support of the families of bardic poets, genealogists, and lawyers. To this extent priests could be seen to be clients of the local lord, and the concern of these lords to exercise control over the church and its resources was most evident when episcopal vacancies were being filled. Then

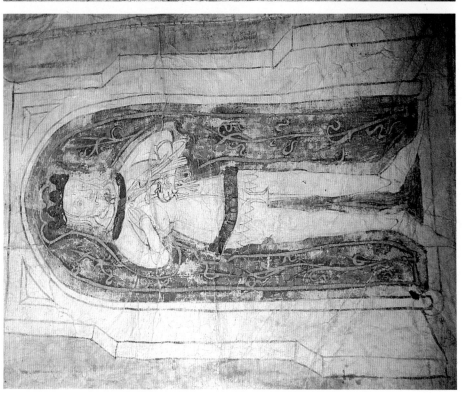

THE CHARTER ROLL OF WATERFORD CITY, inspected by Richard II during his second expedition to Ireland in 1399, gives us a series of Anglo-Irish portraits of their English kings, here on the left King John, on the right Edward III.

GERALDVS·FILIVS·GERALDI·COMES·
KILDARIE·ÆTATIS·43·Å·DNĨ·1530·

they did everything possible to ensure that close kinsmen were appointed to serve as bishops in their local diocese.

Lay interference in ecclesiastical affairs was not quite as blatant in the Anglicized areas of Ireland, but it was none the less a constant reality. Bishoprics in these areas were frequently held by members of the principal noble houses, or by individuals who were favourably disposed to the ruling dynastic lord. This trend was even more evident when it came to the appointment of parochial clergy. The wealth of the monasteries in these areas had also been brought firmly into secular hands through the appointment of abbots who were kinsmen of the ruling landowners. The most obvious consequence was the summary termination of monastic building programmes after worldly minded abbots gained control of institutions which had once been the bedrock of Irish spirituality.

The power of local lords was, therefore, at the end of the fifteenth century the dominant political influence in Ireland. The fact that this was as evident in the Anglicized as in the Gaelic lordships indicates the weakness of central institutions. But the essential proof of that weakness was the fact that most of the country was under the rule of Gaelic or Gaelicized lords. These would have known of the existence of English Crown claims to rule over Ireland but would have rejected them, while the vast majority of the residents within their lordships would have known of no king besides their immediate rulers. Neither would the population have known any language besides Irish, and the only legal system with which they were acquainted was that administered for the chieftain by the local *breitheamh*. The church to which they belonged was, in matters of discipline and organization, far removed from the norms that obtained in England and Continental Europe; the effort that was under way to improve upon this position was being promoted by Observant Friars rather than by the institutional church.

These friars, whose purpose was spiritual renewal, concentrated their energies upon the Gaelic population of Ireland. Their efforts were matched in the Anglicized areas by the endeavours of an earnest group of educated laymen who persistently called upon the English Crown to involve itself in Irish affairs so that the perceived drift towards political and social chaos could be halted. But, while they advocated reform, the leaders of each of these movements must have recognized that theirs was a forlorn hope as they witnessed both central government and Christian church surrender to the voracious demands of the nobility in all parts of Ireland.

This portrayal of the realities of life in late medieval Ireland highlights the contrast with social conditions at the end of the seventeenth century. Furthermore, it focuses attention on the great discontinuity that had occurred during

GERALD ÓG FITZGERALD, ninth earl of Kildare, who like his father and grandfather strove to convert the chief governorship of Ireland into a hereditary office.

the intervening centuries. How had such an exceptional transformation been achieved?

Ireland Transformed, 1500–1700: Government and Religion

The principal instruments of the transformation that was effected in Ireland during the sixteenth and seventeenth centuries were the English state and the Catholic church, which became a reformed and reinvigorated institution in the later sixteenth century. To this extent, those who had emerged as reformers in Ireland at the beginning of the sixteenth century had their wish—although neither body of reformers would have been satisfied with the changes that were implemented over the course of these tumultuous centuries. But, while we may identify the English state and the Catholic church as the instruments of change, it is significant that the more intense efforts at transforming Irish society were always undertaken in response to demands from an established element within Irish society.

This point becomes immediately evident when we survey the involvement of the government in London in Irish affairs. This involvement was for the most part reluctant, deriving principally from the concern of successive English rulers to honour their obligation to defend their inheritance and to prevent Ireland from falling prey to foreign intruders. Occasionally, and almost without warning, rulers in England became engaged in frenzied efforts to draw Ireland to a desired social model, declaring that nothing would block their ambition to attain the desired objective. Later, when it became clear that the defined goal could not be readily attained, English official interest in Ireland waned, and governors who had been specifically appointed to pursue a forward policy were instead directed to wind down the very schemes that they had initiated.

All monarchs were concerned to uphold the English Crown position there; but they could be persuaded to take decisive action only when disorder in Ireland threatened the security of Britain, or compromised the continental involvement of successive rulers. Furthermore, the concern of these monarchs that they should be seen to be just and equitable meant that they gave ear to the overtures of Irish-born noblemen, many of them Catholic, whose advice ran directly counter to that of the serving officials in Ireland. The result of this conflicting counsel was political paralysis; and it was during these interludes of inaction that Catholic reformers in Ireland had the opportunity to mould Irish society after their own prescription.

The first of these Catholic reformers were, as was noted, the Observant Friars, who were already a potent influence in the Gaelic parts of the country during the closing decades of the fifteenth century. There they had acted as defenders of the community and of the church against the incursions of rapacious lords, but they emerged as opponents of Crown government in Ireland once King Henry VIII had denied the authority of the papacy in spiritual matters, and set the English Reformation in train. The Observant Friars were the first to state their opposition to the changes in church government proposed by the monarch and to this end they mobilized support for the FitzGeralds of Kildare, who had risen in arms against the Crown. Their endeavour to depict this revolt as a religious crusade may explain why it received such extensive support in the Gaelic lordships; the Friars certainly heightened the awareness in Ireland of what was involved in the religious changes being promoted in Ireland by the English Crown.

Some clergymen in Ireland were even persuaded to resign their positions in the church rather than bend to the dictates of monarchs who assumed first a schismatic and then a heretical position in relation to the Roman Catholic church. Of far greater consequence for the future religious loyalties of the Irish population was the tendency of many Old English officials and lawyers to withdraw their sons from English universities, lest they be exposed to the instruction of Protestant divines who had come to dominate intellectual life in several Oxford and Cambridge colleges. Instead these young men were dispatched to Catholic universities in Continental Europe where they were taught by teachers who were imbued with the reforming zeal of Counter-Reformation Catholicism. Some students decided to abandon the secular life and become priests; those who remained laymen in London were equally committed to Catholicism and were opposed to having any dealings with the state church in Ireland. The result of these developments was that a generation of Catholic enthusiasts came to maturity within the Old English community in Ireland, and tried to dissuade their relatives and associates from following the dictates of the English state in matters spiritual. Some of these in the 1570s and 1580s carried their convictions to the point of recommending a communal withdrawal of allegiance from a monarch who, in 1570, was excommunicated by the pope. More commonly, however, these zealots sought to draw a distinction between spiritual and temporal allegiance. Thus they recommended to their kinsmen that they should refuse to attend at any services of the state church, but that they might continue to support the English Crown in temporal affairs.

The 'Old English' in Ireland

The general success of these Catholic zealots in the matter of persuasion meant that the one element of the Irish population which had been most consistently loyal to the Crown now refused to participate in services of the state church. Their refusal to do so meant that they rendered themselves ineligible for appointment to government office because Queen Elizabeth and her successors, like their counterparts on the Continent, insisted that all people appointed to positions of trust within their service should acknowledge the authority of the monarch in spiritual as well as in temporal affairs. Gradually, therefore, as positions fell vacant in the Dublin administration these were filled by English-born Protestants—often the only people who fulfilled this one necessary condition for appointment. The Old English lawyers who would ordinarily have expected preferment to these administrative posts were naturally resentful, and it was they who devised the formula that political loyalty did not involve the acknowledgement of Crown supremacy in spiritual matters.

No Protestant ruler in England or elsewhere could have accepted this formula; it was in clear contradiction of the principle steadily gaining acceptance throughout Europe, that the prince should dictate the religion of the community. None the less, successive rulers in England (except Oliver Cromwell) did indicate a willingness to receive delegations from the Old English community, and were sometimes guided by their advice. The leaders of such delegations were usually

THE BUTLER CASTLE AT CARRICK-ON-SUIR was completed about 1565. Its modern appearance is proof of the confidence and resilience of the Old English population just at the moment when they were being subjected to severe criticism by English Protestant officials.

members of the nobility or gentry from the Old English community. But the formulators of advice were always the lawyers who, in this sense at least, had become the leaders of the Old English community.

Their advice was always prefaced by profuse professions of the traditional loyalty of the Old English community to the Crown, and by expressions of their willingness to provide military and financial support for any reasonable policy of reform that the Crown might wish to pursue in Ireland. Such sentiments, however, were intended as a preliminary to a comprehensive critique of the policies being advocated by the English Protestant officials in Ireland, and to the assertion that these individuals were not fitted for the positions they held. This latter point was sustained by the argument that only those who were native to a community were truly concerned for its welfare, and that appointees from outside were interested only in personal gain. In support of this they contended that those Protestant officials who advocated the rigid enforcement of penal legislation against Catholics, and those who suggested that all Catholic landowners should be dispossessed, were in fact seeking to provoke a revolt that would create circumstances from which they themselves would derive benefit. Substance was provided for these charges when they pointed to the corruption of military or civil officers, and to the worldly concerns of some of the English appointees in ecclesiastical positions.

Such challenges were certain to win the attention of monarchs who were conservative by inclination and who were, in any event, keenly interested in saving money on the government of Ireland. As a consequence, successive monarchs allowed themselves to be persuaded to place a restraint upon the endeavours of their officials in Ireland, or even to cancel their reform programmes. This was the fate of the administration of the earl of Sussex, who had sought to provide a lasting solution to Ireland's political problems as Lord Deputy from 1556 to 1558; the same befell the reforming administrations of Sir Henry Sidney (1565–71 and 1575–8) in the following decade; and the ambitions of Arthur Lord Grey de Wilton were also summarily curtailed by royal intervention during the early 1580s. The example thus set by Queen Elizabeth was imitated by her successors, and even the forceful Thomas Wentworth, earl of Strafford and favourite of Charles I, had to suffer the indignity of having some of his specially favoured schemes cancelled by his royal master at the behest of spokesmen for the Old English interest. And where Charles I revealed himself to be pliant in the face of impassioned petition, after 1660 his son Charles II would prove himself to be even more so—especially if the petitioner had been consistently supportive of the royal cause during the interregnum.

It might seem, with the advantage of hindsight, that the Old English succeeded only in winning a stay of execution by deflecting the monarchs from schemes of government that were eventually implemented in full. This is to ignore the fact that the Old English—and particularly the Old English priests—took advantage of these lulls in government activity to proceed with reform endeavours of their own. These reformers sometimes supplemented the official effort by trying to make Irish lords abandon their Gaelic or military ways to embrace English justice and settled living. Their principal concern, however, was to confirm their fellow-countrymen in their attachment to Catholicism and to familiarize the principal Catholic landowners with current Catholic arguments. Thus they would be equipped both to counter the efforts of Protestant ministers and to protect their subordinates from the evangelization efforts of these missionaries of the state church.

The Catholic reformers were remarkably successful during the sixteenth century in securing the allegiance of the Old English population to the reformed Catholicism of the Council of Trent, and in developing a new church community which stood apart from, and opposed to, that of the established Protestant church. Their principal successes came in the late 1570s and again in the early 1580s, when the aggressive schemes of the officials were held in check. By the 1590s the Catholic reformers had succeeded in extending their message to such remote Old English outposts as County Galway and the province of Munster. Then, in the aftermath of the Gaelic defeat under Hugh O'Neill, earl of Tyrone, in the Nine Years War (1594–1603), these Old English reformers were joined by a substantial number of Gaelic Irish recruits. Some were already priests; others were from learned families of bards, *breitheamhs*, or genealogists who had found their way to the Continent where they had enlisted as seminarians. Together, they strove to extend their message to the previously Gaelic areas of the country, concentrating particularly upon those Gaelic landowners who had escaped the confiscations of the early seventeenth century and who continued to exert considerable influence in the provinces down to the outbreak of insurrection in 1641. The efforts of these missionaries again produced dramatic results whenever the assault against Catholicism was abated, and they had succeeded by 1641 in persuading the vast majority of the Gaelic as well as the Old English population to give their full allegiance to Catholicism. This success was largely cancelled by the Cromwellian onslaught of the mid-century. But such recovery was accomplished during the reign of Charles II that a vibrant Catholic community still existed in Ireland in 1685 to greet the accession of James II—the first Catholic monarch since Henry VIII had broken with Rome.

The Irish population of the sixteenth and seventeenth centuries were thus subjected to two opposing reform strategies, each calling upon different allegiances. That sponsored by the government emphasized the obligation of the subject to provide proof of loyalty to the Crown, while the reformers of the Counter-Reformation called upon individuals to remain true to the religion of their ancestors and kinsmen—though they knew that that religion too had been transformed by the Council of Trent. Each was a compelling summons (at least for the Old English population), and many strove to answer both calls. But they were eventually forced to recognize the impossibility of their situation, and to choose between accepting the state religion and taking a stand in the interests of the Counter-Reformation. This realization did not, however, come to all Irish leaders at the same time, and those who eventually chose the course of resistance to the government reform programme failed to muster the wholehearted support of their fellow countrymen. Resistance in Ireland therefore intensified rather than hindered the official reform effort. The sporadic nature of this resistance explains both the pace and profundity of the change that was effected in early modern Ireland.

CATHOLIC INSTRUCTIONAL LITERATURE was concerned both to retain the allegiance of the Irish population to Catholicism and to explain the Catholic doctrine as it had been newly defined at the Council of Trent. This illustration was designed to explain how Extreme Unction should be administered.

THE LORD'S PRAYER IN THE IRISH LANGUAGE PRINTED AT ANTWERP (*right*). The missionary effort of the Catholic church was opposed by the state but it could rely upon the support of the Counter-Reformation movement in Continental Europe.

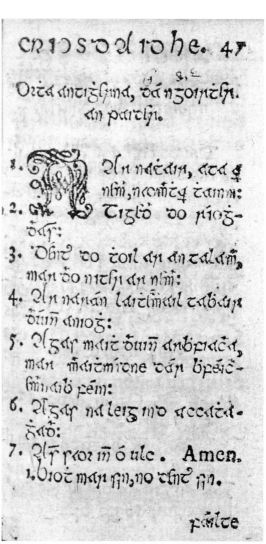

Strategies of Control, 1534–1565

The pace of political and even social change was, as has been suggested, largely dictated by the occurrence of resistance to English government authority. The first major resistance of the sixteenth century was that led in 1534 by Thomas Lord Offaly, son of the ninth earl of Kildare. This movement was simply intended as a show of force by the FitzGeralds of Kildare; their purpose was to convince Henry VIII that the power enjoyed as Lord Deputy of Ireland by the ninth earl of Kildare should not be interfered with, lest he withold his traditional loyalty and thus render Ireland ungovernable. Because the move was correctly interpreted as being a symbolic one, it enjoyed the support of all within the Anglicized community in Ireland who were traditional supporters of the Kildare house. This support quickly fell away, however, when the king made his purpose clear by appointing as deputy Sir William Skeffington at the head of a well-equipped army of 2,300 men. Then the hapless Lord Offaly was forced to depend on the military resources of his own lordship together with the extensive support he was able to muster in Gaelic Ireland and in the province of Munster.

What was intended, therefore, as a protest within the context of loyalty to the Crown thus assumed the appearance of a direct attack upon Crown government, and an assault upon the Anglicized population in Ireland by its traditional enemies. This turn of events gave the king and his advisers the pretext to impose the most severe penalty upon the FitzGerald family: their lands were declared confiscate to the Crown and all male members of the family, with the exception of an infant half-brother to Lord Offaly, were put to death.

Why the government of King Henry engaged upon such stern action is not clear, but it was partly motivated by the fact that the inexperienced Lord Offaly denounced King Henry as a heretic and declared himself champion of pope and emperor. This would certainly have stung the king, who was as yet uncertain of continuing support in England for his recent break with Rome. But it also drew attention to the fact that the ecclesiastical changes, and even the king's matrimonial status, that had been sanctioned by the English parliament, had no legal standing in Ireland. The Kildare challenge left the king with no choice but to convene a parliament in Ireland which would declare him to be supreme head of the church in the same way that the English parliament had done. Moreover, when this parliament was convened in 1536 the members, who were mostly from the Anglicized areas that recently had been in revolt, had no choice but to prove their loyalty by complying with the king's wishes. Therefore a body of religious legislation almost identical with that which had been approved by the English Reformation parliament was summarily passed by the Irish parliament of 1536–7. The only serious objection that arose there was quickly satisfied by the assurance that the secular landowners in Anglicized Ireland would be included in the division of the Irish monastic property that was being declared confiscate to the Crown. Thus the Kildare rebellion of 1534 paved the way for a successful reformation parliament in Ireland, and the state Catholicism which had recently been created in England also became the sole legal religion in the lordship of Ireland.

The passing of this legislation opened the way for the appointment of some Englishmen who were enthusiastic supporters of religious change to senior positions in the Irish church. This did not result, however, in any major drive to convince the population in the Anglicized area of Ireland of the need for religious reform. People generally acquiesced in the official religious position that was adopted both in the reigns of Henry VIII and Edward VI because these changes impinged little upon their spiritual lives. This is not to suggest that the English governors, officials, and clergy who came to dominate political life in Dublin were neglectful of their duty to promote a spiritual renewal in Ireland, but rather that they were so preoccupied with recurring political crises that they had little opportunity to deal with religious matters.

The political crises stemmed directly from the overthrow of the Kildare house. With the FitzGeralds removed, an end was brought to the dominance which they had previously exerted over the Gaelic lords of the midland area. These lords immediately took arms on the pretext of upholding the FitzGerald interest, and when this movement had been defeated they continued to launch sporadic onslaughts against the settled community of the Pale for the simple purpose of taking booty. Such disruption forced the government to undertake a series of military expedients—some aimed at suppressing the dissidents through military forays far beyond the confines of the Pale, and others at securing the frontiers of the Pale by establishing a series of military garrisons. Both schemes proved expensive and ineffectual, and the government eventually stumbled upon a strategy which contained elements of both. This involved the restoration of the surviving FitzGerald heir who had found refuge on the Continent, the return to him of his ancestral title and a portion of his family lands, and the dispossession of the discontented lords of the Gaelic midland area. These were to be replaced by English army captains who would have command over the garrisons that were erected, and who would derive revenue from the lands around each fortified position. The dispossessed lords and their followers were then pushed back into the boggy terrain of the west midlands, and those Gaelic lords who wished to make peace with the government were provided with the opportunity of doing so through the arrangement that has come to be known as the policy of surrender and regrant.

This policy (if a series of *ad hoc* arrangements deserves that description) involved the ruling Gaelic chieftains in making submissions to the government and in recognizing the monarch in England as their legitimate ruler. In return the

THE INAUGURATION STONE OF THE O'NEILLS. The rite of inauguration was particularly important to Gaelic chieftains because it occurred only after they had prevailed over their kinsmen for succession to power. Places of inauguration were therefore revered in Gaelic Ireland just as they were reviled by English officials who decried Gaelic succession procedures.

monarchs, who were styled kings and queens of Ireland by the Irish parliament of 1541, recognized these lords as their liege subjects and guaranteed to uphold their authority and that of their designated successors against local challenges. On the other hand, the lords were expected to assist the extension of English legal administration to their territories; they were required to abandon their military ways and to collect definite revenues from their followers instead of extracting uncertain military exactions; and they were enjoined to facilitate the gradual Anglicization of their lordships by having their nominated heirs raised in the houses of gentlemen either in England or in the English Pale.

It was unclear throughout the 1540s and 1550s whether the purpose of the government was to maintain its foothold in Ireland or to extend its influence to all parts of the country. Whatever the purpose, the reality was a sporadic interference in all areas, and occasional blistering attacks when negotiated arrangements were subsequently cast aside. This meant that the cost of governing the country escalated rapidly, as the small force of 300 fighting men that was made available to the governors of the 1530s had increased to become an army of 2,500 men by the middle decades of the century. Administrators in London were at first agreeable to this increase in military support, because they believed the cost would be borne by the rents which would accrue to the Crown from the confiscated monastic and secular lands. Once it became apparent, however, that these anticipated profits had been filched away from the Crown by the community of the Pale and by the English governor Sir Anthony St Leger and his cronies, the government in London became alarmed. The priority shifted to discovering a scheme of government whereby the existing English influence in the country would be upheld, but without any recurring cost to the English exchequer.

Plausible schemes were brought forward by Thomas, earl of Sussex, and by Sir Henry Sidney; their efforts to enforce these contradictory schemes were to dominate Irish politics from 1556 to 1579. Each of these young men was identified with one of the two opposing noble factions at the Elizabethan court, and each was concerned to earn a reputation for himself while denigrating that of his rival. Each solicited the position of governor of Ireland; the two together have been described as 'programmatic governors', because each devised a scheme for the long-term government of Ireland which they hoped to put in place in a short period of time, usually three years. These schemes were both devised in England without any consultation with interested parties in Ireland; both received the prior approval of Queen Elizabeth and her principal advisers; and both men hoped to return to England crowned with glory in the wake of a short, sharp period of rule in Ireland. Both were sorely disappointed and learnt that the promised official support would quickly disappear as soon as it became apparent

THOMAS RADCLIFFE, EARL OF SUSSEX, AND SIR HENRY SIDNEY. These two governors of Ireland dominated policy-making from 1556 to 1578. Although brothers-in-law they were bitter rivals and they promoted policies which were diametrically opposed. Ironically the more moderate Sussex fell foul of the Old English community because of his irascible character while the more amiable Sidney retained their affection even when he advocated a scheme of colonization that was opposed to Old English interests.

that increased cost was involved. Their experience created the situation whereby senior figures in English political life were subsequently reluctant to accept service in Ireland, and demonstrated to the several elements of the Anglicized population in Ireland that they could defeat even senior English statesmen if they combined their resources against them.

Sussex believed that the key to long-term political stability lay in the consistent adherence to the groundwork that had been laid down by his predecessors. To this end he was a forceful advocate of the military settlement of the Gaelic midland area; the arrangement which has come to be known as the Laois–Offaly plantation was finalized during his years of government. Stability in Gaelic Ireland was, he believed, best assured through the enforcement of the surrender and regrant contracts that had been already agreed upon, and he was particularly concerned to see that power and property were transmitted to the designated heirs under the original agreements. Then, for the reform of the provincial areas which were ruled over by lords of Anglo-Norman descent who had lapsed from English civility, Sussex recommended the institution of provincial councils or presidencies which would revive English legal procedures in those lordships.

This third element of the Sussex programme, although outlined, was never attempted, because his energies were concentrated upon the introduction of stability to the Gaelic areas. His attention was particularly focused upon Shane O'Neill, a spectacularly independent Gaelic lord who had chosen to disregard the surrender and regrant arrangement that had been negotiated for the lordship of Tyrone, laying claim to political succession according to Gaelic procedures. Should this defiance be permitted to prevail, contended Sussex, there was no hope for the survival of any other arrangements that had been negotiated. He therefore set himself to oust Shane O'Neill from Ulster to make way for Matthew O'Neill, baron of Dungannon, and his sons.

This decision required an unprecedented build-up of military forces, but the government became reconciled to this on the understanding that the campaign would be of short duration and a substantial portion of the cost would be borne by the community of the Pale. However, Sussex's attempt to raise local revenue without parliamentary sanction roused a predictable protest, reaching a crescendo when exactions were continued over four successive years. This was so because continuing military incursions into Ulster proved futile and the Palesmen were fearful lest the exactions become a permanent tax. To prevent this they commissioned delegations to lodge formal complaints with Queen Elizabeth; it was their arguments which decided the queen to bring an end to the rule of Sussex.

After the end of Sussex's government it was expected by the Old English community that Sir Henry Sidney, appointed governor in 1565, would prefer conciliation where Sussex had favoured war. Sidney did not discourage this view, though he had in fact presented to the government a policy far more aggressive than anything contemplated by Sussex. Sidney's scheme of government did not depend upon winning the support of any Gaelic lords by persuasion. He planned to dispossess those who engaged in military action against the Crown, or who could be shown to occupy Crown land. Their territories would then be parcelled out into smaller units. Some would be granted to the kinsmen of rebellious lords and the rest assigned to English adventurers who would engage, at their own expense, to settle English families upon their estates. These communities were to be responsible for introducing English law into these previously Gaelic areas, and would act as the eyes and ears of the government in the provinces while providing an example in civil living to the native population. Like Sussex, the new governor favoured the erection of provincial councils to strengthen the authority of the government in the previously Anglo-Norman areas that had become degenerate. The presidents of these councils were to enjoy both the sole authority to raise money in the provinces for the maintenance of soldiers, and the responsibility to recover property into Crown possession. Whatever was recovered through the scrutiny of ancient titles was to be used, as in the Gaelic areas, to encourage the settlement of English communities on Irish land.

Colonization, Resistance, and Plantation

The launching of this scheme aroused much interest in England. Ireland was quickly invaded by a group of adventurers who had ambitions to revive dormant titles to land which had been occupied by their ancestors at the time of the Norman conquest. Such intrusion, including that on the Old English areas of the country, aroused immediate hostility and suspicion in Ireland—especially when these efforts at reclamation were supported by private armies, raised by the more enterprising individuals with state approval. Not surprisingly, these ventures aroused a series of insurrections, apparently welcomed by Sidney as a pretext to extend private plantation schemes far beyond what had been originally envisaged. This did not meet with the agreement of the queen, however—particularly since three brothers of her favoured Thomas, earl of Ormond, were involved in the rebellion. Instead she recommended mercy for all the leaders except James Fitz Maurice FitzGerald, cousin to the earl of Desmond, who had advanced a religious justification for his actions. Moreover, she implied that the impetuosity of her governor was primarily responsible for these revolts when she directed that an end be brought to the private attempts at colonization. In the 1570s Sidney was forced to pursue a scheme of government which was closer to that of Sussex.

This royal intervention forced Sidney to abandon his scheme of colonization through private endeavour. But it did not cancel the provincial councils that had

SIR THOMAS LEE, English Captain General of the kern. This stylized portrait, painted in 1594 by Marcus Gheerhaerts, symbolized the extent to which English captains in Ireland were caught between two worlds. Lee is portrayed in conventional Elizabethan dress to the waist but carries the lance of an Irish kern and, like them, goes barefooted. The painting must have reminded observers of the possibility that servants of the Crown in Ireland would lapse to Gaelic barbarism if the conquest was not completed.

been erected, nor did it affect the English officials appointed to serve in the central and provincial administrations during Sidney's period of rule. These officials clung rigidly to the opinions of their patron, and they lost no opportunity to compel the provincial lords in Ireland to abandon their military ways, and to discredit them in the eyes of the Crown. Their hostility towards Irish society was heightened by the fact that these young men had emerged from an English society that was becoming intensely Protestant, and they were genuinely shocked at the feeble condition of Protestantism in Ireland. This moved them to shrill criticism of all elements in Irish society and their actions, combined with their sentiments, irritated all political leaders in Ireland.

These, however, were reluctant to engage in any actions that could be interpreted as disloyal to the Crown. They remained quiescent—if disgruntled—until 1579 when James Fitz Maurice FitzGerald, who had been forced to flee to the Continent, returned to Ireland with a small military force preaching a crusade against the heretic queen. This intervention aroused widespread support in Munster and also some within the English Pale; the movement assumed major dimensions when it was joined first by a brother to the earl of Desmond and then by the earl himself. Such a challenge could not go unanswered if the Crown was to maintain any credibility, and the queen was moved to put together a major army of 8,000 men under the command of Arthur Lord Grey de Wilton.

The fact that the English government took such a determined action inspired some of those who had wavered on the brink of rebellion to come to the support of the government. Some who had moved beyond the brink also sued for mercy, but no favour was to be shown to the ringleaders of the revolt in either Munster or the Pale. Those in the Pale who were captured were deprived of their property and were subjected to exemplary death by hanging, drawing, and quartering. The zeal of the executioners was made manifest by the efforts of the officiating clergymen to persuade those about to be slain that they should recant their allegiance to the papacy. In Munster the concern was to pin down the expeditionary force, which was duly put to the sword, and the English army then gradually wore down the local opposition to the point where the province was devastated and the leaders of the revolt either executed or slain in battle. Never before had such destruction of property or such systematic slaughter been witnessed in Ireland. The steely determination of the government to inaugurate a new era in Ireland was demonstrated by its scheme to introduce a coherent English settlement of 20,000 people on the lands of the earl of Desmond and his confederates, which were now declared forfeit to the Crown.

This plantation scheme resulted in a massive transfer of property from Irish to English ownership, and the settlement of 4,000 English people on the Desmond lands by the mid-1590s. As such, it fell considerably short of its target. But the settlement in Munster consolidated the Protestant interest in Ireland, and provided the officials with the hope that the policy that had been implemented there would soon be followed up in the other three provinces. For these officials, the test of loyalty was no longer obedience to the Crown but acceptance of the Protestant faith; and they identified as enemies of the English interest all who refused to subscribe to the oath of supremacy. Those who refused to do so should, they averred, be deprived of any official positions they held under the Crown. It was further recommended that heavy financial penalties should be imposed upon all landowners in Ireland who refused to conform in religion. The systematic application of such a measure would have meant the effective dispossession of many native landowners; the English-born officials who were recommending these schemes were hoping to benefit from their eclipse.

All of this seemed consistent and reasonable in the circumstances of the 1580s, but it none the less failed to meet with the approval of Queen Elizabeth who again favoured temporizing measures over a comprehensive policy. She was advised on this by the earl of Ormond, but she was herself naturally reluctant to engage upon any action that was likely to provoke military resistance in Ireland at a time when she was becoming embroiled in war with Spain, first at sea and then in the Spanish Netherlands. The caution of the queen was not, however, shared by her officials in Ireland—or at least not by those who held positions in the provinces, who took advantage of English preoccupation with Continental affairs to engage upon a rampage of freebooting. Their immediate purpose was to establish possession of whatever property they could through legal or extra-legal devices; some hoped to provoke an insurrection which would force the government to proceed with further plantation schemes similar to that in Munster. Sir William FitzWilliam, who served as governor 1588–94, seems to have agreed with this general strategy, and he supported piecemeal settlements that were imposed first in the province of Connacht and then in the southern reaches of Ulster.

But, while agreeing on such schemes of reorganization for the Ulster borderlands, the question still remained of how to deal with the heartland of the province where the O'Neill family held sway. All in government were agreed that this great lordship should be dismembered into several segments, and all were agreed that the government of one of these segments should be assigned to Hugh O'Neill, heir to Matthew, baron of Dungannon. Most officials were also of the opinion that favour should be offered to others of the O'Neill dynasty, but that some land should be reserved for English settlement. What they did not allow for were the ambitions of Hugh O'Neill. As it transpired, it was his ambitions, and their ultimate failure, which dictated the course of change in this previously Gaelic province.

Hugh O'Neill was the claimant to the earldom of Tyrone, which had been constituted at the time of his grandfather's surrender to the Crown in 1542. His

HUGH O'NEILL, EARL OF TYRONE, was the most formidable opponent of Elizabethan rule in Ireland. His memory was hateful to English observers but he was recognized on the Continent as one of the outstanding soldiers of his generation.

father Matthew had never made good his claims to succeed to the earldom against the challenge of Shane O'Neill, and the young Hugh had spent most of his early career as a client of the various English adventurers who had attempted to establish themselves in Ulster. In this capacity he had familiarized himself with modern methods of warfare, and he succeeded with English help in wresting control of the south-east portion of the Tyrone lordship from his dynastic rivals. As time progressed, his English supporters came to recognize the prowess and talents of this shrewd and subtle tactician; while on the other side, O'Neill himself came to see that English adventurers were a greater threat to his advancement than were any of the O'Neills.

Therefore he set himself to recover the entire lordship to which he could claim title and to establish a palatinate jurisdiction over that lordship. Such an ambition ran contrary to the aims of the minor officials, and conflict developed in the 1590s when O'Neill, who had become earl of Tyrone in 1585, tried to expel them from the province of Ulster. What was initially a conflict of wills between a provincial lord and minor officials soon became a squabble between O'Neill and the Lord Deputy, and O'Neill raised an army of defence and equipped it after the English fashion. Early successes on O'Neill's part strengthened the resolve of the government to bring him to heel, while he in turn solicited the aid of all discontented lords in Ireland and further sought to broaden his appeal by advancing himself as a champion of the Counter-Reformation. The Old English population of the country were generally not impressed with this appeal from one whose career had been far from that of an exemplary Catholic; but O'Neill's call made a favourable impression upon King Philip III of Spain, who in 1601 supplied him with a well-equipped force of 4,000 men that established itself at Kinsale in Munster. Even before then, the government of Queen Elizabeth had come to recognize this as the most formidable challenge to her authority that had yet arisen, and an army of 20,000 men had been dispatched to deal with the contingency. This was the army which was in 1601 ranged against the Hiberno-Spanish force at Kinsale. The English victory in that battle marked the collapse of the military coalition that had threatened the very survival of English rule in Ireland.

The fact that this was the most formidable resistance to English authority

that had yet occurred meant that its failure would be followed by the most comprehensive settlement yet proceeded with in Ireland. Accidents intervened to delay the offensive; but it had become clear in 1607, when the previously recalcitrant lords fled the country, that major changes in Irish society would soon be effected.

The argument of the officials on this occasion was that the recent rebellion had shown that the continued existence of Catholic landowners in Ireland was a threat to the very security of England. Immediate steps should be taken, they contended, to ensure that those who were potential rebels should no longer have

THE SIEGE AND BATTLE OF KINSALE, DECEMBER 1601. This drawing from *Pacata Hibernia* shows, on the left, how the Crown forces were mobilized to besiege the Spanish troops within the walled town, and on the right, how they positioned themselves against the oncoming army of Tyrone and O'Donnell. The only action described is on the bottom right, but the illustrator was concerned to distinguish the several constituent elements of the royal army. These included companies under the command of the earls of Clanricard and Thomond as well as MacCarthy Reagh.

control over large numbers of people. This justified the extension of English common law to all areas in Ireland as well as the application to Ireland of English statutes against Jesuits and other seminary priests. Both measures, it was believed, would weaken the moral authority of existing Catholic lords; but the further step that was recommended was the expropriation of the property of all Catholic landowners in Ireland.

James I, who in 1603 became king of England and Ireland while continuing to reign as James VI of Scotland, was generally impressed by this argument. He was satisfied that no further tolerance should be shown to those landowners who had been involved in the recent rebellion, and he saw no reason why those who held property that belonged rightfully to the Crown should be left undisturbed. This meant that he would continue his protection as monarch only to those landowners who could show good title in law for their property, and who had been continuously dutiful to the Crown. Even such landowners, who were mostly Old English, were expected to conform in religion; but those who did not meet these qualifications could no longer expect any favour. To this extent, the monarch offered his approval for a systematic process of colonization in Ireland. The most threatened regions were the entire province of Ulster, substantial areas in the province of Connacht, the Gaelic parts of the Leinster midlands, and the unplanted lands in Munster.

Officials in Ireland needed no more than this nod of royal approval before they set about the work of introducing plantations to six of the nine counties in the province of Ulster, to Counties Wexford, Leitrim, and Longford, and to particular baronies in the King's and Queen's counties and in County Tipperary. These same officials ardently sought approval for further plantations in the province of Connacht and in Counties Tipperary and Clare. This issue of further plantations was to dominate Irish politics down to 1641, with spokesmen from the Old

THE SURVEYOR AT WORK. The seventeenth century witnessed the migration to Ireland of thousands of workers with new and varied skills. One of the more pervasive was the surveyor (interpreted here by an eighteenth-century illustrator) who obtained ready employment from both settler and native proprietors who had increasing need to establish precise boundaries to their properties.

MONEA CASTLE, CO. FERMANAGH. This artist's impression is derived from the surviving ruin and reveals the Scottish influence upon the architecture of the plantation in Ulster. Scottish undertakers wisely took the precaution of placing security above comfort.

English community declaring their opposition to the proposal just as stridently as the English-born officials supported it. But while this burning issue remained in contention, there was no doubting the fact that the position of the Protestant officials in Ireland had been greatly strengthened as a result both of the plantations that had been put into effect, and of the sizeable emigration from Britain into Ireland that ensued.

The plantation in Ulster was similar to what had been attempted in Munster in that a scheme of settlement was detailed in advance, and grantees were required to meet certain plantation requirements or to risk forfeiting their estates. Those English and Scottish grantees who had no previous experience of Ireland were bound by the most rigid conditions, which included an obligation to construct defensible buildings and to introduce ten British Protestant families on each unit of 1,000 acres. The scheme differed from that in Munster, however, because provision was made for the allocation of land to natives who had a proven record of loyalty to the Crown, and because most land was reserved for those described as servitors. These latter were Englishmen who had rendered service to the Crown either in a civil or military capacity; they had a responsibility to preserve order among the natives while introducing some British settlers on their estates and developing model settlements.

This special provision for servitors meant that the plantation in Ulster was particularly pleasing to the official group in Dublin. They saw to it that the land in the subsequent plantations was almost all assigned to servitors and natives,

with scant provision for English and Scottish grantees. These servitors were permitted to retain native tenants on their lands. They frequently did so in the early years, with a view to obtaining an immediate income that would enable them to construct residences suited to their new-found status as landowners, or to modify existing towers to bring them closer to the appearance of the residences of English or Scottish gentlemen. Later, however, they displaced their native tenants, who usually held by short leases, substituting Scottish or preferably English tenants who were given long leases at low rents on condition that they invest their money and skills in the improvement of their farms. By thus proceeding cautiously the servitors among the planters had arrived at a strategy whereby they would enjoy a steady income from their estates at the outset, with the prospect of a dramatic increase in income once the improvements of the first generation of tenants had added to the value of their property. But, while aiming at long-term profits from their rents, like all British proprietors in Ireland they benefited enormously from the exploitation of the natural resources on their new estates. The most spectacular profits were derived from the felling and processing of timber, which found a ready market in England, the Netherlands, and further afield. Fortunes were also made from the export of live cattle to England. And while the new landowners and their tenants were thus able to generate a cash income for themselves, they also expanded tillage farming and in some cases introduced to Ireland the most advanced methods of cultivation then known to Western society.

Settlers and Natives

The combination of these innovations dramatically altered the physical appearance of rural Ireland, far beyond the confines of the seventeenth-century plantations. This was the case because British settlers, particularly those Eng-

JOYMOUNT AT CARRICKFERGUS became the residence of Sir Arthur Chichester, Lord Deputy of Ireland and principal beneficiary of the land settlement in Ulster. The luxury of the building is even more striking when it is contrasted with neighbouring Carrickfergus Castle (on the left of the picture). The name chosen for the house was a play upon that of Lord Mountjoy, Chichester's original patron. This view of Carrickfergus in the early seventeenth century may be compared with the depiction c.1570, p. 111 above.

lishmen who had served under the Crown, were adept at acquiring further Irish property wherever Crown title could be established or weaknesses discovered in the titles held by native proprietors. The most dramatic successes were recorded in Munster, where most of the plantation lands were recovered and developed by English landowners; but there was no county in Ireland where some Englishmen did not establish themselves as new, progressive landowners.

However, while the changing character of the physical environment was

DISTRIBUTION OF ENGLISH SETTLERS IN MUNSTER. This map of English settlement in Munster about 1641 is based upon the distribution of depositions taken in the aftermath of the rising of that year. It shows that the pattern of settlement was principally related to natural resources and the quality of the land.

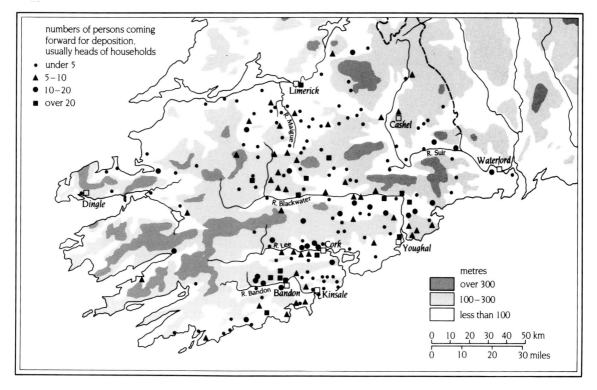

THE TOMB OF SIR RICHARD AND DAME ANNE HANSARD
(*right*) in Clonleigh parish church at Lifford bears
testimony to the simple piety of the great majority of
the Protestant settlers who engaged in the plantation in
Ulster.

RICHARD BOYLE, 1ST EARL OF CORK, AND HIS
COUNTESS ALICE FENTON (*below*). Richard Boyle was
the most spectacularly successful of the first-generation
English settlers in Ireland. The most ostentatious
proclamation of his success was the tomb he had
erected for his wife in St Patrick's cathedral, Dublin.
We here see the sketch made by Thomas Dineley of
that massive monument, and a detail of the effigies. The
sculptor devoted more attention to portraying the
coronets and robes of nobility of the Boyle family than
to representing any human likeness. Attention was also
devoted to illustrating the distinguished lineage of the
Countess of Cork, and her parents and grandparents
who had served as officials in the Dublin government
were included on the superior tiers.

LEMENAGH CASTLE, CO. CLARE, the home of Máire Rua O'Brien. This depicts in its crudest form the effort of a conforming Irish landowner to convert an existing tower into an English-style residence.

closely related to the spread of British landowners and settlers, it was not completely dependent upon this factor. Native proprietors also saw the need to promote innovation, both because they wanted to be considered worthy subjects of the Crown and because innovation could add to their wealth. The more their role in Ireland was questioned by the Protestant officials, the more they saw the need to demonstrate that they were promoters of English civility in Ireland. They did this by adopting the English language, by supporting the spread of English law into their territories, by dressing after the English fashion, and by modifying their houses or by constructing new residences to conform with English tastes. And just as the British settlers (particularly the servitors) saw the need to proclaim their newly attained status by loud display, so also the indigenous landowners displayed their 'Englishness' by purchasing carriages, erecting elaborate tombs, and putting on lavish displays at family funerals.

All such conspicuous display did, of course, cost money. The only way that the native proprietors found to meet this cost, besides the sale and mortgage of their land, was to introduce British or other foreign tenants to their estates. These tenants were always offered their farms at low annual rents and were, like the tenants of British-owned estates, bound by contract to improve the condition of their farms. This in itself would have made foreign tenants attractive to native

THE GREAT BANNER. The most arresting artefact at an Irish noble funeral of the seventeenth century was the Great Banner. This was devised by a herald and it presented a graphic depiction of the genealogy of the deceased person by detailing the coats of arms of his or her ancestors. The banner was displayed prominently in the church and was carried before the funeral carriage to the place of interment.

THE FUNERAL CARRIAGE bore the remains of the deceased noble person to their final resting place. Even this sombre vehicle drew attention to rank and wealth because it was borne by six horses clad in expensive black fabric.

proprietors; but a far more important consideration was that all such tenants were required to pay high entry-fines which provided native proprietors with the cash injection that they required for their recently adopted extravagant style of living.

Migration from Britain into Ireland was greatly increased by such considerations, and the total movement of people in the decades before 1641 cannot have been much less than 100,000. The highest concentration of settler population was understandably in the areas that had been planted, but British settlers on the plantations tended to gravitate towards the more fertile lands, or to places that had easy access to the sea or were near natural resources. Similarly, those who accepted tenancies on non-plantation estates tended to be attracted to the more productive regions, and they sometimes formed themselves into nucleated settlements there, as settlers almost always did on the plantation estates.

The arrival of so many settlers, some of them skilled craftworkers as well as farmers, added enormously to the country's productivity, and seemed to suggest that the government's programme of Anglicization was proving successful. But, while it was unquestionably succeeding in social terms, this was not so in its religious dimension. The position of the Counter-Reformation church was being consolidated rather than weakened with each passing decade. This was so because James I and later Charles I did not wish to have their diplomatic relations with foreign governments damaged by the excessive religious zeal of their officials and clergy in Ireland. Therefore, they restrained the Dublin government from enforcing the penal statutes against Catholics in full. Charles I went so far as to promise Irish Catholic landowners that they would be freed from the threat of further plantation, and he directed that the imposition of fines upon landowners for non-attendance at Protestant services should be suspended.

The Crown and the Catholics: War and Restoration

These concessions, which were wrung from the monarch in return for substantial payments, gave tacit toleration to the existence of Catholicism in Ireland as a separate religion from that of the state. This was how the position was interpreted by the Catholic church, and the clergy set about organizing an unofficial parochial and diocesan structure. They greatly increased their numbers, and devoted themselves to missionary work at all social levels in rural as well as urban society. This turn of events was most offensive to the Protestant officials, who were particularly annoyed that their reform programme should be hindered just at the time when the established church was, for the first time, prepared to engage upon a missionary offensive. Many of the Protestant clergy who were thus constrained in their pastoral work believed that the efforts of their Catholic rivals would make it impossible for them to convert the native population through

BANGOR, CO. DOWN in 1625, together with the manor house (to the left of the picture) and demesne. This shows what could be achieved in a short time by an enterprising planter in Ireland. The naïve sketch of the rabbit warren is particularly arresting because it is being suggested that this could serve as a poor man's substitute for a deer park.

THE VINTNERS' SETTLEMENT AT BELLAGHY in 1622 conveys an accurate impression of the building programme that was required of 'undertakers' in the Ulster Plantation. A church and defensible castle were essential, but details are also provided of the mill with its water-wheel, of the two-storey residences of the settlers with their garden allotments, and of the stocks at the foot of the town cross. To the right are some houses of natives.

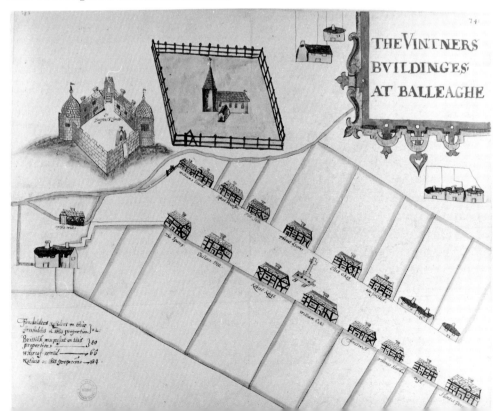

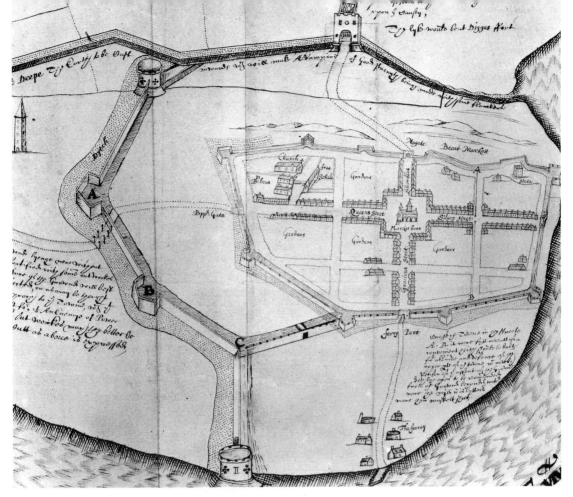

THE TOWN OF DERRY was the principal urban development that resulted from the plantation in Ulster. This sketch made in 1625 by Thomas Raven shows that the town was carefully designed and contained some imposing buildings. However, there was still considerable scope for expansion towards the walls which protected the outer perimeter of the town.

DESIGN FOR A FORTIFIED CITADEL FOR THE TOWN OF DERRY prepared in 1622 by Sir Thomas Phillips but never executed. This was intended as a substitute for the market house that was erected in the Diamond of Derry. Phillips intended that his building would serve as town hall and market place but the grim character of the upper portion shows that he anticipated the difficulties that the settlement in Ulster was to confront in subsequent decades.

LUKE WADDING, Franciscan priest and
founder of St Isidore's College, Rome, 1625.
His foundation was one of several seminaries
on the Continent that made possible the
survival of Catholicism as a popular religion in
Ireland. He was active in training priests for
the Irish mission, in composing spiritual
literature, and in negotiating political support
for Irish Catholicism.

THOMAS WENTWORTH, EARL OF STRAFFORD,
AND SIR PHILIP MAINWARING (*below*),
painted by Anthony Van Dyke. Wentworth
was delegated by Charles I to govern Ireland
from 1633 to 1640 and he was commissioned
specifically to promote the interests of the
Crown at the expense of all local interests.
This he did with a will and he trampled
gleefully upon the rights and privileges of
Protestant and Catholic leaders alike. This
arrogant behaviour and haughty manner left
Wentworth an isolated figure in Ireland but he
shared confidences with his faithful followers
including his secretary Sir Philip Mainwaring,
who accompanied him to Ireland.

BALLINDERRY MIDDLE CHURCH, CO. ANTRIM, was completed about 1668. The oak for the pulpit and pews came from the nearby Killultagh woods. The small size is explained by the existence of a rival Presbyterian church in the neighbourhood, and by the growing conviction of settlers that the native population would never be persuaded to join them in Protestant worship.

persuasion alone, and they came to place increased emphasis on the power of the state as the necessary instrument to effect conformity. This view also gained ground in Protestant lay society, and they were forced to admit that they would remain a minority until more favourable circumstances permitted them to take the offensive. This admission was best symbolized by the new churches constructed in the planted areas, which were usually designed to accommodate no more than the settler population in each parish.

It becomes clear, therefore, that two separate societies were developing in Ireland and that it was religious rather than cultural factors that now distinguished them. The appointment of Thomas Wentworth, later earl of Strafford, to serve as governor in Ireland, 1633–41, tended to blur these distinctions because his effort to extract money for the king from all groups in Ireland compelled them to join forces to achieve his destruction. Such a coalition of convenience did not, however, ease the enmities that existed between the two groups in Ireland. Strafford's period of rule served to drive many Catholic landowners to despair, because he made it clear that they could no longer rely upon the support of the king to save them from the venom of their local adversaries. Instead, Strafford worked energetically to prepare the way for a fresh wave of confiscation in Ireland. It had become clear by 1641 that if this was not instituted by the king's nominee, it would certainly be undertaken by the English parliamentarians who were then challenging royal authority in England.

These are the circumstances which explain why some Catholic landowners in Ulster decided in 1641 to strengthen their claims for special consideration by having resort to arms. The recent example of the Scottish Covenanters and their success in achieving a special recognition for a Presbyterian church in Scotland must have encouraged the Ulster lords to seek by force what they had failed to achieve by negotiation. But while the members of the Catholic social élite who precipitated the crisis of 1641 may have viewed war as an extension of diplomacy this opinion was not shared by their social inferiors. The stored-up bitterness that derived from the systematic loss of property and status spilled over in an onslaught against the persons and belongings of the foreign Protestants who had settled in Ireland during the preceding decades. As many as 2,000 Protestant settlers were killed in the ensuing chaos; tens of thousands were stripped of their clothes and chattels and driven destitute to the few remaining places of refuge. Even those Catholic landowners who always favoured caution were driven by their inferiors to participate in this desperate action.

What began as an Ulster phenomenon thus quickly spread to all parts of the country and involved most Catholic landowners to some degree. The many atrocities that were committed were greatly exaggerated in the telling in England and in Scotland; the belief that a general massacre of Protestants had occurred in Ireland caused all elements of the English and Scottish populations to demand that the government should take immediate revenge upon all who had been implicated in the Irish uprising. Circumstances did not permit the government of Charles I to take the decisive action that he favoured, because tension between himself and his parliament was mounting and soon erupted in a bitter and prolonged civil war. This interlude should have given the dissidents in Ireland

THE ATROCITIES ASSOCIATED WITH THE IRISH RISING OF 1641 provided useful material for the propagandist's art. Many Protestant settlers in Ireland were subjected to the humiliation of stripping but this woodcut implies that all Protestants in Ireland were stripped and banished into the wilderness.

English Proteſtantes ſtriped naked & turned into the mountaines, in the froſt, & ſnowe, whereof many hundreds are periſhed to death, & many liynge dead in diches & Sauuages upbraided them ſaynge now are ye wilde Iriſch as well as wee,

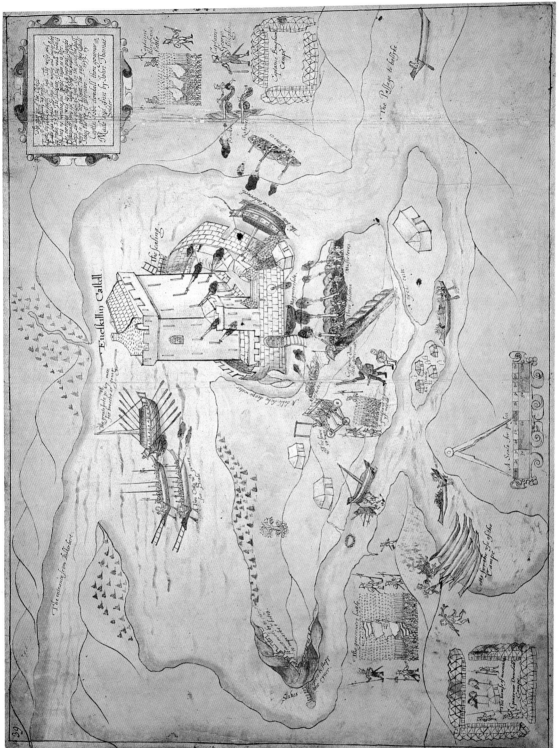

THE SIEGE OF ENNISKILLEN CASTLE, 1594. This previously impregnable fortress of the Maguires is here shown to have been unable to withstand the amphibian assault of the Elizabethan army.

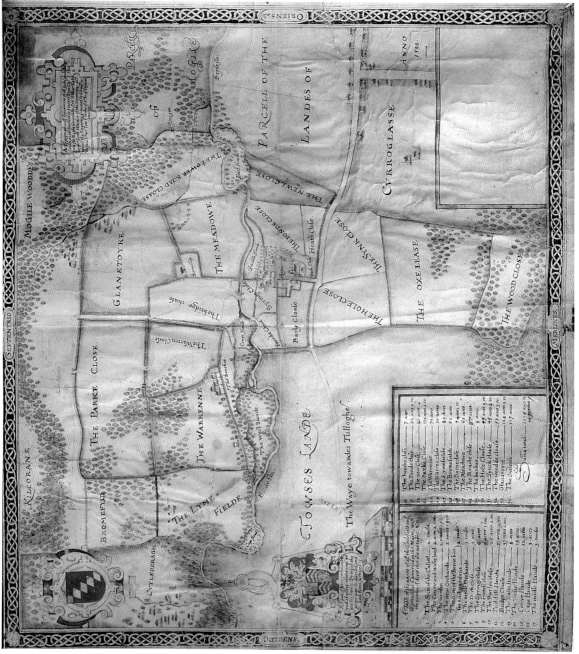

WALTER RALEIGH'S LANDS AT MOGEELY, CO. CORK, 1598. This, the earliest estate map for Ireland, was intended to illustrate the order that could be imposed upon the uncivil Irish environment by a conscientious planter.

JOHN BAPTIST RINUCCINI, ARCHBISHOP OF FERMO was appointed as papal nuncio to Ireland during the years 1645–9. Coming from a Continental background, he had little sympathy with the arguments of Old English Catholics that they could hope for religious toleration from a Protestant monarch. Instead, he wanted all Catholics in Ireland to combine their resources to achieve a political situation whereby Catholicism would be established as the exclusive religion in Ireland.

the opportunity to mobilize themselves for a final onslaught against the British settlers in Ireland, but divisions quickly appeared in the Irish Catholic ranks. The essential problem derived from the hope of the Old English that they would still be received to mercy by their king; they refused to concede military leadership in Ireland to Colonel Owen Roe O'Neill. Owen Roe, the nephew of the great Hugh O'Neill, had spent his career in the Spanish army of the Netherlands and knew from his experience with religious conflict on Continental Europe that the Irish lords had now no choice but to make a determined effort to eliminate the last vestiges of British power in Ireland. This appraisal was not welcomed by the Old English landowners who stood to lose most, and they consistently refused to provide adequate support to O'Neill in his attempt to confront and expel the Scottish Covenanter army that had been dispatched to Ulster to support their kinsmen and co-religionists there. At the same time, the Leinster lords were unable to expel government forces from Dublin without the aid of Owen Roe O'Neill, and the hopelessness of their diplomatic manœuvres was exposed when it transpired that it was the parliamentary army and not that of the Crown that emerged victorious from the civil conflict in England.

The leader of that army was Oliver Cromwell. He was determined both to take revenge for the supposed massacre of Protestants in Ireland, and to introduce order and stability where chaos had reigned since 1641. Cromwell was not at liberty to devote attention to Ireland until August 1649. He then launched a three-pronged programme aimed at the elimination of all military resistance to

ST GEORGE TRAMPLING UPON THE IRISH DRAGON. This vignette reveals the intensity with which the Cromwellian soldiers engaged upon the reconquest of Ireland believed themselves to be pursuing a mission of vengeance for the supposed massacre of 1641. The illustration is from the record of a military visitation of 1649 by Leveret, the Athlone pursuivant.

government authority; the removal of all priests and landowners who were in any way implicated in the insurrection that had taken place; and the promotion of an evangelization drive, supported by the state, that would bring the entire population of Ireland to the Protestant faith. These various elements of the Cromwellian programme were not very different from what had previously been advocated by the Protestant reformers in Ireland. What was different was the fact that the Irish insurrection in 1641 had alerted all elements of English and Scottish society to the need for drastic action in Ireland.

The Cromwellian regime was the best possible to deal with the military situation in Ireland because the army of 20,000 men that was placed at the disposal of Oliver Cromwell was perhaps the best fighting force in all of Europe. It came as no surprise therefore that all military opposition in Ireland was summarily crushed. The atrocities associated with this exercise can be likened to the excesses associated with the taking of fortified towns in Germany during the course of the Thirty Years War: the armies in both instances were imbued with religious zeal which in a seventeenth-century context involved a detestation of opposing religions. Zeal also meant that individuals were ready to invest enormous energy to achieve goals which they believed were determined by God, and the Cromwellian effort to eradicate Catholicism from Ireland was one case in point. Priests were hunted down with such energy that the entire Catholic church structure that had been erected with such painful dedication was swept aside in a few years. The Cromwellians also decided to confiscate all Catholic estates in the country, and to provide partial compensation in the area west of the river

Shannon to those Catholic proprietors who could prove that they had not been involved with the rebellion. The blueprint envisaged only Protestant proprietors in the three provinces of Leinster, Munster, and Ulster; those Catholics who were to be conceded small estates west of the Shannon were to be cut off from foreign contact by a colony of soldier settlers, who were to occupy a four-mile line along the coast and the boundary of the river Shannon. This massive exercise in social engineering was to be facilitated by a comprehensive survey of land ownership in Ireland that was directed by William Petty, a noted scientist, statistician, and Protestant enthusiast.

The work of Petty was completed in record time and with remarkable accuracy; Ireland enjoyed the doubtful distinction of being the most accurately surveyed and mapped country in Europe. The work of dispossession also proceeded rapidly; the estates thus vacated were assigned to Cromwellian soldiers and to those in England who had financed the Cromwellian conquest of Ireland. The work of transplantation to Connacht was given less careful attention by the government, but the surviving Catholic proprietors in Ireland were bundled across the river Shannon and left to scramble as best they could for whatever

SIR WILIAM PETTY was the most talented of those who made their careers in Ireland in the aftermath of the Cromwellian settlement. It is appropriate that he who 'anatomized' Ireland with a view to prescribing a remedy for its reform (*c*.1649–51) should be here depicted with a skull.

land they could occupy. Thus at one fell swoop the Catholic landed interest was shifted from the most prosperous to the poorest province in Ireland, and Catholic control over tenants was greatly weakened.

The third element of the Cromwellian scheme, which related to the promotion of Protestantism in Ireland, also went ahead energetically. Measures were taken to provide an income both for clergymen and schoolmasters, land was assigned for the endowment of schools, and some enthusiastic educators and preachers were recruited among the ranks of the Cromwellians in England. More importantly, strenuous efforts were made to force the Irish population to attend designated places of worship: a campaign rewarded with considerable success. Difficulties arose, however, when the clergymen could not address these people in their own language. The evangelization drive was also hindered by the unwillingness of many of the serving Protestant clergy in Ireland to work within a Cromwellian church framework. Therefore, for lack of skilled manpower, the government lost this great opportunity of bringing the Irish population to the Protestant faith.

While it is possible to talk of loss of opportunity, it must also be emphasized that the Cromwellians did not have much time to advance their programme in Ireland. Fighting continued into 1652 and the future of the regime in England was already doubtful by the mid-1650s. Furthermore, the true zealots quickly gave way to more accommodating figures, and Oliver Cromwell's son Henry tried to consolidate the regime by joining forces with the Protestant leaders in Ireland who had tried to hold ground after 1641. In the longer term, it was these rather than a new generation of proprietors who were the principal beneficiaries of the Cromwellian land confiscation, because they purchased considerable holdings from Cromwellian grantees who had no wish to remain permanently in Ireland.

Such transactions bonded together Protestant landed families who had been established in Ireland before 1641, and those who settled there in the aftermath of the Cromwellian conquest. Each group was greatly concerned with the maintenance of political order; and to this purpose they welcomed in 1660 the restoration to the throne of Charles II, once it had become evident that the Cromwellian regime in England had ceased to command the moral respect of the political nation. But while these Protestant proprietors supported the Stuart restoration, they never enjoyed the trust of their monarch because of their close association with Cromwellian government. Instead they had to yield place to James Butler, duke of Ormond, who enjoyed the particular favour of Charles II, both because he was an Irish Protestant of impeccable ancestry and because he had gone into exile with his king rather than become tainted by association with regicide.

The restoration of the king thus brought about an immediate recovery of their ancestral property by those Irish landowners, whether Protestant or Catholic, who had found refuge in France with their king and been deprived of their property as royalists. Ormond would have welcomed an altogether more drastic reversal of the Cromwellian land settlement: it was largely at his instigation that machinery was established whereby dispossessed landowners would have the opportunity to prove themselves innocent of insurrection against the Crown and thus worthy of recovering their property. Once it became evident, however, that undue leniency towards Catholics would provoke a Protestant backlash, Ormond drew back from the full implementation of this scheme. Instead he recommended to the king that, with minor modifications, the Cromwellian land settlement in Ireland should become permanent.

The acceptance by Charles II of this advice proved severely disappointing for dispossessed Catholic landowners, and particularly for those Old English Catholics who had expected favour through their contacts with the duke of Ormond. The amount of land in Catholic ownership remained limited, and was concentrated west of the river Shannon where Catholic landowners had continued to be tolerated by Cromwell. This meant that the only tangible improvement in the position of Catholics after the Stuart restoration was relief from the intense religious persecution of the Cromwellian era. Once again it was possible for the Catholic clergy who had found refuge on the Continent during the Cromwellian interlude to resume their missionary work in Ireland. Even this benefit was fortuitous, resulting not from any official toleration of Catholicism, but from the new government's concern with re-establishing an episcopal Protestant church rather than persecuting Catholicism. The change therefore provided a breathing-space for Catholicism in Ireland, despite the outbreak of occasional acts of persecution such as the execution of Archbishop Oliver Plunkett of Armagh at the time of the Titus Oates plot in England. This interim proved crucial for the survival of Catholicism in Ireland. Interruptions like the Plunkett affair notwithstanding, the breathing-space lasted from 1660 to 1690; it enabled the Catholic clergy to re-establish Catholicism as the religion of the people in most parts of Ireland, except in those areas where Protestant settlement was most intensive.

This reality, which we can recognize with the benefit of hindsight, was not obvious to those Catholics who lived in Ireland in the decades after 1660. For these their period of glory was past, and they could see nothing but further defeat as they looked into the future. This pessimism is most evident in the Gaelic poetry that was composed at this time; and so is the sudden optimism that was expressed in this poetry when in 1685 the Catholic duke of York ascended the English throne as James II. This, claimed the poets—and their opinions were shared by Catholic clergy and landowners alike—presaged a turn of fortune's wheel in their favour: recovery of their land and their lost glory and an official position for their religion would follow.

RICHARD TALBOT, EARL OF TYRCONNELL, is here depicted on an English playing card of about 1689 as the knave placing arms in the hands of Irish Catholics. Tyrconnell was viewed with equal hatred by Irish and by English Protestants who held him responsible for corrupting James II and luring him towards Catholicism.

Tyrconel arming ỹ Papists in Ireland.

What was articulated by the poets was attempted by the political leaders of Irish Catholic society. The most vehement was Richard Talbot, a favourite of James II, who was now elevated to become Lord-Lieutenant of Ireland with the grandiose title of duke of Tyrconnell. This impetuous *arriviste* set about the business of restoring public office to Catholics in Ireland; he began to mobilize a Catholic army that would be available to the king for whatever purpose he might require; and he set in train the procedures whereby a parliament would be convened in Dublin which would consist primarily of Catholic members, enthusiastic supporters of his ambition to reverse the Cromwellian confiscation.

The hasty and ill-considered actions of Tyrconnell alarmed Protestant opinion in Britain as well as in Ireland, and greatly encouraged those in Britain who favoured offering the throne to Prince William of Orange and his English wife Mary. Their claims were quickly made good by force of arms and the desperate King James, once ousted from his throne in England, was forced to seek military support from his Irish subjects and the French army that had been dispatched to Ireland to support him. The Catholic landed interest in Ireland as well as the Catholic clergy responded enthusiastically to the call; the Protestant community stood amazed and feared that a repetition of the 1641 rising was about to be enacted. Some Protestant towns in Ulster, notably Derry and Enniskillen, denied

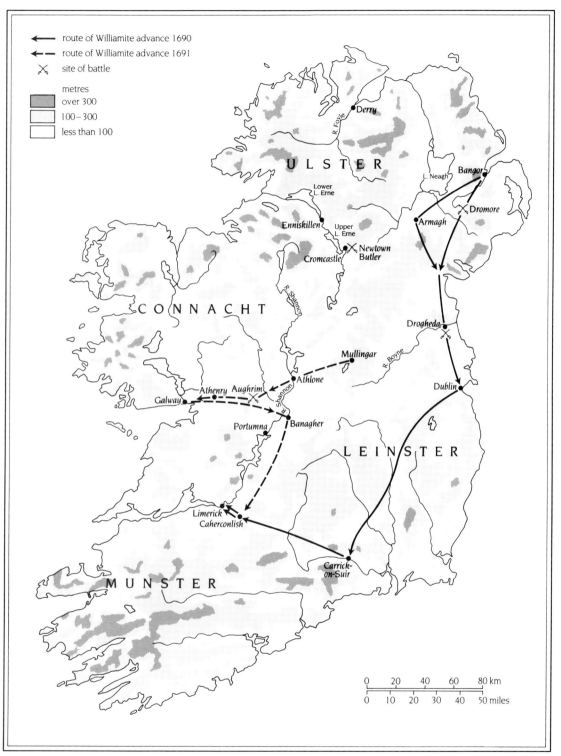

route of Williamite advance 1690

route of Williamite advance 1691

site of battle

metres
over 300
100–300
less than 100

R. Foyle

Derry

ULSTER

L. Neagh

Bangor

Lower
L. Erne

Dromore

Armagh

Enniskillen

Upper
L. Erne

Cromcastle

Newtown
Butler

R. Shannon

CONNACHT

Drogheda

R. Boyne

Mullingar

Athlone

Dublin

Athenry Aughrim

Galway

R. Shannon

Portumna

Banagher

LEINSTER

Limerick
Caherconlish

Carrick-
on-Suir

MUNSTER

0   20   40   60   80 km

0   10   20   30   40   50 miles

THE WILLIAMITE CAMPAIGN, 1689-91

THE BATTLE OF THE BOYNE, 1690, was not an engagement of any great military significance but it became an encounter of prime symbolic importance. This contemporary engraving by Theodor Maas shows the Williamite forces in the act of crossing the river at Oldbridge.

the authority of King James; by holding out against him they provided a bridgehead for the army that King William brought to Ireland to confront the forces of his rival. The first major conflict in the struggle between the two kings occurred at the River Boyne in July 1690, when the army of King William was attempting to move southwards from Ulster in the direction of Dublin. The failure of the forces of King James to prevent the southwards march of the Williamite army forced them onto the defensive. Those in Ireland who had identified with the cause of King James and the revival of a Catholic interest had to defend the line of the Shannon, with a view to preserving the bulk of Catholic-owned estates which lay to the west of that river. Stern resistance to the Williamite army was presented at the Bridge of Athlone, on the field of Aughrim, and twice at sieges

of Limerick: but all proved futile. This sequence of defeats prepared the way for the final surrender of the Catholic landed interest; the departure from the country of most Catholic officers who had fought in the Jacobite army; and yet another confiscation of Catholic property, consolidating the Protestant interest and facilitating a rigid penal code against Catholics. However, while the political war was lost, the battle for souls had been won. Ireland at the outset of the eighteenth century was English and Protestant in appearance, but still predominantly Catholic in religion.

Conclusion: A European Society?

A glance at social conditions in Ireland at the onset of the eighteenth century reveals that Ireland was a truly European society—both by virtue of its structure and because its development was constricted by factors that were general

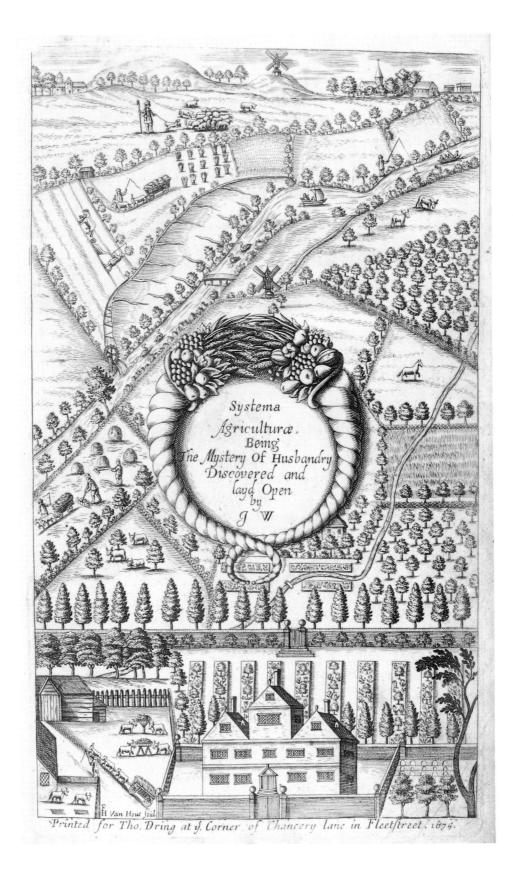

Systema
Agriculturæ.
Being
The Mystery Of Husbandry
Discovered and
layd Open
by
J W

H. Van Houe Sculp.

Printed for Tho. Dring at ye Corner of Chancery lane in Fleetstreet. 1675.

throughout western Europe. We have it on no less an authority than Sir William Petty, who was perhaps the most respected European statistician of his generation, that the total population of Ireland in 1687 was 1,300,000—which reveals a density of population that matched that of all but a few particularly wealthy regions of western Europe. The vast majority of these people were settled on farms or smaller agricultural holdings, they were engaged principally in tillage and stock raising, and the poorer of them supplemented their farming incomes by their involvement with the spinning and weaving of woollen and linen cloth. These textiles, together with barrelled meat and animal by-products, constituted the principal export commodities of Ireland at this time, and the bulk of the wealth that was thus generated by the farming population went towards the payment of rent to their social superiors for the use of the land which they occupied.

Some of these superiors were themselves tenants to head landlords, owning vast estates which sometimes extended to several thousands of acres. These head landlords, together with the middlemen and the established church, owned almost all the landed property in the country. The principal landowners made manifest their social dominance principally through the construction of comfortable and sometimes ornate houses, embellished by ornamental grounds and model home farms. These same people constituted the Irish political nation; the more affluent of them would have aspired either to become members of parliament or to hold office under the government. To this end they needed to be in regular attendance at Dublin Castle, particularly whenever the Lord-Lieutenant, who was the Crown's representative in Ireland, was in residence. This tendency led to the development of Dublin as a metropolitan city of some consequence, and the marks of its future magnificence were already evident in 1700. Its population stood at about 50,000 and some fine suburban building had already been executed to provide appropriate housing for the visiting gentry and for the serving members of the government administration. The existence of two ancient cathedrals in the city further contributed to its dignity as a capital, and so did the formation of learned societies—most notably the Dublin Philosophical Society, which included both Robert Boyle and William Petty among its members.

The presence in Dublin of an affluent leisured population explains its development as a service centre, while the commercial importance of the city was enhanced by the appetite of these people for luxury goods. The export trade of the city was greatly expanded through a road and water communication network which brought most of the province of Leinster as well as north-east Ulster and

LANDOWNERS IN IRELAND who wished to develop the environment of their great houses after the English fashion had some fine examples available to them in print. One of the most compelling was that depicted in *Systema Agriculturae* of 1675. This indicated that the promotion of improved agriculture on the entire estate was as essential to good management as the development of ornamental grounds.

even sections of eastern Connacht within Dublin's expanded hinterland. The export of produce from the rich farming lands of the province of Munster was channelled through the ports of Cork, Youghal, and Waterford, and the town of Derry catered for the commercial needs of west Ulster and north Connacht. The towns of Limerick, Galway, and even Sligo on the west coast were also of some commercial importance, and the service needs of the inland areas of Ireland were met by a regular series of towns that were situated at the sites of traditional markets or at river crossings.

Because of the existence in Ireland of this relatively sophisticated commercial infrastructure, the several local economies that had developed over time were closely interrelated and complementary. The integration of the country into a single coherent unit was also facilitated by the provision of a single code of common law which was administered from the central courts in Dublin, through the provision of circuits of assize which moved about the provinces on a seasonal course and supplemented the manorial, baronial, and county courts that operated continuously within each locality. A sense of unity was also fostered by the existence of a chain of garrison towns where the country's standing army was maintained, and even more so by the pattern of intermarriage that had been established between the country's principal landed families.

There is plenty of evidence, therefore, that Ireland in 1700 bore all the marks of a highly centralized European kingdom, albeit a kingdom that was subsidiary to the kingdom of England. The inferior constitutional status of Ireland was revealed by the presence in Dublin of a viceroy, and by the refusal of all English rulers except two, during the years 1500–1689, even to consider visiting their remote kingdom.

Members of the Irish political nation were wont to object to the treatment of Ireland as anything less than a sister kingdom, complaining bitterly over the pretensions of the English parliament to pass legislation that would have force in Ireland. But for all their complaints they chose to be guided entirely by English fashion even to the point of having their sons educated in England rather than at Trinity College, Dublin, whenever they could afford this luxury. The wealthier of them always preferred to marry into English landed families rather than their peers in Ireland. Experience was to show, however, that such matches were extremely difficult to negotiate on advantageous terms, and only the exceptionally wealthy among Ireland's landed families could expect to arrange English matches on a continuing basis.

Ireland's reputation for cultural backwardness and political instability helped obstruct such ambitions; but more important was the inescapable reality that Irish society was poor by English standards. Landowners in Ireland derived their income almost entirely from rents and office, and only the exceptional few enjoyed the prosperity that came the way of their English counterparts who had

H. The Work of the Mine
T. The melting houses
S. The Water that turnes y Wheele
K. A new Work beginning 1681.
O. The new Inn at the mines
M. The old Inn y signe y Holy Lamb
A. The Road to Limerick
D. The Mountaines.

SILVER MINES

THE SILVER MINES, CO. TIPPERARY, about 1681. English settlers in Ireland were always alert for the existence of mineral deposits and spared no effort to exploit such resources. The existence of silver in Tipperary was discovered before 1641 and the deposits there were quickly exhausted. By the late seventeenth century it was being exploited as a lead mine by Henry Pretty, Esq., and the illustration here shows the melting house that had been erected together with the water which turned the wheel and gave power to the great forge bellows.

The silver mine was found out by an English man a little before the late Rebellion, who observing a sheep killed in the shambles to be extream yellow, enquired where it grazed, who told him upon the aforedescribed mountaines, whereupon he concluded in that place to be and discovered the Silver mine. The Soyle is short and crumbling, not a clay though of a clayish colour in some almost of a bright yellow in others darker: it abounds with Yellow Oker and Umber, which burnt in a crucible turnes to a red this the Proprietor sells as such. Whilst it produced silver it was held by Pattent It is now possessed by Henry Pretty Esq who onely rayseth lead Concerning the Veines, the flakey and shineing is best for silver the glittering and sparkey next, but the white crusted with Oker is the best for Lead, this last the Workers in the Mine call Catts Teeth and with a blow pipe Cole and Candle will melt into plain lead it is very weighty and resembles white enamell or glass. The melting houses and Mill marked with T. hath a large Water Wheele by whose motion a Great Forge bellows

diversified their investments into commercial enterprises. This heavy reliance on rent meant that the income of Irish landowners was largely dictated by the markets that could be found for the country's export commodities; and the harsh reality was that these markets were constantly shrinking during the recessionary decades of the late seventeenth and the early eighteenth centuries. If any markets remained consistently open to Irish products, they lay in Britain's Atlantic colonies and in supplying the needs of the British navy. Repeated efforts to improve upon this situation by creating a more diversified economy came to little, and this growing dependence on British overseas markets more than anything else illustrated the extent to which Ireland had become tied to England for its economic survival.

Survival is an apt term to employ in this context because, as a consequence of growing population levels during years of diminished opportunity, great numbers at the lower end of the social scale were teetering at the brink of subsistence. Many English commentators considered this remarkable, and some were at pains to compare the menial living conditions of Irish cottiers with those of their counterparts in England. Such comparisons were hardly fair, because post-restoration England was one of the few areas of Europe that experienced continuous economic expansion and some of the prosperity that had derived from commercial improvement had filtered down to the lower levels of society. In reality, therefore, the precarious position of the poorer Irish peasantry at the end of the seventeenth century was no different from that of European peasants generally, and like them their numbers were quickly cut back by famine whenever they were beset by poor harvests or by adverse market conditions. And whenever they experienced adversity, so also did their social superiors—who were immediately hit by the reduction in the purchasing power of tenants and sub-tenants, and even more by the inability of tenants to pay rent. To the extent that all social classes in Ireland were victims of the recession that gripped most of western Europe, it can be said that they were all members together of a common European community.

While considering those social characteristics which justify the inclusion of Ireland within a European community of nations, attention must also be devoted to features unique to the Irish social condition. This is all the more necessary because these very features are evidence that the social forms that have just been described were the product of draconian measures such as had been attempted in few other European societies. Moreover, the survival of these features from an earlier dispensation suggests that the social experiment that had been attempted in Ireland had been only partially successful.

The most glaring anomaly, and the factor which made Ireland different from all other European societies, was that most landowners and most senior officials were of a different ethnic background and a different religion from the population at large. The social élite in Ireland at the close of the seventeenth century was composed principally of first-generation English settlers, together with the descendants of those Englishmen who had made successful careers for themselves in Ireland during the reigns of Elizabeth and James I. To these was added a significant group of landowners of Scottish descent, who were concentrated in Ulster, together with some landowners of Anglo-Norman or even Gaelic origin who had succeeded in accommodating themselves to English ways and had begun to marry with settler families in preference to those that were indigenous to Ireland. All members of this ruling group were Protestant in religion; all but a few of the Ulster-Scots landowners were staunch upholders of the established church; and all were firm believers in the advantages that had accrued to Ireland as a consequence of the introduction there of English civil standards. These enthusiasms notwithstanding, the landed élite in Ireland had failed in their efforts to draw the native population to the Protestant faith. While they devoted much thought to how this could be achieved, they repeatedly failed to agree upon a common strategy to achieve the work of conversion. The result was that the élite held dominance over a population of land occupiers which was generally Catholic in religion and frequently Gaelic in origin, language, and culture—despite their acceptance of the tenurial conditions that were usually attached to their leases.

The religious and cultural polarization between landowners and land occupiers was most pronounced in the province of Connacht. Here the land was frequently of poor quality, and the only Protestants in effect were the proprietors themselves and their dependants, together with the clergy and other professionals who catered for their needs. Divisions were not quite as acute in the other three provinces, where the plentiful availability of good quality land made it easy for the proprietors to introduce principal tenants of the same religion and outlook as themselves. A dense population of English, Scottish, or even Continental Protestants had been introduced wherever economic opportunities were favourable, or where formal settlement had been promoted by the government. Even in such areas a substantial residue of native occupiers remained; and while many had learned to speak English they remained conversant in the Irish language, providing patronage to priests and Gaelic poets. Thus they received constant reminders that they were the descendants of glorious ancestors who had been wrongfully dispossessed of their rights and property during the century of confiscations—making way for Protestant intruders who had no legitimate claim to the estates which sustained them in wealth and luxury.

The prevalence of such beliefs within a peasant community was not, of course, confined to Ireland; the notion of the world being turned upside down achieved almost universal popularity in this era. However, there was probably no other society in Europe where the propagation of the message was so institutionalized as it was in Ireland, nor any other where the belief was so generally fixed in the minds of the peasantry that they were the dispossessed who would one day recover that of which they had been so unjustly deprived.

If the peasants had but known, they had not technically been deprived of anything: land under the old dispensation had belonged to ruling kinship groups rather than to communities of peasants, and most of the ruling families who had not conformed to English ways had either been killed in battle or had abandoned the country at the conclusion of one of the several political tumults of the previous era. Of the survivors from the old order, it was the previously privileged groups such as priests and poets who had lost status; and it is significant that it was these who fostered the myth of a lost golden age which might again be recovered. That it was possible for them to do so, and to have myth accepted as reality, is explained in large part by the comprehensive nature of the change that had taken place; by the brutality with which change had been effected and resisted; and by the resulting sharp discontinuity with the past. It is the scale of this discontinuity which sets apart the Irish historical experience of the early modern centuries from other European societies.

4

Ascendancy and Union

R. F. FOSTER

The Formation of Ascendancy

A BROAD view of Irish history in the eighteenth and early nineteenth centuries necessarily leads to well-worn generalizations: themes of dispossession, poverty, and the dominance of a landed élite underlie rebellion, constitutional union, Catholic *révanche*, famine, and the rise of popular nationalism. Looked at more closely, however, the received images become less clear-cut; equivocation and ambiguity blur many corners of the picture. This is particularly true of the long Irish eighteenth century, which began with the victory of the Williamite dispensation in the early 1690s.

The harrowing defeat of the Irish Jacobites at the Boyne and Aughrim in 1690-1 had been succeeded by the equally traumatic Treaty of Limerick, enabling an exodus of Jacobite soldiers to the Continent and supposedly ensuring some degree of toleration for the Catholic population. But the apparently generous terms agreed by William's Dutch commander were not carried through. For the events at the Boyne, Aughrim, and Limerick had followed the powerful Catholic challenge mounted since 1685, when the army and the law had been rapidly and dramatically 'Catholicized': the process climaxing in the 1689 parliament convened by James in Dublin, which apparently threatened the land settlements made in the Protestants' favour over the previous century. Given this threat, the Irish Protestant sense of heartfelt deliverance after Aughrim was inseparably linked to an equally intense feeling of insecurity. The years 1689, 1690, and 1691 were linked back to 1641: Irish historical obsessions, precociously developed and artificially nurtured, kept alive perceived continuities throughout the period of Protestant 'Ascendancy' and afterwards. In this sense, the characteristics of the Irish eighteenth century began in the 1690s and continued well into the nineteenth century.

There are elements, however, which tidily expired in 1800—notably the replica Irish parliament, which met regularly as an integral part of government from the 1690s until its abolition by the Act of Union which took effect in 1801. And the Irish parliament, meeting in the tremendously grand Parliament House at College Green (begun in 1729 and designed by an Irish architect, Sir Edward

TRINITY COLLEGE through the portico of the Houses of Parliament, College Green. Malton's contemporary engravings of Georgian Dublin preserve its ambitious style. This one shows the close relationship between Trinity College's great west front, rebuilt in the 1750s, and Lovett Pearce's Houses of Parliament (now the Bank of Ireland).

Lovett Pearce), remains a potent image of certain Irish achievements and Irish aspirations in the Georgian era. But the dependent and essentially colonial derivation of the institutions of Irish government was also true of the Dublin parliament. Though it had a lower and an upper house, a Speaker, and followed from time to time the party-political splits at Westminster, it retained a different, querulous, and often impotent relationship *vis-à-vis* the apparatus of government. The question of what powers were actually possessed by the Irish parliament remained curiously uncertain. Articulated by Anglo-Irish polemicists like William Molyneux and Jonathan Swift, the claim for restitution of autonomous parliamentary authority would carry forward to the campaigns of Henry Grattan towards the end of the century; a retrospective continuity was (inaccurately) asserted by the cry for Repeal of the Union in the 1830s; and 'Home Rule' from 1870 would take up the claim. But though proponents of parliamentary 'independence'—like Grattan in 1782—legitimized their arguments by invoking those of their predecessors, they were in fact calling for different things.

The fundamental question debated from the 1690s was not that of independence in a 'national' sense, but of how far the Dublin assembly had the right of originating legislation without subsequent adaptation in London. (The point was sharpened by an economic controversy over the apparent challenge being presented by the Irish woollen trade, and by British efforts to restrict it.) Later Westminster legislation attempting to define the Irish parliament as subordinate was never accepted by a certain strain in Irish political thought. The fact that this contributed largely to the faction of opposition called 'Patriots' should not conceal the fact that it was completely consistent with a commitment to the British connection and the Protestant faith; and both these identifications characterized the political 'nation' who made up the little world of Irish parliamentary society. For the parliament represented the post-1690s élite, and symbolized the domination of a class or caste defined by religion and social status: the Protestant 'Ascendancy'.

Those who constituted the Ascendancy were established by the land redistributions of the seventeenth century, and by the fact that they had withstood the threat to the property settlement posed by the Jacobite parliament of 1689. Insecurity was therefore an essential part of dominance. They were also those who had adhered (or adroitly turned) to the established Protestant Church of Ireland: the faith of a small minority of the Irish population, but the official religion of the state. The Church of Ireland represented a curious mixture: a decrepit and undermanned organization, backed by great reserves of landed property, and embodying some very rich sinecures as well as many poor livings. Some contemptuous contemporary descriptions notwithstanding, it was founded on the definition of privilege.

And here, too, privilege implied insecurity. As with the disposition of landed wealth, religious dominance looked uneasily back to the upheavals of the seventeenth century. The speed with which Catholics had been reinstated in power between 1685 and 1689 could not be forgotten; nor, further back, could the events of 1641, which were built into the Irish Protestant iconography of betrayal, siege, and deliverance. (Annual church services commemorating the providential escape of loyal Protestants in 1641 had been a fixture since the seventeenth century.) But on the other side, the adherents of the majority—if unofficial—faith, Catholicism, had their own memory of betrayal. This involved the promises of religious toleration embodied in the disputed terms of the Treaty of Limerick. To be a Protestant or a Catholic in eighteenth-century Ireland indicated more than mere religious allegiance: it represented opposing political cultures, and conflicting views of history.

FAMILY PORTRAIT ATTRIBUTED TO PHILIP HUSSEY, *c*.1770. The style of Irish Ascendancy life is indicated by distinctive items like the wallpaper and the fireplace, and the dining-chairs waiting around the walls. It possibly represents the Corbally family of Rathbeale, Co. Dublin.

Containment of the Catholic presence in Irish life, and the maintenance of Protestant Ascendancy, were expressed in legislative terms by a complex apparatus of penal laws formally excluding Catholics from participation in most areas of public life. Oaths denying the doctrines of transubstantiation and papal power were imposed on Irish MPs from the 1690s; the Popery Bills of 1703–4, following English legislation of 1700, limited the rights of Catholics to inheritance rights and secure leases. Further restrictions followed in 1709, after which the practice of legal conformity to retain an estate became more common. In 1729 the right to vote was specifically removed from Catholic freeholders; the Parliament now formally represented Protestant opinions only, inside and outside its walls.

Support for such measures was always more vehement among the MPs at Dublin than the government in Whitehall, or in Dublin Castle; indeed, anti-Catholic legislation could be—and was—used by the government as a *douceur* in their bargaining for support with recalcitrant Irish politicians. A general suspicion persisted that English government was soft on the vital question of 'Protestant liberties'. It was certainly true that, whatever some zealots may have hoped, the imposition of the penal laws as a unified 'code' never achieved a very high standard of efficiency, and small-minded restrictions like forbidding a Catholic to own a horse worth more than five pounds, or to bear arms, rapidly fell into desuetude. Additions to anti-Catholic legislation in the early eighteenth century generally came about as a result of *causes célèbres* in the courts apparently revealing loopholes to be blocked; the idea of an overall plan is not convincing. A more helpful image might be that of a power held in reserve, which enabled the continued exclusion of most Catholics from landowning, and of all Catholics from political representation. Given the simple fact of their large majority, the way they conducted their religion and led their private lives was necessarily left as largely their own affair. But by the early eighteenth century Catholics, though about 75 per cent of the population, owned only 14 per cent of Irish land.

Thus, despite the letter of the law, Catholic religious communities existed in surprising numbers during the first half of the eighteenth century, and masses were being said without interference from an early stage; there is evidence of decent urban churches being built by the 1720s. Priests were being trained in Irish seminaries by the 1750s; by the 1790s Catholics could buy and sell land, and educational restrictions had been repealed. The right to marry Protestants, practise at the bar, and vote followed in 1792–3. The organization of the church reached further and further into Irish life, notably after the foundation of the seminary at Maynooth in 1795, though the gap between formally structured Catholicism and the traditional religious practices of rural Ireland remained large. The status of Catholicism as an 'unofficial' religion helped perpetuate the pilgrimages, holy wells, and sacred bushes which had transferred into popular faith from far older practices.

At more sophisticated levels, Catholic 'society' remained, especially in certain areas, something to be taken into account. A residual Catholic gentry survived, especially across the Shannon, often retaining their land with the complicity of Protestant neighbours; there is evidence that the 'popery laws' were manipulated by such allies to ensure continued ownership. The importance of the Catholic merchant classes in the towns was attested to by all contemporaries, and highlighted by the controversy that arose over their exclusion from guilds. Commercial predominance was, in some ways, reinforced by social and political exclusion—a process which may also have applied to the other out-group restricted by religious exclusivity, the Dissenters. While elements like the important Huguenot colony

ST PATRICK'S CATHOLIC CHURCH, WATERFORD (1764), which demonstrates that even before the relaxation of the penal laws Catholic congregations were assembling publicly in handsome and dignified buildings—though often situated, like this one, down a discreet alley rather than on a main street.

in Dublin managed to evade many restrictions, sacramental tests formally kept religious nonconformists from public office, the army, and local government as well as parliament. Though practical discrimination against them was not often implemented by the government and some Dissenters even entered parliament, their exclusion was of great importance in helping form the adversarial Presbyterian political culture of Ulster: where their congregations increased in great number, and they remained unrepresented in the local government of a province which many saw as particularly their own.

The Political Base

The nature of eighteenth-century Irish politics revolved, as in England, around the landed nexus; in the counties and in most boroughs, landowners controlled representation. The boroughs comprised the usual eighteenth-century variety of qualifications and erratic distribution of population (their medieval origins are discussed above, pp. 60–1). Defined as a property interest, they could be easily organized—though 'open' boroughs epitomized a livelier and more independent political culture than is often realized. The 'forty-shilling freeholders', who possessed votes in the counties, were closely marshalled, but less easily controlled. The powers of local grandees, while they counted for much, were constrained by a variety of expectations, assumptions, and conventions.

The same might be said for the relationship between government and parliament. A comparatively small number of Irish landowners could control a large number of seats; this, combined with fundamentally uncertain notions as to how far the powers of the College Green Parliament might stretch, created potential difficulties for the Dublin Castle administration, headed by the viceroy and his chief secretary. The system that emerged in the mid-1690s amounted to political management by means of tacit co-operation between the Castle and the borough-owning grandees. The passage of government bills was ensured by a combination of patronage and a certain amount of favourable or locally demanded legislation. The system was temporarily disrupted by a brief period of party-political divisions in Anne's reign, when the 'rage of party' prevalent at Westminster was replicated (with certain local variations) at College Green. The old method of 'management' subsequently reasserted itself; but the fundamental constitutional uncertainty continued. And significantly, it was following this period of instability that an attempt was made to resolve it. A controversy over the right of the House of Lords at Westminster to act as a higher court of appeal for cases referred to the Irish Lords led to an Act of 1720 ('the Sixth of George I') which defined the constitutional status of the Irish legislature as subordinate. This scenario was reinforced by the medieval 'Poynings' Law' limiting the right of the Irish parliament to originate legislation (discussed above, p. 103). Together, the two laws provided the target for Irish 'Patriot' rhetoric declaimed over the next sixty-odd years.

The fact that many of the office-holding élite found such legislative trammels as offensive as did 'Patriotic' demagogues is a helpful pointer towards an understanding of Ascendancy political culture. *Causes célèbres* like the Crown's inept attempt at arranging an Irish minting monopoly to the advantage of a royal mistress (the 'Wood's halfpence' affair, 1722) focused Irish political energies into a generalized campaign for independence under the Crown, couched in language characteristic of a colonial élite. Jonathan Swift, political polemicist and dean of St Patrick's, took the issue as the basis for his 'Drapier's Letters', subjecting the Anglo-Irish relationship to devastating analysis; his subsequent career expresses the contradictory, vehement, intractably Protestant, but politically Anglophobic character of a uniquely Irish Tory tradition.

In the case of Swift and others, Ascendancy political culture was founded firmly on the principles of 1688—as these were interpreted in Ireland. When party labels crossed the Irish sea, they underwent a subtle but significant change.

Irish Toryism, for instance, while it existed, was not Jacobite or even pro-Stuart; it stood for hard-line Protestantism, an independent line in politics, with an affinity to what would later be called 'Patriotism', and a cynical view both of Hanoverianism and of the intentions of English government. Irish Whiggery was seen as trimming, latitudinarian, soft on Catholics, and too pro-English for its own good.

In the Irish political world, Toryism of the old stamp dwindled after 1714; family connections became the conventional cement of politics, with factions jockeying against each other for access to government patronage. The government's practice of co-operation and bargains, first adopted in the 1690s, evolved into the 'undertaker' system: large-scale political patrons among the Irish Ascendancy families 'undertook' to manage parliamentary factions, in return for access to the baroque and complex ramifications of the 'jobs' system which spread through the government, the civil service, the army, and the church. (There were recurrent spasms of fury when these preserves were invaded by Englishmen.) In this, the Irish political system operated according to the conventions of the time.

This was one aspect of Ascendancy politics; another is summed up by the developing 'Patriot' tradition, which called on the tradition of constitutional independence as expressed by Molyneux, Swift, and Charles Lucas—an unlikely trinity. Lucas was a radical darling of the Dublin mob during the 1740s, a traducer of 'privilege' as well as English usurpations, and a self-styled tribune on behalf of interests which Swift and Molyneux would have ignored or despised: his epic battles with the closed shop of Dublin aldermen provided constant political theatre, and he used the press and pamphlets to mount a radical, almost Wilkesite, critique of British misgovernment in Ireland. 'Patriot' opposition at all levels concentrated on resentment of English placemen, the necessity of a secure settlement of lands, the need to keep the Catholic threat contained, the desire for cheap government (sustained by low taxes), and for investment in certain areas of the Irish economy. Patriot spokesmen jealously guarded the Irish parliament's right to initiate money bills and critically examine government accounts. And though Lucas's radical posture and Swift's vituperative polemic were part of the tradition, much of the 'Patriot' ethos had to do with the priorities of landed Protestants. Though the rhetoric was later borrowed by those seeking Catholic redress, a closer connection should not be inferred.

Though the Dublin political world contained these volatile elements, activity from mid-century was dominated by internecine struggles between the great 'undertaking' interests (in which Patriotic rhetoric could easily be adopted). The tempo was heightened by the advent of new political brooms in England, with the accession of George III in 1760, and by a local campaign for an Irish Octennial Act limiting the duration of Irish parliaments (eventually passed in 1768). A new viceroy, Townshend, wrestled with over-mighty 'undertaker' factions, and tried

CHARLES LUCAS, the popular
Dublin radical, represented in 1772
by the sculptor Edward Smyth as
tribune of the people: hero of the
Dublin mob, he remained a thorn
in the side of 'respectable' politics.

to build up support for the administration among independent elements—in a
sense paralleling the efforts of George III to free himself from the great Whig
factions at Westminster. And the significance of the Townshend viceroyalty lies
in the fact that viceroys became, from the 1760s, more generally resident in
Dublin, negotiating with the local politicians directly from Dublin Castle rather
than delegating parliamentary management to undertakers, and setting up a
'Castle party' of local supporters. From this period until the abolition of the Irish
parliament at the end of the century, a larger number of hands were dealt in to
the political game.

But players at the table were still restricted to the Ascendancy caste: and this,
though socially mobile within its limits, was limited to the world of Protestants.
The frenetic, introverted nature of Irish Georgian politics reflected the insecure
basis of Ascendancy: symbolized by the existence of a large standing army in
Ireland—12,000 in 1699, augmented to over 15,000 a few years later. Regiments
were continually moved around: Irish recruitment was considered a risky policy
until after the apparent débàcle of Jacobitism in 1745. In the following era, the

danger seemed to come more immediately from France, to which the Irish coastline was obviously vulnerable; the army in Ireland was also used to confront unrest generated by the endemic rural 'secret societies' and to restore order after faction fights. Later, they were supported by locally raised militia and yeomanry corps. But the eighteenth-century army barracks remained an essential part of the way Irish towns were 'landscaped', along with the market square and the row of estate cottages. This, as much as the Georgian grandeur of Dublin architecture, is part of the inheritance of Ascendancy.

Irish Life in the Georgian Era

The Irish economy had entered upon a rapid post-war recovery by the late 1690s, though the fluctuating value of Irish coinage and the recurrent spectre of war led to great financial insecurity in the early years of the new century. Local conditions, notably a run of bad harvests in the late 1720s and 1730s, caused much rural destitution. But the Irish population subsequently entered a period of sustained growth, and this was matched by economic expansion too. Though food shortages recurred (on occasion, as in 1740, amounting to famine), they did so on a highly regionalized pattern; here as elsewhere, the variety of Irish experience in the eighteenth century is striking. Life in Connemara, or on the Kerry peninsulas, remained fixed in the old modes which were being abandoned by the increasingly Anglicized and commercialized east and south. The picture of a dispossessed Gaelic rural proletariat eking out an embittered existence in smoke-filled cabins is partial, to say the least. For one thing, farming developments complicated the rural class structure; the pasture-farming belt, spreading over north Munster, Leinster, and east Connacht, was sustaining a prosperous farming class by mid-century. Short-term price fluctuations (especially in the foreign market for butter) would have a severe effect on agricultural prosperity, especially in the first half of the eighteenth century; but from about 1750, a new phase of economic activity was marked by the inflow of capital, low interest rates, and a rise in agricultural prices. Those who were landless and insecure—and they were many—were exploited by the cattle-farming classes at least as much as by the supposedly alien landlords. And the idea of Irish rural life as universally and ostentatiously poverty-stricken owes more to polemical pamphleteers than to dispassionate observers.

On other levels too, the economic history of the period had been highly coloured by political preconceptions. This was true at the time as well. For instance, the boom in Irish woollen exports from the 1690s caused great political as well as economic controversy, which eventually ended in an export ban and a tariff on Irish woollens entering England. But whether this really meant the strangling of an infant industry in its cradle has been disputed. Diversification took place, into yarn production rather than fabric; while the encouragement of the linen industry formed the basis of a new domestic economy in Ulster and elsewhere. The recent consensus is that trade was not greatly hampered by colonial restrictions, despite a few high-profile (and highly specific) measures. In fact, one of the success stories of the eighteenth-century Irish economy is the growth of foreign trade.

This was mirrored by the expansion of trading networks within the country. Both public and private patronage emphasized the improvement of internal transport facilities—not only the turnpike roads which radiated out from Dublin, but also an ambitious inland waterways system. The prosperity of market towns and large ports like Cork, Limerick, and Waterford was evident in their commercial buildings as well as in the fortunes made by merchants—often Catholic, linked by influential networks of family relationships stretching as far as Spain or the West Indies, but also representing other subcultures like the Quakers (prominent in textiles and milling). The spread of a cash economy was further encouraged by the importance of the cattle-market, based on regional specializations in rearing, fattening, and breeding, and feeding the increasingly insatiable English market. The institution of the cattle fair made the fortunes of

DOMESTIC LINEN PRODUCTION IN ULSTER as shown in an engraving by William Hincks (1783). The women of the family are spinning, reeling, and boiling yarn.

many small towns; there were over 3,000 by the end of the century. Great butter-markets flourished in places like Cork. Tillage began to increase again from the 1770s, responding to market demands and government bounties. Economic growth and expansion, founded on a highly active agricultural sector, was evident from the middle of the century.

Agricultural exports, however, like textiles, remained directed largely towards the English market. And with the industrialization of the British economy, this would have an ominous implication. While rural industry existed in Ireland, it was highly regionalized—notably in the north. The domestically based linen industry predominated, possibly producing as much as 40 million yards per annum by the last quarter of the eighteenth century—half of it for export. The bleach greens stretched out by northern rivers were a feature of the Ulster landscape; and the domestic nature of production transformed the family economy. And in bleaching as many other livelihoods, a Protestant monopoly was noted by nearly every observer.

There were other enterprises too. Late in the century 'cotton villages' began to appear, encouraged as a mechanism for industrial relocation; fishing and distilling provided useful additions to farming incomes, especially in Ulster. But where a varied local economy did not take root, small farmers and cottiers became increasingly dependent on two elements: the pig and the potato. The latter crop was uniquely well adapted to Irish conditions—prolific, nutritious, and useful as a rotatory crop. But dependence on it for sustaining the tiny holdings especially characteristic of the underdeveloped south and west would bring a terrible nemesis.

Where the rural economy expanded, this was evident in the physical landscape. Roads, bridges, mills, and barracks were built; landlord villages accompanied the growth of the medium-sized, centralized estates which in many areas replaced the sprawling *latifundiae* accumulated in earlier eras. The Palladian pattern of the country house was followed and adapted by small country builders as well as the architects of the breath-taking classical mansions which epitomize the Georgian Ascendancy's obsession with laying ostentatious claim to the land. 'Improving' landlords existed, and their activities are recorded by travellers like Arthur Young as well as in the activities of the Royal Dublin Society (founded in 1731). But the inexorable logic of the Irish agricultural estate, especially in less fertile parts of the island, dictated the letting out and multiplication of holdings (outside a showpiece demesne), rather than organized commercial farming in large units.

This development also reflected the dramatic demographic growth which probably began around mid-century. Already rising, the Irish population graph started a sharp ascent; figures probably doubled by the end of the century, reaching a total of nearly five million by 1800. This process interacted with economic ex-

RUSSBOROUGH HOUSE, CO. WICKLOW, built in 1742 for the earl of Milltown (grandson of a brewing fortune, soon dissipated), by Richard Cassels and Francis Bindon. The Palladian lay-out, much adopted in Irish houses of the period, concealed kitchen and stable-block in the form of pavilions.

COLGANSTOWN, CO. DUBLIN by Nathaniel Clements (c.1760) carries the same principles down to farmhouse proportions, and epitomizes the markedly Italian style of many Irish Georgian houses.

pansion and altered farming patterns to drive rents inexorably up. Significantly, the counties of domestic linen production –Armagh, Antrim, Monaghan—were most densely populated, leading later in the century to tension over the occupation of land. Moreover, population growth was particularly concentrated towards the lower end of the social scale. The class above labourers but below 'solid' farmers had increased noticeably by the 1790s; as had the cottier class, dependent on the proceeds of migratory labour and the cultivation of a potato-garden, and vulnerable to rising agricultural prices. Above them, the strong-farming elements consolidated their position, economically and socially, subletting land to labourers as well as profiting from the grazing and dairying boom. The extent of such 'middleman' activity provoked a great deal of subsequent commentary: often inaccurate. Re-letting tenanted land was, in fact, an activity engaged in by a wide variety of farmers and investors, and the generalized denunciations of Arthur Young are an oversimplification at best.

The complexity of class structure and landholding arrangements in rural life was echoed by equally complex social relations. An exhaustive study of leases in the Kenmare area in the early eighteenth century, for instance, shows a surprising picture of prosperous ex-Jacobite tenants, many of Gaelic stock, holding profitable leases in perpetuity: the survivors of the old landed class, pushed down the scale to subtenants, but retaining more status than often supposed—especially where the head landlord was an absentee. Under subsequent penal laws, the terms of their leases may have been questioned: fifty years later, the agent of the same head landlord was trying to weaken their position but found it difficult to deal with 'a people who consider themselves gentry', as he noted to his surprise. The 'middlemen' condemned by Arthur Young and others for their parasitism were often just such survivors of the old landed families, who felt they had a right to a living from the land. By the last decade of the century, significantly, the Kenmare tenantry were thoroughly embittered by the attempts to reorganize their leases; elsewhere too, resentments were rising.

The social geography of rural Ireland reflected a history of settlement and dispossession; in several areas, the Protestant artisanate and small-farming class (much more widely distributed throughout the island than they would be later on) were brought into conflict with upwardly mobile and land-hungry Catholics. The endemic faction-fighting and violence of Irish life fits into this context: and confrontational attitudes were further sharpened by the levelling off of growth in incomes, consumption, and output by the last decades of the eighteenth century. Outbreaks of violence by secret societies, often grouped under the 'Whiteboy' label, were recurrent; though often connected by the official mind with sectarian animosity, some manifestations at least were inspired by resentment at taxation, or opposition to social changes attendant upon the spread of the dairying economy. Agricultural crisis was almost invariably accompanied by rural protests, often highly structured in form, but none the less reliant on the ultimate sanction of violence.

The dislocations of the 1790s, however, followed an era whose prosperity and apparent stability have not always been recognized. The physical evidence of this remains in the sophisticated standard of Irish-manufactured artefacts—silver, glass, jewellery, and furniture; the innovative and accomplished achievements in the decorative arts, notably plasterwork; and most of all in the uniquely satisfying traditions of Irish Georgian architecture, preserved all over the country in houses which represent different levels of social standing and aspiration, but which all adhere to conventions of elegant simplicity and assured style. In many ways, Dublin represented the apex of this achievement: a showpiece city, laid out with grandeur and imagination. Even before the Wide Streets Commission

IRISH PLASTERWORK again owed much to Italian influence, but Michael Stapleton was just one local master. The staircase hall of Belvedere House, Dublin (1786) characteristically contains tremendously ornate decoration behind a severely austere façade.

was appointed in 1758, the spacious and carefully interrelated pattern of squares, streets, malls, and bridges was being constructed; the Parliament House and the reconstruction of Trinity College had begun early in the century. Gandon's great Customs House and Four Courts put the coping on a conception of unrivalled style, much of it tragically and wilfully destroyed only in very recent memory.

Balancing this achievement was the civic culture of Belfast: not yet the industrial boom city it would become, but by the end of the century taking over from Dublin as the chief export centre for textiles. Its vigorous, independent, Dissenter merchant classes dominated the ethos of a town whose slightly suspicious relationship with Dublin was akin to that between Glasgow and Edinburgh. Here too can be seen another facet of the variety and tension implicit in Irish eighteenth-century life. Perhaps the intellectual reaction to this is best epitomized by the *Irish Querist*, an exasperated pamphlet of rhetorical questions put together by Bishop Berkeley of Cloyne (an eccentric, much loved, and very sharp for his purposes). Many of Berkeley's interrogations strike at the heart of eighteenth-century Irish dilemmas. 'Whose fault is it if poor Ireland still con-

BISHOP BERKELEY OF CLOYNE, a dominating figure in eighteenth-century Ireland, whose philosophical theory about *The Principles of Human Knowledge* (1710) was to be far more influential than his many panaceas for bettering the lot of Ireland. The ship in the background represents his interest in far-flung colonization schemes, notably Bermuda.

The gent' in blacke
sat on this Syde/

The ladyes women in
blacke attieres on this Syde/

ye Alter table

Thes Bannarolls

to Stand w:thout ye herse/

La
mist

La
mist

La

Aslistant

Aslistant

La

Aslistant

Aslistant

Aslistant

Aslistant

La
vicounte

La
vicount

ye corps

Aslistant

Asl:

ye chefe morner

place for
or lyt

ye great banner to stand
w:thout ye rayle·

PLAN FOR THE FUNERAL OF ELIZABETH, COUNTESS OF ORMOND, in 1601, which became a prototype for noble funerals. The mourning ritual was enacted within the funeral hearse erected in the centre aisle of the church. The hearse was covered in rich black tapestry which showed off the vivid colours of the banner rolls and the great banner.

JAMES, DUKE OF ORMOND. This portrait by William Wissing reveals the aloof grandeur that was associated with those few Irish lords who had gone into exile with Charles II. As a consequence of his travails Ormond was certain of the king's favour in the decades after the restoration.

MÁIRE RUA O'BRIEN, c.1640, was one of the great survivors of the Cromwellian conquest. The widow of Conor O'Brien of Lemenagh, who died fighting against the Cromwellian forces, she married a Cromwellian officer and raised her existing children as Protestants. The lavish dress indicates something of the cost involved in conforming to English ways.

STATE BALL IN DUBLIN CASTLE, 1731, painted by William van der Hagen (below). The occasion was recorded by Mrs Delaney in a letter to a friend: 'The room . . . was finely adorned with paintings and obelisks and made as light as a summer's day. I never saw more company in one place; abundance of finery, and indeed many very pretty women . . . Vast profusion of meat and drink, which you may be sure has *gained the hearts of all guzzlers!*'

VIEW OF WATERFORD, 1736, by William van der Hagen. The town was a major port, and an outlet for the prosperous south-east. The arcaded quayside buildings are striking, and the many churches; also the Norman fortress, 'Reginald's Tower', on the extreme left. In 1795 an ambitious 832-foot bridge of stone and oak was built, lasting well into the twentieth century.

tinues poor?' 'Whether it would not be more reasonable to mend our State than complain of it; and how far this may be in our power?' And, finally, 'Whether our parties are not a burlesque upon politics?'

Crisis and Union

By the later eighteenth century, then, Irish society was subject to several hidden tensions. The population boom was threatening the stability of rural life; areas dependent on domestic industry were vulnerable to economic fluctuations; and increasing resentment at taxation (in several forms) had reactivated rural unrest. From the late 1770s, the crisis in the British empire set off echoes which re-sounded through Ireland. The lurch towards war in America, and the ac-companying battle of rhetoric, focused the attention of 'Patriotic' Irish politicians on their own position. Anti-ministerialist, anti-corruption, and anti-Catholic lines of argument all tended to support the American case, and to stimulate comparison with that of Ireland. The process was encouraged by the fact that some of the Rockingham Whigs at Westminster opportunistically made the same link; the unofficial alliance thus set up between Irish and English oppositions led to prom-ises which were unexpectedly redeemed in the 1780s.

Moreover, the strong links between Ulster and America, forged over gen-erations of emigration, reinforced the current of radical anti-government feeling in that province. Irish unrest was suddenly manifested at all levels, and the beleaguered British government had to make some kind of response. One result was the policy of relaxing penal laws against Catholics—which was usually the result of pressure from London against local resistance. The disadvantage of alienating the Irish élite was considered to be outweighed by the advantage of securing a loyal and grateful majority population, and also enabling Catholics to join the army—which was increasingly overstretched. At the same time, the policy of encouraging the training of priests in Ireland was embraced with the foundation of Maynooth College: the theory was that an Anglicized Catholic church would evolve if priests were not trained in Europe, and were not drawn from the Irish-speaking peasantry. But though the clergy were locally trained, and the Maynooth priests came to represent the families of strong farmers and shopkeepers rather than cottiers, the Catholic church in Ireland remained inescapably and unmistakably Irish.

In other areas of life too, the American War provoked self-examination and aggressive demonstrations of discontent. A powerful and articulate campaign calling for the reconstruction of commercial legislation to give Ireland un-restricted access to world trade escalated from 1778; as part of the process, 'Patriotic' and other discontents had been channelled into a military volunteering movement. Detachments of Volunteers, uniformed and partially armed, springing

'THE IRISH HOUSE OF COMMONS', 1780, by Francis Wheatley shows Grattan, standing to the right of the table, urging that the Irish Parliament should have the exclusive right to legislate for Ireland. Twenty years later, however, the impressive chamber of 'the old house' was the setting for the Debate on the Union when members voted themselves out of existence.

from a variety of local bases, were set up by individual grandees or professional associations; they were reluctantly recognized by the government and commandeered by Opposition political interests. The Volunteer demonstrations out of doors, the pressure on Lord North's government from the inflamed rhetoric of 'patriot' political leaders like Henry Grattan and Henry Flood, threats of non-co-operation in the Irish House of Commons, the disastrous events in America, and finally a change of government in Britain: all helped bring about first the repeal of the remaining restrictions on Irish commerce, and then the constitutional concessions of 1782, which were intended to face up at last to the uncertainty of the Irish parliament's constitutional position by amending Poynings' law and repealing the 'Sixth of George I'. The assembly at College Green now enjoyed an ostensible independence in originating its own legislation: nineteenth-century nationalists would christen it, as a rather misleading tribute, 'Grattan's parliament'.

Behind the rhetoric, what had 1782 delivered? The Crown and parliament of Ireland were defined as the law-giving authority; heads of bills could originate in Ireland. But the power of the Privy Council over Irish legislation, not to mention that of the monarch, still remained—as did the troubled relationship between the Dublin Castle executive and the Irish parliament. A recognition of this inconclusiveness prompted Flood's successful campaign for a statute formally renouncing all external controls over the Irish parliament. But the wheels of Irish government still had to be oiled by the aid of local politicians, notably a hard core of powerful and implacably conservative Ascendancy figures, with deep reservations about the Patriotic campaigns which climaxed in 1782. One of these was John Fitzgibbon, earl of Clare, who blocked the idea of any further concessions to Catholics; he expressed an authoritarian rationale of Irish government which stressed the insecurities, tensions, and resentments below the surface of

Portrait of an Irish Chief: drawn from Life at Wexford.

HENRY GRATTAN (*left*), seen as a contemporary Augustan representing the virtues of learning and dedication to public service, in the country house bequeathed to him by 'the nation'.

GILLRAY'S VERSION OF GRATTAN violently but inaccurately puts him at the head of the rebels in 1798. In fact, he had by then repudiated even the moderate demands for political reform articulated by the Volunteers.

Irish society, and threw sardonic doubt on the euphoria of the Patriot victory. The events of the subsequent decade provided—to those of his own mind at least—some kind of a vindication.

The instability caused by war with France in the 1790s, and the increasingly radical demands for political reform from Volunteer demonstrations, was exacerbated by Earl Fitzwilliam's brief appearance as viceroy in 1795. Attempting to overturn existing power-brokers and offer total Catholic emancipation, he opened a Pandora's Box; Fitzwilliam was repudiated by his government and recalled. But the gilded world of Ascendancy politics was already cracking apart. British political opinion was increasingly worried about the unstable political and constitutional status of the Irish assembly and the ominous effect of political alliances across the Irish sea—especially as the Irish movement for political reform gathered pace. Nor did the government's own initiatives defuse the situation. In 1793 legislation had been forced through, giving the vote and civil rights to Catholics; the liberalization of land laws had already heightened sectarian tension in certain 'frontier' areas, notably south Ulster. Secret societies, under the generic name of 'Defenderism', were taking a more openly political form. Politicians at College Green were split on the issue of total Catholic emancipation (the right to sit in parliament and hold high office)—a cause embraced as much from opportunism as from enlightenment. Fitzwilliam's failure raised the temperature, but events were already setting towards a crisis. Most of all, a native political radicalism had taken light from the fuse that had been lit in France.

This was especially true in Belfast, where the radical, egalitarian predisposition of the Presbyterian bourgeoisie seized readily upon 'French ideas'. (The doyen of Belfast radical politics, Revd Sinclare Kelburn, allegedly began prayers with 'O Lord, *if it be possible*, have mercy on the king.') Even before France and Britain went to war, conspiracy theories were circulating; by the mid-1790s, the Ascendancy politician John Beresford painted a dramatic picture in a letter to Lord Auckland.

We are in a most desperate situation. The whole north, south, Meath, Westmeath, Longford, Roscommon, Galway, Co. and city Dublin ready to rise in rebellion; an invasion invited by ambassadors; our militia corrupted; the dragoons of Ireland suspected; the United Irishmen all organized; the people armed; while we are without military stores, magazines, etc., and where things will end God only knows, but our heads are in no small danger I promise you.

'Where things ended' was in a bloody, sectarian *jacquerie* which sputtered through the summer of 1798. This fused together several very disparate strains of resistance. But the ideological impetus towards radicalization was supplied by the movement mentioned by Beresford; the United Irishmen.

The United Irishmen began life as a sophisticated, radical debating club, French-influenced but in the tradition of Irish constitutional opposition. The original Belfast society represented middle-class, radical Presbyterianism—the articulate, anti-government commercial classes, political reformers by inclination, whose leading spirits veered increasingly to radicalism and eventually to republicanism. Their original prospectus was written in 1791 by William Drennan, who described himself as an 'aristocratical democrat'. But the most celebrated United Irishman was not an Ulsterman. Theobald Wolfe Tone was a *déclassé* Kildare Protestant, who moved from youthful ambitions to be a servant of the empire, through constitutional Whiggery, to pro-Catholic campaigning (bringing a sharp new edge to the cautious Catholic Committee), and eventually steered the transformation of the United Irishmen into a 'French Revolutionary' movement with powerful links to the rural underground of 'Defender' societies.

The bewildering speed of this radical evolution, for Irish radicalism at large as well as for Tone in particular, was accelerated by the government's hasty and ill-considered crack-down on all radical activity as the war with France reached a crisis point. The Dublin United Irishmen, suppressed in May 1794, were reconstructed underground into what was apparently a much tougher and more ruthless organization than heretofore. It certainly involved a *sans-culotte* element, later defined by a prominent United Irishman: 'mechanics, petty shop-keepers and farmers who wanted a practicable engine by which the power of men like themselves might be most effectually combined and employed; accordingly the scheme was calculated to embrace the lower orders and in fact to make every man a politician.' But this underestimates the continuity with middle-class radical leadership, now driven underground; and it leaves unstated the corollary of an appeal to sansculottism, Irish style. This was the inevitability of releasing sectarian antipathies, especially in rural areas where tension was already high. Here the confrontation that eventually took place had very little to do with the secular republicanism officially preached by Paris and Belfast.

Three developments characterized the drift towards crisis: the United Irishmen's cross-fertilization with Defenderism, the government's provocation of resistance by the draconian activities of the yeomanry (often led by the most paranoiac of the country gentry), and the general collapse of Protestant morale, as the succession of Catholic Relief Acts encouraged challenges to their local authority. By 1795, Defenderist offensives had inspired opposing Protestant societies, notably the Orange lodges founded after a celebrated sectarian confrontation. At the same time, Defender ideology began to spread among the artisans of country towns, probably encouraged by mounting resentment at the taxation system, which was restructured and steadily expanded from the early 1790s: the high point of resistance was reached in 1797. Meanwhile Tone, in French exile, represented Irish republicanism to the revolutionary government

'THE UNFORTUNATE WOLFE TONE', as envisaged in 1798 by *Walker's Hibernian Magazine*. Later representations became progressively more idealized.

with extraordinary aplomb, and remarkable effect. Due to his efforts, a large-scale invasion force arrived off Bantry Bay in December 1796, but was dispersed by storms. Later expeditions followed in 1798, including General Humbert's brief but legendary invasion of Connacht: but by then the rebellion was over.

The United Irishmen and their Defender allies apparently planned a rising for the early summer of 1798; but in May, a preliminary swoop on known radicals defused the explosion. What broke out instead was a localized *jacquerie*, taking hold in Wexford and east Leinster, leading to bloodletting and massacre on an appalling scale. The rationale was more aggressively sectarian than United Irishman theory had ever allowed for; the Ulster rising, led by old-guard radicals like Henry Joy McCracken, was late and ineffectual. It was the Wexford war, led by priests, with celebrated engagements at New Ross and a tragic last stand on Enniscorthy's Vinegar Hill, that entered nationalist mythology. How far a 'national' spirit inflamed the rebels is very doubtful; land hunger, increased taxes, crisis in the local agrarian economy (notably the grain market) all helped dictate the pattern of the rising. The surprising emergence of several members of the gentry as local leaders certainly indicates widespread alienation after several years of repressive government. But generally, the radical alliance that had attempted to combine so many disparate elements split apart in confusion. The idea of a secular combination across the classes, in opposition to British government and in favour of national independence, had conspicuously failed to take hold. Older antipathies emerged and older allegiances were confirmed.

The inheritance of the Irish eighteenth century was, therefore, at once potent and strangely confused. In recent, traumatically vivid memory, there was the great myth of 1798: 'The Memory of the Dead', in the title of a rousing Young Ireland ballad of the next generation ('Who fears to speak of '98?'). Tone had died in a clumsy suicide, after being taken prisoner in a French expedition to Lough Swilly late in 1798; less well known to contemporaries than most of the rebel leaders, his memory was ensured by an influential filial biography, the publication of extracts from his marvellous journals, and eventually his elevation to the pantheon of nationalist heroes set up in 1916 by Patrick Pearse. The reality of 1798 was later transformed into an expression of what Pearse would call 'the separatist idea'. Something similar happened to the remembered tradition of 'Grattan's parliament'. Far from separatism though it really was, 'the old house at College Green' was represented throughout the nineteenth century as the home of an ideal of national independence. With the abolition of the Irish parliament in 1800, and its Union with Westminster in a radical act of reform, the idea of British treachery was also enshrined in the memory of 'independence'. The Act of Union had been managed through the Irish House of Commons in the accepted manner, though patronage and bribery were used more blatantly and more extravagantly than usual; the fact that such tactics had always been a necessary if venal part of Ascendancy politics was forgotten, and the stolen parliament became linked with the broken Treaty of Limerick in the long tradition of Albion's perfidy. The fact that the Union was not accompanied by Catholic emancipation, as originally intended, helped sustain the parallel further. As for the civic culture of the Georgian Ascendancy, it declined along with the decay of Dublin—generally represented by early nineteenth-century observers and novelists as an echoing shell, full of grand but redundant buildings. The House of Parliament, symbolically, became and remained the Bank of Ireland.

The political élite of eighteenth-century Ireland, many of whom had fought hard to preserve their own parliament, by and large adapted to the new dispensation: several great names from the palmy days at College Green transferred their eloquence and their career prospects to Westminster, including Grattan himself. With the rise of Catholic democracy, this class—by an ironic reversal of their original attitude—would cling to 'the Union' as their guarantee of survival (or of privilege). But an anti-Union tradition of constitutional nationalism continued, in a muffled way: adhered to by some members of the more liberal country gentry, whose representatives would help found the early Home Rule movement more than fifty years later.

Other underground traditions also continued from the eighteenth century: notably the world of organized rural disaffection, with 'secret societies' and allegiance to alternative traditions of authority, following their chosen (and readily mythologized) 'Captains', and often harking back to an imagined Golden Age of 'right' economic relationships. But they also remembered, and used, the language of Defenderism, and their imagery and aspirations were often frankly sectarian. A millennial day of justice for the Catholic cause, with the attendant extirpation of Protestants, was part of this half-hidden popular culture; elements of what it represented haunted many aspects of political activity in the subsequent era.

The Rise of the Catholic Democracy

The changes in the Anglo-Irish relationship after 1800 were in some ways more apparent than real. The Dublin Castle system continued, with a resident viceroy and an increasingly authoritative chief secretary. Irish representation in the House of Commons was fixed at 100 members (out of the total 658), involving the disenfranchisement of the more blatantly 'pocketed' boroughs: the arrangements made for Ireland in the 1832 Reform Act did not modify matters much, and more sweeping political changes had to wait until 1850, when the franchise was considerably extended.

In economic terms, the Union meant that Ireland entered a free trade area with Britain: an arrangement often solicited, and one of the reasons why the Union gained some support among the Catholic bourgeoisie and Belfast businessmen. But, given the pace of British industrialization and the collapse of the inflated agricultural market with the coming of peace after Napoleon's defeat in 1815, the economic future was not to Ireland's advantage. The apparent exploitation of the less developed economy, together with the continuing failure to grant Catholic emancipation, created the terms in which nationalist rhetoric denounced the Union: a recurring metaphor being that of the failed marriage. The very validity of the contract was denied by many: the attempted rebellion of Robert Emmet in 1803, a continuing inspiration for nationalist balladeers, set the tone of rhetoric which claimed the right of Ireland to 'take her place among the nations of the earth'. Those who were prepared to support the rhetoric with anything more than words were an infinitesimal minority. But the tradition of Anglophobia, and the recital of historical grievance, was built into the framework of Irish nationalism under the Union.

This development was aided by the outward trappings of British power in Ireland, now divorced from any relationship (however uneasy) with a local parliament (however unrepresentative). Besides the viceroy presiding over an increasingly gimcrack and shabby court in Dublin Castle, there were the appurtenances of a large army establishment, an increasingly professional police force, and the dominating presence of solidly built barracks in most provincial

REVEREND HENRY COOKE, whose endorsement of hard-line Presbyterian orthodoxy triumphed over the more libertarian ideas of Henry Montgomery in the 1820s and helped settle Ulster Protestantism further into an inflexible mould. He was a powerful opponent of government schemes for interdenominational national education.

towns; the intentions and record of the Irish administration, though on occasion energetic, constructive, and well-meaning, could not compete against this. Nor was the credibility of benevolent government enhanced by the blatant continuation of many Protestant monopolies—in the civil service, the legal profession, and most of all local government. In the first decades of the nineteenth century, resentment at this was focused in the sporadic outbreaks of violent resistance to the collection of church tithes. Violent confrontations, and the sense of an underlying alienation, continued as a theme of rural life up to the 1830s.

In some ways, a similar syndrome also characterized the Protestant world outside the landed classes who went to Westminster. With the rapid development of Belfast as an industrial phenomenon, and the influx of a Catholic proletariat into the city, religious tempers ran high. The debates which racked Ulster Presbyterianism in the early nineteenth century had nearly as much to do with political ideology as with religion: the recurrent clash between orthodoxy and liberalism was fought out once again, taking Catholic emancipation as a touchstone. Fundamentalism won out, dominated by the figure of Dr Henry Cooke: the language of the Ulster Protestant, while on many levels egalitarian and democratic, continued to see righteousness as their monopoly, both in political and in religious terms. The religious geography of the north-east settled into a three-way division between Church of Ireland, Presbyterian, and Catholic: a population fractured along invisible frontiers. These years also saw the re assertion of the Orange lodges, as a popular Protestant movement uneasily watched by government and gentry; it was closely connected with the high profile of Protestant political activity in towns like Cork, where oligarchic privileges remained to them until the Municipal Corporations Act of 1840. Most of all, the emphatically confessional framework of political activity in the early nineteenth century reflected the phenomenon of the mass Catholic political movement led by Daniel O'Connell.

The Irish Catholic cause in a sense transcended the simple claim for an 'emancipation' which would allow them to sit in parliament and hold high office. The peculiar status of the Irish Roman Catholic Church, its informal but tacitly acknowledged power, its Gaelic strain combined with powerful Roman links, the power of its priests and bishops as agents of social control, most of all the way it symbolized an Irish identification which repudiated English efforts at conversion and colonialism—all this conferred a necessarily political dimension upon Catholicism in Ireland, despite disclaimers. Daniel O'Connell, Gaelic folk hero and legendary lawyer, used the issue of emancipation to build a prototype popular mass movement, orchestrated by the Catholic Association (founded in 1823) and financed by a vast number of small subscriptions: the 'Catholic Rent'. But the potency of its appeal arose from more than the simple injustice of the denial of Catholics' civil rights. By the 1820s, government commitment to some kind of measure hovered in the air, probably involving a veto on the appointment of bishops and a salaried priesthood. Political ineptness and procrastination enabled the Catholic campaigners to harden their line; issues like the veto provided grounds for a split from the traditional aristocratic leadership. But the real revolution in the 1820s was O'Connell's mobilization of mass politics, led by an élite of Catholic lawyers, later joined by provincial merchants and journalists. The new militant rhetoric demanded rights rather than concessions; the language was, in a real sense, democratic. The chapel-yard and the courthouse were used as political forums; the tactics were those of sensationalism and brinkmanship, great public demonstrations were mounted, symbolic issues brought triumphantly to law, and an 'alternative parliament' effectively met in O'Connell's Dublin headquarters, the Corn Exchange Building on Burgh Quay. What it amounted to was a political education for the classes outside the Ascendancy.

This was put in concrete form by the Waterford election of 1826, where a candidate backed by the Catholic Association challenged and vanquished the nominee of the local grandees, the Beresford family (who had symbolically been one of the greatest 'connections' of the eighteenth-century political dispensation). Other challenges followed, mobilizing the votes of the forty-shilling freeholder cottiers; they culminated in O'Connell's own election as MP for Clare. This

DANIEL O'CONNELL, hailed by Catholic and nationalist Ireland as 'The Liberator' in the early nineteenth century, but decried for his pacifism and compromises by the later 'physical force' spokesmen. He used the framework of the law to win greater achievements than many of his traducers. This picture, significantly, hangs in the Reform Club, London.

highlighted the absurdity of imposing oaths of supremacy and abjuration as a means of excluding Catholics from parliament: it was now obvious that O'Connellism could return a phalanx of popularly mandated MPs who would have no alternative but mass secession. The measure so long debated was introduced in 1829; Catholics could sit in parliament and hold most high offices. But the forty-shilling freeholder class, on which their electoral triumphs had been based, were disenfranchised by the raising of the county franchise to £10. As so often under the Union, an overdue gesture of concession was made in as deliberately grudging a manner as possible.

In practical terms, O'Connell and his followers could now graduate from the out-of-doors tactics of Irish political demonstrations to the political establishment at Westminster: which they did. Irish nationalist historiography has dismissed the effectiveness of O'Connell's manœuvres in alliance with English Whigs and Radicals through the 1830s, and has chosen to see his subsequent reversion to mass-movement tactics in a campaign for Repeal of the Act of Union as an admission that the Westminster route was a dead end for Irish political nationalist organization. But O'Connell's decade of ceaseless political activity in London was yet another facet of his protean personality, and by no means the least effective. Improvements in the structures of Irish government, education, and health care, the achievements of a sympathetic and radical Under-Secretary in Thomas Drummond, the reorganization of the Church of Ireland (including the commutation of the ever-rankling tithe problem) were at least decent payments on account. Actual measures of reform often fell short of what was needed. But the psychological breakthrough of giving Catholics access to senior legal positions, for instance, should not be underestimated. Nor did the 'Repeal' campaign so prominent in the early 1840s occur as a reaction to a decade of supposedly fruitless endeavour; the objective to restore an Irish assembly of some kind was there throughout. What happened was that the tactics changed with the fall of Whig government in 1841; O'Connell and his allies felt (in some ways inaccurately) that much less was to be hoped for from Sir Robert Peel. The tactics of challenging the government by means of popular assembly, however, when exercised as part of a campaign to repeal the Act of Union, released emotions and provoked confrontations which had not accompanied the campaign for Catholic

A MONSTER REPEAL MEETING, significantly held at the historically resonant location of Tara in 1843 ('Repeal Year'). This contemporary drawing shows banners carried by trades unions; the characteristic O'Connellite iconography of harps, wolf-dogs, and round towers; and even a reconstituted Irish harper enthroned in the centre of the picture.

REPEAL MEETING AT TARA.

emancipation. Repeal of the Union did not arouse the support of liberal Protestants and sympathetic British politicians; and it raised up memories of rebellion
and sacrifice which even O'Connell—a life-long pacifist and constitutionalist—
could not control. The crisis came when O'Connell cancelled a banned 'monster
meeting' at Clontarf in 1843 under threat of military intervention. But his emotive
and carefully ill-defined objective of 'Repeal' was already being pushed further
by a discontented wing of more radical nationalists called the 'Young Ireland'
movement. And the political language of the Repeal movement utilized a militant
view of Irish history which was becoming increasingly important in the formation
of Irish nationalist ideology.

It was significant that O'Connell's banned Repeal meeting had been scheduled
to take place at Clontarf: the scene had been deliberately chosen to rouse
memories of Brian Boru's confrontation with the Norsemen in 1014 (described
above, p. 40). This encounter, like so much else in Irish history, had by the early
nineteenth century been incorporated into an inspirational tale of an un-
suppressible Irish nation constantly struggling against invaders and sustaining
an indomitable cultural identity going back to Gaelic (and, implicitly, Catholic)
roots. The process by which Irish history became an instrument of political
rhetoric as well as national assertiveness is a complex one: its roots lie in the
eighteenth-century Ascendancy fashion for antiquities and archaeology, as well
as in the innovations in history-writing pioneered by apologists for the Irish
Catholic cause, at home and abroad. By the early nineteenth century, European
notions of immutable national character, and a Romantic preoccupation with the
culture of the 'folk', were also coming into play; these generalized and often
inchoate themes received specific expression in a variety of ways during the
first decades of the Union, not all of them ostensibly 'nationalist'. Besides the
numerous ambitious histories, written to invalidate or to justify the Union, there
were novels like Lady Morgan's *The Wild Irish Girl* (1806), which helped market
the ideas of Irishness so influential later in the century (and ever since). The
same might be said of Thomas Moore's sensationally successful *Irish Melodies*
(1807–34). Both Moore and Lady Morgan were successful and fashionable figures, who made their careers in England; but both analysed and expressed
Irishness in a manner which used the symbolic trappings of nationalism. Lady
Morgan (and her Wild Irish Girl, Glorvina) adopted the harp as a symbol of Irish
cultural differentiation; it was also a recurrent motif with Moore, expressing the
remnant of a once-great Gaelic civilization. The 'last Irish harper' became a
powerful image of cultural deracination, much used in the historical narrative
paintings of the time. And the long historical memory, together with the idea of
an apostolic succession of national martyrs, was sharply expressed in popular
lyrics like Moore's 'Let Erin Remember'—published with detailed historical
footnotes.

LET ERIN REMEMBER THE DAYS OF OLD

Let Erin remember the days of old,
　　Ere her faithless sons betray'd her;
When Malachi wore the collar of gold,[1]
　　Which he won from her proud invader,
When her kings, with standard of green unfurl'd,
　　Led the Red-Branch Knights to danger;[2]
Ere the emerald gem of the western world
　　Was set in the crown of a stranger.

On Lough Neagh's bank as the fisherman strays,
　　When the clear cold eve's declining,
He sees the round towers of other days
　　In the wave beneath him shining;
Thus shall memory often, in dreams sublime,
　　Catch a glimpse of the days that are over;
Thus, sighing, look through the waves of time
　　For the long-faded glories they cover.[3]

[1] 'This brought on an encounter between Malachi (the Monarch of Ireland in the tenth century) and the Danes, in which Malachi defeated two of their champions, whom he encountered successively, hand to hand, taking a collar of gold from the neck of one, and carrying off the sword of the other, as trophies of his victory.'—WARNER's *History of Ireland*, vol. i, book ix.

[2] 'Military orders of knights were very early established in Ireland: long before the birth of Christ we find an hereditary order of Chivalry in Ulster, called *Curaidhe na Craiobhe ruadh*, or the Knights of the Red Branch, from their chief seat in Emania, adjoining to the palace of the Ulster kings, called *Teagh na Craiobhe ruadh*, or the Academy of the Red Branch; and contiguous to which was a large hospital, founded for the sick knights and soldiers, called *Bronbhearg*, or the House of the Sorrowful Soldier.'—O'HALLORAN's *Introduction*, &c., part i, chap. v.

[3] It was an old tradition, in the time of Giraldus, that Lough Neagh had been originally a fountain, by whose sudden overflowing the country was inundated, and a whole region, like the Atlantis of Plato, overwhelmed. He says that the fishermen, in clear weather, used to point out to strangers the tall ecclesiastical towers under the water. *Piscatores aquae illius turres ecclesiasticas, quae more patriae arctae sunt et altae, necnon et rotundae, sub undis manifeste sereno tempore conspiciunt, et extraneis transeuntibus, reique causas admirantibus, frequenter ostendunt.*—*Topogr. Hib.* dist. 2, c 9.

The obsession with the Irish past, and the search therein for validation of one national experience or another, may have originally owed a good deal to Ascendancy dilemmas of identity, intensified by the traumatic Union. This tradition continued in the 'Orange Young Ireland' movement of the 1830s, where Protestant intellectuals like Samuel Ferguson and Isaac Butt used the *Dublin University Magazine* as a forum for ideas which were 'national', in many ways anti-English, but unashamedly Protestant. (It was a tradition which would re-emerge in 1870, when Butt founded the Home Government Association.) All could agree on the evident shortcomings of the Union. But the popular market was captured by the emotive ideas of the Irish past and Irish identity marketed by the Young Irelanders through their extreme Repealer newspaper, *The Nation*, and the accessible, racy, and moralizing treatments of Irish history circulated

THOMAS DAVIS, much loved ideologue and idealist of the Young Ireland movement: remembered after his premature death for his emotional nationalist ballads preaching pluralism and anti-Englishness, and for his editorship of *The Nation*.

through reading-rooms and public libraries as the 'Library of Ireland'. Thomas Davis, the movement's chief ideologue, preached that Ireland could become 'A Nation once again' through reconciliation of its various elements and recognition of its exploited and oppressed history: but the latter realization in a sense invalidated the former. The emphasis on past battles, and rebellions, and the high value put on 'dying for Ireland', helped inculcate a verbal cult of physical violence; threatening to the Irish Protestant establishment as well as the British government, and inseparably part of Irish nationalism from this time on.

The fact that the Repeal movement sputtered out with the onset of economic crisis in the mid-1840s, while the Young Ireland Movement dispersed after a failed skirmish of a 'Rising' in 1848, made these ideas no less potent: transported with ex-Young Irelanders to the world of American journalism and expatriate political organizations, they entered a new sphere of influence. The rhetoric of the nationalist argument from history, together with the phenomenon of O'Connellism and the advent of the priest in politics, helped create the terms of future Irish political mobilization—which would owe far more to confessional identification and to agrarian secret-society traditions than to the class-orientated politics of more industrialized societies elsewhere.

Society and Economy in the Early Nineteenth Century

How far was Ireland in decay after the Union? 'Society' was supposed to be less exciting than in the days of the colonial parliament; the great days of urban architecture were over, except for the ostentatiously splendid Catholic churches that began to dominate cities and towns. Yet in the countryside, some palatial neo-classical mansions were built during the early decades of the nineteenth century; and Belfast entered upon its great expansion. Elsewhere in Ireland too, industrial development continued in this era; the great Malcolmson cotton factories at Portlaw, Co. Waterford, providing one example. In many sectors of the Irish economy, there was evident prosperity. But it was those industries based on agriculture and well adapted for exporting to Britain, like linen and brewing, that continued prosperous. Other industries, exposed to competition from British factories, could not cope with the rigours of the free market which had been established by the end of the 1820s. Unemployment and industrial decline followed. Moreover, life in the countryside continued to dominate the perceptions of most observers; and with the post-war collapse of agricultural

PANORAMA OF DUBLIN, 1840. Though the city had already spread up river and to the south, the plan is still compact and clearly shows the wide eighteenth-century boulevards around Trinity College in the centre, as well as the buildings fronting the quays instead of backing on to them. Also note Gandon's great Four Courts and Customs House on the north quays, and the lay-outs of the Royal Hospital, Kilmainham, and Dr Steevens' Hospital to the west. But here factory-chimneys are beginning to appear as well; while important termini for communications are the canal basin to the left of the picture, and the Westland Row railway station on the right.

prices after 1815, and the working through of the population explosion, rural tensions often exploded into violence. James Grattan, a liberal Wicklow landlord, wrote gloomily in the early 1830s that Irish society was 'ignorant, prejudiced, vulgar, brutal', with 'a gentry embodying the character of a military without the discipline. . . . The people in many places are insufficiently civilised, pursued by tithes, habituated to see a great military force and to think that the law depended upon them; for the most part unacquainted with an active magistracy or an efficient police, kind or indulgent landlords, or a respectable clergy, they are what they have been and will continue to be until a milder government and system changes their character and education changes their habits.'

Certainly, early nineteenth-century Ireland continued to be marked by the activities of the agrarian underground, mobilized by issues like tithes, land

'SOCIETY' BY CAROLINE HAMILTON (1801). The date of this satiric water-colour is an intrinsic part of the title, since it expresses the common perception that life for the Ascendancy classes after the Union became characterized by ennui, and a provincial yearning after past glories or metropolitan glamour. Psychologically this may be true, though at a less rarefied level the early nineteenth century saw considerable social and economic advances.

hunger, the invasion of common bog or grazing. Their panaceas involved the fixing of prices, and a reversal to 'old ways'; though anti-modern, pre-industrial, and often anti-Protestant, such activity was not necessarily nationalist. Their identifications were usually local, like their names (Thresher, Caravat, Shanavest, Rockite); they dealt in the language of oaths, badges, vendettas, and millennial 'prophecies'. In their struggles, a certain latent class conflict between different levels of the peasantry can sometimes be inferred; the marked regionalization of secret society activity (north Munster prominent, Connacht much less so) indicates an underlying economic pattern. What cannot be clearly established is when, and by what channels, this activity became 'politicized'.

The movement named 'Ribbonism' or 'Ribbonmen', which finds its way into police reports by the early nineteenth century, draws on many of these traditions, but also mobilized some working-class elements in the small towns; strongly

PORTLAW VILLAGE was another example of 'planning', but this time as an industrial community, with carefully designed housing schemes for different levels of workers, and factory shops. The Malcolmsons also laid out the thatched village of Dunmore East on the Waterford coast.

THE MALCOLMSON COTTON MILLS in Portlaw, Co. Waterford, which dominated the local economy until the 1860s.

Catholic, there are connections back to Defenderism. But Ribbonism was a protean and shadowy movement, often merely used as a generic term for all such activity. And what the continuation of rural unrest signifies is more important than what is actually achieved. In fact, levels of violence were, by many criteria, quite low. What was worrying was the implication of such unrest. It indicated, for one thing, a dogged belief in legitimate alternatives to the developing apparatus of the Victorian state. And it also implied a stubborn popular perception of a right order of propertied and religious relationships, which had been disrupted by settlement. In a sense, of course, O'Connellism answered both these needs too, and answered them more safely.

But the problem of evident rural poverty in the subsistence areas remained, not met by the panaceas of improving landlords, or the increasing resort to emigration—both seasonal and permanent. The 1830s were a decade of particular unrest; and by then, the ideology of administrative modernization was being embraced by Whig governments working in alliance with O'Connell. O'Connell, in fact, opposed some of the initiatives attempted by the British state in this period—notably the ambitious scheme of secular primary education mounted by Stanley in 1831 (a classic rationalist response, in the spirit of James Grattan's critique quoted above). He was more supportive of the government

ENNISKERRY VILLAGE, CO. WICKLOW, in the later nineteenth century. Again, not all villages were as squalid as the prejudices of travellers described them. Enniskerry was one of many villages 'planned' by a local estate, in this case Powerscourt.

policies aimed at whittling down the autonomous powers of the local gentry. Particularly in law enforcement (again, a problem singled out by James Grattan), a series of measures from the 1820s culminated in the centralizing and professionalizing of the police force in 1836. Known as the Royal Irish Constabulary, the highly organized, disciplined, salaried Irish police later became the model for colonial police forces throughout the empire. Their identification remained largely Protestant (though many Catholics joined); but they were controlled by government-appointed officials, and preserved a fair degree of impartiality. By the same token, Whig government introduced stipendiary magistrates, centrally appointed; Catholic lawyers were advanced within the judicial system; the Irish Municipal Corporations Act reformed urban politics, introducing elective councils and rationalizing the franchise; tithe charges were commuted to payments added on to rents; the structure and endowments of the Church of Ireland were reorganized, to the bitter resentment of Irish Protestants; an Irish Poor Law Act was passed, against the advice of the experts and at odds with the underlying pattern of Irish poverty, but which at least provided a new political forum in the Boards of Guardians. In all these measures (even if often ill-conceived or inadequate) and in the immortal lecture from Under-Secretary Thomas

' "THE PATRON", OR THE FESTIVAL OF ST KEVIN AT THE SEVEN CHURCHES, GLENDALOUGH', by Joseph Peacock (1817). This shows a 'pattern', exactly the kind of popular religious festival which the modernizing Catholic church was trying to suppress because of the attendant indiscipline, merrymaking, and distracting commercial activity—all indicated here. In this case, the artist would also have been attracted by the venue, an increasingly fashionable (and recently excavated) early Christian monastic site.

Drummond that 'property had its duties as well as its rights', the Irish Protestant Ascendancy discerned a concerted if temporary attack on its privileges.

There were other, more autonomous, responses to the perceived problems of life in early nineteenth-century Ireland—no less important for being equally transient in their effects. The Temperance movement, inspired by a Cork priest Father Mathew, began in 1838, and by late 1842 an estimated five million Irish people had taken the pledge of total abstinence. The organization of the movement involved medals, speeches, bands, and banners: it was related to

attempts by the church to stamp out traditional and more subversive pastimes, like 'patterns' (celebrations of a patron saint's feast day) and wakes, which brought together great convocations of disorganized (and often disorderly) people. Some contemporaries worried that the temperance crusade might have a potentially subversive effect of its own, in regulating the masses, *à la* O'Connell. The movement was primarily characterized by an atmosphere of revivalism and 'improvement' (and affected the Irish economy in a way by no means universally welcomed). Father Mathew's crusade, disrupted like so much else by the trauma

ST MARY'S DOMINICAN CHURCH, CORK, designed in 1832 but nearly 50 years in the completion (like the great Pugin cathedral in Killarney and many other contemporary Catholic edifices). It is a characteristic expression of the splendour and formality of nineteenth-century Irish Catholicism.

of the famine years, should take its place with other phenomena of increased efficiency, organization, and interventionism in early nineteenth-century Ireland.

The Conservative government of Peel in the early 1840s, however decried by Irish politicians, helped contribute to this: notably in legislation which favoured the Catholic church in terms of the making of charitable bequests, and in endowing seminarian education. This reinforced the process whereby the Catholic church rationalized and modernized its structure, and broadened its apparatus of social control: reflected in strikingly ambitious developments in church architecture during the period, as well as the introduction and systemization of ritual practices. But up to the 1840s, rates of attendance at mass—for instance—varied surprisingly between regions, and the ratio of clergy to populace, in an expanding population, became inevitably overextended. These were just two of the phenomena which were drastically altered by the great dislocation of 1845–9.

The variety of agricultural problems, and the prevalence of bare subsistence standards in regions like the west, had been repeatedly described by foreign travellers and perceived despairingly (if often impotently) by government officials. This climaxed, horrifyingly, with the potato famine of the mid-1840s. Under-invested and labour-extensive agrarian practices coexisted with inadequate smallholdings and congested populations; temporary employment, endemic poverty, and a universally execrated land system were the usual targets of contemporary criticism. How far 'the landlord system' exacerbated the situation is arguable: the fundamental fact of a backward agrarian system, linked to a largely unindustrialized economy, and supplying the market created by British industrialization, was strained to breaking point by an uncontrollably expanding population (of over eight million by the early 1840s). Though there is disagreement about the responsibility of the potato economy for bringing the situation about, it certainly enabled the fragile equilibrium to be sustained. Tiny, subdivided holdings could feed a family on potatoes (and feed them well, when combined with buttermilk and occasional bacon); early and fecund marriages were the rural norm, if we are to believe the evidence constantly reiterated by observers. Economic historians have demurred, postulating an altering picture by the 1830s—later marriages, mounting emigration, less automatic resort to subdivision, and a levelling off of population growth. But when the potato crops in 1845 were ravaged by a new and fatal fungus disease, the situation had reached a point where the removal of that one means of sustenance meant a sentence of death for those trapped in the subsistence economy of the west and south-west, and great suffering elsewhere.

Need this have been so? The reactions of government policy, constrained by the economic ideology of the day, were by any modern standards inadequate: the self-congratulatory hard line of *laissez-faire* economists makes chilling reading

RATION CARDS issued during the Famine, as part of an early attempt at organizing relief.

nowadays. If Peel's early measures—creating public works, pegging prices, and distributing food—were on more or less effective lines, his successor Lord John Russell adhered to free-market dogmas which attempted, hopelessly, to—at very best—place the burden on Irish property rather than state hand-outs. And this was never feasible. Poor Law Boards were inadequate in terms of resources and powers (though in some areas their record was both admirable and effective). Some landlords and strong farmers bankrupted themselves in trying to cope with their starving dependants; many others simply closed their gates and demanded their rents. Regions with varied local economies (notably Ulster, and the east coast) escaped lightly; but the densely populated 'clachan' villages of cabins in the west lived through nightmares of starvation, fever, and death. By 1849, after repeated harvest failures, an observer described such settlements as resembling 'the tombs of a departed race': which, in a sense, they were.

'Departure' took the form not only of death, but of frantic emigration—to Britain, Australia, Canada, and particularly America. Some of those who stayed struggled against the visitation: some grain convoys were attacked, and radical Young Irelanders (reconstituted as the 'Irish Confederation') attempted a tiny and inchoate 'Rising' in 1848. But the general reaction was the passive one: emigration or death. The result was selective depopulation, and the export of a race-memory of horror.

Ireland after the Famine

Irish life and Irish history from the 1850s were, in a sense, reconstructed by the effects of the Famine: many patterns were set which would dictate the shape of things over the next century. The population was declining; by 1847, nearly a quarter of a million were emigrating annually, often comprising the most

SCENES OF IRISH LIFE: potato-weighing at Youghal, showing the staple ingredient of the Irish diet; kelp-gathering, a widespread local source of fertilizer; and selling a pig, an important component of the potato ecology.

'THE TOMBS OF A DEPARTED RACE': a drawing of the village of Tullig, abandoned just after the Famine. Note the density of settlement: such villages were described in 1845 as 'a congeries of hovels thrown indiscriminately together, as if they fell in a shower from the sky'.

potentially fertile sector of the population; the rural landscape which they left would be more and more characterized by deserted villages, the bachelor farm, and the late marriage. The dispersal of the cottier class, and the rough but vital life of the clachans described by so many pre-Famine travellers, was accompanied by the slow disappearance of the agricultural labourer. Another casualty was the Irish language—driven out as much by the growth of the market economy and the transport revolution, as by the Famine dislocations.

Accompanying this process was the consolidation of the large or middle-sized farm. Holdings below 15 acres declined; at the other end of the scale, many landlords went bankrupt and were bought out under the provisions of the 1849 Encumbered Estates Act. The successor class were not, generally speaking, absentee investors; when the marquess of Thomond's 40,000 acres were sold off in 183 lots during 1850, three-quarters of the purchasers were locals. But new landlords, however Irish and Catholic, did not make the system any easier on the small tenants: often the opposite. The pasture economy was encouraged by depopulation (as well as international price movements); in high-emigration counties like Mayo, there was a dramatic shift to grazing at the expense of tillage, accompanied by displacement of population as graziers 'cleared' the land—often through eviction. The evolution of the 'strong farmer' class moved on a stage. Meanwhile the rocky western fringes remained 'congested' by a population which, if reduced, still outpaced the available resources. In certain areas, elements of the pre-Famine dispensation lasted on.

Moreover, agricultural consolidation was not accompanied by industrial take-off. Nascent industrial developments like the Malcolmson cotton village at Portlaw went into decline (given the *coup de grâce* by backing the wrong side in the American Civil War); only in Ulster did industrialization proceed apace, where a massive shipbuilding industry arose on the Lagan, rivalling the Clyde. The town of Belfast was now a city—a development helped by the readiness of its spectacularly indebted landlord, the marquess of Donegall, to alienate land by means of perpetual leases from the 1820s. With the advent of power-looms a factory culture finally displaced the outworker textile industry; the urbanization of eastern Ulster and its booming industrial activities combined with its peculiar religious mix to make the separate nature of the north-east clearer than ever.

In political as in economic life the famine marks a clear divide. British government had conspicuously failed to solve the problems of Ireland, generally tagged 'the Irish question': even hard-line Liberals had to concede that the Famine years and ensuing changes raised questions about the administration of

A KITCHEN INTERIOR, EARLY NINETEENTH CENTURY by F. J. Mulvany. The standard of comfort and equipment in a 'strong farmer's' house at this period is quite impressive, and should be noted as an antidote to the prevailing image of western cottiers' cabins retailed by foreign travellers.

CARDINAL PAUL CULLEN, the architect of reorganizing Irish Catholicism by a 'devotional revolution', introducing systematic Roman practices and discouraging the more latitudinarian traditions of Irish Catholicism. He remained inflexibly opposed both to physical-force nationalism and English influences.

ANNVALE, CO. ARMAGH. By the nineteenth century, though domestic spinning continued, factory linen production had reached the scale indicated by this panoramic view of a bleach-green.

Irish affairs. From the 1860s William Ewart Gladstone (an ex-Peelite, now leading the Liberals) attempted a series of political measures (not necessarily inter-connected, for all his retrospective claims). The 1869 Act disestablishing the Church of Ireland (although on very favourable terms) was one response; another was the 1870 Land Act, giving the right of compensation to evicted tenants for expenditure made on their holdings, and applying the supposed 'Ulster custom' of tenant right all over Ireland. These measures were inadequate responses to the problems of alienation and poverty which they were designed to meet; but they were of symbolic importance in implying the end of the Ascendancy of Protestants and landlords, many of whom angrily interpreted Gladstonian legis-lation in just these terms.

This reaction was intensified by another post-famine development: the solidi-fying of politics into a confessional framework. The 1850 Reform Act, increasing the electorate and basing the franchise on occupation (rather than property-owning) built on a lively if locally orientated political culture and helped create a new political nation. This was distinctively Catholic, largely rural, and sustained the lessons of O'Connellite democracy in implicitly admitting the church to a position of political leadership. Archbishop (later Cardinal) Paul Cullen ex-emplified the new face of the Catholic church—Romanist, authoritarian, and ready to make pronouncements on any political questions which might be ac-counted to have a bearing on faith and morals. On the other side of the divide,

JAMES STEPHENS is generally supposed the originator of the Fenian movement, though much of his reputation is due to assiduous self-publicity. Here he is addressing an American Fenian demonstration in 1864. There are similarities to the Repeal meeting illustrated on p. 188, but the banners here assert a rhetorical association with Wolfe Tone and the separatist tradition. The function of Fenian support organizations, however, was often less single-minded than this.

the 1850s saw a great wave of evangelical Protestant revivalism, particularly in Ulster: and in proletarianized Belfast, confessional politics took a strong root too. The sectarian geography of the city was more and more firmly demarcated: despite the official dissolution of Orange lodges in 1836, the potency of that demotic political identification remained violent and undiminished. Sectarian riots were endemic from the 1850s. Already in mid-nineteenth-century Ulster, the lineaments of the political culture that would be called 'Unionist' was coming into view.

Also in the 1850s, the opposing political culture of Irish nationalism became expressed in a new movement which carried through many of the traditions already surveyed: 'Fenianism'.

'Fenians' became the name most generally applied to the Irish Republican—or possibly Revolutionary—Brotherhood, a separatist secret society which emerged

"'BURKEING' THE CONSTITUTION OF ENGLAND.' The introduction of Catholic Emancipation is presented as Peel and Wellington murdering John Bull to provide a corpse for the Pope and Satan—a play on the celebrated contemporary scandal of Burke and Hare, who stifled their victims and sold the bodies for dissection. It is given added piquancy by the fact that Burke was an Irish immigrant.

THE MARRIAGE OF STRONGBOW AND EVA (painted in 1854 by Daniel MacLise), is a characteristically grandiloquent representation of a theme from Irish history (see above, p. 189): this is a water-colour study for the celebrated heroic oil-painting. The lamenting harpist in the foreground, left, and Strongbow's foot planted on the broken cross, symbolize the oppression of native Irish culture. The theme of the Anglo-Irish relationship as a forced marriage is recurrent.

(rather than being 'founded') in the late 1850s. The doubts about its name are symptomatic, as are the various strands which went into it. Remnants of the 1848 Confederate clubs, Irish-American exiles, the agrarian secret-society tradition, and Continental exemplars all played their part: represented by inspirational figures like James Stephens and John O'Leary. Also influential in the formation of Fenianism was the political mobilization of distinctive sectors in post-Famine Ireland: classically, Fenianism represented the journalist sons of the farming classes, and the clerks of market towns. Clubs, cells, conspiracy, and Anglophobic rhetoric were characteristic of the movement; so was a readiness to embark upon sacrificial gestures (a dynamite explosion, a hopeless 'Rising') in order to sustain nationalist energy. The movement was much preoccupied by the version of Irish history created by John Mitchel, an ex-Young Irelander whose *Jail Journal* and other writings brilliantly constructed an apocalyptic tale of eight hundred years of national struggle against a sadistic oppressor, whose last, genocidal act had been the deliberate depopulation of Ireland through an artificially sustained

JOHN O'LEARY, editor of the *Irish People* and lifelong Fenian. The quintessence of idealistic nation-alism, he lived on to become the mentor of W. B. Yeats and Maud Gonne in the 1880s and 1890s. This drawing is by his friend J. B. Yeats, father of the poet.

John O'Leary

JOHN MITCHEL, usually seen as the extremist face of Young Ireland. The son of an Ulster Presbyterian manse, he progressed to a violent espousal of the blood-cult, and advocated race war between England and Ireland.

famine. In Mitchel's Carlylean rhetoric, nationalism became a secular religion: an attitude subscribed to by the Fenian spirit. The church's relationship with it was correspondingly uneasy: individual priests might be sympathetic, but the hierarchy condemned the organization. Fenianism's subversive spirit was seen as dangerous and destabilizing. None the less, like Cullen's church itself, the movement was built on the basis of Ireland's post-famine 'modernization', in terms of increased literacy, education, and politicization: as well as an Anglophobic rhetoric which owed a great deal to the Young Ireland version of Irish history and the perceived lessons of the Famine.

In *The Red-Haired Man's Wife*, a story written just before his death in 1869, the novelist William Carleton forecast that though Fenianism was the current vogue, a coming land war would prove the greatest movement Ireland had seen. His prophecy was accurate. Post-Famine Ireland saw the arrival of the land question on the political agenda, with the formation of tenant societies from the late 1840s, and an attempt at a national organization in the 1850s. This represented well-off farmers rather than the landless or the labourers—as was acidly pointed out at the time. It had a brief and uncertain success: political organization at Westminster never really took it up. By the late 1860s, the resentments built up are indicated by a threatening notice posted in Westmeath in February 1869:

We do hereby warn all landsharks not to take or have anything to do whatsoever with house or land from which a tenant is evicted. We also warn those landjobbers who are in the habit of taking large tracts of grazing land from year to year that was let to the public heretofore, that they must give it up, as these lands must be let for the use of the public as formerly—and any tyrant-landlord who turns out a tenant will meet with his reward—any person who acts contrary to this notice will be shot.

Incidents like this were interpreted by the magistracy as 'revived Ribbonism'; but this was erroneous. What matter are the issues detailed and the fact that the prospect of an imminent Land Act was raising expectations; and that, according to local clerics, everyone was now determined 'to have a bit of land'. The landlords, still socially powerful, had become the perceived enemy. The position of some (often the most ruthless) had been strengthened by the collapse of their less efficient peers in the 1850s. But landlords can be too easily grouped together as a homogenous class; they constituted a very varied stratum of Irish society, especially with the recruitment of new—often Catholic—members to their ranks after the Famine. For many of them the system was coming under stress by 1870. The strong-farming classes had benefited most from the price and production increases building up after 1851. Landlords had tended to identify the Tenant Right Movement as 'socialistic' or even 'communistic'; but this was ludicrously wide of the mark. It represented, more accurately, the first stirrings of the successor élite.

Many landlords still exercised energetic influence at local elections (though rarely in the draconian manner sometimes claimed). But post-Famine politics had shown new lines of division appearing at local levels, with decisive clerical leadership, and an increasingly high profile being taken by well-off farmers. A special study of Mayo identifies the dominant class of the 1860s as 'the post-famine élite of strong farmers, shopkeepers, merchants and traders': the picture was being repeated all over Ireland. Favoured by price movements and market demands, the large-scale graziers would play a vital part in future political movements. Disadvantaged by low levels of rent returns and mounting debts to be serviced, the writing was on the wall for many of the landlord class. By 1870, the social and religious dominance of the 'Ascendancy' outside Ulster was effectively broken; the power of Catholic nationalism was on the edge of realization. But the attitudes of both sides continued to be conditioned and confused by historical obsessions inseparable from events in Ireland since the late seventeenth century. All that had happened in the era of Ascendancy and Union was built into the artificially contrived but extremely potent construction of Irish nationalist history.

MODERN IRELAND: TOWNS, COUNTIES, AND PROVINCES

5

Ireland Since 1870

DAVID FITZPATRICK

Progress and Stagnation after 1870

By 1870 Ireland had assumed an appearance of economic, social, and political stability unknown since the eighteenth century. Despite the Famine catastrophe, the residual rural population had preserved much of its familiar way of life while achieving unfamiliar prosperity. Destitution was no longer sufficient to exhaust the capacity of the Poor Law system; emigration continued to ameliorate underemployment by removing surplus population. A generation was reaching maturity which had never known economic collapse, social breakdown, or fear of starvation. The depletion of the poorest classes and the optimism of those more privileged had weakened social animosities, while Gladstone's 1870 Land Act offered the promise of further and more effective state intervention in the troubled relationship between landlord and tenant. Manufacturing industry in the Belfast region was attracting massive capital investment, in engineering and shipbuilding as well as the long-established linen sector. Ulster Protestants were beginning to relish the Victorian sensation of Progress, while the growing Catholic middle class and the Catholic church attained a new respectability in Irish social and political life. The appearance of political stability was enhanced by popular indifference to the Fenian insurrection of 1867, though subsequent agitation once the crisis was safely over induced Gladstone to grant a partial amnesty to those punished after the rising. Many Irishmen as well as Englishmen looked forward to a belated realization of O'Connell's dream of an Ireland transformed into a 'modern' industrial society modelled upon England. Their confidence was sorely misplaced.

Ireland's apparent stability was dangerously dependent upon population drainage through emigration. This in turn depended upon the persistence of demand for Irish labour, service, and marriage overseas. By 1870 more than half as many natives of Ireland were living overseas as at home. Three-fifths of the three million emigrants were in the USA, a quarter in Britain, and about one-thirteenth in Australia as in Canada. The unique decline of Ireland's population for nearly a century after the Famine was mainly caused by structural emigration which removed up to half of each generation from the country.

EMBARKATION OF EMIGRANTS at Queenstown (now Cobh), the major port for this activity in the later nineteenth century. This drawing from the *Graphic* (27 May 1893) shows an orderly and adequately clothed group of passengers, very different from the wailing mobs of paupers depicted in comparable scenes from the Famine period. The small child in the foreground was an increasingly atypical emigrant.

Women were roughly as likely as men to emigrate, and in some years stronger foreign demand for female labour combined with declining domestic opportunities to produce a female majority. All classes, religions, and regions were drained by emigration, but the intensity of overseas movement was greatest from the poorer counties of the western seaboard. Short-distance migration in search of urban employment was more characteristic of Leinster and Ulster. Not all migration was irreversible: seasonal movement to Britain was commonplace among north-western adolescent males, while many 'returned Yanks' and holiday-makers brought back personal tidings of the good life abroad and often invested their savings in Irish farms, pubs, or marriages. Emigration was concentrated among young adults at the threshold of employment and marriage, so tending to create a swollen proportion of old people in Ireland itself. So long as demand for emigrant services endured, Ireland could safely reproduce more children than its households could support. Yet any stoppage of the 'safety valve' would soon generate a surplus of frustrated young people competing for survival in Ireland's congested markets of marriage and employment. The American recession of the 1870s and the First World War both resulted in population congestion which contributed heavily to the social unrest of the land war and revolutionary period, when young men and women who would otherwise have been making their way up foreign social ladders instead devoted their enforced leisure and indignation to collective protest at home. Even so, Irish people were ingenious and adaptable in face of fluctuations in foreign demand, often switching to Britain, Canada, or Australia when the American welcome cooled.

Emigration was the key to Ireland's unusual and remarkably stable demographic system between 1870 and 1914. While fertility within marriage declined elsewhere in Europe, the average completed Irish family remained at about six children. Children were 'reared for emigration' in the hope that they would not only fund further emigration but also provide social insurance for their parents

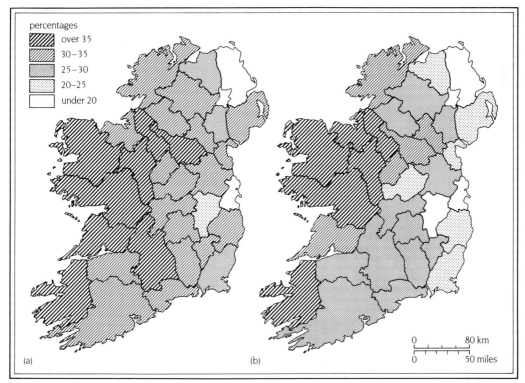

DEPLETION OF AGE-COHORTS, 1851-1911. Cohort depletion is defined as the percentage of people aged 5-24 at one census who had 'disappeared' from each county's population a decade later, judging from the population aged 15-34 recorded at the second census. Each map shows the average cohort depletion for three successive decades: (*a*) the average for 1851-61, 1861-71, and 1871-81; (*b*) the average for 1881-91, 1891-1901, and 1901-11. In the Irish context this provides the best available estimate of net outward migration among young people, though mortality rather than migration accounted for a few of those who disappeared.

through remittances, which helped pay rents, rates, and shop-debts. The Christmas 'American letter' became an essential prop of the western rural economy, supporting an archaic system of farming and landholding. At least a million pounds annually were sent home from America alone, a sum equal to about 2 per cent of the added value of agricultural output. By comparison, expenditure on rearing, outfitting, and transporting emigrants seemed insignificant to most parents. The 'stream of gold' enabled Irish families to extend their reciprocal obligations effortlessly across oceans, so relieving tensions within Irish households while maintaining a modified version of the conventional kinship network. Meanwhile the marriage institution became increasingly rigid. In rural areas the acquisition of spouse and farm became almost inseparable, so facilitating smooth transfer of property control between generations by a means which would scarcely have been tolerable without the option of emigration and marriage overseas. Yet emigration, though heavy, was insufficient to cope with the surplus 'unmatched' population. By 1911 over a quarter of 50-year-old women as well as men had never married, a fact which placed Ireland very high in the European celibacy league-table. Even in Connacht, male celibacy and also age at marriage were beginning to rise alarmingly as the demographic system started to falter. Yet for most of the century after 1870 Ireland maintained a unique combination of infrequent marriage, high marital fertility, and heavy emigration.

The survival of archaic demographic patterns was facilitated by sluggish urbanization, industrial growth, and agricultural modernization. Despite the activity of official agencies such as the Congested Districts Board (1891) and missionary bodies like the Irish Industrial Development Association (1905), industrial expansion remained concentrated in the Belfast region. Serious decline in the Ulster linen industry was delayed until the First World War, while undertakings such as Harland and Wolff (1858) and Workman Clark (1880) transformed the north-east into Clydeside's major rival as the British centre of engineering and ship-building. Meanwhile provincial towns such as Cork and Galway continued to shrink, while even Dublin's development as a mercantile centre was unaccompanied by marked industrial expansion. On the eve of war the majority of occupied Irishmen were still engaged in agriculture or casual rural labour, while other employment was actually becoming less accessible in some poorer counties. Investors remained reluctant to sink capital in what was still pictured as a lawless and undisciplined society, while the impact of industrial stagnation outside the north-east was softened by emigration to foreign rather than Irish cities and by the revival of commercial agriculture.

By the 1870s the value of farm output exceeded that for the 1850s, despite continuing reduction of the rural population. Farmers' responsiveness to the growing commercial attractiveness of pasturage as against tillage had been enhanced by two related factors. Depopulation had reduced the social costs of

THE CONGESTED DISTRICTS BOARD was established in 1891 to reorganize the economic and social structure of the poorest regions of the West of Ireland. The lure of public funding for schemes of 'improvement' such as road-building proved attractive enough to allay popular misgivings at the imposition of social revolution from above.

abandoning labour-intensive cereal cultivation, while the elimination of cottiers and diversification of diet since the Famine had enabled more land to be switched from subsistence to commercial production. The reduction of tillage affected all regions and sizes of farm, and continued until the First World War. Yet the structure of Irish agriculture escaped many of the disruptions associated with Britain's agricultural 'revolution'. Technological innovation and improved systems of crop rotation and manuring were slow to affect Ireland. In 1870 the sickle had yet to be displaced by the scythe in many districts, while even in 1917 there were only 70 tractors, 311 hay balers, and about 40,000 double-furrow ploughs in the country. Drainage and other improvements were hampered by the chronic indebtedness of tenant farmers and the reluctance or inability of landlords to sink capital in Irish estates. Despite the growing sophistication of marketing networks, co-operative farming and wholesaling were slow to take off after the foundation in 1894 of Horace Plunkett's Irish Agricultural Organization Society.

In many respects the Irish rural economy remained archaic far into the twentieth century.

The most severe constraint upon agricultural restructuring was the virtual closure of the land market after the Famine convulsion. As prosperity returned landlords and tenants reached a new *modus vivendi*, whereby tenants at will and expired leaseholders passed farms to their chosen successors as if they held a heritable estate. In many parts of Munster and Leinster as well as Ulster, 'tenant right' amounted to an established custom which was given some legal standing by Gladstone's Land Act of 1870. Cohabitation collapsed only in the late 1870s, when agricultural recession, stoppage of emigration, and partial failure of food supply brought landlord and tenant into conflict. Many landlords were bankrupted, while others sought to evict defaulting tenants whose ability to withstand loss of income was smaller than their own. Michael Davitt's Irish National Land League (1879–82) provided a formidable national network which co-ordinated local tenant associations and incorporated radical and Fenian ele-

THE MELODRAMA OF THE LAND WAR is suggested by the depiction in the *Illustrated London News* (8 January 1881) of the burning of the Duke of Leinster's leases at a meeting in Kildare. The bearded arsonist is Michael Boyton, an Irish-American member of the Central Land League who was charged with Parnell and others in November 1881 with conspiracy to prevent rent payments. He is said to be wielding a pike dating from the 1798 insurrection, a weapon of symbolic rather than military power whose manufacture was revived as late as 1917.

ments not hitherto active in tenant agitation. Most farmers were happy to exploit the rhetorical, political, legal, and financial amenities of the Land League in so far as it protected them from eviction. Their primary demand was security of tenure; and when the League espoused more radical demands such as expropriation of landlords, non-payment of any rent, or non-observance of legislative reform, it lost much of its support.

Security of tenure was reinforced by Gladstone's land acts of 1881 and 1882, which gave most tenants a recognized interest in their holdings and the right to seek judicial reduction of rents. Despite widespread exploitation of these reforms, the successors of the suppressed Land League were able to organize further acrimonious tenant agitations throughout the decade, such as the 'Plan of Campaign' (1886–9). For most Irish farmers, however, rents were now endurable, eviction improbable, and tenure secure. Security was reinforced by the sequence of land purchase acts initiated in 1869 and culminating in Wyndham's Act (1903). By 1914 most farmers were paying annuities to the state which had advanced their purchase money, rather than substantially higher rents to their landlords (whose co-operation was usually secured not by compulsion but by the carrot of an attractive bonus in cash or stocks). The effect of achieving security of tenure

THE BATTERING RAM recorded in this possibly staged photograph from the Lawrence Collection was a form of machinery actually seldom required in evictions for non-payment of rent.

was to freeze the distribution of holdings, prevent consolidation of 'uneconomic' farms, increase indebtedness, and discourage innovation. However, since lands held under lease were scarcely affected by reform, many grasslands continued to attract bidders and provoke agrarian agitation. Graziers or 'ranchers' were the major target of protest by the United Irish League, especially between 1906 and 1910, when 'cattle drives' became commonplace in Connacht and the midlands.

Catholic Nationalism, 1870–1914

The 'Land War' of 1879–82 had political significance far beyond the successful struggle for tenant power. Its immediate effect on government was to revive 'coercion' through suspension of *habeas corpus* and creation of special courts, in response to the unprecedented frequency of 'agrarian outrages' arising from collective action or conspiracy. Yet violence was repudiated by the Land League, which aimed to intimidate landlords and government through peaceable combination and 'boycott' rather than murder and destruction. Its objectives included self-government, and by 1880 it was in effect the constituency organization of parliamentary nationalism, with its demand for devolution of control over Irish affairs to a 'Home Rule' parliament in Dublin. The effect of collaboration was to transform the Home Rule body from a loose medley without local organization except at elections into a tight-knit political party whose parliamentary weight was immeasurably increased by the menace of mass mobilization. Parliamentary nationalism had been disorganized and ineffectual under the leadership of Isaac Butt, the Protestant lawyer, freemason, and former Orangeman who had initiated the Home Government Association in 1870 and the broader Home Rule League in 1873. The grim and autocratic Charles Stewart Parnell, whose status as a Protestant landlord gave unique bite to his rhetorical assault upon his own class, was able to forge a disciplined populist party united on a far wider range of issues than Home Rule. Popular participation, already encouraged in 1872 by introduction of the secret ballot and removal of the ban upon party processions, was further facilitated by extension of the franchise under the 'Mud Cabin' reform act of 1884, which more than trebled the electorate. In the general election of 1885 Parnell's party not only won four-fifths of the Irish representation, but also completed its transformation into a team of Catholic merchants, shopkeepers, lawyers, and journalists pledged to vote in accordance with party directives. Parnell thus created Westminster's first modern political party.

The integration of most nationalist factions into the networks of a parliamentary party gave unprecedented stability to politics in Catholic Ireland. The failure of Fenians to rise in 1867 had persuaded many 'physical-force men' (they were hardly ever women) that independence was more likely to be achieved

PARNELL'S INTROSPECTIVE PERSONALITY
and physical tension are partly caught by
this cartoon from *Vanity Fair* (4 September
1880).

through parliamentary agitation than insurrection. Though some Irish and American factions continued to deplore the movement's 'new departures' into constitutional alliances, the majority accepted the revision in 1873 of the Irish Republican Brotherhood's constitution. Thenceforth, Irish Fenians were bound to confine themselves 'in time of peace to the exercise of moral influences', such as supporting 'every movement calculated to advance the cause of Irish independence'. War against Britain was to await 'the decision of the Irish nation, as expressed by a majority of the Irish people' (a most improbable event). The Land League, whose early branches were mainly organized by Fenians, acted as a bridge for Fenian pragmatists weary of awaiting the call to arms. The transition from gunman to parliamentarian was easily achieved, since Parnell took care to pack his new party with ex-Fenians and to tolerate their sentimental approbation of the past and future use of violence. It was Parnell who subdued the Fenians rather than the reverse, though their genuine co-operation misled

THE GRAND OLD MAGICIAN'S IRISH POLICY.

A **WONDERFUL REMEDY** No settlement of any question, great or small, can be equitable and permanent which is not approached by all concerned in a perfectly unprejudiced spirit; no person who is in any way affected in health can be for long in a truly unbiassed and judicial frame of mind; therefore—to secure a lasting and **GREAT IRISH PROBLEM** it is absolutely necessary that the satisfactory settlement of the whole English-speaking race should be able to bring the full powers of the mind to bear upon the subject, untrammelled by any disease or ill-humours of the body.

To gain this end there is no better means than **BEECHAM'S PILLS,** which are well known to carry off all the gross humours and impurities of the system, and thus, by sweeping and garnishing the temple of the soul, set the mind free to bring all its powers to bear on this, the most momentous question of modern times. Sold everywhere, in Boxes, 1s. 1½d. and 2s. 9d.

GLADSTONE a fortnight after the introduction of his first Home Rule Bill, depicted by the *Illustrated London News* of 24 April 1886.

governments into futile calumnies and prosecutions of the parliamentary leader as front man for a treasonable conspiracy. Butt had accomplished short-term tactical alliances with frustrated Fenians, whereas Parnell was able to integrate that significant minority into his new populist movement.

Parnell's greater triumph was to mobilize the Catholic church in pursuit of Home Rule. The church under Paul Cullen's shadow had avoided overt commitment to political movements not under its own patronage, issued maledictions against Fenianism, distrusted Butt's ineffectual attempt to solicit Protestant support, and offered only partial support to the Land League. Yet Parnell's evident success in suppressing factionalism, discouraging seditious conspiracies, and mobilizing popular support left the church with the options of co-operation or withdrawal from politics. For most Irish churchmen, the latter alternative was unthinkable. Instead, the hierarchy endorsed the Home Rule demand in 1886, in return for the party's support on issues such as denominational education which affected the church's institutional interest. The parochial clergy became indispensable as local organizers, officers, and subscribers to party funds, while church porches provided the forum for political oratory and debate. Despite this mutually beneficial bargain, 'church, state, and nation' were not permanently welded together in the 1880s. Instead, Parnell demonstrated that such an alliance was workable under certain conditions. The cost of even partial alliance between nationalism and the church was enhanced and perhaps irreversible alienation of Irish Protestants from the Home Rule cause.

Parnell's third significant alliance was accomplished in 1886, when his party briefly gained the nominal balance of power in the House of Commons after helping the Conservatives to eradicate Gladstone's majority. This circumstance encouraged Gladstone to rescind his once impassioned objection to Irish Home Rule, and to draw up a Government of Ireland bill which the party could support. Despite deep rifts between Gladstone and leading Liberals such as Chamberlain and Dilke, which had precipitated the previous Liberal government's defeat and the subsequent election, Gladstone formed a new administration and introduced the promised bill in April 1886. Chamberlain (who had himself been advocating an alternative scheme for Irish devolution) resigned and led a secession which resulted in defeat of the bill, collapse of the government, and formation of a Liberal Unionist party with ever closer ties to the Conservatives. Despite the manifest expediency of Gladstone's 'conversion', Home Rule quickly became a fundamental tenet of Gladstonian liberalism which nevertheless achieved high priority only when the Irish Party held the balance in a 'hung' parliament. The Liberal–Nationalist alliance proved robust enough to withstand the splintering of the Irish Party in 1890 and persistent non-conformist hostility to Catholic causes such as state-funded denominational education. After 1886 Liberal candidates only occasionally contested Irish elections even in Ulster, while in Britain the nationalist United Irish League was by 1914 little more than a Liberal constituency organization.

The Irish Party's association with Liberalism was not a predictable outcome of Conservative aversion to Irish reform. Indeed, the most lasting Irish innovations of the two decades after 1886 were initiated by Conservative chief secretaries such as Arthur Balfour (1887–91), his brother Gerald (1895–1900), and George Wyndham (1900–5). In addition to creating a 'peasant proprietary', Conservative administrations helped modernize agriculture through state agencies such as the Congested Districts Board and Department of Agriculture and Technical Instruction (1899). Nationalist control of local government was made possible by the belated extension to Ireland in 1898 of the reform which widened the franchise to incorporate parliamentary electors and certain women; while Wyndham and his controversial Under-Secretary Sir Antony MacDonnell toyed six years later with a devolution scheme which fell not far short of Home Rule. It is significant that nationalists found rhetorical alliance with Liberalism more comfortable than association with the substantive reforms of 'constructive unionism'. Leaders such as Parnell and John Dillon were often indifferent or hostile to reform, fearing that material comfort and equitable treatment would render Irish Catholics uninterested in national freedom. The Irish Party proved as ambivalent towards land reform in 1903 as in 1881, giving its grudging support only when public enthusiasm became undeniable. Its alienation from the Conservative programme was sharpened by its alarm at the apparent strategy of 'killing Home Rule by kindness', and its indignation at the concomitant coercion. While neither coercion nor conciliation was the preserve of either party, Irish nationalists preferred to deal with governments which sought consensus before imposing reform.

Parnell's delicate array of working alliances was shattered in November 1890, when Gladstone made it known that he would resign as Liberal leader unless the Irish Party found a new chairman. His threat echoed Nonconformist outrage at Parnell's identification as co-respondent in the divorce suit of his former parliamentary associate, Captain William O'Shea. A protracted Party meeting in early December repudiated his leadership by a large majority, encouraged by the discreet intervention midway through that meeting of the standing committee of Irish bishops. Both resolutions were controlled responses to the menace facing the alliance with Gladstone rather than heartfelt outpourings of moral indignation, which had been notably muted in the week following the award of Captain O'Shea's decree nisi. Parnell's rejection was facilitated by widespread disenchantment with the leader's capricious blend of protracted inactivity interrupted by dictatorial intervention. Brutal central discipline and contempt for local interests were tolerable only for so long as they seemed likely to hasten Home Rule.

Even after his death in October 1891, Parnell's cult retained considerable support in the major towns and a few rural midland constituencies. The anti-Parnellites were fragmented among a bewildering range of often warring factions under leaders such as Justin McCarthy, John Dillon, Tim Healy, and William O'Brien, whose differences diminished the attractiveness of the Irish Party to both the church and the Liberal Party. Parnellism, whose parliamentary representation amounted to only nine members in 1892 and twelve in 1895, became more and more the faith of the disaffected. Those worried by clerical interference in politics were driven towards Parnellism by the snarling partisanship of much of the priesthood, encapsulated in the bishop of Meath's assertion that 'Parnellism, like paganism, impedes, obstructs and cripples the efficiency and blights the fruitfulness of the preaching of the gospel'. Parnell's Fenian associations, which he had opportunely resuscitated in 1891 by appealing to the 'men of the hillsides', formed the dubious foundation for the equally opportunist Fenian cult of the dead leader. This cult enveloped many writers, intellectuals, and cultural revivalists who hoped to create a nationalism far broader than the constitutional campaign which the living Parnell had brought to ascendancy. The eclectic character of the new Parnellism was epitomized by the close collaboration between the poet William Butler Yeats and John O'Leary, president of the supreme council of one faction of the Irish Republican Brotherhood. Yeats portrayed the dead leader as a 'tall pillar' burning in the gloom, and later set in rhyme the alluring but deceptive thesis that 'the Bishops and the Party that tragic story made'. The excited coteries of wild men and literary revivalists, mainly belonging to the urban and often emigrant middle class, were still more faction-ridden than the parliamentarians: at least three vying committees tried to commandeer the legacy of 1798 for the centenary celebrations. By comparison with the disciplined nationalism of the previous decade, the 'split' seemed to inaugurate chaos. In fact, nationalist disunity had been equally embittered in the 1850s and 1860s. It was the unity of the 1880s that was aberrant.

Foremost in the cultural revival of the 1890s were the medley of scholars, politicians of many factions, and enthusiasts of many religions who believed that the pursuit of nationality would be futile unless the language were revived. Whereas parliamentary leaders from O'Connell to Parnell had envisaged self-government untrammelled by British maladministration but enlightened by British virtues, the 'Irish-Ireland' movement aimed to 'de-Anglicize' the Irish in preparation for a pseudo-Gaelic social order. The language revival was initiated in the 1870s and 1880s by a sprinkling of enthusiasts, often with Trinity College connections; among whom was Douglas Hyde who founded the Gaelic League in 1893. The Gaelic League did much to eliminate the sense of shame formerly felt by many native Irish speakers, and to teach the rudiments of the language to schoolchildren and enthusiastic clerks and shop-assistants in provincial towns. It also popularized 'Irish' entertainments such as fiddling, piping, dancing, reciting poetry, and listening to history lectures. Like all 'non-political' organizations in Ireland, it was subject to vicious factional struggle between rival manipulators. Most of its early Protestant leaders (such as the novelist 'George Birmingham') were forced out of office in the Edwardian decade, while Hyde himself was induced to resign the presidency in 1915 after a Fenian takeover. Fenian control was more overt and complete in the case of the Gaelic Athletic Association (1884), though a 'clericalist' faction following Archbishop Croke of Cashel remained active after the acrimonious split of 1887. Neither faction paid much attention to either athletics or (initially) hurling, their principal concerns being football and factional scheming under cover of team training.

Many Irish-Irelanders became enmeshed in the succession of bodies organized by Arthur Griffith, an ex-Fenian, anti-semitic, and anti-Labour journalist who promulgated the 'Sinn Féin' policy of exploiting local authorities while ignoring or sabotaging other state institutions, rather than seeking either violent revolution or legislative reform. Despite its professed contempt for 'politics', Sinn Féin unsuccessfully contested one by-election (North Leitrim in 1908) with the promise of 'abstention' from parliament if elected. After this defeat Sinn Féin's always small popular support outside certain Dublin suburbs virtually dissipated, and the movement posed no political menace to constitutional nationalism until 1917. The political significance of the Irish-Ireland movement consisted not in its negligible impact on contemporaries, but in the training and ideology with which it equipped a small knot of enthusiasts who by a strange accident came to dominate nationalism after 1916.

If cultural nationalists distrusted the narrowness of the constitutionalist strategy, militant Labour distrusted its eclecticism. The belated growth of the 'new' trade unionism in Ireland was crowned in 1909 by the creation of the Irish Transport and General Workers' Union, whose British-born syndicalist leaders Jim Larkin and James Connolly organized a sequence of major industrial disputes culminating in the Dublin lock-out of 1913–14. This bitter and sometimes violent confrontation between 400 Dublin employers and 20,000 workers caused the loss of 200,000 working days before the union's resistance collapsed. The strike's failure exposed Labour's industrial weakness and the futility of its leaders' syndicalist rhetoric. Labour's political development was also tardy, despite formation of the Irish Trades Union Congress in 1894 and its nominal conversion into a Labour Party in 1914. United political action was inhibited by the conflicting affiliations of Catholic and Protestant workers and the attachment of many Irish trades unionists to British-based bodies supporting the English or Scottish Labour Parties. National co-ordination remained ineffectual until 1930, when the Irish Labour Party was belatedly separated from the Trades Union Congress. Most workers gave their political allegiance to nationalist or unionist rather than

JIM LARKIN, the Labour leader: a melodramatic representation *c*.1913.

Labour organizations, their interests being proclaimed by bodies such as the Ancient Order of Hibernians and Ulster Unionist Labour Association. Militant Labour exercised only marginal political influence over the Irish proletariat, its significance being grossly inflated by the spectacular involvement of Connolly and a handful of followers in the 1916 Rising.

The predominance of the constitutionalist approach to nationalism was re-inforced in 1900, when the warring factions of parliamentarians were reunited under the Parnellite leader John Redmond. Though unable to control Party bosses such as John Dillon and Joe Devlin, Redmond was remarkably successful in papering over divisions in the Irish Party and its associated organizations in both Britain and Ireland. Parliamentary selection was passed over from central managers to constituency conventions of priests, local administrators, and del-egates of approved organizations. The Party's chief instrument was the parish network of the United Irish League (1898), initially a radical agrarian movement but increasingly devoted to electoral politics and fund-raising for Home Rule.

Other societies entitled to participate in conventions were Labour and Irish-Ireland bodies as well as nationalist fraternities such as the Irish National Foresters (1877) and the Ancient Order of Hibernians (reorganized under Party control by the 'Board of Erin' in 1905). As agrarian animosities softened while sectarian conflict intensified, the aggressively Catholic AOH gradually displaced the UIL as the Party's major vehicle for popular mobilization under the Home Rule banner. Home Rule generated an acceptably vague and grandiloquent political rhetoric for groups with disparate sectional aims and social functions, whose active participation in the nationalist movement maintained the Irish Party's vitality in periods of constitutional quiescence. The dream of national solidarity among both leaders and followers was never fully realized, being spoiled by reiterated opposition to the Party line from Tim Healy and William O'Brien. O'Brien deplored the increasingly sectarian tone and composition of the Irish Party, and formed the secessionist All-for-Ireland League (1910) in a vain attempt to win Protestant enthusiasm for Irish nation-building by dangling an 'olive branch'. Outside O'Brien's Munster strongholds, the Party's central and local machinery became so effective that its electoral candidates were mostly returned unopposed. The deals and confrontations were prudently confined to committee rooms and convention halls rather than polling stations, so giving credence to the Party's formidable image as representative of the united Catholic population. By 1914 that monolith had scarcely been dented by the pebbles flung at it by conciliators, conspirators, or Irish-Irelanders.

Redmond's party eventually regained the respect of both the Catholic church and the Liberal party, though the bishops found Redmond's education policy insufficiently sectarian while Campbell-Bannerman's Liberal ministry (1905–8) showed little enthusiasm for Home Rule. Under effective pressure from Irish members, wide-ranging Irish reforms were carried through by the seemingly effete and whimsical Augustine Birrell (chief secretary, 1907–16), who in reality combined tactical acumen with matronly good sense and an uncommon if condescending enthusiasm for Ireland and the Irish. Under Birrell so much state funding was directed to Ireland that its chronic 'overtaxation', as documented by the Childers Commission of 1895, had been reversed when the Primrose Committee reported 17 years later. The most important reform measures were the Old Age Pensions Act (1908), which raised the income and social status of most Irish people claiming to have reached 70 years; the Land Act of 1909, which facilitated land purchase and introduced powers of compulsory acquisition of estates in congested districts; and the National Insurance Act (1911), which compelled certain groups of employers and workers as well as the state to contribute towards benefits in case of sickness and unemployment, though not for medical treatment. The Irish Universities Act (1908) neglected to dismantle the archaic structure of Trinity College, but gave university status to Queen's,

Belfast, and to the colleges grouped under the Catholic-dominated National University of Ireland. Though the Asquith government failed to reform the Poor Law or to improve urban housing, the cumulative effect of Irish legislation between 1881 and 1914 was that of social revolution. Moreover, the application to Ireland of expensive reform measures gave substance to a 'union' which, for most of the nineteenth century, had seemed but a shoddy disguise for colonial occupation. Popular alienation from government was further mitigated by introduction of competitive examinations for the civil service (1876) and more eclectic exercise of official patronage. The British presence in Ireland, however unwelcome in principle, came to be widely tolerated as a practical source of employment and material benefit.

Protestant Unionism, 1870–1914

Ireland's apparent stability was undermined by a flaw which, though fundamental, failed to penetrate the complacency of either nationalists or their clerical and Liberal allies. The cost of collaboration between those groups was embitterment and further alienation of Ireland's economically formidable Protestant minority. The 'Ascendancy', though enfeebled by indebtedness and state intervention, conducted furious propaganda against church disestablishment (1869), land reform, and Home Rule. Yet the most savage resistance to *rapprochement* between Britain and Catholic Ireland came from the Protestants of urban Ulster, whose economic strength waxed as the influence of landlords waned. Though liberalism was never quite eradicated among Belfast's Presbyterian bourgeoisie, their distrust and contempt towards 'backward' southerners intensified. Sectarianism was most virulent within the Belfast proletariat, in which most workers of all religions preferred to promote their interests through factional conflict rather than trades unionism. Between 1871 and 1911 Protestant workers were chillingly successful in reversing the trend towards a mixed workforce, as Catholics were edged out of better paid and more skilled employment. It was Protestant workers rather than employers who drove Catholic rivals out of the Belfast shipyards on many occasions between 1864 and 1912. The accompanying violence was routinely deplored by unionist spokesmen; yet, under firebrands such as William Johnston of Ballykilbeg, many Orangemen and Blackmen employed rioting and drilling as political tools. Each Home Rule initiative (in 1886, 1893, and 1912) was answered by public reorganization of militant Orangeism as well as supportive propaganda by Irish and British unionists. Protestant and Catholic Ulstermen reaffirmed their sectarian identities by attachment to separate networks of secretive and ritualistic fraternities: indeed, their political cultures grew more similar in structure as their political objectives became more irreconcilable. Protestant attempts to find a middle way, such as

THE CLOSE LINKS BETWEEN LOYALIST ORGANIZATIONS are illustrated by this scene of an undated procession with drum and fife band, from a glassplate negative. The silk banner belongs to the Belfast 'Ulster Volunteers Loyal Orange Lodge', while the mace-bearer wears a sash of the Royal Black Preceptory.

Robert Lindsay Crawford's dabbling with devolution through the Independent Orange Order (1903), had no more enduring success than O'Brien's olive branch. Protestant opposition to Home Rule was periodically enriched by evangelical crusades, in which political and spiritual terrors were ingeniously woven together by bigots such as the Revd Hugh Hanna of Belfast, progenitor of the Revd Ian Paisley. The characteristic Protestant response to the new Anglo-Irish polity was to foster an alternative, mutually supportive Ulster Protestant polity incorporating all classes and all but a few courageous dissidents.

This simmering sectarian antagonism boiled over after Asquith's electoral quasi-victory in December 1910, which ensured that the Lords' right to veto major legislation would be diminished to suspension for two sessions of parliament. Since Unionists and Liberals achieved equal representation, Asquith's retention of power was contingent upon support from the Irish Parliamentary Party. It was generally assumed that Asquith would follow Gladstone's example (when managing hung parliaments in 1886 and 1893) by introducing a Government of Ireland bill, which this time would be enacted. Even before the bill's introduction with nationalist backing in April 1912, Home Rule had been selected as the primary target of unionist venom against Asquith and his fellow 'radical conspirators' against the constitution. Though unionist opposition in both islands applied to any measure of Home Rule, the practical alternative gradually emerged of enacting Home Rule with exemption or special status for some part of the province of Ulster. In public, the Irish Party insisted upon an act covering all Ireland with inbuilt safeguards for Protestant interests, while the Ulster Unionist Council (1905) and still more emphatically the landlord-dominated Irish Unionist Alliance (1891) demanded unaltered preservation of the Union. In private, under pressure from their parliamentary allies, both sides contemplated the option of exclusion for Ulster. Agreement could not be reached over the number of counties involved, the period of exclusion, or the range of powers to be granted to the Dublin parliament. Partition, whereby two autonomous administrations would be created, was not discussed. The attempt to negotiate an Ulster compromise ended in July 1914 with the failure of the Buckingham Palace conference.

Confrontation in Ireland developed with alarming rapidity after the initial parliamentary skirmishes of 1912. Protestant intransigence was affirmed by over 200,000 men and rather more women who signed the covenant or pledge on Ulster Day (28 September 1912): the recorded signatories amounted to almost three-quarters of all Ulster Protestants over 15 years. The women's pledge expressed the deferential 'desire to associate ourselves with the men of Ulster in their uncompromising opposition to the Home Rule Bill'. The men's 'Solemn League and Covenant' used pugnacious though ambiguous terminology, promising to employ 'all means which may be found necessary to defeat the present conspiracy to set up a Home Rule Parliament in Ireland', and 'to refuse to recognise its authority'. The appropriate means and identity of those deciding them were not specified, while the territorial scope of resistance was left unresolved in the claim that 'Home Rule would be disastrous to the material well-being of Ulster as well as of the whole of Ireland'. These ambiguities were clarified by a sequence of defiant initiatives. An Ulster Volunteer Force was established in January 1913, whose 90,000 members including many ex-servicemen soon achieved formidable military discipline under the command of the retired general Sir George Richardson. In April 1914, with police connivance, the Ulster Volunteers imported and distributed illegally some 30,000 service rifles

LOYALISM IN BELFAST. A cyclist detachment of the Ulster Volunteer Force.

each with a hundred rounds of ammunition. A few weeks earlier, senior intriguers at the War Office had induced fifty-eight army officers at the Curragh camp to threaten resignation unless assured by the government that they would be exempted from military operations against the Ulstermen. Meanwhile the Ulster Unionist Council had resolved in September 1913 to constitute its standing committee as the 'central authority for the provisional government' which Sir Edward Carson would lead in the event of Home Rule. When this body convened in July 1914, both the means and leadership of resistance had become unambiguous. The choice of Ulster's nine counties as the territory to be defended was also explicit, though many southern unionists stirred uneasily in their Big Houses upon this 'betrayal'. Despite nationalist incredulity, there seems no good reason to doubt that Home Rule would have been greeted in Ulster with armed rebellion. It is equally clear that Carson, soon to become a minister in Asquith's wartime coalition, expected parliamentary and propagandist pressure to prevail with the help of the menace rather than reality of violence. In July 1914 Asquith's resignation seemed the most probable outcome of the impasse in Ulster.

The spectacular effectiveness of the unionist campaign outside parliament persuaded a group of Fenian militants to create the Irish (National) Volunteers

THE IRISH NATIONAL VOLUNTEERS of Ennistymon, Co. Clare, unlike the Ulster Volunteers, used their feet rather than motorcycles and wooden guns rather than service rifles.

in November 1913, in the hope of counteracting its propagandist impact. The new force was self-consciously modelled upon the Ulster Volunteers and eventually enrolled twice as many members. It was slow to attract recruits under the improbable command of Eoin MacNeill, medieval historian and vice-president of the Gaelic League. In April 1914, however, the AOH began to give practical assistance to the force by providing drill-halls and advising all male nationalists with two functioning legs and a mouth to join up. Within two months the Volunteers had become in effect a Party organization, with Redmond as president and the Fenian founders of the provisional committee outnumbered by his nominees. Army veterans were prominent as drill-sergeants and (after the outbreak of war) as officers hoping to see the force transformed into a militia for home defence against German invasion. Despite this unexpected adherence of bellicose country gentlemen, the Volunteers became firmly committed to the defence of Home Rule without developing any contingency plans matching those of the Ulster Unionist Council. Their armament was puny by comparison with that landed at Larne by the Ulster Volunteers: only 1,500 rifles with 25 rounds each were landed at Howth and Kilcoole in July 1914, though about 6,000 weapons were clandestinely but legally imported after relaxation of arms control at the outbreak of war. For Redmond and his party the Volunteers provided a counter-bluff to Ulster's supposed bluff, so raising the stakes in the extra-parliamentary battle to influence Asquith's conduct of Irish policy. Yet for many of the 200,000 Volunteers, perplexed by the sophistries of politicians, participation raised the prospect of future armed conflict with the Ulster Volunteers. Recruitment was most intensive in mid-Ulster where Protestant and Catholic communities were evenly matched. In July 1914 it seemed unlikely that two armed forces could long coexist without outbreaks of sectarian conflict possibly erupting into bloody attrition. Civil war loomed.

War and Upheaval, 1914-1918

The outbreak of European war in August 1914 postponed the threat of armed conflict in Ireland by offering each protagonist a line of dignified retreat under cover of patriotic necessity. After some weeks of negotiation the government suspended the implementation of Home Rule for six months while allowing the act to receive Royal Assent unamended. Asquith promised verbally to make unspecified provision for part or all of Ulster before the suspension expired. Though Bonar Law's unionists left the Commons in a huff, their continued adherence to the 'party truce' implied acquiescence, and the act's suspension was periodically extended by order in council. Redmond's response to war was two-fold. His spontaneous response to Sir Edward Grey's undertakings on 3 August was to offer the Volunteers for home defence against invasion. Seven weeks later, when the need for vast forces for foreign combat had become apparent, he celebrated the enactment of Home Rule by calling upon Volunteers to enlist for service 'wherever the firing line extends'. Redmond hoped that these affirmations would reassure the cabinet of nationalist Ireland's patriotism and fitness for self-government, conciliate Irish unionists, and encourage the War Office to establish the Volunteers as a militia force or Irish division under their current command structure. The War Office sabotaged both schemes, instead creating two 'Irish divisions' (the 10th and 16th) under regular officers who were sometimes Irish but seldom Catholic nationalists. Redmond's gestures drew tears of gratitude from politicians of all parties but failed to move the granite face of Ulster unionism. Until suspension of Home Rule was assured, Ulster leaders had avoided organized involvement in war against the Germans, their erstwhile suppliers of armament and inspiration. At last, on 3 September, the Ulster Unionist Council sanctioned an unconditional offer by Carson and his chief associate James Craig to provide Kitchener with 35,000 Ulster Volunteers. Their reward was the creation of a 36th (Ulster) division under officers nominated by the Volunteers, the very bargain which Redmond's magnanimity had failed to secure. The immediate effect of war was to divert the most active sections of Ireland's paramilitary organizations towards the European conflict, without achieving lasting reconciliation between the parties left at home.

Irish popular response to hostilities was level-headed, and some weeks passed before recruits in great numbers began to join the 50,000 Irish regular soldiers and reservists automatically mobilized on 4 August. Despite War Office obduracy and the insensitivity of the Irish recruiting campaigns, about 90,000 men were enlisted in Ireland before 1916 (3.7 per cent of total recruitment in the United Kingdom). This fell not far short of Ireland's share of the non-agricultural male population (5.7 per cent in 1911), while few agricultural recruits were obtained in either island. The imposition of conscription in Britain but not Ireland caused the Irish contribution to drop to 1.7 per cent in 1916–18. All told about 200,000 men joined the colours in Ireland as well as numerous expatriates in Britain, the empire, and the United States. National Volunteers slightly outnumbered the 30,000 Ulster Volunteers who were enlisted, and the bare majority of recruits were Catholics. Though Protestants were indeed over-represented, this fact was entirely attributable to high recruitment rates in Ulster, with its large proletariat and heavy unemployment affecting Catholics at least as much as Protestants. It is significant that in Belfast in 1915, Catholics were actually more likely than Protestants to join the army: economics rather than politics or religion best explain the variations in Irish as in British recruitment. Those with insecure employment had least to lose by trading danger for free food, lodging, and foreign travel, a fraternal structure well adapted to Irish preferences, and 'separation allowances' for wives. Ireland's response to war was remarkable not for the fervour of its patriotism or disloyalty, but for its hard-headed readiness to accept the king's shilling.

For many who remained in Ireland, the war period brought unexpected prosperity. After initial economic dislocation, urban unemployment fell well below pre-war levels as a result of recruitment into the forces and munitions factories (mainly in Britain rather than Ireland). Yet the reduction of unemployment was relatively modest by British standards, and there was no dramatic 'dilution' of the workforce by veterans, juveniles, or women. Only forty-three Irishwomen had joined the Women's Land Army by late 1917, one-thousandth of the total. Dublin female workers suffered from contraction of demand for textile operatives and domestic servants; while proletarians of both sexes had to endure inflation and scarcity despite unprecedented state regulation of prices and wages. The major beneficiaries of war were farmers, who profited from the reduction of Continental and foreign competition for the British market. The doubling of food prices between 1914 and 1918 benefited farmers as much as it harmed consumers, and Irish producers willingly acceded to demands for increased tillage production. Inflation generated easy agricultural credit, which was recklessly exploited by farmers eager to acquire machinery and join co-operative societies. Ag-

THE 36TH ULSTER DIVISION
(*above*) parading past the City
Hall, Belfast, in May 1915; and a
recruiting parade (*right*), *c*.1915,
passing down St Patrick's Street,
Cork.

ricultural prosperity scarcely affected the few remaining farm labourers, whose earnings only kept pace with inflation as a result of state intervention. The small farmers of Connacht and the western seaboard also gained little, partly because of household congestion caused by the virtual stoppage of emigration between 1915 and early 1920. Yet many rural Irishmen enjoyed jangling pockets, brimming overdrafts, and well-rounded stomachs testifying that they were doing well out of the war.

Since it was a nationalist commonplace that England's necessity was Ireland's opportunity, it was to be expected that a small but ingenious band of conspirators would plan a wartime insurrection. This was evidently discussed at a meeting in September 1914 attended by Arthur Griffith as well as recent recruits to the supreme council of the Irish Republican Brotherhood such as Patrick Pearse, Seán MacDermott, Tom Clarke, and Eamonn Ceannt. The conspirators induced the provisional committee of the Volunteers to repudiate Redmond's leadership, though only a tenth of the force subsequently joined MacNeill's Irish Volunteers while most followed Col. Maurice Moore into the National Volunteers. The dissidents kept most of the rifles but secured strong support only in Dublin. The American Clan na Gael agreed to pay for an insurrection, and sent Sir Roger Casement (late of the British consular service) to Germany to raise an Irish Brigade consisting of prisoners of war who would accompany a shipment of German arms to Ireland. Soon, however, those who had expected war to revive Irish hostility towards the empire began to despair. Military recruitment, prosperity, and the nominal achievement of Home Rule all suggested closer rather than declining common interest between Ireland and Britain. Although the same factors had robbed the Home Rule organizations of their vitality, the consequences of war for dissident nationalism were still more negative. Sinn Féin and the Gaelic League were moribund and membership of the Irish Volunteers remained static, though the IRB managed to reverse its decline by energetic recruitment of MacNeill's followers. It was frustration at organizational failure as well as fanaticism which induced a minority of activists within each body to continue preparation for revolt in the teeth of popular contempt, and with the certainty of military defeat at the hands of the vastly swollen army across the water. Similar frustration inspired James Connolly, acting president of the Irish Transport and General Workers' Union, whose defeat and near-bankruptcy in the Dublin labour struggle of 1913–14 had been compounded by loss of half its membership to the army by 1916. Early in 1916 Connolly was co-opted to the IRB's military council, a shadowy group formed in May 1915 to execute the plans discussed in September 1914. Just as Connolly acted without authority from his union or its vigilante force (the tiny Irish Citizen Army formed in 1913), so the military council bypassed Denis McCullough whom its members were bound to acknowledge as president of the Irish Republic. Far from being the predictable outcome of growing popular antipathy to Britain and her war effort, the Easter Rising emerged from the fragmentation and demoralization of the anti-war movement.

Birrell's Irish administration, though aware of the conspiracy, employed ridicule rather than coercion to undermine it. Though it suppressed some 'seditious' journals and excluded several Fenian organizers from their recruiting areas, Dublin Castle was able to confute republican expectations of counter-productive wartime coercion. It acted as a caretaker administration pending implementation of Home Rule, and held secret meetings on the transfer of powers with Redmond and Dillon during 1915. In return Redmond and many other nationalist members, though not Dillon, became active in the recruiting campaign. Birrell's dealings with Ulster unionists were less happy. Despite unionist participation in Asquith's coalition ministry after May 1915, Birrell virtually ignored the Ulster lobby in Ireland and bitterly opposed it in Westminster and Whitehall. By April 1916 his relationship with church and nationalist leaders was imperilled by cabinet insistence that Sir James Campbell, a bitter unionist who was to achieve further notoriety as speaker of the Free State's Senate, be appointed as Attorney-General for Ireland. The Castle continued to discount intelligence warnings of imminent rebellion: its forbearance seemed justified when the only shipload of German arms was sunk, Casement was arrested in Kerry after a submarine mission to ensure abandonment of the insurrection, and orders for Volunteer exercises were cancelled publicly by MacNeill. Rebellion seemed inconceivable, and the Castle looked forward to relaxation at the Easter Monday races before rounding up the demoralized conspirators after the holiday.

The military council's decision to rebel in the certainty of military defeat, though incomprehensible to most Volunteers as well as administrators, was in keeping with a familiar theme of republican rhetoric. Joseph Mary Plunkett and Thomas MacDonagh, like Pearse, revelled in the vulgar wartime lie that the shedding of blood was 'a cleansing and a sanctifying thing', and imagined that a race of resurrected Gaelic heroes would emerge out of the bloodied gutters of Sackville (alias O'Connell) Street. To achieve 'bloody sacrifice' they employed diverse tools of deception in order to mobilize the Irish Volunteers and Irish Citizen Army. The location of buildings chosen for occupation in Dublin served to maximize injury to persons and property rather than to immobilize the key institutions of Irish government. No serious attempt was made to occupy Dublin Castle or even Trinity College, whose strategically sited and stoutly walled campus was virtually empty of soldiers and students. Instead rebel headquarters were established at the General Post Office, a building hitherto without symbolic connotations but at the heart of Dublin's main shopping zone. A medley of parks, factories, bridges, and public buildings, mainly south of the Liffey and in no sense constituting an encirclement, were also seized and defended by small parties.

Only about 1,600 members of the Irish Volunteers and Irish Citizen Army turned out in Dublin, while activity elsewhere (apart from minor incidents in a few country towns) was restricted to route-marching and parading. Troops were promptly shipped from Liverpool and Aldershot, carnage and devastation ensued, and after six days Pearse called upon his forces to surrender; 132 soldiers and policemen were killed and 397 wounded, whereas civilian deaths amounted to 318 and woundings to 2,217. Only about 64 rebels were killed in action (excluding 15 executed 'martyrs'), a minuscule loss by comparison with the 25,000 Irish recruits who died from war injuries. The main victims of the 'proclamation of the Irish Republic' were thus unarmed civilians, whose suffering was compounded by the wreckage of central Dublin, widespread looting, disruption of employment, and interruption of postal services.

Initial popular response to the Rising was general fury and disgust at the human and material wastage. Rebels were roughed up on active service by

AFTERMATH OF 1916. Beresford Place, Dublin, showing the wreckage of Liberty Hall, headquarters of Connolly's ITGWU, and also of the Irish Women Workers' Union founded by Jim Larkin's sister Delia.

enraged women and pelted with tomatoes after surrendering. Had Birrell's astuteness been shared by his successors, Pearse's suicide squads would probably have died or languished unregretted by most nationalists. Instead, Asquith's government over reacted beyond even the dreams of the conspirators. Birrell and his senior advisers resigned without being replaced for several months; General Sir John Maxwell was given command under martial law without explicit restriction or definition of his powers; 3,500 people were arrested, courtmartialled, or deported for internment in Britain. The number of arrests was double that of rebels, and included a representative range of dissident nationalists from groups and districts untouched by the conspiracy. The indiscriminacy and brutality of the military response could scarcely have occurred except in wartime, when those who had dared to 'stab the Empire in the back' could be treated as 'traitors' rather than dissident citizens. The effect of repression upon public opinion was insidious and irreversible, despite rapid release of those interned, Asquith's stoppage of further executions, relaxation of martial law long before its abrogation in November, and appointment of a new chief secretary (Henry Duke) in July 1916. Communities previously indifferent to republican slogans were outraged at victimization of hitherto innocuous idealists, who nevertheless benefited from detention by meeting enthusiasts from other localities, learning Irish, mastering Gaelic games, and so receiving elementary training in revolution. While the new revolutionary élite crystallized in detention, a sentimental cult of veneration for the martyrs developed outside as after previous failed risings. The conspirators thus achieved their aim of reversing the movement towards Anglo-Irish reconciliation. Their greater dream of reversing Anglicization remained as elusive as before.

Within a month of suspending Irish policy to permit military vengeance, Asquith had reverted to prudence by burdening Lloyd George with responsibility for immediately putting through an amended Home Rule settlement. As after 1867 and 1880, a Liberal ministry required the menace of revolution to activate its desire for Irish reform. Lloyd George very nearly succeeded in negotiating a compromise under which six Ulster counties would be excluded from Home Rule for the duration of the war. Redmond and Carson were placated by his apparent assurances that exclusion would be temporary and indeterminate respectively. Despite popular misgivings in both communities and strenuous opposition from northern Catholic bishops, this ambiguous resolution of the pre-war impasse was accepted by conventions of northern nationalists and Ulster unionists. The agreement was soon sabotaged by unionist magnates such as the marquess of

IRISHMEN ALL. These illustrations of emblematic national 'types' from George Birmingham's book of 1913 were taken from paintings by Jack B. Yeats, brother to the poet: they show The Police Sergeant, The Lesser Official, The Publican, and The Politician.

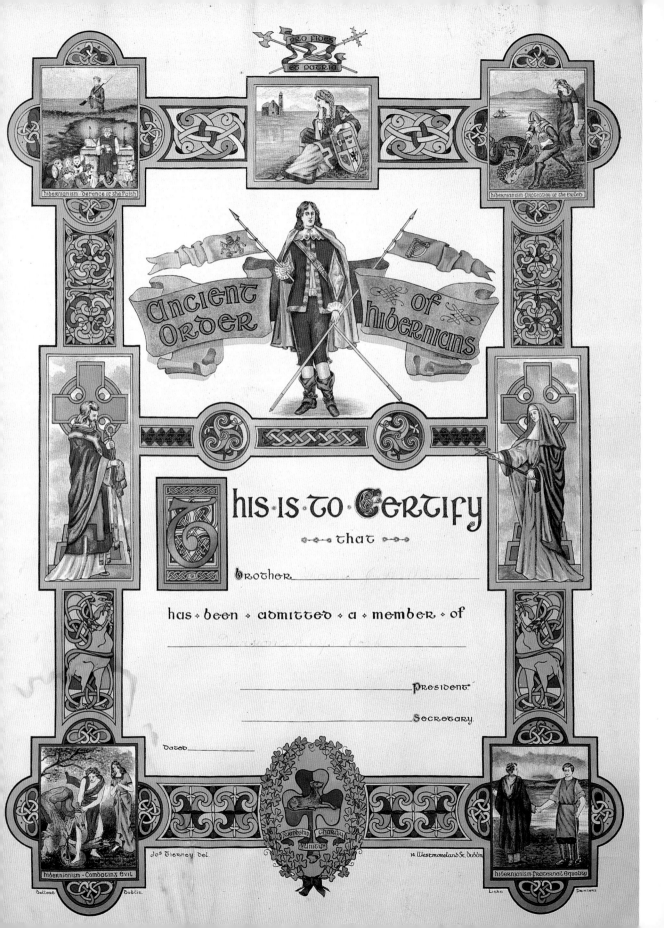

PRO FIDES ET PATRIA

hibernianism - defence of the Faith

hibernianism - protection of the exiled

Ancient Order of hibernians

This is to Certify

that

brother _____

has · been · admitted · a · member · of

_____

_____ President

_____ Secretary

Dated _____

Friendship Charity Unity

Jos Tierney del

14 Westmoreland St. Dublin

hibernianism - Combating Evil

hibernianism - Fraternal Equality

Dollard

Dublin.

Litho

Printers

Lansdowne, who induced the cabinet to restrict the operation of Home Rule in wartime and prolong exclusion until the north-eastern population voted for extension of Dublin's authority. The collapse of Lloyd George's plan wrecked the Irish Party, which was execrated for acquiescing in 'partition' without winning the solace of immediate assumption of power. It also sapped the government's will to accomplish a wartime settlement. Lloyd George's only initiative after replacing Asquith was to convene a nominated and un-representative 'Irish Convention', which met under Sir Horace Plunkett's inept chairmanship between July 1917 and April 1918 without influencing policy.

Catholic alienation from constitutionalism was not immediately expressed in the creation of a new populist party committed to institution of the republic proclaimed on Easter Monday, 1916. The rebels themselves had distrusted popu-lism, and many survivors looked forward to further bloody sacrifice in pursuit of further repression and resurrection of the Gaelic spirit. The survivor who did most to confute that strategy by encouraging mass political participation in re-publicanism was Eamon de Valera, the courageous if reluctant commandant at Boland's Mills whose American birth had probably saved him from execution. While still imprisoned at Lewes, the former teacher began to educate the evolv-ing revolutionary élite in the advantages of political struggle and dangers of renewed urban insurrection. He argued that a further rising, however appealing, could not be justified without reasonable hope of military victory. Instead, he and Arthur Griffith urged republicans to engage in an international propaganda campaign to seek recognition as a separate nation entitled to self-government. For two years after early 1917 their plan was to mobilize popular support for the republican demand in order to win American backing for Irish representation at the eventual peace conference. Electoral contests were used to demonstrate the popularity of republicanism, though in conformity with Sinn Féin's policy republican candidates were pledged to 'abstain' from taking up their par-liamentary seats. Between the Rising and the Armistice abstentionists were nominated for nine of the nineteen Irish by-elections, winning six of the seven southern contests. In the north-east, where the sectarian appeal of the AOH remained strong while the Irish Party declined elsewhere, Sinn Féin lost both contests to constitutionalists. De Valera's own victory in East Clare (July 1917) was notable for his success in winning support from many old nationalist bosses and priests, who were placated by his warnings against futile violence and 'doctrinaire' republicanism. Until October 1917 no unified party existed, beyond a loose coalition of previously bickering dissident groups assembled at the Mansion

THE ANCIENT ORDER OF HIBERNIANS, membership certificate issued in Cork in 1913. The four alleg-orical scenes (clockwise from top left) represent four functions of Hibernianism: Defence of the Faith, Protection of the Exiled, Fraternal Equality, and Combating Evil. The left-hand and right-hand panels show SS Patrick and Brigid, while in the top panel Erin mourns past glories.

WHICH?

VOTE FOR *DE VALERA*, A Felon of Our Land

GRACE PLUNKETT

EAST CLARE BY-ELECTION, JULY 1917. In a cartoon poster by Grace Plunkett, widow of the 1916 'martyr' Joseph Mary Plunkett, Sinn Féin's de Valera awaits sentence of death as demanded by the Crown Prosecutor—a post once held by his nationalist opponent Patrick Lynch, KC, who in later life became de Valera's Attorney-General.

House, Dublin, in April 1917 by George Noble Plunkett (father of the executed Joseph Mary). Finally, de Valera and Griffith agreed upon a revised version of the Sinn Féin constitution which won general acceptance, becoming president and vice-president in turn. At the *ard fheis* (convention) the gunmen were out-talked, the clergy were charmed, veteran Irish Party fixers were welcomed into the republican fold, and subsequently parish branches proliferated until membership far exceeded 100,000. With impressive pragmatism and efficiency, Sinn Féin absorbed and exploited much of the personnel and technique of its bitter antagonist. Only the slogans had changed.

While Sinn Féin consolidated its popular support, the republican élite re-grouped itself in the IRB, the Irish Volunteers, and its energetic women's counterpart (Cumann na mBan). The IRB soon came under the sway of Michael Collins, a London clerk whose astuteness and record in the Rising enabled him to become a key manipulator in most republican bodies. Collins and his fellow

Fenian Dick Mulcahy also took crucial parts in the Volunteers' new national executive (October 1917) and general headquarters staff (March 1918), though nominal control rested with de Valera as president and with Cathal Brugha, who like de Valera had broken with the IRB after the Rising. The Volunteers remained a defensive force, committed to drilling, parading, defying judicial and military authority, but also to avoiding armed attacks upon soldiers and policemen. Though short of serviceable arms and with less than 30,000 members known to the constabulary, the Volunteers exuded menace through their effective 'protection' of republican politicians and disruption of the prison system in pursuit of 'political status'. Throughout 1917 they solicited arrest and martyrdom by hunger strike, until Duke spoiled the fun by allowing illegal drillers to read, dress, assemble, and entertain almost as they pleased. By April 1918 most Volunteer organizers were back home, awaiting the call to arms which did not come.

Renewed rebellion seemed probable when Lloyd George, urged by panic-stricken generals to draft further soldiers for service against the rampaging Germans, rushed through a new military service act which allowed the Lord Lieutenant in Council to extend conscription to Ireland. The Irish administration objected that this would further alienate 'moderate' nationalists, provoke violent resistance, and necessitate deployment of more soldiers than it would secure for foreign service. Once again military crisis outweighed political expediency, and Lloyd George installed a tame administration whose chief secretary (Edward Shortt) was to assist Lord French as 'viceroy' with the powers (or so French supposed) of a military governor. The effect of this affront was to bring together delegates of Sinn Féin, organized Labour, the Irish Party, and dissident nationalism in a conference convened at the Mansion House on 18 April 1918. De Valera and John Dillon, Redmond's successor upon his recent death, collaborated in propaganda and won the surprisingly explicit support of the Catholic hierarchy for resistance 'by the most effective means at our disposal' (if 'consonant with the law of God' as infallibly interpreted by bishops).

Implementation was postponed after widespread though uncounted adhesion to the 'solemn covenant to resist conscription' after mass on 21 April, followed by a one-day general stoppage two days later. Co-ordination of 'passive resistance' fell largely to Labour after the arrest of most Volunteer leaders upon the spurious revelation of a 'German plot'; while the Volunteers, not separately represented at the conference, made contingency plans for armed resistance through 'ruthless warfare' should peaceful protest prove ineffectual. In the event, Lord French introduced a quota scheme for voluntary recruitment as an alternative to conscription; and by extension of deadlines and trimming of quotas the need to revert to compulsion was evaded up to the armistice of 11 November. The prevention of conscription was justifiably regarded as a vindication of the propagandist strategy, from which all participants in the conference derived

ANTI-CONSCRIPTION PLEDGE being signed by parishioners outside an unidentified church on Sunday, 21 April 1918.

credit. Sinn Féin spread into dormant counties and organized Labour allayed republican distrust of its political ambivalence; and even the Irish Party regained support, before suffering blame for the breakdown of solidarity in June 1918 when a constitutionalist vainly challenged Griffith's candidacy in Cavan East. The effect of the campaign was to reinforce reliance upon political struggle and undermine the military case for direct action.

Revolution, 1919–1922

The return of peace in Europe rapidly altered the terms of conflict in Ireland. Despite Asquith's intention in 1914 to implement an amended form of Home Rule when the war ended, the unionist-dominated post-war coalition made no attempt to resolve the constitutional impasse. The Irish Party's collapse was demonstrated at the general election of December 1918, when it won only six seats of which most were secured by an electoral pact with Sinn Féin in Ulster.

Sinn Féin secured seventy-three seats and 48 per cent of votes cast, compared with 29 per cent for unionists and 23 per cent for constitutionalists. Those Sinn Féin members who were still at liberty convened as a national assembly, Dáil Éireann, on 21 January 1919. Its functions were at first propagandist rather than administrative, and the Republic's inauguration was designed primarily to win international confidence and a hearing (if no longer recognition) at the peace conference. After May 1919 the hope of a hearing dissipated, and republican propaganda was redirected towards mobilizing the Irish abroad in verbal and financial support of self-determination. De Valera's protracted American tour as 'president of the Irish Republic' raised over five million dollars in republican 'bonds', despite bitter opposition from entrenched Irish-American organizations. The campaign in Britain was less remunerative and more muted, being headed by an Irish Self-Determination League which tactfully desisted from affirming its republicanism for fear of alienating moderate well-wishers. Even Ireland's revolution was moulded, in its priorities and funding, by emigration.

Despite Sinn Féin's electoral success, the political unity of Catholic Ireland

DÁIL ÉIREANN: when Sinn Féin members of parliament first assembled in the Mansion House, Dublin, as Dáil Éireann, their intention was to publicize the respectability and determination of their movement through open proceedings. Only three further public sessions followed this ceremonial occasion on 21 January 1919 before the Truce of July 1921. Within a few months Dáil Éireann had been proclaimed, and its members embroiled in a war involving more than lofty words and illuminated addresses directed towards the pressmen on the balcony.

was fragile. Between 1918 and 1920 class conflict became a major problem for the first time since the Land War. Trade union membership and industrial conflict increased sharply after 1917, reflecting the benefits of low unemployment for collective action. Strike activity spread from cities to provincial towns, and from skilled trades to casual labour, clerical occupations, and even domestic service. Outside Ulster the major missionary force was the revived ITGWU, which by 1920 had 100,000 members of whom over a third were agricultural workers. Labour's continued efflorescence was made possible by fear of post-war recession combined with its postponement; though working-class solidarity was disrupted in 1919 by demobilization of ex-servicemen who found employment elusive, organized Labour unwelcoming, and the new politics incomprehensible. When civilian unemployment exceeded pre-war proportions late in 1920 trades unionism declined, wages fell, and class conflict shifted from broad-based collective action to local eruptions of 'soviets' advocating industrial management by workers. Agrarian unrest likewise diminished after approaching Land War levels in 1920. Even at its peak, class conflict was too diffuse and localized to generate effective political expression. The Irish Labour Party maintained close though informal liaison with the republican government, causing further alienation of northern Protestant workers whose discontent was harnessed by the Ulster Unionist Labour Association (June 1918). As unemployment worsened two years later, sectarian conflict was revived in Belfast when Catholic workers were again expelled from shipyards and factories in the bloodiest episode since the Rising. Factionalism and unemployment undermined class protest, to the relief of republican organizers who had been active in suppressing labour and agrarian disputes.

As northern sectarianism intensified, Irish Protestants split asunder over the partition issue. Many southern unionists worked hard to reverse sectarian polarization and conciliate the Catholic majority among whom they lived. Viscount Midleton's conciliatory faction was forced to secede from the Irish Unionist Alliance and form the Irish Unionist Anti-Partition League in January 1919. Their aversion to partition exceeded their fear of self-government, and southern unionists were prominent in several futile attempts to obtain dominion status for the entire island. The 'diehards' supported the Ulster Unionist Council in its determination to establish Protestant Ulster's right to determine its own constitutional status. Despite this provocation, few attacks upon southern Protestants were reported during the 'Troubles' though many vacant houses were burned. In Ulster the UVF was revived in June 1920 to the disgust of General Macready (Irish army commander between 1920 and 1922), but its activities were largely confined to the six most Protestant counties. Despite post-war disruption of the shipbuilding, engineering, and linen industries, the Belfast bourgeoisie remained confident of the economic viability of a six-county unit. The growing alienation

A SECTARIAN RIOT in York Street, Belfast, on 2 September 1920. Protestant shipyard workers are shown driving back Catholics on their way to work on Queen's Island.

of the Catholic minority and its Hibernian defenders only reinforced Protestant preference for a compact, Protestant-dominated state.

Menaced by growing disorder and unionist as well as nationalist militancy, Lloyd George's second coalition ministry resolved to tackle the status of Ulster before the national issue. The contradictory advice from Lord French and his post-war chief secretary (Ian Macpherson) was ignored, and formulation of Irish policy passed to a cabinet committee chaired by Walter Long, a former unionist chief secretary. In February 1920, Lloyd George introduced a bill 'for the better government of Ireland' which broke new ground by proposing two Home Rule administrations rather than one. Next month the UUC accepted this principle, so acknowledging that Protestants cared more for consolidation of their local power than for maintenance of the union. Passage of the bill occupied nearly a year, yet no serious effort was made either to gather nationalist support for a separate southern state, or to provide for future reunification except through a clawless Council of Ireland. Instead, the new Castle administration installed in spring 1920 under the innovative direction of Sir John Anderson continued to contemplate dominion Home Rule for all Ireland. Lloyd George and other ministers also conducted secret negotiations with republican leaders through episcopal and Labour intermediaries, so intimating that the partition plan was negotiable. Yet in May 1921 elections were held in Northern Ireland, a unionist ministry installed under Sir James Craig, and the slow process of transfer of powers initiated. The subsequent southern elections were subverted by Sinn Féin's unopposed triumph in all but four seats in the House of Commons, as a result of which the southern parliament was never convened.

The government's granting of priority to the Ulster issue reflected the surprisingly slow development of terrorism and violence in the south. De Valera continued to seek freedom through international propaganda rather than revolution. But in Ireland itself, an unexpected alternative to emancipation by propaganda or by terrorism was taking shape by early 1920. In response to the virtual breakdown of local government, the police, and the lower courts, local republican organizers responded to popular demand by devising republican institutions with similar functions, structure, and sometimes personnel. The Dáil ministry was faced with the embarrassment of having to implement or repudiate its own propagandist pronouncements, such as the Democratic Programme of January 1919 with its reiteration of Griffith's and Pearse's policies for administrative reform and land nationalization. The ministry responded reluctantly but with flair by co-ordinating, ratifying, and extending the more successful local initiatives. It promulgated schemes for civil and criminal courts, rate-collection and local administration, industrial development and land purchase, and even (though without effect) redirection of income tax. Though no scheme was fully implemented, enough local participation and central funding was involved to prompt the startling retrospective admission from Lloyd George that 'the Irish Republican Organisation had all the symbols, and they had all the realities of a Government'. This assessment reflected official demoralization without persuading the government of the urgent need for constitutional settlement which Ulster's sectarian unrest had provoked.

The 'constructive programme' developed in parallel with military defiance, yet the two strategies were unco-ordinated and often at odds. The shape of Volunteer activity was similarly formed by local initiative, though Mulcahy's GHQ attempted to regularize command structures, improve military proficiency, and import arms. The force still rested on the network of parochial companies, swollen with unarmed and inattentive Volunteers often more absorbed with factional than national objectives. Contrary to historical fiction, there was no 'declaration of war' in January 1919 when two constables were killed at Soloheadbeg in Tipperary. The 'War of Independence' resulted in only about 18 deaths in 1919, 282 in 1920, as well as 82 in Ulster's sectarian riots, but 1,086 in 1921 before the Truce. Nearly half of the victims were soldiers or policemen. Until spring 1920, Volunteer activity was largely confined to arson, arms raiding, intimidation, and ostracization rather than murder of the constabulary. GHQ resisted demands for renewed urban insurrection by zealots such as Terence MacSwiney, the blood-thirsty Cork commandant who achieved droll apotheosis as martyr and man of peace when he died on hunger strike in October 1920.

The slide towards terrorism was largely precipitated by increasingly brutal repression, which forced armed Volunteers to 'go on the run' and band together for protection. After reintroduction of massive internment under the Restoration of Order in Ireland Act (August 1920), these groups began to crystallize as 'flying columns' plotting pre-emptive ambushes against 'enemy' parties. Between September 1920 and April 1921 several bloody ambushes were executed, mostly in Munster by guerrilla heroes such as Tom Barry, Dan Breen, and Liam Lynch. The flying columns often despised GHQ and its 'paper army', which itself remained formally independent of the Dáil's authority until imposition of an oath of allegiance to the Republic during late 1920. In many counties the Volunteers were never active or effectively organized, while even in Munster the improved performance of the Crown forces in 1921 forced the gunmen to resort to sniping, small-scale attacks, and murder of 'informers'. Many organizers were

GUERRILLA DISRUPTION OF MILITARY MOVEMENTS, probably in the Bandon area in 1921. The Essex Regiment, here halted by a detonated bridge, met with fierce opposition from the West Cork Brigade and its Flying Column under Tom Barry.

demoralized by this descent into terrorism, despite attempts to revive morale such as the showy if futile burning of the Dublin Custom House in May 1921. The three or four thousand armed activists had no practical hope of military victory, yet their defiant survival frustrated the army and police and augmented political pressure for a truce and settlement.

The rapid intensification of violence after 1919 was largely caused by the disorganization and savagery of the 'occupying' forces. The worst atrocities were committed not by the army but by the reconstituted Royal Irish Constabulary, which was swamped in 1920 by ex-soldiers enrolled as special constables or 'Black and Tans', as well as 'auxiliary cadets' under separate command who were recruited from the wartime officer corps. Crown 'reprisals' against persons and property in disaffected localities ranged from beatings and murders to the destruction of fifty-three creameries; from window-smashing to the ransacking of towns such as Balbriggan, Fermoy, and Ennistymon, and the wreckage of central Cork in December 1920. The reprisal always seemed more vicious than the incident provoking it, as in the slaughter of twelve football supporters at Croke Park on 21 November 1920 in revenge for the assassination of fourteen suspected spies by Collins's infamous 'Squad'. Popular outrage at reprisals was sharpened by the justified suspicion that the government was secretly conniving at a practice in keeping with its policy of punishing localities which harboured rebels by applying economic sanctions. Reprisals provided the focus for republican propaganda and provoked formation of influential protest groups such as the Peace With Ireland Council, which worked effectively to persuade British politicians to seek a settlement. At the end of 1920 the manifest disorganization of the Crown forces induced the government to reimpose martial law in the most disturbed southern and western counties. Both within and outside the martial law zone police and military interference in civilian life became ever more intrusive, with innumerable raids, searches, proclamations of meetings and of societies. Arrests were followed either by internment or by summary conviction at the hands of special tribunals or courts martial. Popular disgust at the licence allowed to marauding bands of 'law-enforcers' was most intense among Ulster Catholics whose livelihood and lives were menaced by the grim reserve of Protestant part-time constables known as the 'B Specials'. The militaristic tenor of Irish government between 1916 and 1919 was superseded in 1920–1 by a savage and calculated arbitrariness which shattered the residue of the pre-war Anglo-Irish polity.

Eventually international outrage and military stalemate created the conditions for a truce and peace conference. Under the 1920 Government of Ireland Act, Southern Ireland was to become a Crown colony under martial law if its parliament were not functioning by 12 July 1921. Hostilities were suspended successfully by both armies with a day to spare. Killings and outrages virtually

NOT CONQUERING HEROES. The Irish peace delegation and other officials and ministers of Dáil Éireann are shown, stiff and apprehensive, upon arrival at Euston station, London, on 8 October 1921. Arthur Griffith is pictured (third from right); but Michael Collins slipped into London two days later, unnoticed by photographers.

ceased, though the police could not prevent the Dáil from rebuilding its administration and the Volunteers from reorganizing themselves into a force more worthy of the prevalent sobriquet 'Irish Republican Army'. Lloyd George, hopeful at last of having identified a republican leader capable of carrying the 'murder gang' with him, initiated contact with de Valera before the Truce and met him on 14 July. After two months a bilateral conference between the representatives of 'Britain' and 'Ireland' began in the absence of delegates from Northern Ireland, so allowing national status to the Dáil ministry. Lloyd George offered dominion status rather than Home Rule, while de Valera vindicated his denial of doctrinaire republicanism by proposing 'external association', whereby Ireland would acknowledge the monarch as head of the Commonwealth with which Ireland would be associated for 'purposes of common concern'. For over two months, the surprisingly astute Irish delegation headed by Griffith and Collins tackled Lloyd George and other senior ministers. They secured substantive concessions concerning defence, taxation, tariffs, and policing as well as verbal victories in nomenclature. The majority of the delegation accepted Lloyd

George's final draft treaty as an objectionable but tolerable basis for future step-wise progress towards broader self-government; but de Valera and several ministers in Dublin repudiated the agreement on the grounds that Irish representatives should never express even 'fidelity' to a British monarch. In the bitter Dáil debate which followed de Valera tried unavailingly to table an alternative draft omitting the oath and altering nomenclature, but leaving virtually intact all specific restrictions upon Irish autonomy. On 7 January 1922 the Treaty was approved by a small majority of deputies.

The most curious aspect of the Anglo-Irish agreement was the indifference shown by both parties towards the response of Ulster Protestants, who already controlled a functioning parliament in a rapidly evolving state. The Treaty purported to apply to all Ireland, the Northern Ireland parliament being allowed either to keep its current status or to transfer its subordination from Whitehall to Dublin. Northern Ireland duly repudiated the Treaty and subsequent constitution just after they came into force in December 1922. The only remaining constraints upon partition were the inoperative Council of Ireland, and the prospect of a tripartite Boundary Commission charged with determining the border 'in accordance with the wishes of the inhabitants, so far as may be compatible with economic and geographic conditions'. This waffle was initially accepted by de Valera, though under republican pressure he later asserted the Dublin parliament's 'supreme authority' over Northern Ireland, which should nevertheless be granted 'privileges and safeguards not less substantial' than those in the Treaty. Most southerners remained naïvely confident that Northern Ireland would soon seek reunification since it could not survive without southern co-operation. In de Valera's words, the Ulster question was in practice merely a 'Belfast question', the proper answer to which was a judicious alternation of bribes and punishments. Though invasion was no longer envisaged, the Dáil ministry had implemented a damaging 'Belfast Boycott' against products of firms discriminating against Catholic workers in 1920. Collins, while suspending the boycott and reaching two short-lived pacts with Craig in early 1922, covertly supplied arms to northern Catholics and sought to destabilize the northern state. Partition was thus tolerated by opponents as well as supporters of the Treaty in the belief that it was unsustainable, coupled with concealed relief at the exclusion of a hostile minority while the new state was being constructed out of the revolutionary rubble. Southern nationalists were almost as content as Ulster unionists to abandon their beleaguered co-religionists in order to consolidate their local supremacy. Partition had practical appeal to every party but one, the vulnerable and confused Catholic population of Northern Ireland. For the time being, their voice was scarcely heard. Such was the basis for the claim by one historian that 'Lloyd George found the key to the Irish puzzle where all before him had failed'.

Partition, 1922–1949

Both Irish states survived initiation by civil turmoil, while avoiding open conflict with each other. Sectarian violence in Northern Ireland, though quiescent by summer 1922, generated an enduring and formidable state apparatus for entrenching Protestant supremacy. During the two years following the Derry riots of June 1920, over 400 people died as a result of sectarian or 'political' conflict. Most of these deaths occurred in 1922, when twice as many Catholics were killed as Protestants. Though sometimes spuriously ascribed to 'indiscriminate IRA firing', Catholic casualties were commonly caused by sectarian attacks condoned and often perpetrated by the seemingly uncontrollable 'B Specials'. By comparison, Catholic gang organization was feeble and the IRA remained small and inactive, despite sporadic provision of armament and training by southern supporters as well as opponents of the Treaty. Sectarian violence was matched by state coercion, using the familiar instruments of internment, banishment, and summary justice. The Civil Authorities (Special Powers) Act of April 1922, modelled upon the Restoration of Order in Ireland Act, provided the statutory basis of coercion until 1972. The new government slipped easily into reliance upon political and physical mobilization of Protestant 'loyalists' through sectarian fraternities such as the Orange Order and the Grand Black Chapter.

Protestant supremacy was facilitated by the refusal of many Catholics to exploit their admittedly restricted access to nascent state institutions such as the Royal Ulster Constabulary (May 1922) and the new system of schooling administered by local authorities (1923). The police quota of one Catholic in three could not be filled, while Catholic school managers preferred to retain 'voluntary' status despite loss of state funding. Egged on by the southern provisional government with its strategy of destabilizing Northern Ireland, many Catholic teachers followed the southern curriculum and drew southern salaries until payment was terminated in October 1922. Northern nationalists as well as republicans boycotted parliament until 1925 and participated only fitfully in local government, so making it all the simpler for unionists to gerrymander constituencies and abolish proportional representation at both local and national level (in 1922 and 1929 respectively). The Catholic posture was that of a frightened and alienated minority, sheltering behind priests, fraternities, and Catholic socio-economic networks from the twin menaces of Protestant hostility and unemployment. Protestant ascendancy in Northern Ireland was reinforced though not caused by Catholic repudiation of the new state.

In southern counties the division over acceptance of the Treaty with its oath of fidelity provided enduring rhetoric for future political conflict, and rationalization for civil war. That war did not, however, originate in the collision of incompatible ideologies. De Valera's supporters only gradually slipped from would-be pragmatism into 'pure' republicanism; while Collins's reluctant acceptance of the temporary curtailment of Irish freedom was only slowly translated into the enthusiastic endorsement of the Commonwealth principle voiced by Desmond FitzGerald as minister for external affairs, after the Imperial Conference and 'Balfour Declaration' of 1926. Tactical disagreement erupted into civil war because of the weakness and fragmentation of the agencies which normally restrain armed disputation between citizens. In early 1922 state authority was awkwardly distributed between Griffith's Dáil ministry and Collins's more functional provisional government. The civil service, almost entirely composed of officials from the former administration, operated effectively and conventionally upon transfer of services during 1922. But the provisional government controlled no worthwhile army, police force, or court system, instead being encumbered with the decentralized and squabbling remnants of the revolutionary Volunteers, intelligence network, and Dáil judiciary. The weakness of state authority and elimination of the common adversary allowed factions to flourish in these and other institutions, generating a chessboard pattern of conflict in which neighbouring potentates vied to extend their territorial supremacy.

The strongest Volunteer opposition to the Treaty came from counties such as Cork and Tipperary, where many local warlords were encouraged by their past successes in guerrilla struggle to defy central authority and renew the fight for freedom. Opposition was further concentrated in Dublin itself and in Connacht, where autonomy from central direction had been associated with guerrilla inactivity rather than vitality. Volunteer support for Collins and Mulcahy came from midland commandants such as Michael Brennan of Clare and Seán Mac-Eoin of Longford, whose personal effectiveness had not blinded them to military feebleness elsewhere. The majority of active Volunteers and also republican justices probably opposed the Treaty, as did the bulk of organizers in Sinn Féin and the Cumann na mBan. The obvious fragmentation of the IRB prevented Collins from successfully following Ulster unionist precedent by harnessing the state to the interests of clandestine fraternal networks. This was demonstrated by the 'army mutiny' of 1924, after which Mulcahy's IRB clique as well as the mutineers' Irish Republican Army Organization were thwarted in their competing attempts to control personnel and determine promotions. Meanwhile, the government had hastily constructed a new national army, civic guard, and court system drawing heavily upon former British servicemen, RIC officers, and conventional juridical practice and organization. In the absence of serviceable alternatives, the architects of the new state cobbled together a rough replica of the machinery of coercion and law-enforcement which they had helped overthrow.

Meanwhile, the fracturing of revolutionary structures had made civil war possible but not yet certain. The dissident army council was left undisturbed for eleven weeks after its occupation of the Four Courts in April 1922, while repeated

A SECOND ASSAULT UPON THE FOUR COURTS, this time by the Dublin Fire Brigade, after its surrender by Rory O'Connor's 'Irregular' IRA Executive on 30 June 1922. The seizure of this building by Michael Collins's forces, aided by two 18-pound guns lent by the British army, initiated the Civil War.

attempts were made to retrieve political unity by twisting the draft constitution into a blueprint for external association. Collins and de Valera agreed to inhibit voters from expressing their overwhelming support for the Treaty by presenting a common panel of electoral candidates, retaining the former balance of parliamentary support and rejection. The basis of accord collapsed when Churchill and the cabinet repudiated the proposed mutilation of the Treaty's provisions, forcing the provisional government to give constitutional voice to every element of dominion status. Collins then neatly sabotaged the pact by advising voters to support Labour, farmers', or unaligned candidates in preference to anti-Treaty Sinn Féiners. The effect was to augment support for the new constitution, sharpen political polarization, and ensure republican abstention from the provisional parliament elected on 16 June by an electorate extended to include adult women six years in advance of Northern Ireland.

Fear of armed resistance had already persuaded Collins to procure armaments from his unexpected ally, the colonial secretary Churchill; and British artillery was used to recapture the Four Courts on 28 June after the kidnap of Mulcahy's deputy as chief of staff. Major 'Irregular' military operations were mainly limited to Munster, and Brennan's bloodless occupation of Limerick played a key part in isolating the rebels and making possible their virtual defeat within three months. Resistance then reverted to sniping and assassination (as practised less ruthlessly in early 1921), until despair overcame the remaining terrorists upon execution of seventy-seven untried prisoners beginning in November 1922. Many leaders of both blocs died, including Griffith (of a heart attack), Collins (in an ambush in August), and his old adversary Brugha (in an ostentatious bid for martyrdom). The viciousness exhibited by both factions by comparison with 1920–1 reflected not merely the corrosive effect of war, but also the fact that in 1922 both parties were struggling for military victory rather than seeking the world's admiration for their idealism and virtuous conduct.

Both sides in this sordid conflict nevertheless felt the need to enhance their tarnished legitimacy by regularizing the civil–military relationship. The new provisional government established after Collins's death by William T. Cosgrave placed greater restraint upon the war council and army command; while in October the republican army council gave allegiance to a provisional government of its own under de Valera. In practice the two armies paid scant attention to their political mentors, though Mulcahy exploited the legislature to secure still greater statutory curtailment of civil rights than any enacted in Northern Ireland. About 12,000 opponents of the Treaty and miscellaneous trouble-makers were interned or imprisoned between 1922 and 1924, compared with only 728 internments in the northern state over a similar period; and successive governments of the Free State were all too ready to introduce further 'public safety' measures against militant opponents. Military resistance had, however, crumbled after the death of the republican commander, Liam Lynch. On 24 May 1923 de Valera instructed the quaintly named 'legion of the rearguard' to cease hostilities, so ending a campaign which had caused the death of 800 troops and thousands of 'Irregulars' and civilians (far more than in the War of Independence). The violent challenge to the state then degenerated into a dolorous sequence of murders, robberies, burnings, and kidnappings which has not yet ceased. So the state survived its painful baptism into a faith whose first article was the consolidation of state authority rather than the welfare of the nation.

In contrast to Northern Ireland, most of the victims of state repression were of the majority religion. Since the religious minority of the Free State constituted less than a tenth of the population compared with a third in Northern Ireland, sectarian conflict was more easily avoided. Far from condoning victimization of religious minorities, the Cumann na nGaedheal administration relied increasingly upon their political participation and financial support. The constitution not only avoided reference to the Catholic church and its moral code, but also provided for a second chamber (Seanad Éireann) which was designed to represent minority interests unvoiced in the Dáil, as demanded by southern unionists. Cosgrave nominated a bizarre *mélange* of independent-minded landlords, businessmen, lawyers, trades unionists, and writers, ranging from W. B. Yeats to Lord Glenavy (James Campbell). Apart from occasional murmurs over repressive or divisive measures (such as the inconclusive attempt in 1925 to stifle divorce bills), the senators usually supported the government and worked to avert sectarian confrontation. Cosgrave's success in soliciting co-operation from Protestant bankers and businessmen helped the economy to avoid disaster in the early 1920s. Unlike Collins, Cosgrave made no serious attempt to undermine Protestant supremacy in Northern Ireland. The futile boundary commission of 1925, to which Northern Ireland had refused to accredit a representative, collapsed when Eoin MacNeill resigned upon leakage of its draft report recommending transfers of territory to as well as from the northern state. The Irish Free State then publicly accepted the boundary as set in 1921, virtually terminating its shrill propaganda against partition and its tenuous association with northern nationalist groups.

The stability of the new order was reinforced rather than disturbed by de Valera's secession from Sinn Féin and formation of the Fianna Fáil party in 1926. In August 1927 he led his forty-two elected followers into the Dáil to take the execrated oath of fidelity. Many of his former associates continued to repudiate the legitimacy of the constitution and to subscribe to arcane authorities and dissident organizations ever more torn by faction. But Fianna Fáil at once became the 'slightly constitutional' opposition to a government rattled by the recent assassination of Kevin O'Higgins (Cosgrave's formidable minister for home affairs) and dependent upon minor parties for its survival. The ministry later betrayed its own rather than the state's insecurity by insinuating that Fianna

Fáil was a front organization for revolutionaries scheming to destroy the state, capitalism, and Catholicism. In fact, de Valera was content to use democratic and parliamentary means to achieve power and dismantle the Treaty. After forming its first government with Labour support in February 1932, Fianna Fáil soon discarded the armed IRA well-wishers who had so vigorously protected its candidates during the campaign. Far from abolishing parliament or incarcerating Cumann na nGaedheal, de Valera proceeded over the next decade to observe parliamentary forms, to suppress paramilitary bodies when they menaced state security, and eventually to imprison, intern, and execute republican terrorists.

At first, however, the most alarming challenge to parliamentary rule came not from the IRA but from the National Guard or 'Blueshirts', a professedly Christian and anti-communist volunteer force derived from an association of national army veterans and led by Eoin O'Duffy (whom de Valera had dismissed as commissioner of the civic guard). The Blueshirts aimed from the first to 'promote and maintain social order' and establish corporative organizations to prevent

THE BLUESHIRTS' debt to Mussolini's fascist salute is illustrated by this photograph taken in 1934 at the Bluebell cemetery, Dublin. Yet the choice of location and the use of drums suggests the Irish flavour of this proto-fascist organization.

industrial disputes, offering a blend of muscle and ideology which proved so attractive to opposition politicians that Cosgrave consented to serve under O'Duffy as president of the new United Ireland party (Fine Gael), formed in September 1933. After a year of chaos and violence the opposition repudiated O'Duffy, who soon called upon his diminishing circle of admirers to emulate Mussolini by introducing a vocational register once they had gained control of parliament. By 1935 both major parties had severed their overt links with paramilitary populism and demonstrated their preference for working within the parliamentary system bequeathed by Britain.

By ingenious manipulation of that system, de Valera contrived to undermine first the symbolism and later the substance of dominion status. By doing so he confirmed the truth of Michael Collins's claim that the Treaty gave Ireland 'the freedom to achieve freedom'; though all his zeal and ingenuity could not restore the Gaelic mentality without which Irishmen would not (as Collins wrote in 1922) 'be worthy of the fullest freedom'. Though probably entitled to implement unilateral constitutional amendments under the Statute of Westminster (1931), de Valera's government insisted on deriving its authority 'from the people' rather than imperial enactments. The effect on Anglo-Irish relations was to substitute confrontation for Cosgrave's strategy of reconciliation and constitutional evolution. During 1933 the oath of fidelity and the right of appeal to the privy council were abolished, while the governor general's powers were trivialized. Three years later the increasingly restive senate was indefinitely prorogued, the governorship abolished, and the doctrine of external association given statutory force by restricting the monarch's functions to the accreditation of Irish diplomats. Yet de Valera refrained from proclaiming a republic, ostensibly because no Irish state bereft of its fourth 'green field' deserved that august description. Instead he devised and enacted, in 1937, a new 'constitution of Ireland' on behalf of 'the people of Éire', which laid claim to the entire 'national territory' but limited its jurisdiction to the twenty-six counties 'pending the re-integration of the national territory'. De Valera's constitutional initiatives provoked fury and economic reprisals from Britain's national government, but not Ireland's expulsion from the Commonwealth. Ulster unionists responded to the irredentist claim with anger and contempt, and the cabinet briefly contemplated changing the name of the state to Ulster as a gesture of its separateness.

De Valera's paper victories were offset by the economic costs of confrontation. Under Cosgrave the Free State had achieved marked improvement in real income per capita despite its unadventurous strategy of balancing the budget, avoiding heavy borrowing, limiting state intervention, and merely dabbling in protective measures against British imports. The Irish economy was still tied to the British through absence of alternative trading partners and retention of a unified currency. Irish agricultural exports remained competitive in the British market, though industrial growth was negligible and emigration heavy. This modest achievement was enhanced by comparison with Northern Ireland, where unemployment among insured workers averaged 19 per cent between 1923 and 1930 as a result of industrial decline in shipbuilding and linen production. After 1931, of course, both states suffered heavier unemployment and dislocation of trade as a result of world recession. In Belfast, discontent at the niggardly outdoor relief available to uninsured workers when unemployed was sufficient to generate multi-denominational riots in 1932; while average unemployment among the state's insured workers reached 27 per cent between 1931 and 1939. In the Free State, the effect of recession was greatly intensified by the 'economic war' of 1932–8, the regrettable outcome of British indignation at de Valera's refusal to transfer receipts of land annuities payable by farmers who had received loans under the pre-war land purchase acts. The resultant application of competitive tariffs and quotas on trade between the Free State and the United Kingdom caused irritation in Britain and Northern Ireland but immiseration in the southern state. The subsequent collapse of livestock exports and prices was only feebly counterbalanced by de Valera's ostentatious programme for reviving tillage and subsidizing industrial development. The tariff war proved more effective than partition in separating the economic markets of the two Irish states, to the benefit of Northern Irish agriculture which enjoyed government subsidies and preferential access to the British market. Trade between Éire and the United Kingdom was somewhat revived after April 1938, when Chamberlain applied his appeasement strategy to Ireland by settling the dispute over annuities, removing punitive duties, and surrendering the naval facilities and ports reserved to the United Kingdom under the Treaty. Yet even in 1938 Irish national income per capita was only about 3 per cent higher than in black 1931.

Economic stagnation and isolation fostered the cult of self-sufficiency without frills. Already under Cosgrave the state had intervened to restrict cultural and sexual freedom, by introducing systematic censorship of films (1923) and publications including those promoting contraception (1929). Fianna Fáil reinforced this puritanical code by banning importation and sale of contraceptives in 1935, and by extending the Censorship Board's 'black list' until it provided a comprehensive index of official anxieties as well as a handy guide to modern literature. The state's controls over cinema, reading, and contraception were not substantially relaxed until 1964, 1967, and 1979 respectively. These forlorn attempts to insulate the people from 'Anglicization' were accompanied by still more futile measures to restore the national language and hence, perhaps, the supposed values of Gaelic civilization. Cosgrave's ministry immediately made Irish a compulsory subject in national (primary) schools, and briefly attempted to compel nursery teachers to use the medium of Irish. Fianna Fáil made spirited efforts to infuse the history curriculum with Gaelic and patriotic precepts, and

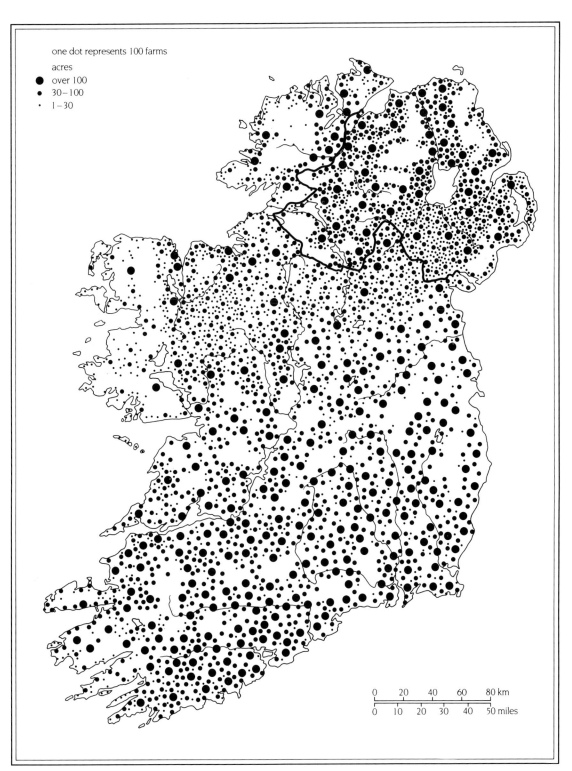

one dot represents 100 farms

acres
● over 100
• 30–100
· 1–30

0   20   40   60   80 km
0   10   20   30   40   50 miles

DISTRIBUTION OF FARMS BY SIZE, *c*.1930

THE IRISH CENSORSHIP BOARD periodically published a 'Black List': this extract drolly brings together Aldous Huxley, Marie Stopes, Radclyffe Hall, and Paul Gauguin as representatives of several shades of obscenity.

SAORSTAT EIREANN.

REGISTER OF PROHIBITED PUBLICATIONS (BOOKS) AS ON THE 31st MARCH, 1931.

No. on Register	Name of Book.	Edition or editions to which Prohibition Order relates.	Name of Author.	Name of Publisher.
			If and as stated in Book.	
1	Point Counter Point ...	All	Aldous Huxley ...	Chatto & Windus, London.
2	Family Limitation ...	All	Margaret Sanger	Rose Whitcop, London.
3	Wise Parenthood ...	All	Marie Stopes ...	G. P. Putnam's Sons, Ltd., London.
4	Home to Harlem ...	All	Claude McKay ...	Harper & Bros., New York and London.
5	On Conjugal Happiness	All English versions	Hofrat Dr. L. Lowenfeld ...	John Bale, Sons & Danielsson, London.
6	Married Love ...	All	Marie Stopes ...	G. P. Putnam's Sons, Ltd., London.
7	Early days of Birth Control.	All	do.	do.
8	Contraception ...	All	do.	do.
9	Radiant Motherhood ...	All	do.	do.
10	The New Motherhood	All	Margaret Sanger	Jonathan Cape, London.
11	The Pivot of Civilisation	All	do.	do.
12	What every Mother Should Know.	All	do.	do.
13	The Well of Loneliness ...	All	Radclyffe Hall ...	Civici Friede, New York.
14	Marriage and Morals ...	All	Bertrand Russell	Geo. Allen & Unwin, Ltd., London.
15	Class 1902	All English versions	Ernst Glaeser ...	Martin Secker, London.
16	The Intimate Journals of Paul Gauguin.	do.	Paul Gauguin ...	W. Heinemann, Ltd., London.
17	Schlump	All English versions	—	Martin Secker, London.
18	The Ant Heap ...	All	Edward Knoblock	Chapman & Hall Ltd., London.
19	The Party Dress ...	All	Joseph Hergesheimer.	A. A. Knopf, London.
20	Brief Candles... ...	All	Aldous Huxley ...	Chatto & Windus, London.
21	Redheap	All	Norman Lindsay	Faber & Faber, Ltd., London.
22	Sex and Its Mysteries ...	All	George Ryley Scott.	J. Bale, Sons & Danielsson, London.

declared Irish to be the 'first official language' in the 1937 constitution. The effects of cultural coercion were often negative. Censorship nurtured a dissident counter-culture which generated much of the finest Irish writing of the century; compulsory inculcation of the language failed to revive its vernacular use and virtually killed the Gaelic League and cultural revival; even subsidies for 'Gaeltacht' regions with clusters of Irish speakers failed to counteract the brighter attraction of American and English life for young people still largely reared for emigration. Only in Northern Ireland did Irish speech and culture retain their glittering appeal in the teeth of Protestant and official antipathy.

In one respect, however, social practice largely coincided with state ideology. To a greater extent than in most countries, the institution of marriage continued to contain most sexual activity. Despite abnormally late and infrequent marriage for both sexes, illegitimate births, infanticide, and abortion remained rare. The illegality of abortion was given constitutional force in 1983, while the interdiction of remarriage after divorce contained in the 1937 constitution was confirmed by huge majorities in most constituencies at a referendum held in 1986. Within marriage fertility remained relatively high despite long-term decline which accelerated in the 1960s. In Northern Ireland, where statutory controls over family and sexual life were progressively though tardily relaxed according to British precedent, the demographic profile was more 'Irish' than British despite evidence of more extensive use of contraception within marriage by northern Protestants than by Catholics. Emigration from both states continued to provide an essential

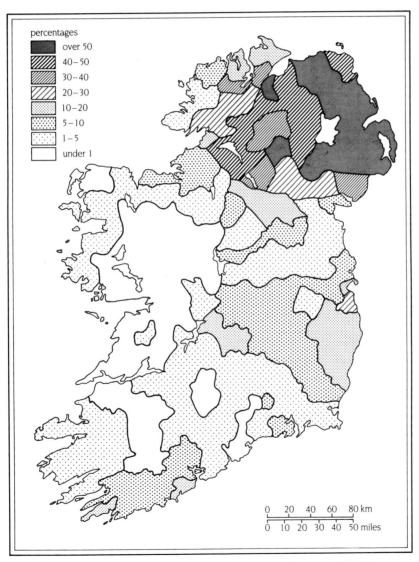

PERCENTAGE OF PROTESTANTS IN EACH RURAL DISTRICT, 1936-7

CROWDS LEAVING CATHOLIC MASS at Finglas, Dublin, in 1950, indicating heavy male attendance, absence of contraception, and (less typically of Ireland) sunshine.

escape route for men and particularly women who found the property match repugnant and the repression of sexuality outside marriage unacceptable. For the residual Catholic population, the moral code which governed the public expression of their private lives was closer to Victorian puritanism than to Gaelic licentiousness. Victorianism had its last and least predictable efflorescence in the country whose political rhetoric was most Anglophobic.

The family and sexual organization of modern Ireland, though ultimately the product of economic stagnation and selective emigration, was vigorously monitored and reinforced by the Catholic and to some degree the Protestant churches. Despite the misgivings of many bishops, the social programmes of 'Catholic Action' were implemented with spectacular effect in the Irish Free State. Menaces to public morality such as communists, bigamists, and prostitutes were pursued relentlessly by lay organizations including the Knights of St Columbanus (1915), the Legion of Mary (1921), and a host of parish guilds, sodalities, and fraternities. Catholic pressure groups skilfully manipulated journalists and politicians in their pursuit of communal purification; while fraternities such as the Hibernians and the Knights furthered the process of securing preferential employment for Catholics in competition with the freemasons and the forces of evil which they allegedly represented. The hierarchy rapidly achieved Catholic supremacy in the Free State despite the constitutional guarantees of religious liberty. After their excommunication of all practising Irregulars in August 1922, the bishops were rewarded for their support by Cosgrave's insistence that all legislation with moral implication be submitted to church leaders for approval before its introduction in the Dáil. Cumann na nGaedheal and the church were at one in regarding the Free State as a Catholic rather than pluralist society, a precept which went unchallenged by both the Labour Party and Fianna Fáil. The hierarchy, though hostile to de Valera up to 1932, soon succumbed to his honeyed if convoluted flattery, permitting the 'long fellow' as well as Cosgrave to bear the papal legate's canopy at Dublin's eucharistic congress in June 1932. Fianna Fáil proved to be less deferential but more adroit than its opponents in handling the hierarchy, and as a result of extensive prior consultation with Jesuit theologians secured church endorsement for the controversial 1937 constitution, with its grandiloquent preamble 'in the Name of the Most Holy Trinity'. Though the church remained unestablished in a state required to 'respect and honour religion', its 'special position . . . as the guardian of the Faith professed by the great majority of the citizens' was constitutionally recognized until 1972. By discarding the forms of secularism de Valera added new flavour to the sectarian apologetics of Ulster unionism, confirming Craig's dictum of 1934 that 'they still boast of Southern Ireland being a Catholic State. All I boast of is that we are a Protestant Parliament and a Protestant State.' In both states, the twin evils of secular education and sexual licence were ecumenically condemned. The Irish museum of puritanism straddled the border.

In September 1939, the declaration of war on Germany brought Éire's separation from the United Kingdom under renewed strain. Having retrieved the 'Treaty ports' in 1938, de Valera reversed his earlier assumption that Éire would be sucked into any European conflict on Britain's side, and proclaimed its neutrality during the 'National Emergency'. Neutral status enabled Dublin to become a thriving centre for mutual espionage despite British and later American indignation at German activity. Churchill's choleric demands for reoccupation of the ports were stifled, but Éire suffered from secret reimposition of trading sanctions in December 1940 and derived little economic benefit from the war. American aid was also curtailed in response to de Valera's refusal to close enemy legations despite the pugnacious campaign conducted in 1943 by Roosevelt's minister in Dublin (David Gray). De Valera rejected bribes and threats with equal disdain, ignoring Chamberlain's offer in June 1940 to barter the 'declaration of a United Ireland in principle' for Éire's entry into the wartime alliance. In practice Éire gave extensive informal help to the United Kingdom by initiating joint military consultations in May 1940, releasing Allied but not German airmen and planes violating its aerospace, and abetting the enlistment in the RAF and other forces of tens of thousands of its citizens. Had Germany threatened to invade Ireland, de Valera's covert support for the Allies would undoubtedly have given place to overt desire for their military assistance. As it was, neutrality endured and Éire's wartime losses were minimized by de Valera's adroit manœuvring; though German bombers ignored the border and killed 34 Dubliners in May 1941, six weeks after the death of 700 people in Belfast's most lethal raid. Neutrality was so clearly expedient that no influential politician save James Dillon (son of John and deputy leader of Fine Gael) dared demand military co-operation with the Allies. In Britain and Northern Ireland, where unionist indignation was compounded by the success of the nationalist campaign against conscription, neutrality had strongly negative consequences. The Emergency thus softened domestic political conflict at the cost of further isolating Éire within the British Isles, as became evident in 1949. On Easter Monday (18 April), John

Aloysius Costello's inter-party government belatedly filched the old slogan of its Fianna Fáil antagonist by inaugurating a republic. Though an empty and hasty gesture, Costello's severance of the rusty Commonwealth link provoked the bleak undertaking in the subsequent Ireland Act 'that in no event will Northern Ireland or any part thereof cease to be part of His Majesty's dominions and of the United Kingdom without the consent of the parliament of Northern Ireland'. The Treaty had been shredded at last, yet partition endured, jagged as a seismic fault.

Fragmentation Since 1949

In the aftermath of the war, both states experienced economic and social transformation. Northern Ireland's economic revival had begun during the war, causing real income per capita to rise by 84 per cent between 1938 and 1947 (six times the increase recorded for Éire). After the war Northern Ireland, but not yet the Republic, replicated the novel amenities of Labour's welfare state, developing an educational system and health service scarcely less ambitious than those created in Britain. During Sir Basil Brooke's term as prime minister (1943–63) industrial expansion was encouraged by state intervention and extensive foreign investment. In the Republic average income remained lower, social

GERMAN AIR-RAIDS ON BELFAST, 1941, left much of the city devastated. On 4 May 204 aircraft dropped 95,000 incendiaries on the harbour and shipyards, killing 150. This shows the view from High Street across Bridge Street during the clearing-up operations afterwards.

ORDERLY REMOVAL OF QUEEN VICTORIA'S STATUE from the courtyard of Leinster House, seat of the Irish parliament. The statue's humiliation occurred on 22 July 1948, shortly before Costello's declaration of the Republic.

welfare more restrictive and parsimonious, industrial growth more sluggish. Indeed, it was not until just before de Valera's ascension to the presidency in 1959 that a policy of economic expansion was first implemented under Sean Lemass as minister for industry and taoiseach (1959–66). The foundation of the 'economic miracle' was provision of inducements for foreign investors within a tightly balanced budget, as proposed by the orthodox secretary to the Department of Finance (T. K. Whitaker). The great Irish experiment in deficit financing was delayed until the mid-1970s, when successive governments responded imprudently to the energy crisis and entry to the European Economic Community in 1973 by accumulating crippling debts with consequences yet to be exhausted. Urbanization and rapid expansion of public-sector employment were achieved at the expense of simultaneously high rates of inflation and unemployment. The overall impact of economic expansion since 1958 has been to destroy the predominance of the rural economy and to destabilize the associated social and family structures. Even in agricultural regions the property match and the 'stem family' system of farm succession could no longer be sustained, though the massive emigration which formerly propped up that system has outlived it. During the 1970s civil conflict caused still sharper economic decline in Northern

THE ECONOMIC MIRACLE. A Dublin beggar of the 1950s, whose children probably have similar occupation today.

Ireland than in other peripheral regions of the British Isles, the impact being mitigated by abnormally generous state subventions in such sectors as shipbuilding. Urban unemployment became still greater than that in the Republic, though the disparity in average income and welfare provision has yet to be eliminated. Despite the improvement in living standards in both states, Ireland is still one of the poorest parts of Europe and seems likely to remain so.

The political cultures of Ireland have proved more resilient than the economic and social structures from which they emerged. Urbanization and social disruption have failed to break the dominance in the Republic of the two parties which grew out of the civil war, despite their steady convergence in ideology and class support. Fianna Fáil has long since shed its spurious social radicalism and Fine Gael its conservatism, while parties such as Labour remain unable to

WAITING FOR THE END, BOYS. Good-humoured policemen and a patient crowd await civil rights demonstrators in Derry on 16 November 1968.

induce most voters to determine their political affiliation according to class rather than faction. The recent referenda on abortion and divorce demonstrated the undiminished supremacy of Catholic moral precepts in politics, and the church's determination and ability to counteract the cultural 'pluralism' promulgated by Garret FitzGerald as taoiseach and Fine Gael leader in the 1980s. In Northern Ireland, political affiliation remains almost exclusively sectarian despite attempts to diminish discrimination against Catholics during Terence O'Neill's tenure as prime minister (1963–9) and after imposition of direct rule from Westminster. The cross-denominational Alliance Party, founded in 1970, remains short of Catholic and indeed Protestant support. Since 1965, when Eddie McAteer's Nationalist Party at last became the official opposition to O'Neill's unionists, politicians of the minority have become more integrated than before in the political process without broadening their appeal beyond the Catholic population. Yet the sad consequence of O'Neill's half-fulfilled promise of reform and reconciliation was to raise Catholic expectations without satisfying them, so creating the conditions for renewed collective protest after formation of the Northern Ireland Civil Rights Association in February 1967. The major alignments of Irish politics today are those of 1922, religion being the primary affiliation in Northern Ireland and civil war pedigree in the Republic.

The first official gestures indicating shared desire to diminish cross-border polarization were performed in January and February 1965, when Lemass and O'Neill met first in Belfast and then in Dublin. These meetings inaugurated no process of administrative integration, though similar discussions were held at Stormont in December 1967. *Rapprochement* was reversed in 1968–70, when members of Jack Lynch's Fianna Fáil ministry were implicated in the provision of arms for the IRA in its supposed role as protector of the Catholic community during the campaign for civil rights in Northern Ireland. This astonishing indiscretion persuaded many Ulster unionists that subsequent southern governments were disingenuous in their condemnation of terrorism, despite the vigorous suppression of the IRA accomplished in the Republic as well as Northern Ireland during the 'border campaign' which had ended in February 1962. Militant Protestants, increasingly bellicose in their assertion of an 'Ulster' identity distinct from both Irish and British nationality, have continued to oppose British attempts to involve Dublin overtly in northern political management. The Sunningdale conference of December 1973, which established a 'power-sharing executive' incorporating unionists, the Alliance Party, and the nationalist Social Democratic and Labour Party (founded in 1970), included representatives of the Dublin as well as London governments. Though the issue of reunification was shelved, the conference agreed to establish a new Council of Ireland with equal northern and southern representation and wide-ranging powers. After a devastatingly methodical and effective stoppage of essential services by the Ulster

A LOAD OF RUBBISH. Some consequences of the strike organized in May 1974 by the Ulster Workers' Council in Belfast.

Workers' Council in May 1974, Britain abandoned the agreement and reimposed direct rule (first applied in March 1972). In 1985 the British government tried to circumvent unionist intransigence by negotiating a bilateral agreement for liaison in security and civil administration with the Irish government at Hillsborough. The granting of a consultative role to southern politicians and civil servants immediately reunited Ulster unionists in their insistence that 'Ulster says no'. That negation seems as unanswerable today as it did in 1914 or 1922.

The significance of the 'Troubles' which have destabilized Northern Ireland since the disturbances over Catholic civil rights in 1968 cannot be assessed while

AN ELABORATE RECRUITING POSTER, issued in 20,000 copies by HMSO in July 1916. It sought to excite nationalist sentiment by depiction of a piper with a beast reminiscent of an Irish wolfhound, a sunburst, and the unofficial national flag with its uncrowned gold harp on green. Despite inclusion in the canton of a device suggesting the Royal Inniskilling Fusiliers, these colours could not have been carried by any wartime regiment.

THE CALL TO ARMS

IRISHMEN
DONT YOU HEAR IT?

DAVID ALLEN & SONS Ltd
40. Gt. Brunswick St.
DUBLIN.
(Copyright Apd.)

TWO ALLEGORICAL IMAGES OF WOMEN. A postcard published by William Strain and Son (Belfast) depicts Ulster as a female able if not eager to handle a rifle. By contrast, the poster showing 'The Birth of the Irish Republic—1916' (produced at the Art Depot, 6 Mary Street, Dublin) pictures an unarmed female figure ineffectually waving an olive branch as she is borne aloft upon the backlash of her menfolk's rifle-fire.

they continue. The carnage has somewhat exceeded that recorded for the much briefer War of Independence. Between 1969 and mid-1983 some 2,305 deaths were officially attributed to political or sectarian conflict, of which about 700 depleted the security forces. Since 1972, the year of most intensive civil conflict during which 467 people died, casualties have tended to diminish as a result of more effective policing and military deployment as well as more precisely targeted terrorist activity. There is, however, no clear negative correlation between the intensity of state coercion and of carnage. The period of internment of both republican and loyalist suspects (1971–5) coincided with the years of heaviest fatality. Moreover, the transition from relatively peaceful collective protest to lethal violence was a calculated response by frustrated republicans to the British government's attempt to reorganize policing and provide military backing, even though the army's initial function was to protect Catholics from attack by Protestant gangs. The 'Provisional' faction of the IRA, which has dominated the fractured networks of militant republicanism since December 1969, adroitly exploited military insensitivity in order to redirect Catholics' indignation from their Protestant neighbours towards Britain and its 'army of occupation'. Anglophobia was intensified after 'Bloody Sunday' (30 January 1972) when thirteen people were killed by soldiers in Derry. As the security forces rendered themselves less vulnerable and eventually less obnoxious, terrorism was readdressed to sectarian and factional targets, which accounted for the majority of killings in 1975. Recently many killings, knee-cappings, and other 'punishments' have affected suspected 'informers' and deviants within religious groups rather than targets across the communal divide. The political organizations associated with terrorist gangs have achieved only modest support, and the tiny cells of gunmen and bombers cannot claim the communal loyalty which sustained the Volunteers of 1920–1. Yet the separation of both Catholic and Protestant terrorists from most of their co-religionists has not undermined the military effectiveness of gangs whose level of training and armament exceeds the dreams of their less cynical precursors. The killing of eleven bystanders awaiting the Remembrance Sunday ceremony at Enniskillen on 8 November 1987 demonstrated the resilience as well as the vindictiveness of the IRA despite the protracted struggle by the security forces to suppress terrorism. Even so, the state's achievement in reducing the intensity of violence is heartening by comparison with, say, Lebanon. Life goes on.

The outbreak of armed conflict between northern Catholics and Protestants marked the failure of partition. We have seen that partition created two states whose legitimacy was long denied by substantial minorities and whose survival was secured through initial repression. Each state confounded the prediction of the other that it would prove incapable of averting economic, social, or political breakdown. The Troubles have belatedly demonstrated the futility of a constitutional 'settlement' which left the Catholic third of Northern Ireland's population to fend for itself in a state whose rulers regarded Catholics rather as Joshua and the chosen people regarded the unfortunate inhabitants of Jericho. No doubt more sensitive and skilful government might have averted the translation of disaffection into violence; yet it is difficult even with hindsight to propose an alternative settlement capable of eradicating the underlying disaffection. Yeats has yet to be proven wrong in his pessimism:

> Out of Ireland have we come.
> Great hatred, little room,
> Maimed us at the start.

6

Irish Literature and Irish History

DECLAN KIBERD

Irish Literature and Irish Politics

THE points in history at which literature and politics meet have been described as a 'bloody crossroads'. Romantic impulses, derived from literature, allegedly lead to carnage and terror in a city's streets. Conor Cruise O'Brien has gone so far as to deride the ancient Irish collaboration between nationalism and art as 'an unhealthy intersection'. There is, however, a counter-argument to the effect that art is too potent a force to be left entirely in the hands of its creators, and politics too pervasive in its effects to be left in the sole control of politicians. There is no doubt that most conservative nationalists seek, at a certain point, to aestheticize politics, if only to distract attention from their failure to redistribute economic wealth; but, as Walter Benjamin said, it is always possible, by way of response, to politicize art.

Ever since the Romantic movement, critics have been properly distrustful of the claim of poets to be the unacknowledged legislators of the world. Shelley, when he lodged that claim, emphasized that the power was unacknowledged, even by poets themselves; but, in our own century, W. H. Auden took those reservations a stage further, arguing that such a description better fitted the secret police. In his elegy for W. B. Yeats he remarked that 'poetry makes nothing happen'; and elsewhere he contended that 'art is not life and cannot be / a midwife to society'. Yet Oliver St. John Gogarty, one of the first senators of an independent Ireland could stand and suggest, in full seriousness, that without the poetry of W. B. Yeats, he and his colleagues would not be representatives of an independent state. That was an exaggeration, but not a swaggering one. Yeats's poetry had, after all, entailed a repossession—a revision, in the sense of 'seeing again'—of an authentically Irish landscape; and it is for this that he is celebrated throughout the world as one of the foremost poets of decolonization. Michael Collins, one of the military leaders of the Irish independence movement noted: 'We only succeeded after we had begun to get back our Irish ways . . . after we had made a serious effort to speak our own language, after we had striven again to govern ourselves.'

This is to say that Ireland's successful declaration of political separation occurred after, rather than before, those assertions of cultural independence implicit in the foundation of the Gaelic Athletic Association (1884) and the Gaelic League (1893). This is, by most standards, unusual. The United States had, after all, enjoyed political sovereignty for more than half a century before Ralph Waldo Emerson's lecture on *The American Scholar* signalled the start of the American Renaissance. The relationship between politics and culture in Ireland, by way of contrast, was dialectical. The institution of literature was not just a storehouse of lore and wisdom over centuries for a dispossessed people; it was also a kind of dynamo, gathering energies into focus and releasing more. Standish James O'Grady, the man dubbed by Yeats as 'the father of the Irish Revival', caught the balance exactly when he predicted, towards the end of the nineteenth century, that a cultural movement ('which will not be very important') would be followed by a political movement ('which will not be very important'), and that, in turn, would give way to a military movement ('which would be very important indeed').

w. b. yeats by john butler yeats. 'Every Irish writer must either express Ireland or exploit her', wrote Yeats. Tiring of a career as a professional Celt in London, Yeats returned to Dublin in the 1890s with the aim of creating a national literature and gathering a native audience. He made folk-tales and fairy-lore the basis of his own poetry, and of the major plays of the Irish National Theatre Society. This romantic portrait by his father emphasizes their common conviction of the enduring importance of emotion and their distrust of the calculating intellect of the emerging middle class.

men of the south by sean keating. A major burden of the War of Independence was borne by 'flying columns', which traversed the countryside, launching surprise attacks on British forces and enjoying sanctuary with sympathetic farmers. Though treated as terrorists by the British authorities, they were cast by Irish artists in heroic mode.

STATUE OF CUCHULAIN. 'A statue's there, by Oliver Sheppard done', wrote Yeats, 'there' being the General Post Office, Dublin, site of the Easter Rising in 1916. Many rebels saw themselves as re-enacting the warrior-exploits of Cuchulain, who defended the Gap of the North despite many wounds, until a raven alighted on his shoulder and drank his blood.

Many of the young men who joined the rebels of 1916 did so in the belief that they were re-enacting the sacrifice of Cuchulain, that ancient Celtic hero who defended the Gap of the North against all comers, even unto death. This knowledge of Cuchulain had been reopened to them by O'Grady's *History of Ireland* (1878–80); but, by a paradox of history, the author's intention had been to employ the figure as a model to regenerate the declining pride and self-esteem of the aristocracy. That Cuchulain should have been appropriated by the lower-middle-class clerks and schoolmasters who wanted nothing more than to erase that aristocracy was just the first of many ironies, the most recent of which is the adoption of the hero as a role-model by the Protestant paramilitary grouping known as the Ulster Defence Association. There is poetic justice in this, for what Cuchulain defended, after all, was the entry-point to the north of Ireland. Clearly, there are those in the private armies, as well as those in public houses, who believe that, in certain circumstances, life may and should be made to imitate art.

The Social Power of Art

This is, among other things, a tribute to the abiding power in Ireland of an ancient literary tradition which was, from the outset, heavily implicated in the world of politics and militarism. Battles were fought over books. St Colmcille went into exile on Iona as an act of reparation, it is said, for a battle triggered off by his illicit appropriation of a sacred text. The number and exactions of poets grew to such an extent that political leaders felt obliged to control their behaviour and regulate their recruitment at the Convention of Druim Ceat (575), or so later priestly historians claimed.

These critics of the poets had their reasons, for the ancient Gaelic *file* was believed to have semi-mystical powers, thought by some to overlap with those of the Druids. Certainly, the poets were issued with a wand at their ritual investiture; and it is said that they, in turn, had a central role to play in the

BOOK OF KELLS. The pictured scribe in a scriptorium is a detail from the eighth folio of this illuminated manuscript of the four Gospels. The coiled, snakelike circularity of the initial lettering is typical of much early Celtic art, which found in circles intimations of eternity. Centuries later, the citizens who walked in circles through Joyce's Dublin found in that shape the sign of monotony, repetition, and boredom—but the obsession with circles remains.

investiture of a chieftain or king. Even the more powerful rulers treated poets with some circumspection, for it was widely believed that they had the capacity to curse their enemies, including those chieftains who refused patronage, and to bless with prosperity those who looked after them. They could raise blisters of shame, like the legendary harlot's curse, on the foreheads of their victims, with the result that chieftains preferred to harness these forces against their enemies rather than risk the sharp cuts of a spurned bard's tongue. As is usually the case when satire flourishes, the underlying attitude to poetry was classical, in the sense that the artists saw themselves as gifted verbalizers of certain social and political norms, whose infractions were mercilessly punished by a power that verged on enchantment and was based on a culture of shame.

The ancient *file* was celebrated for two basic functions—he kept a record of laws, and told fluent, magnificent tales. All laws are, in one sense, lies, representing as they do an ideal aspiration rather than actual practice, but the way in which the work of *file* (poet) and *breitheamh* (judge) overlapped in ancient times suggests that Irish cynicism about the forces of law and order has an ancient pedigree, predating by centuries the onset of English colonialist codes. Nobody was more cynical than the law-makers themselves. They told wild stories of violent deeds and hard travelling, and to these stories even the canny and hard-headed men of Ulster gave their assent. 'What you say is incredible', they told their chief poet Aimhirgin, 'but we believe you, because you are a poet, and if a poet says that a thing is true, then it is indeed a fact.' This may be interpreted to mean that the poets have the power to change reality by their words, or as an early Celtic affirmation that 'a poem should not mean but be': poetry being based on a truth of internal coherence rather than on external correspondence to a known world.

No matter how far back one looks in Irish experience (or forward to the plays of Oscar Wilde and J. M. Synge), one comes upon regimes or rebels devoted to the sanctification of the lie—a process augmented, though not originated, by the arrival of Norman colonizers in 1169. Words have always been the last weapons of the disarmed, and the elaboration of a compensating inner world of fantasy is a feature of the psychology of most colonized and even post-colonial peoples, apparent today in the fabulistic techniques which link many Irish novelists to those of India or Latin America. But there were eminently practical uses for this tradition as well. In countryside overrun by foreign armies, lying to officials could be seen as a highly moral activity, which could save a family or even a whole townland from ruin. The Irishman's reputation for deceit, guile, and wordplay is not only the result of the distrust nursed among natives of all colonizers; it is also the logical outcome of a life of political oppression. Sir John Davies, the poet who presided over the Ulster Plantation of the early seventeenth century, admitted this when he wrote: 'This oppression did of force and necessity make

MACSWEENEY DINES AS BARD RECITES. The work of the *file* or poet was recited to the accompaniment of a stringed instrument, a tradition revived by Yeats, who had Florence Farr speak his poems to the psaltery. The *reacaire* or reciter was a subordinate employee of the bardic composer, who sat by the chieftain (his patron) enjoying his own composition. Note the strategic use of a fire to warm frozen posteriors.

the Irish a craftie people; for such as are oppressed and live in slavery are ever put to their shifts.' Irony, ambiguity, and downright lying flourished as modes of self-protection as well as being graces of literary style.

Gaelic bards were perceived as a particular obstacle by the colonizers, not just because they epitomized a cultural tradition which the occupiers hoped to destroy, but, more practically, because they were figures of political influence in their own right, second only to the chieftains, to whom they sat next in council. They were, in effect, publicists, appointed to celebrate the exploits of their ruler in strict quatrains, or to mourn the dead warriors who fell while fighting for him in battle. Eochaidh Ó hEodhusa, bard to Maguire of Fermanagh from 1586 to 1602, was his chieftain's foremost strategist, as well as his lyric celebrant. It is true that some poets offered their services to the highest bidder, with all the cynicism of latter-day advertising executives, even if that bidder was part of the new colonial dispensation. This tradition went back at least to the fourteenth century, when Gofraidh Fionn Ó Dálaigh wrote:

> I ndán na nGall gealltair linne
> Gaodhil d'ionnarba a hÉirinn;
>   Gaill do shraoineadh tar sáil soir
>   I ndán na nGaoidhil gealltair.

> In a poem for the foreigner we promise
> That the Gael will be driven from Ireland;
>   The expulsion of the foreigner eastwards across the sea
>   Is promised in a poem for the Gael.

In general, however, it is fair to say that most of the bards were identified irrevocably with the destiny of their Gaelic patrons, not just in their own minds, but in the mind of the colonizer. As Edmund Spenser wrote: 'It hath ever been the use of the conqueror to despise the language of the conquered, and to force him by all means to learn his. . . . the speech being Irish, the heart must needs be Irish.' Accordingly, during Spenser's own sojourn in Munster, its president, Sir George Carew, had the Gaelic manuscripts of the province cut up to make covers for the English-language primers even then being put into circulation among schoolchildren. 'We must change their course of government, clothing,

Iryſhe,   Latten,   Engliſhe,

IRISH PRIMER PREPARED FOR QUEEN.
A knowledge of Latin is as helpful to the student of today's Irish language as it was to those Irish-speakers compelled to learn English in the days of Elizabeth I. However, today's primers would show fewer errors in the English translation!

Iryſhe	Latten	Engliſhe
Coney ta tu,	Quomodo habes,	How doe you.
Taim ɣo maih,	Bene ſum.	I am well,
ɣo ʃo maih aɣav,	Habeo gratias,	I thancke you,
Jn tolʋ ɣt ɣealaɣ	Poſſis ne }	Cann you }
vo lauaiʃv, }	hibernice loqui, }	ſpeake Iryſhe
Abaiʃ laʋven.	Dic latine.	Speake Latten
Dia leʃiuean }	Deus adiuat }	God saue the
ʃaɣona }	Regina Angliæ }	Queene off Englande.

customs, manner of holding land, language, and habit of life', he explained; 'it will otherwise be impossible to set up in them obedience . . .' Sir John Davies, writing out of his Ulster experience in 1612, claimed that these policies were already bearing fruit, having 'reclaimed the Irish from their wildness, caused them to cut off their glibs and long hair; to convert their mantles into cloaks, to conform themselves to the manner of England in all their behaviour and outward forms. . . . So as we may conceive and hope, that the next generation will in tongue and heart and every way else become English: so as there will be no difference or distinction but the Irish Sea betwixt us.' Even in 1612, the clothes a person wore were seen as a political statement, no less than the language in which that person chose to speak.

Philip Edwards has found most remarkable in the writings of Elizabethan intellectuals concerning Ireland 'their inability to contemplate, even as a thesis to be disproved, that the Irish might have a case for resistance'. Certainly, the blustering Irish officer Macmorris in Shakespeare's *Henry V* betrays those propensities for violence, excitability, and garrulity which would soon become the hallmarks of the stage stereotype. Nor was Sir Walter Raleigh alone in his imperviousness to Irish culture. Spenser scanned the work of some Gaelic bards with amused curiosity and made a polite noise about its flowery imagery; but, in general, he concurred with the colonialist view that the bards were abettors of barbarism, because 'by their ditties, they do encourage lords and gentlemen', by which he meant Gaelic lords and Gaelic gentlemen.

Ireland as Woman

One of the most ancient and, in the event, subversive conceits in bardic tradition was the notion that the land was a woman, to be worshipped, wooed, and won, if necessary by death.

A full understanding of this conceit, however, can only be gained by analysing a prior metaphor, according to which the poet was *married* to his chieftain, with whom he had the right to share a bed. This has led some readers to posit a homo-erotic content in many praise-poems, especially in view of the fact that the physical attractions of the ruler's visage were described by many poets in precisely the same terms which they had already used to celebrate their actual lady-love. It has recently been suggested that the Hag of Beare poem from the ninth century, in which a spent and discarded old harlot recalls her varied lovers before retiring in repentance to a monastery, is really a metaphorical account of an aged bard who, having served disparate masters, has nowhere to go but into a Christian monastery. This tradition of androgyny, by which a male poet speaks in the persona of a woman, was taken up by many poets of the Irish revival, from Pearse to Yeats. The latter's Crazy Jane poems were, indeed, prompted by the Hag of Beare sequence.

In his symbolic marriage to the chieftain, the poet foretold the fortunes of the actual land under that lord's jurisdiction. The underlying thinking is almost universal—if the ruler was wise and good, then the land was fertile and beautiful, like the splendid woman of tradition; but, if he was incompetent or wicked, and the poet went uninspired and unrewarded, then the land lay unproductive and fallow, like a cursed bride. From this conceit sprang the perennial notion of Ireland as a woman. Sometimes she was imagined as a mother, with strong or betraying sons, depending on the mood of the poet. Patrick Pearse's *The Mother* (spoken in the persona of his own mother, as her sons prepare to face the firing-squad for their part in the 1916 Rebellion) is a version of the optimistic tradition of strong sons, whereas his *Mise Éire* is the classic version of the pessimistic moment:

> Mise Éire;
> Sine mé ná an Cailleach Béarra.
>
> Mór mo ghlóire;
> Mé do rug Cuchulain cróga.
>
> Mór mo náire;
> Mo chlann féin do dhíol a máthair.
>
> Mise Éire;
> Uaigní mé ná an Cailleach Béarra.
>
> (I am Ireland;
> I am older than the Hag of Beare.
>
> Great my glory;
> I who bore the brave Cuchulain.
>
> Great my shame;
> My own children who sold their mother.
>
> I am Ireland;
> I am lonelier than the Hag of Beare.)

In the 'optimistic' tradition, the strong sons would willingly go into battle to redeem their mother's shame. A variant of this may be found in W. B. Yeats's explosive drama *Cathleen ni Houlihan* (1902), in which a withered hag walks again like a radiant young queen, but only when young men are willing to kill and

MAUD GONNE IN *CATHLEEN NI HOULIHAN*. Her performance in Yeats's play stirred its audience with the prospect of revolution. To the insurrectionist republican P. S. O'Hegarty it was 'a sort of sacrament'; to the rebel countess Markievicz 'a kind of gospel'; but the constitutional nationalist Stephen Gwynn left the theatre convinced that such plays should not be produced unless people were willing to shoot and be shot. A Belfast production in the 1980s was backed by a banner quoting Pearse: 'Ireland Unfree Shall Never Be At Peace.'

die for her in a political insurrection. This had such a heady effect on the young men who first saw it—with Maud Gonne the nationalist leader in the title role—that it fed the forces of extra-parliamentary separatism, leading the constitutionalist Stephen Gwynn to ask whether such plays should be permitted unless young men were willing to pay with their lives. In a late poem, Yeats asked himself if 'that play of mine sent out / Certain men the English shot?'

There were, inevitably, other versions of Ireland as woman, with England most often cast in the part of invasive and predatory male. Even in our own time, a poem like Seamus Heaney's *Act of Union* can describe the Anglo-Irish relation in terms of a doomed marriage between a pregnant wife (the baby battering the walls of her womb being, presumably, the embryonic violence in the north of Ireland) and an aloof, unconcerned husband:

> Your back is a firm line of eastern coast
> And arms and legs are thrown
> Beyond your gradual hills. I caress
> The heaving province where our past has grown.
> I am the tall kingdom over your shoulder
> That you would neither cajole nor ignore.
> Conquest is a lie. I grow older
> Conceding your half-independent shore
> Within whose borders now my legacy
> Culminates inexorably.
>
> And I am still imperially
> Male, leaving you with the pain,
> The rending process in the colony,
> The battering ram, the boom burst from within.
> The act sprouted an obstinate fifth column
> Whose stance is growing unilateral.
> His heart beneath your heart is a wardrum
> Mustering force. His parasitical
> And ignorant little fists already
> Beat at your borders and I know they're cocked
> At me across the water. No treaty
> I foresee will salve completely your tracked
> And stretchmarked body, the big pain,
> That leaves you raw, like opened ground, again.

The metaphor seems by now too blatant to be truly poetic, and too archaic to capture the complex psychology of the contemporary Anglo-Irish confrontation; but it would be hard to overestimate the force of the tradition in its day. (For a fourteenth-century version, see p. 89 above.) Outlaw poets of the seventeenth and eighteenth centuries spoke of a woman, variously named Cathleen ni Houlihan or Cáit ní Dhuibhir, who would duly be liberated by the proper male. Many ostensible love-poems such as *Éamonn an Chnoic* turn out under scrutiny to be patriotic or insurrectionary statements, which could not be overtly made for fear of summary execution; just as, at a much later stage, many apparently political poems, like Yeats's *Easter 1916*, may also be read intelligently as love-lyrics.

The authors of the eighteenth-century *Aisling* poems evoked in luscious detail the image of a passive, blonde *spéirbhean* (skywoman), filled with vague longing and half-articulated desire, awaiting her deliverer—a figure, in short, who would not seem incongruous as a centre-fold pin-up. There was, however, a more libertarian native tradition of self-possessed and masterful women, such as the mythic Deirdre of the Sorrows, or the warrior-queen Maeve, or the pirate Grace O'Malley. These figures were an inspiration to the radical nationalists Maud Gonne and Constance Markievicz (who became Minister for Labour in the First Dáil of 1919). The culture which rediscovered these literary stereotypes was also the culture which sponsored the manly women of Shaw and Wilde and Joyce, as well as the adventurous heroines of Synge and Seán O'Casey.

In O'Casey's play *The Plough and the Stars* (1926), set in the week of the 1916 Rebellion, there are clear echoes of the preceding tradition:

> CLITHEROE. You have a mother, Langon.
> LIEUT. LANGON. Ireland is greater than a mother.
> CAPT. BRENNAN. You have a wife, Clitheroe.
> CLITHEROE. Ireland is greater than a wife.
> LIEUT. LANGON. Th' time for Ireland's battle is now—th' place for Ireland's battle is here.

Why, then, this need to imagine and worship Ireland as an unliberated woman? A number of reasons present themselves. Throughout the nineteenth century, the proponents of Anglo-Saxonist theories had spoken and written of the Celtic temperament as 'feminine', and this, most significantly, in an age when women were not deemed worthy of participation in the processes of government. The implication was that, as long as they remained 'feminine', the Celts would scarcely be ready for the discipline of self-government. The liberationist response to this stereotyping would have been for Irish men to acknowledge, celebrate, and explore their female dimension, in the manner of Leopold Bloom in Joyce's *Ulysses* or, indeed, as Yeats did through Crazy Jane. There are unmistakable traces of that tradition in the writings of Synge, Wilde, and Shaw as well; indeed, the latter liked to joke that 'all good women are manly, and all good men womanly'. The nationalist response, among political analysts and speechmakers, was to admit the female dimension—a radical enough concession by the prim standards of the time—but to admit it only as a massive liability. The Irish-

Irelander D. P. Moran, for example, castigated the want of manliness in the Irish who permitted even their most trenchant protests to become an undignified, female screech; and Archbishop Croke recommended the pursuit of physical-contact Gaelic games as an antidote to such emasculation.

The Search for a Hero: Poetry and Violence

The hypermasculinity of the heroic figures of the Ulster Cycle was a major part of their attractiveness to the revivalist generation, whose models were no longer constitutional activists such as Henry Grattan (see above, p. 178). For many, the aspiration to a Home Rule parliament in Dublin was no longer quite enough and the republication of many Gaelic texts which satirized parliamentary procedure (as, indeed, Joyce parodied it in *Ulysses*) seemed to validate those traditions which issued in physical-force nationalism. For example, the publication by Osborn Bergin of *Parlaimint Chlainne Tomáis* in a relatively obscure learned journal of 1912, whether that gentle scholar intended it or not, can only have had this effect. Its aristocratic disdain for the Cromwellian invaders of the 1650s and for their middle-class hangers-on was a godsend to those militants who were visibly tiring of parliamentary pusillanimity in the years immediately after the Ulster Covenant of 1912. Moreover, in their naked appeal to the aristocratic mentality, such texts allowed the schoolmasters and clerks of the Gaelic League and Sinn Féin to assert a new kind of self-image and a proud lineage of their own. Revivalists could see themselves as the lawful descendants of dispossessed noblemen. This aristocratic self-image undoubtedly blinded many of them to the real class-interests which they represented, the interests of just the kind of emergent bourgeoisie satirized by the anonymous bardic author of *Parlaimint Chlainne Tomáis*. This kind of contradiction was noted at the time only by the acutest minds, such as that of James Joyce in his early short story *A Mother*. In this dry, acerbic anecdote, the respectable Mrs Kearney sees in the Gaelic League a chance to promote not so much the cause of the Irish language (to which she pays the necessary lip-service) as the material and careerist aspirations of her daughter. Already, as O'Casey bitterly noted, the 'fight for Irish' was being transformed into a 'fight for collars and ties'.

The aristocratic fetishism of revivalists led them, inevitably, back to O'Grady's supermale Cuchulain. If the degenerate and doomed landlords could not model their lives on his, then perhaps the rising bourgeoisie could, in accordance with the theory (soon to be proposed by Gramsci) that every class defines itself by aping its immediate superiors. Sensing, however obscurely, that the middle class throughout the world holds power by force of a violence that can never afford to reveal itself as such, they installed Cuchulain as their role-model. He went rapidly downmarket, without so much as a blush. The Ulster Cycle was characterized by

its capacity to glamorize Cuchulain's violence and, by means of poetic retelling, to render that bloodletting heroic. The link between sedition and literature had always been strong in Ireland, but, in the years of national revival, that link became a version of the connection between violence and poetry, a bloody crossroads indeed.

One young student at St Enda's College—an institution founded on Gaelic principles of education at the opening of the century—was astounded when, on school prize-day, he was rewarded for victory in a poetry competition not with a book, nor even a Bible, but a gleaming new rifle. Already his headmaster Patrick Pearse, present poet and future rebel, was making explicit for his students the intimate connection in nationalist culture between poetry and violence, a connection cemented throughout the eighteenth and nineteenth centuries in thousands of rebel ballads and recitations. The motto of St Enda's College was an aphorism attributed to Cuchulain: 'I care not if I live but a day and a night, so long as my deeds live after me.' To Yeats, also, Cuchulain appeared as an exponent of the legitimate violence of rulers.

In his controversial *The Playboy of the Western World* (first performed, to a rioting audience, in 1907) J. M. Synge re-created some of the heroic qualities of an ancient Cuchulain in a peasant youth, in order to explore the relation between the ancient aristocratic tale and the debilitated rural Ireland in which it still lingered. For Synge, as for James Connolly, the worship of past heroes was nothing other than an evasion of present mediocrity; and his play uncompromisingly suggests that the cult of Cuchulain, or of anyone else for that matter, is more a confession of impotence than a spur to self-respect. Nevertheless, he follows Yeats and Pearse in their exploration of the relation between poetry and violence; but, against his chosen mock-heroic backdrop, Synge can conduct his investigation in a more critical way. The village girls in *The Playboy of the Western World* turn out to be more in love with Christy the poet than father-slayer; and, when Pegeen Mike rejects him with the rueful observation that 'there's a great gap between a gallous story and a dirty deed', she has, in

SYNGE BY JACK B. YEATS. Synge set out to depict not the sociology of rural Ireland so much as 'the psychic state of the peasantry' in plays, poems, and essays. He did, however, tour the Congested Districts of the West, reporting his impressions in a series of articles for the *Manchester Guardian*. These were illustrated by his travelling companion Jack B. Yeats, whose stencil portrait likens Synge to the craggy, stoic countrymen who were his constant study.

effect, dismantled Pearse's equation between poetry and violence. Through her, Synge is suggesting that the myth of the fighting Irish is only a myth; and that, in fact, the Irish can only bear the *thought* of violence if it is committed elsewhere, or in the past, and dressed up in a suitably remote and glamorous kind of verbiage. A killing in one's own back yard is quite a different story. This was the dilemma which Yeats eventually faced, years after Synge, in *Easter 1916*, a poem in which he was forced, for the first time, to distinguish his admiration for the ancient violence of Cuchulain from his manifest distaste for the sight of dead bodies in the streets of his native city.

The Collapse of the Gaelic Order

The beautiful dialect in which Synge's plays were written was, after all, made possible only by the ritual slaughter of the Irish language, which provided, even as it collapsed, the potent *substratum* of Hiberno-English. That slaughter occurred over three centuries in the slowest of slow-motion sequences.

The most graphic example of the relation between poetry and violence is the painful fate of Gaelic poets, after the defeat of the old Gaelic order at the Battle of Kinsale (1601). This mainly hereditary caste now faced ruin and, rightly or wrongly, they found inscribed in their fall the defeat of an entire people. Aindrias Mac Marcais bluntly equated the ruin of Ireland with the decay of Gaelic tradition:

> Gan gáire fá ghníomhra leinbh
> Cosc ar cheol, glas ar Ghaeilg.

> (Without laughter at the antics of a child;
> Music censored; and Gaelic banned.)

After the initial Plantation of Munster, poets feared that they would have to live in 'Saxa nua darb ainm Éire' (a new England named Ireland). In their desperation, during this period of retrenchment, many bards went downmarket, playing less austere metrical schemes, and hawking their wares to a wider audience in works like *Ceist, cia cheannóidh dán?* (A Question, who will buy a poem?). Mathúin Ó hIfearnáin advised his son, a bard by rightful inheritance, to abandon the poetic arts:

> Ná lean do dhíogha ceirde,
> Ná cum do ghréas Gaeilge.

> (Do not follow your trade,
> Do not compose your Gaelic patterns.)

In a notable political poem of the mid-seventeenth century, *An Síogaí Rómhánach* (The Roman Fairy), the anonymous author makes a significant equation between the enemies of Ireland and 'bodaigh an Bhéarla', the English-speaking churls. The term *English language* ('Béarla') is used, instead of *foreigner* ('gaill'), to represent the new element in the population, as the poets began to show a deeper awareness of the long-term cultural implications of the conflict.

It was in this post-Reformation period, also, that many authors began to identify the precarious state of Gaelic culture with the cause of a threatened Roman Catholicism. Irish colleges were founded in Continental Europe to service the young clerical students in flight from the Protestant occupiers of their native country. Scholars in places like Louvain printed many religious texts in Gaelic, thereby maintaining a tradition of intellectual discourse in the language. And many young men who might in other circumstances have become professional poets instead pursued a life of learning in the religious orders. One commented: 'Is treise Dia ná bodaigh an Bhéarla' ('God is stronger than English-speaking churls'). To those English spies who monitored them, the Irish colleges seemed to harbour only 'traitors and breeders of treachery'; but Daniel Corkery wrote in his short history of the Irish language that 'such groups in Europe, keeping Irish alive, counterpoint the attempts to anglicise the wards of court, the sons of Irish princes, in London'.

By 1603, the English abolished the Brehon Laws, but, even before that date, the more astute Gaelic writers had sensed that the game was up. Learned poets and priests had already set about gathering the lore of Ireland into book form. Geoffrey Keating's *Foras Feasa ar Éirinn* (The Basis of Knowledge Concerning Ireland) was explicitly composed as a comprehensive reply to such English historians as Spenser and Stanyhurst, attempting to clear the ancient Irish of numerous charges including cannibalism and sexual irregularity. In a similar mode, the Four Masters produced their annals, in an attempt to systematize the facts of Irish history.

Such collections of past lore and narrative went hand-in-hand with the writing of a vibrant new chapter in Gaelic literary history. The artists of the seventeenth century conspired in a veritable swan-song to Gaelic civilization, comparable in many respects to the flowering of Anglo-Irish literature which also coincided with the collapse of another ascendancy at the start of the twentieth century. W. B. Yeats saw many correspondences between the predicament of an Anglo-Irish artist who was spurned by the philistines of a modern Catholic middle class, and the plight of a figure like the poet Aogán Ó Rathaille, a ruined aristocrat too proud to beg on his deathbed for help that would not be forthcoming anyway. Ó Rathaille's closing lines in *Cabhair Ní Ghairfead* (I shall not summon help)

> Rachad a haithle searc na laoch don chill,
> Na flatha faoi raibh mo shean roimh éag do Chríost.

were rendered by Frank O'Connor as

> I shall go after the heroes, ay, into the clay;
> My fathers followed theirs before Christ was crucified.

This version is clearly echoed in Yeats's *The Curse of Cromwell*

> The lovers and the dancers are all beaten into the clay,
> And the tall men and the swordsmen and the horsemen, where are they?
> And there's an old beggar, wandering in his pride.
> His fathers served their fathers before Christ was crucified.

The Curse of Cromwell is, of course, in an ancient tradition of laments for fallen nobles and great houses, a tradition epitomized by *Cill Cais* (Kilcash), also looted by Yeats in the lines just quoted:

> Níl trácht ar Chill Cais ná a teaghlach,
> Ní chluinfear a cling go bráth.
> An áit úd a gcónaíodh an deighbhean
> Fuair gradam is meidhir thar mnáibh,
> Bhodh Iarlaí ag tarraingt thar tuinn ann
> Is an tairfreann doimhin dá rá.
>
> (Kilcash and the house of its glory
> And the bell of the house are gone;
> The spot where that lady waited
> Who shamed all women for grace
> When earls came sailing to greet her
> And Mass was said in the place.   O'Connor version.)

There is an even wider sense in which many of Yeats's laments for ancestral houses are conscious reworkings of this tradition.

Nor was Yeats the only major artist of the Irish Renaissance to feel haunted by the ethos and imagery of the earlier literary revival. Geoffrey Keating's keen ('caoineadh') for Ireland as outraged woman

> Deor níor fágadh i gclár do bhrollaigh mhínghil
> Nár dheolsad ál gach cránach coigríche.

was rendered by Synge as

> A drop was not left in the plane of your smooth and fair bosom
> That was not eaten by the farrow of every foreign sow.

In *A Portrait of the Artist as a Young Man* (1916) James Joyce shrewdly recruited the Gaelic tradition to give evidence against itself, by inverting the basic meaning of Keating's image, while retaining its elements: 'Ireland is the old sow that eats her farrow'—a wicked reversal also of Pearse's *Mise Éire*. The poems of Keating had been published in 1901, at a time when Joyce was attending Pearse's classes in the Irish language.

Why this sedulous cultivation of a parallel between two literary periods, themselves separated by more than three centuries? The history of literature, as Carlyle said, is a history of revivals; but there were specific reasons for favouring the seventeenth-century Renaissance. The decades after Kinsale represent not just a poignant late-flowering of art, but of an art forged very consciously against a wider European backdrop. Ever since the first Christian missionaries from Ireland had founded monasteries in places like Bobbio, there had been a strong connection between Ireland and Continental Europe; and even the professional bards and noblemen who composed love-lyrics ('dánta grá') between 1200 and 1600 had been working deliberately in an *amour courtois* tradition. But now, after the bardic collapse, many of the greatest Gaelic texts, such as Tadhg Ó Cianáin's *Imeacht na nIarlaí* (The Flight of the Earls), Flaithrí Ó Maolchonaire's translation of the Spanish *El Desseoso* as *Desiderius*, or the lyrics of Keating and Haicéad were actually composed in European cities and towns. Hence their

PATRICK PEARSE. Though immortalized in Irish iconography as a soldier-rebel, Pearse was temperamentally ill-suited to the military life, and surrendered to Crown forces in 1916 rather than prolong the slaughter of civilians. He was more attuned to the life of the mind, winning recognition as poet, playwright, and educational theorist, as well as being editor of the Gaelic League paper *An Claidheamh Soluis* (*The Sword of Light*).

attraction for a modern generation of revivalists, who wished to free Ireland of its nineteenth-century provincialism by what Yeats would term 'an exacting criticism, a European pose'. Similarly, Joyce's Stephen Hero 'was aware of some movement proceeding out of Europe. Of this last phrase he was fond, as it seemed to him to unroll the measurable world before the feet of the islanders.' Padraic Colum's tribute to the seventeenth-century figures—'they Europeanised Irish literature without deGaelicising it'—well represents the ideals of another literary generation that attempted to look outwards.

That generation was painfully aware that, for more than two centuries, the Irish language had been, with few exceptions, bereft of serious intellectual content; and its members were impatient with men who believed that *caint na ndaoine*, the daily speech of small farmers and fishermen on western seaboards, was sufficient for a literary language, and produced simple texts for Irish classes on that basis. As Patrick Pearse commented: 'A living literature cannot be built up on the folk tale. Why set up for today a standard at which Seathrúin Céitinn (Geoffrey Keating) and Aodh Ó Dálaigh (Hugh O'Daly) would have laughed? If Irish literature is to live and grow, it must get into contact on the one hand with its own past and on the other with the mind of contemporary Europe.' In poems like *A Mhic Bhig na gCleas* (Little Lad of the Tricks), Pearse sought to re-create the direct lyricism as well as the mandarin syntax of Keating:

> Tá cumhracht id phóig
> Nochar frith fós liom
> I bpógaibh na mban
> Ná i mbalsam a gcorp.

> (Your kiss has a fragrance
> That I have yet to find
> In the kisses of women
> Or in the balsam of their bodies.)

In *Fornocht do Chonac Thú* (Naked I Saw Thee), Pearse is beguiled by a very real *Spéirbhean*, but rejects her, paradoxically, to save Ireland. Like *A Bhean Lán do Stuaim* (usually attributed to Keating, the title means 'O Woman Full of Wile'), where the poet rejects a woman for spiritual reasons, Pearse's poem is a clever inversion of the ancient tradition whereby the woman was embraced before *she* disappeared. Keating's poetry is typical of the work of the early seventeenth century in its deeply personal qualities. Most of the bardic poetry of earlier periods had been formulaic and conventional, however well wrought; but the vast social disturbances after Kinsale impelled artists to a more passionate and sincere kind of utterance. Keating saw behind many tired conventions of the poetry new truths which few had dared to face; and so he bravely attacked the convention with its own evasions. Shrewd enough to realize that those who merely replicate a tradition help to deaden and mummify it, he invoked many old-fashioned tropes in order to overturn them. Frank O'Connor thought it revealing that 'one of the finest poems of the period is about a man so old and physically exhausted that he can no longer have sexual relations with the woman he loves'; but, in fact, it is the convention, rather than the poet, which is revealed to be spent.

The art of the poets was reinvigorated not just by a personal and social crisis, but by the new literary conditions which forced the bards—two hundred years before Wordsworth's *Preface to the Lyrical Ballads*—to speak to the masses rather than the classes. The result was a creative fusion of the diction of the mandarins with the robust idiom of the streets. The life of the poetry sprang from an ever-present tension between these extremes, epitomized on the one hand by the *dán díreach* (literally, straight or strict poem) of the bardic caste, with its complex rhyming schemes, and, on the other, the popular *amhrán* (song) metres which the poets appended, with increasing frequency, to their texts. What the best of them achieved was a synthesis between the rigour of their tradition and the informal urgency of the individual talent, a language above grossness and below refinement where propriety might reside. Pearse wrote in celebration of such texts as models for his contemporaries to imitate: 'The ordinary speech of the people is never literature, although it is the stuff from which literature is made.'

Not all the bards, it should be added, were braced to meet the challenge of a more popular market. Eochaidh Ó hEodhasa wrote of crude rhymesters, as Yeats would of 'certain bad poets' three centuries later, refusing to endorse shoddy workmanship, but haunted and baffled by its new popularity:

> Ionmholta malairt bhisigh:
>   tárraidh sinde 'san amsa
> iomlaoid go suarrach sona,
>   do-chuaidh a sochar dhamhsa.
>
> Do thréig sind sreatha caola
>   foirceadal bhfaobhrach ffrithir
> ar shórt gnáthach grés robhog,
>   is mó as a moltar sinde.
>
> (I like the simple ways
> That modern poetry goes,
> Fatuous but worthy praise,
> And lucrative, God knows.
>
> I have left the manly skill
> Of academic art
> For a sort of easy thrill
> That makes men take my part.   O'Connor version.)

The Eighteenth Century: A Confluence of Cultures?

The extremes of bitter poverty to which this caste could be reduced are manifest in the spectacle of Aogán Ó Rathaille celebrating the outset of the eighteenth century in Kerry by feeding his children periwinkles—then, if not now, the most despised of dishes. And that bitterness has led nationalist historians such as Daniel Corkery in *The Hidden Ireland* to posit a thoroughgoing conflict between Gaelic and English cultures in the hundred years which followed. Some Marxist historians have, in recent years, even begun to speak not just of two cultures but of two nations. While commentators continue to disagree about the extent of Anglo-Irish privilege and the scale of Catholic suffering under the Penal Laws, most will agree that there was no significant cultural intercourse between the two sides.

There have, however, been other interpretations, most notably Yeats's attempt in his later years to bring the Anglo-Irish tradition of Swift, Berkeley, and Burke into line with the Gaelic Ireland of Ó Rathaille and Brian Merriman. In *Pages from a Diary in 1930* the poet wrote: 'Preserve that which is living, and help the two Irelands, Gaelic Ireland and Anglo-Ireland, so to unite that neither shall shed its pride.' There is, in fact, a good deal to be said—although, lacking Irish, its author could not have known it—in favour of the Yeatsian analysis.

For one thing, proponents of a 'two-nations theory' take no account of the bilingual nature of many communities, including Jonathan Swift's Dublin, in the period. Swift, who was probably tended by an Irish-speaking nursemaid, noted with interest the spread of Gaelic loan-words and phrases in the Hiberno-English of country squires; and Arthur Young, the English visitor, remarked that it was unusual to find English spoken in Dublin without some admixture of Irish. According to the census of 1736, Roman Catholics formed one-third of the city's population, and many of them were Irish-speaking.

A large Irish-speaking community resided on the edge of the city in poorer suburbs whose names—Irishtown, Baile bocht (Poortown)—tell their own story. The city was still a vibrant focus of Gaelic tradition, with twenty-six poets and men of learning listed in a single text of 1728. One of those named, Aodh Mac Gabhrán (Hugh McGauran), a man accorded the status of squire by his Protestant contemporaries, was the author of verses entitled *Pléaráca na Ruarcach* (O'Rourke's Feast), a jocose celebration of a banquet held by O'Rourke of Bréifne

JONATHAN SWIFT BY FRANCIS BINDON. The greatest writer of eighteenth-century Ireland, his *Drapier's Letters* and *Modest Proposal* articulated the increasing disquiet of the Anglo-Irish with imperial policy towards the colony. He asked why a free man in England seemed to lose his autonomy by simply crossing the Irish Sea. Though never a separatist, he became a forerunner of the campaigns for Irish self-reliance and home rule. He left his fortune to found a mental hospital in Dublin, 'and showed by one satiric touch / No nation wanted it so much'.

in the sixteenth century. The famous harper Turlough Carolan put the words to music and his version so entranced Jonathan Swift that he requested a literal translation, so that he might produce his own rendition of the piece. In *Pléaráca na Ruarcach* a quarrel among the drunken guests concerning questions of pedigree led to a traditionally pugnacious stage-Irish conclusion, captured by Swift as follows:

> What stabs and what cuts,
>   What clatt'ring of sticks,
> What strokes on the guts,
>   What bastings and kicks.
> Come, down with that beam,
>   If cudgels are scarce,
> A blow on the weam,
>   Or a kick in the Arse.

This extraordinary collaboration between three of the greatest talents of the age ensured the popularity of the song, which Lady Morgan reports as having been sung at her christening party.

The life of Turlough Carolan was itself a fine example of the abiding links between Gaelic and Anglo-Ireland. He travelled the west and midlands, playing

CAROLAN BY FRANCIS BINDON. The instrument, the ancient symbol of Irish music, was still played by this 'last of the harpers' for the remnants of the Gaelic aristocracy, but also for such Anglo-Irish patrons as Dean Swift and Dr Delany of Co. Down. After Carolan's death in 1738, however, harp music went downmarket, being played more often by mendicants in the market-place.

music for Roman Catholic and Protestant patrons alike, in the decades which saw the implementation of the Penal Laws; and it was reported that rich and poor, Gael and planter, mingled freely among the thousands at his four-day funeral. He had sedulously avoided either political or religious controversy in his lyrics and, with true bardic diplomacy, served all who were willing to pay for his product. It is significant that a number of planters were happy to support Gaelic culture, and that, where this was the case, bards were still to be found who would celebrate these patrons in praise-poems, such as that written by Ó Rathaille for Warner.

Many influential Protestants—notably the radical Presbyterians of Belfast, who organized the Harp Festival of 1792 and who purchased Charlotte Brooke's *Reliques of Irish Poetry* in good numbers—thus displayed a genuine interest in Gaelic tradition; and it is also clear that there were still Catholic families in a state of sufficient prosperity to offer patronage to Carolan, or to deck their tables with costly foods in the manner of Eibhlín Dhubh ní Chonaill, as described by her in *Caoineadh Airt Uí Laoghaire* (The Lament for Art O'Leary). Nevertheless, Gaelic Ireland was in much disarray, especially after the foundation of the 'charter schools' of 1731, which had the avowed purpose of instructing poorer Catholics in the rudiments of the English language. Moreover, English had by then secured a firm foothold as the major subject of study in the hedge-schools, whose teachers placed great emphasis on skill in reading the language. When Jonathan Swift said that it would be a noble experiment to ban Irish from all markets and places of dealing, he spoke not just to, but for, the emerging Roman Catholic middle class which, though forbidden to practise the learned professions of law and medicine, could become merchants and businessmen. And even the recalcitrant rebels in the hills needed some competence in English, if they were to write threatening messages to landlords, or to secure their own legal rights.

So, by a weird paradox, while Belfastmen with names like Taylor, Bunting, and Craig passed measures in defence of Gaelic culture and studied its spoken language, the rising Catholic bourgeoisie was abandoning the last vestiges of Irish, that 'badge of a beaten race'. This process had begun, in fact, well before the Battle of the Boyne (1690), to the consternation of Gaelic poets like Dáibhí Ó Bruadair, who sighed in a poem *Mairg nach fuil ina dhubhthuata* (A Pity for Him who is not a Black Churl). Almost a century after its defeat at the Boyne, that same Catholic middle class, anxious to show its gratitude for a relaxation in the Penal Laws which allowed for the opening of Catholic colleges in 1782, at once instituted English as the language of instruction. By now, the seventeenth-century equation between 'Gaelic' and 'Catholic'—or, indeed, 'rebel'—had been effectively dismantled. When the Whiteboys rose against unfair rents in 1779, Bishop Troy promptly excommunicated them, ordering his priests to 'read this notice in Irish where the ignorance of the English language among the generality

MAYNOOTH, *c.*1870. The major seminary for the training of Roman Catholic priests, founded in 1795. Its failure to produce, in the ensuing century, a single theologian of international stature led George Moore to conclude that Catholicism depends for its intellectual content on the skills of its converts, because 'after two or three generations of Catholicism, the intellect dies'. During the Irish Revival, James Joyce noted that many priests were supporting the Gaelic League, seeing in Irish culture a bulwark against modernism.

of your parishioners may render it necessary'. English was now the language of all privileged classes, Catholic and Protestant, and it made steady gains in the countryside.

A schematic division between an Irish-speaking peasantry and an English-speaking gentry is, therefore, wrong-headed, if only because it takes no account of the way in which bilingualism had spread through the countryside, as people were shedding one language and acquiring another. As late as 1773, an Irish bishop instructed the pope that students of the Irish College in Rome must be trained 'in both native languages'. A Munster poet like Eoghan Rua Ó Súilleabháin could produce ballads in English celebrating a British naval victory at Fort Royal in 1782; while, in *Suirí Mhuiris Uí Ghormáin* (The Courtship of Maurice O'Gorman), the Ulster poet Peadar Ó Doirnín satirized the broken English of a poetic rival in a macaronic poem that, by very definition, would have been comprehensible only to a bilingual audience. That poem is, incidentally, just one of a host of instances whereby snobbish Gaelic authors showed just as much contempt for the 'brogue' as did the purveyors of stage-Irish plays in London. With his heavy boots, verbal bulls, and hopeless mispronunciation, as well as his penchant for alcohol and obliging ladies, O'Gorman is a thoroughly recognizable figure common to both cultures at the time. Writers of Irish prose were also quick to spot the comic possibilities in a medley of languages. 'Butter is very carpenter', joked Seán Ó Neachtain, 'Tá im an-saor' ('saor' being the Gaelic word for 'craftsman' as well as 'inexpensive'); and in *Stair Éamuinn Uí Chléire* (The Story of Eamon O'Clery), he evolved a strange lingo which, two centuries before Joyce, trembled on the brink of *Finnegans Wake*: 'and 'tis name to him, old hog son foal, and he is in the house of your ear handsome seldom hundred sick . . .'

Such conjunctions might seem unusual, were it not for the more crucial affinities of form and tone, technique and theme, between Gaelic and Anglo-Irish literature in the period. Vast changes in the social order caused a realignment of monied as against landed interests, with a consequent emergence of satire designed to detect and punish infractions of the old norms. Mockery of pushing *arrivistes* and pretentious fops may be found in both traditions. Social standing was now determined by money rather than land; and the Gaelic poets suffered because of their ambiguous class position. They saw themselves as ruined aristocrats who had been deprived of their landed patrons, but to the new moneymen they appeared to be nothing more than beggars with inflated egos. Like Swift and Pope, they consistently used animal imagery to disparage the new predatory interests, among either the laity or (in some cases) the clergy. The ethical priorities of a materialistic priest who sets the welfare of his horses above that of his human parishioners were exposed by Ó Doirnín in *An Dá Sheán* (The Two Johns—contrasting the old and new type of cleric); but such a depressing code will be familiar already to the reader of *Gulliver's Travels*.

The Gaelic Court of Poetry was, in one sense, a continuation of the *file-as-breitheamh* tradition, but, in actual procedures, it was remarkably similar to the Spectator or Scriblerus Clubs of London. While the Augustans met in coffee-houses, the Gaels met in the tavern, but the objective was the same—to read texts aloud for discussion and criticism, to investigate one another's partialities, and to savour the pleasure of winning their way into the intricacies of another man's mind. Just as the coffee-house set chose to admire or abuse one another in the form of a verse-epistle, so the Gaelic authors adopted the genre known as 'warrant' or legal letter. This was, in part, an uproarious parody of the despised English law, but also a variant on the 'familiar epistle' of Augustan England. The High Sheriff of the Court ruled with the same magisterial efficiency of a Mr Spectator in London and his style had the air of persuasive authority quite acceptable to men who looked up to a self-constituted oracle in their debates.

The eighteenth century was, of course, the great age of letter-writing and the members of the Court often preferred to send their message in writing, rather than have an enigmatic text spoiled by tiresome first-hand exchanges. There is a palpable element of stage-management in the warrants and verse-epistles alike, a mock-heroic tongue-in-cheek solemnity visited upon such trivial events as the loss of a pair of spectacles or the failure to return a borrowed book. Ó Rathaille's warrant, on the theft of a goose, is written in *Casbhairdne*, one of the most intricate of bardic metres and a form more appropriate to the death of a king. In that sustained discrepancy between tone and topic may be found a characteristic strategy of the Popian couplet:

> Here thou, great Anna, whom three realms obey,
> Does sometimes counsel take, and sometimes tea.

Both are examples of the domestication of the epic, by an artist trained in obsolete modes who knows all too painfully that the heroic phase of writing is past.

And, indeed, that decline was nowhere more obvious than in the collapse of the old systems of patronage. Ó Rathaille was spurned by one of the new men Valentine Brown, the son of the poet's former patron, to whom he seemed just a shabby mendicant. As he waited in Brown's vestibule, the poet took revenge by comparing the new man to 'a foreign raven nesting in the woods of Ross'.

Ó Rathaille did share with men like Swift a capacity to make a line work on more than one level, to say one thing while intending its opposite. This penchant for irony, so notable in most phases of Irish literature, arises from the difference between the official version of reality and the actual state in which men live. This universal affliction was particularly acute in eighteenth-century Ireland. On the Gaelic side, poets sang of Cathleen ni Houlihan when they really referred to Ireland; they decried the felling of the woods when they were actually be-moaning the fall of the Gaelic aristocracy; and they besought girls to shelter gallants, who turned out on inspection to be rebels on the run. On the Anglo-Irish side, the Penal Laws were equally multivalent in their ironies. Catholics were compelled to work on church holidays, but justices who refused to implement that law were to be gaoled. As Andrew Carpenter has explained: 'the very law which outlaws the Catholics seems to concede the impossibility of its own application. It acknowledges that it is merely one way of looking at life and seems to accept that the other perspective is *de facto* to remain in existence.'

The verbal harshness of the Penal Laws was itself a reflection of their wide-spread inoperability in a land which lacked either a proper police force or a comprehensive system of prisons. This has prompted the historian Louis Cullen to suggest that the account of native Irish poverty and oppression rendered by

Daniel Corkery in *The Hidden Ireland* is vastly overstated. This corrective account was long overdue, but, in redressing the balance, Corkery's critic manages to repeat many of his mistakes, especially his propensity to read highly formulaic love-poetry as actual social documentary. Cullen bases his interpretation on the aristocratic attitudes and imagery which still pervaded much Gaelic poetry, but does not see that these might be merely literary conventions, all the more poignant to a dispossessed people. He interprets the many references to dowries by poets as proof that 'a substantial proportion of the rural population enjoyed some substance'. Doubtless, some middle-class families could afford a dowry for their daughters, but it is equally probable, in a literary tradition notorious for its love of dead or inoperable conventions, that a majority of those who sang these songs had no such affluence. Just as the ritual reference to poetic poverty may be taken (in some cases) with a grain of salt, so should the promises of wealth and abundance. The most common of all compliments to the girl

> Do phósfainnse gan feoirling thú
> Is ní iarfainn ba ná spré

> (I would wed you without a farthing
> And I would not seek cattle or dowry)

may reveal the underlying sociology of rural Ireland at the time. Similarly, when Eoghan Rua Ó Súilleabháin promises a woman a slate-roofed house, it is foolish to deduce from this that the fashion was widespread among the rural Catholics, since the poetry of courtship tells more of imaginative aspirations than actual lives. Or again, if a poet disavows sweaty labour, this does not make him a man of leisure—merely one who feels that, by right and possible future restoration, he was made for better things.

Many of these poems and songs are written either in the future tense or the conditional mood, indicating a Utopian element common to the arts of many oppressed peoples. As Yeats would later say, 'the arts lie dreaming of what is to come', especially if what is to come is the restoration of an imagined golden age. Popular songs—now as then—have always been filled with lists of what people want but cannot have. What matters is not the nearness of such things, but their remoteness; and it is all the better if they evoke the past elegance of an earlier dispensation. The poet who promised a slated roof was, in all likelihood, offering an extravagant compliment to his love, and the pains to which he went suggest just how unusual such a pledge would be. The idea that each class experiences its dream-life in terms of the imagery associated with its superior ruling group seems much nearer the mark—a notion already inscribed in the Gaelic phrase 'ag sodar i ndiaidh na nuasal' (trotting after the nobility). From ancient times, the poor have always taken a great interest in the culture and activities of the rich and the dispossessed Gaelic poets were all the more likely to reflect this, since they felt that, by strict justice, it was with the rich that they should belong.

If the Gael experienced uncertainty and ambiguity in the eighteenth century, so did the Anglo-Irish Ascendancy; and if not all Gaelic and Anglo-Irish shared a common culture, they did at least experience a common predicament. Their joint anxieties may be read in the fondness of their texts for covert implication and for an irony that flashes between Lilliputian and Brobdingnagian extremes. The strategy of Swift's *Gulliver's Travels* (1726), where life among dwarfs and giants is contrasted and compared, had already been employed in the Gaelic prose tale *Imtheachta Tuaithe Luachra agus Aidheadh Fhearghusa*.

Many other parallel developments in both literatures might be more briefly indicated: the growing protest against the domestic enslavement of women in *Parlaimint na mBan* (1703), for example. Dónal Ó Colmáin's subversive text followed hard upon Daniel Defoe's *Essay upon Projects* (1697) and his *Good Advice to the Ladies* (1702), both of which similarly urged a fuller involvement of women in educational and political life. Indeed, throughout the eighteenth century, Gaelic poets consistently complained about the increasing fetishization of the female, as the influence of English fashion and English puritanism spread ever more widely in rural townlands. In *Bodaigh na hEorna*, the Ulster poet Art Mac Cubhthaigh (1738–73) denounced the vulgar feathers and frills sported by the Anglicized females of a successful local family which had made its fortune through the distilling industry. By the century's end, Brian Merriman in *Cúirt an Mheáin Oidche* (The Midnight Court) launched a full-scale assault on the entire apparatus of feminine frippery—stiletto heels, powder and cosmetics, fashionable hoods—as part of his wider plea for a restoration of the sexual liberalism which had characterized the now defunct Brehon Laws. The anger of all these writers is directed not against Anglicization as such, but against the degradation of woman to sex-object and fantasy-machine by the jaded puritan imagination. It is, of course, revealing that this was one aspect of the Gaelic tradition which the selective 'revivalists' of our own century chose to ignore. The revolutionary or Utopian potential of such native texts was kept well concealed by the new breed of Gaelic puritans, who preferred instead to read their own late-Victorian ethical code into their favoured Gaelic traditions.

Enslaved as they were, in their political and sexual unconscious, to English codes and practices, the revivalist historians of Gaelic culture experienced a pathological need to deny any similarities between the native and the English literary traditions at the conscious level. So, they managed not to register the clear overlap between the Gaelic printed sermon and the English periodical essay for the instruction of the emerging middle class; the common emergence of the dictionary and wordlist; or the rise of the anti-hero in both cultures. On that last connection, many Gaelic texts such as *Stair Éamuinn Uí Chleire* (1710) and *Siabhra Mhic na Míochomhairle* (1725) present gangling innocents abroad

LADY LAVERY AS CATHLEEN NI HOULIHAN (painted in 1923 by Sir John Lavery). A controversial representative of Irish womanhood (since she was American), but considered so typical that she featured on Irish banknotes for half a century after independence. The harp is emblematic of Irish music and aristocratic tradition. Fertile as the land which frames her, the lady's image is approximated to that of the landscape to which the ancient chieftains felt bound in a symbolic marriage.

in a corrupt world which they nevertheless manage to survive. R. A. Breatnach found in these anti-heroes 'a noteworthy phenomenon which suggests the decline in cultural standards', but they might, more justly, be seen as the Irish precursors of Fielding's Tom Jones and Joseph Andrews.

If there was no final confluence of cultures in eighteenth-century Ireland, this was due, more than anything else, to the emergence of a lethal sectarianism during and after the bloody rising of 1798. Theobald Wolfe Tone had hoped to put an end to the prevalent anxiety and ambiguity and to widen the meaning of the phrase 'Irish nation'; but when the Act of Union yoked Ireland to England by violence, the divisions ran deeper than ever. It would take more than a century for the wounds to heal, before Yeats, Douglas Hyde, J. M. Synge, and their mainly Protestant collaborators would attempt a more successful *rapprochement* with the Gaelic tradition, and before such bilingual artists as Liam O'Flaherty, Flann O'Brien, and Brendan Behan would fuse both traditions in single works of art, 'so that neither shall shed its pride'. By then, it would be appropriate for the leading Gaelic poet of the twentieth century, Seán Ó Ríordáin, to count among his mentors Wordsworth, Hopkins, and Joyce as well as Pádraigín Haicéad and Piaras Feiritéir; and *de rigueur* for Synge to invoke Keating as well as Swift and Burke.

The Nineteenth Century

The passing of the Act of Union in 1800 prompted a renewed campaign against the stage-Irish stereotype among Ascendancy writers. In their *Essay on Irish Bulls* Richard and Maria Edgeworth warned: 'Let English retailers or inventors of Irish blunders beware of such prefatory exclamations as: By my shoul and St. Patrick, By Jasus, Arrah honey, My dear Joy, all such phrases being absolutely out of date and fashion in Ireland.' In an imaginary conversation between an Englishman and an Irishman, the Edgeworths mocked the expectations of the latter who says: 'I imagined that I should have nothing to drink in Ireland but whiskey, that I should have nothing to eat but potatoes, that I should sleep in mud-walled cabins, and that I should know nothing but the Irish howl, the Irish brogue, Irish answers and Irish bulls.' In novels such as *Castle Rackrent* Maria Edgeworth proceeded to depict the realities of rural Irish life in the years before 1782, in a form which effectively pioneered the regional novel not just for English but for Continental writers. Similarly, Richard Edgeworth wrote many essays in an attempt to correct English misconceptions about Ireland in the wake of the

FAIR DAY AT MISS O'DOWD'S, 1945, by Lilian Lucy Davidson. Small-town profiteers and extortionate hucksters, known as 'gombeen men', held many of the rural poor to ransom. J. M. Synge noted the emergence of the breed at the start of the century and threatened to expose their 'double-chinned vulgarity' in a play.

MARIA EDGEWORTH drawn by Joseph Slater as a cross between plain Jane Austen and Cathleen ni Houlihan, capturing the spiritual hyphenation of one neither Irish nor English, but an occupant of the liminal zones between. Sensing perhaps that the periphery might one day be the centre, she pioneered a consciously regional novel, which in England issued in the art of Trollope and Hardy.

Union. Writing in 1811, he remarked that the peasantry 'have within these few years made a greater progress in learning English, than the Welsh have made since the time of Edward the First, in acquiring the language'.

The emergence of the novel as a major literary genre in the early nineteenth century permitted—at least for a time—a more sophisticated investigation of the language and psychology of the Irish character. At first, such novels were invariably written by members of the Ascendancy, since most country people still lacked a command of the English language. *Castle Rackrent* may have described the close relationship between servant and master in the previous age, but no such trust existed in Ireland after the Union. The Ascendancy novelists' understanding of the countryman was limited by their incomplete rapport with labourers and maidservants. Indeed, so charged did the situation become that Maria Edgeworth abandoned her career as an Irish novelist, writing to her brother in 1834: 'It is impossible to draw Ireland as she is now in a book of fiction—realities are too strong—party passions are too violent to bear to see, or care to look at, their faces in a looking-glass. The people would only break the glass and curse the fool who held the mirror up to nature.' She had come to that moment of decision later described by Yeats—whether to express the emerging people to themselves, or to exploit local piety and local colour for the delectation of a superior English audience. Being too shrewd to hold a mirror up to the people's faces and too honest to employ distorting mirrors for cheap amusement, she opted finally for silence.

'Silence, on the whole, is the real condition of Irish literature in the nineteenth century', wrote Thomas Kinsella. That is, of course, an excessive lament for a period that produced bravura effects like the widely popular songs of Thomas Moore and the acclaimed psychological thrillers of Joseph Sheridan Le Fanu. But silence certainly enveloped many rural communities which, as the century unfolded, were to endure massive depopulation as a result of famine and emigration. And these developments particularly threatened the survival of the Irish language. In the mid-century, the leading novelist William Carleton wrote of a wedding at which the bride spoke only Irish, the groom only English, and 'the very language of love needed an interpreter'. People were now shedding Irish and adopting English at a pace which left them fully articulate in neither. 'I see, sir, how it is', groaned an Irish-speaking judge to a peasant defendant who insisted on conducting his case in very broken English: 'you are more ashamed of knowing your own language than of not knowing any other.' In the face of this crisis, village schoolmasters—like Goldsmith's in the previous century— resorted to 'jawbreakers', words of learned length to amaze the gazing rustics who soon imitated them; and the brogue enjoyed a new lease of life at all levels of literature, as Irish persons, half-ashamed of abandoning Irish, sought to console themselves by demonstrating their matchless eloquence in English. By the 1840s, the stage Irishman re-emerged in the novels of Charles Lever and Samuel Lover.

William Carleton, more than any other author of the mid-century, challenged these stereotypes and spoke out of the experience of a whole people. 'As the son of an Irish peasant he knows his subject better than the Levers and Lovers', wrote Karl Marx to Friedrich Engels, after reading the first volume of *Traits and Stories of the Irish Peasantry*. Carleton had been raised by Irish-speaking parents and would later be praised by J. M. Synge as the father of modern Irish literature, because of his awareness of the true source of the Hiberno-English dialect in the Irish language rather than in the conventions of stage brogue. Carleton himself claimed to be able 'to transfer the genius, the idiomatic peculiarity and conversational spirit of the one language into the other', at a time when many rural people were still thinking in Irish syntax and imagery while using English words. Noting that many conventional idioms in Irish acquire a sudden poignancy when translated into English, Carleton cited 'M'anam istigh thú', 'my soul within you'. His stories did, indeed, capture the psychic state of a peasantry caught between

WILLIAM CARLETON. His instinctive understanding of the peasantry was the envy of later writers like Yeats and Synge, but it was matched by an acute sense of the emerging audience for such material in Ireland, Britain, and the USA. Accused in his day of betraying his Roman Catholicism for success with the largely Protestant readership of the *Dublin University Magazine*, he seems in retrospect to have been one of the first truly national artists seeking an appropriately wide audience.

two cultures; and yet, in the introduction to his collected works of 1860, he declared with some depression that, from the time of Shakespeare, 'neither play nor farce has ever been presented to an Englishman in which, when an Irishman is introduced, he is not drawn as a broad grotesque blunderer'.

The perennial pressure of audience expectations in England had to be met by those who wanted recognition, and not just by playwrights but by novelists too. The novels of Charles Lever and Samuel Lover were populated by feckless, good-natured bumpkins who struck a happy-go-lucky pose in the midst of their poverty and ill fortune. If the life of the peasantry swung between desperation and the healing release of comedy, the homes of the Ascendancy were, by contrast, drab, respectable, and insipid, especially in the decades of their decline after the Act of Union. In Lever's *Tom Burke of Ours*, a character named Darby-the-Blast shrewdly explained the popularity of the rascally peasant among

Ascendancy gentlemen: 'The quality has ne'er a bit of fun in them at all, but does be always comin' to us to make them laugh.'

Decades later, and coming from a drab but respectable Anglo-Irish family herself, Lady Augusta Gregory would walk into a Galway poorhouse, like a tourist among the poor, to take down the tales and anecdotes of the dying derelicts who lived there. In her subsequent collection *Poets and Dreamers* (1903) she registers her surprise at the contrast between the poverty of the tellers and the splendour of their tales. There is a sense in which much of the literature of the Irish Revival at the end of the nineteenth century arises out of the ironies of this master–servant relationship. The affable countryman had discovered that a whimsical mood or a colourful phrase were assets in his dealings with the 'quality', even if they confirmed in his interlocutors a sense of their own superior breeding.

THE MAN FROM ARANMORE, BY JACK B. YEATS. A classic portrait of the upright peasant, quite at variance with the feckless blunderer and fawning mendicant of the 'stage-Irish' mode. This idealized figure, epitomizing a sturdy self-reliance, is clearly ready for the responsibilities of self-government.

Anglo-Irish relations, even in England, seemed throughout the nineteenth century to be conducted on the basis of this stereotype. As early as 1818, John Keats observed in a letter that the Irish in London were 'sensible of the character they hold in England and act accordingly to Englishmen'. Ever since the days of Spenser and Stanyhurst, Anglo-Saxon theorists had presented the English as a cold, refined, and urbane race, so it suited them to see the Irish as hot-headed, rude, and garrulous—the perfect foil, in fact, to set off English virtues. In his introduction to *Foras Feasa ar Éirinn*, Geoffrey Keating had offered a counter-vailing account of the ancient Irish as disciplined, slow to anger but steadfast thereafter in pursuit of their rights, urbane and spare of utterance, and so on—in other words, the very model of an aristocratic English gentleman. But to a scant avail. Even the Irish in England, coming from neolithic windswept communities to the centres of the industrial revolution, found it easier to don the mask of the garrulous Paddy than to reshape a complex urban identity of their own. Acting the buffoon, they seemed harmless and lovable characters to many English who might otherwise have resented their competition for jobs. An art of fawning duplicity was perfected by many Irish builders and businessmen, who acted the lout while making shrewd deals which often took their English rivals unawares.

The career of Oscar Wilde in late Victorian London was, in every respect, an inversion and critique of all these stereotypes. According to the bemused Yeats, Wilde there 'perpetually performed a play which was the opposite of all that he had known in childhood and youth'. The home which he had abandoned in Dublin had been presided over by two eccentric parents who seemed to have stepped out of a bad stage-Irish melodrama. Sir William Wilde, although an eminent surgeon and pioneer in the rediscovery of Ireland's past, was reputed to be one of the dirtiest men in Dublin and the butt of many an undergraduate jibe (Why are his finger-nails so black? Because he has just scratched himself). Lady Wilde was known for her theatrical demeanour, collections of Irish folklore, and outpourings of nationalist verse, under the pen-name 'Speranza'. The father had been unkempt Irishman, so the son became a fastidious, urbane Englishman. From his mother, Oscar Wilde had inherited a gigantic and ungainly body, which recalled all too painfully the gorilla-like form of the Irish peasant in cartoons by Tenniel and others. To disarm such racist critics, the young dandy concealed his massive frame with costly clothes and studied the art of elegant deportment. The ease with which he effected this transition from stage Irishman to stage Englishman was his ultimate comment on the hollowness of the antithesis, on the emptiness of both notions. For Wilde sensed that antithesis was the master-key to the Victorian mind, which delighted in absolute distinctions between men and women, good and evil, English and Irish, and so on. By this mechanism, the English male could attribute to the Irish all those traits of emotion, poetry, and

LADY WILDE, as a youthful supporter of Irish nationalism, wrote patriotic verse for the Young Ireland journal *The Nation*, under the pen-name 'Speranza'. Her famous editorials (written when the editor Charles Gavan Duffy was in prison in July 1848) called for a hundred thousand muskets and said that 'the long-pending war with England has already commenced'. When Duffy was accused in court of writing this sedition, Speranza stood dramatically in the public gallery, saying, 'I and I alone am the culprit, if culprit there be.' She was not prosecuted, however, and Duffy was eventually set free.

soft charm which a stern industrial code had forced him to deny in himself. In rejecting this manic urge to antithesis, Wilde was satirizing the determinism of figures as diverse as Marx and Carlyle, who contended that social conditioning or parental upbringing determined consciousness. The belief that the Irishman was a prisoner of heredity, diet, and climate, like the conviction that woman is by nature docile, subservient, and deferential, were twin attributes of Victorian determinism. This determinism is taken to its *reductio ad absurdum* in the account of two girls, each of whom accepts that it is her ineluctable destiny to love a man named Ernest. The very plot of Wilde's *The Importance of Being Earnest* is an example of a determinism so extreme as to render the concept idiotic and banal.

Yet the Victorian Englishman continued to attribute to the Irish all those

'AN IRISH JIG' BY JAMES A. WALES, from *Puck*, November 1880. Uncle Sam and John Bull despair of their peaceful attempts to control the violent Irish Celt, fattened by the largesse of Britain and the US; and so they roll up their sleeves to implement more forceful methods. Victorian fears of the 'beastly Irish' were connected to popular disquiet at the findings of Charles Darwin, leading cartoonists to suggest that if man really was descended from the ape, then the Irish—like the blacks—must be closer to animality on the ecological scale.

emotions and impulses which his strict code had led him to deny in himself. Thus, if John Bull was industrious and reliable, Paddy was held to be indolent and contrary; if the former was mature and rational, the latter must be unstable and emotional; if the Englishman was adult and manly, the Irishman must be childish and feminine. So the Irish joined hands with two other repressed groups, women and children; and at the root of many an Englishman's suspicion of the Irish was an unease with the woman or child who lurked within himself. This equation contained a political implication: either as woman or as child, the Irishman was incapable of self-government. The flaunted effeminacy of Wilde, no less than his espousal of the inner world of the child in his stories, may well be a sly comment on these hidden fears. Wilde's 'few' writings on Ireland question the assumption that just because the British are industrious and rational the Irish must be lazy and illogical. The man who believed that a truth in art is that whose opposite is also true was quick to point out that every good man has an element of the woman in him. In *The Importance of Being Earnest* it is the women who read heavy works of German philosophy, attend university lectures, and discuss the finer points of male physique, while the men are filled with breathless surges of emotion or else simply lounge on sofas trying to look pretty. On much the same principle, Wilde could see that every sensitive Irishman must have a kind of secret Englishman within himself—and vice versa. He realized that the image of the stage Irishman tells us far more about English fears than Irish realities, just as the still vibrant Irish joke tells us far less about the Irishman's foolishness than about the Englishman's persistent and poignant desire to say something funny. In his case, Wilde opted to say that funny something for the English, in a lifelong performance of Englishness which constituted a parody of the very notion. By becoming more English than the English themselves, Wilde was able to invert, and ultimately to challenge, all the time-honoured clichés about Ireland.

George Bernard Shaw was another writer who treated England as a laboratory in which he could define what it meant to be an Irishman. On the other hand, he observed how 'Ireland is the only spot on earth which still produces the ideal Englishman of history.' *John Bull's Other Island* is Shaw's attempt to show how the two peoples spend most of their time acting an approved part before their neighbours' eyes, and these assigned parts are seen as impositions by the other side rather than opportunities for true self-expression. In the play, stereotypes are exploded, for it is the Englishman, Tom Broadbent, who is a romantic duffer, while the Irishman, Larry Doyle, is a cynical realist. The underlying reasoning is sound, for the Irish have become fact-facers through harsh poverty, while the English have enjoyed a scale of wealth so great that it allows them to indulge their victims with expansively sentimental gestures.

As a consequence, there is a sense in which *John Bull's Other Island* is itself the victim of the vice of 'English compartmentalisation' which it satirizes. The

'ASPECTS OF WILDE.' 'The only way to intensify personality is to multiply it', Wilde told his admirers. His assault on the romantic ideal of sincerity was based on the assumption that, in being true to a single aspect of the self, a man is repressing or denying many other attributes—his femininity, his childishness, his sensuality, and so on. Max Beerbohm's caricature wickedly mocks Wilde's gigantism, while nevertheless managing to capture the artist's versatility (mistaken by some for shallowness).

plot issues in victory for the romantic and efficient Englishman, but all the subversive witticisms have been uttered by the cynical but ineffectual Irishman. This was the same dualism which Shaw detected in the comedies of Wilde, each of which contains a scathing set of witticisms at the expense of upper-class society, but whose power to disturb is wholly disarmed by the reassuringly conventional nature of Wilde's plots. In *The Importance of Being Earnest* the aristocratic society wins out, as Lady Bracknell discovers that she can indeed marry off Gwendolen to a young man of her own exalted class. Both Wilde and Shaw are finally English writers in the strict terms of Shaw's own definition of Englishness as a talent for keeping radical and conservative ideas separate in watertight compartments. All of which is a measure of the constraints on any socialist dramatist who sought a career in the London of the time.

SHAW AT TYPEWRITER. On his ninetieth birthday, after half a century as the world's most celebrated dramatist, he was still at work. His greatest plays, like *St. Joan* and *Major Barbara*, project the ideas of a feminist and international socialist; but he also maintained a steady stream of commentary on Ireland. 'If we could only forget that we are Irish, and become really Catholic Europeans, there would be some hope for us', he wrote, adding the bleak afterthought that 'as long as Ireland produces men with sense enough to leave her, she does not exist in vain.'

Yeats's solution to this dilemma was to gather a native Irish audience and to create a native Irish theatre in Dublin—to express Ireland to herself rather than exploit her for the foreigner. He accepted the Anglo-Irish antithesis, but only on condition that he was allowed to reinterpret it in a more flattering light. Whereas the English had called the Irish backward, superstitious, and uncivilized, the Yeatsian revivalists created an idealized counter-image which saw the land as pastoral, mystical, and admirably primitive. Yet such a counter-image was false, if only because it elevated a single aspect of Ireland into a type of the whole. 'Connaught for me is Ireland', said Yeats; but Ireland was not Connacht—rather she was a patchwork-quilt of cultures and fiefdoms, as indeed before the Normans invaded. George Watson has elaborated this point, showing how the folklorism of Yeats confirmed the traditional image of the Irish as subservient and menial— except that now they were deemed menial in colourful and interesting new ways. 'The cracked looking-glass of a servant' was how Joyce's Stephen Dedalus characterized such an art. It is an apt image, not just of Yeats's doomed re-habilitation of the modes of deference, but also of Joyce's own escape into modernism, for what a cracked looking-glass shows is not a single but a multiple self.

Yeats and Literary Nationalism

Yet it was the very multifariousness of rural Irish life, with its varied classes and groupings, which the revivalist myth of a timeless peasantry was designed to occlude. This myth, like most forms of pastoralism, was a wholly urban creation, the brainchild of authors like Yeats and George Russell, political thinkers like Éamon de Valera and Michael Collins. They were the urbanized descendants of country people and, in their nostalgia for abandoned roots, patented the idea of a rural nation. Those who rioted against Synge's *Playboy of the Western World* in 1907 were not rural dwellers themselves but—as Conor Cruise O'Brien has pointed out—their citified offspring and grandchildren. What galled them was the portrayal of that harsh and violent way of life which they preferred to view in a softer focus. Like Patrick Kavanagh's long poem *The Great Hunger*—which would not appear until 1942—Synge's play was one of the first Irish exercises in anti-pastoral, offered at a time when middle-class nationalists were perfecting an eighth version of pastoral—the timeless Irish peasant noted for Christian stoicism and endurance.

THE REVIVAL OF FAIRY LORE. In the later nineteenth century Roman Catholic priests sought to 'Protestantize' Irish Catholicism by discouraging fairy lore; and so there was an irony in the revival of this very lore by such Protestants as Yeats, Lady Gregory, and Douglas Hyde. This drawing by Max Beerbohm shows Yeats 'presenting Mr George Moore to the Queen of the Fairies'. Ambiguity on the subject persisted well into the twentieth century. A US anthropologist asked a Galway woman in the 1940s if she really believed in fairies. 'I do not, sir,' she replied after some thought, 'but they're there anyway.'

Mr. W. B. Yeats, presenting Mr. George Moore to the Queen of the Fairies.

LANE, SYNGE, YEATS, LADY GREGORY (*left*). Artistic pride shades into aristocratic disdain in Orpen's portrait executed in the year of the *Playboy* riots. Synge never looked as ferocious as this, though Yeats was by now beginning to identify his true antagonists in the emerging Roman Catholic bourgeoisie. Sir Hugh Lane, whose gift of paintings would be rebuffed, looks at once dapper and impassive. Only Lady Gregory (who privately disapproved of *Playboy*) seems anxious and self-effacing.

PROTESTORS AGAINST SYNGE'S *PLAYBOY* CARICATURED (*right*). Gaelic Leaguers protested against 'titillating' love-scenes, little realizing that it was from a book published by the League's president, *Love Songs of Connacht*, that many of the offensive phrases had been taken. Yeats attributed the protests to sexual anxiety brought on by Synge's celebration of the body and he likened the protestors to eunuchs in hell gazing with envy upon Don Juan's sinewy thighs. The protestors insisted on the chastity of the Irish race, but one doctor present at an Abbey riot remarked, 'I can hardly resist pointing out those protestors whom I personally have treated for venereal disease.'

The object of that pastoral was to soften, and even obscure, the class differences which even then were overtaking rural life. Yeats inadvertently gave the nationalist game away in a striking couplet:

> Parnell came down the road and said to a cheering man:
> 'Ireland will get her freedom, and you still break stone.'

His more typical strategy, however, was to emphasize rather than ironize this vision of an ahistorical peasantry unaffected by social change. He does this most succinctly when he adopts the authoritative tones of the aristocratic war-hero Robert Gregory in a poem entitled *An Irish Airman Foresees his Death*:

> I know that I shall meet my fate
> Somewhere among the clouds above.
> Those that I fight I do not hate,
> Those that I guard I do not love.

That much, at least, is an honest account of the difficulties faced by one Irishman in working up enthusiasm for a British imperialist war. But then the poem changes tack:

> My country is Kiltartan Cross,
> My countrymen Kiltartan's poor,
> No likely end could bring them loss
> Or leave them happier than before.

Here, the soft-focus lens obscures those embarrassing class differences just then emerging among Irish country people. These differences had been described in uncompromising terms by Shaw, whose *John Bull's Other Island* depicted the

HYDE, PRIEST, AND CHILDREN ON THE ARAN ISLANDS. The cult of the innocent child was combined with that of the saintly peasant in much revivalist writing, while Abbey actors won praise in England for their childlike spontaneity of movement. Though himself a Protestant, Douglas Hyde recruited many Roman Catholic priests for his Gaelic League meetings, becoming (in George Moore's cutting phrase) 'the archetype of the cunning Catholic-Protestant'. Joyce believed that the clergy saw in the native language a sure barrier against foreign ideas and 'the wolves of disbelief'.

plight of the landless labourer in the wake of the Land Acts. Larry Doyle argued in that play that far from abolishing landlordism, the Land Acts had multiplied the number of petty landlords in every townland, and with them a sinister class-consciousness which would mean that the labourer's last lot would be worse than his first. The old landlords, comments Doyle, were too high in station above the peasant to feel any need to grind him into the ground; but the new peasant proprietors—tuppence ha'pennies effectively looking down on tuppences—will be lethal in writing the labourers out of Irish history. As lethal as they had already been in their campaigns against the persons and property of individual Irish landlords. It is at this point that the real poignancy of Yeats's lines becomes apparent. In the fate of Kiltartan's landless poor, Robert Gregory reads his own, for both will be common victims of the new nationalist regime. The peasant, like the landlord, is mythologized by the new middle class which, at that very moment, is putting both other groups out of business. Every repressive regime first crushes its victims; and, having safely contained them, it sentimentalizes them and reduces them to the status of merely literary material. The myth of a timeless peasantry, like the conceit of a noble aristocracy, is a middle-class invention, purveyed by the *arrivistes* who were seizing the positions of power and influence in Ireland's cities and towns. And in the writings of the impeccably middle-class W. B. Yeats, these conjoint conceits found a trusty celebrant. Hence the rather paradoxical fetishizing of aristocratic values by the insurgent Irish nationalists, who countered Big House culture with the mandarin locutions of the Gaelic bards. The aristocratic self-image of revivalists—all of them descended from kings, of course—blinded many to the economic motivations which impelled them; but, now and again, these hidden forces showed themselves, as when the rebel Cathal Brugha sacked an employee for trying to form a trade union.

That aristocratic self-image had other, equally unfortunate, results. For one thing, it was an abject surrender to the prevailing English categories of thought. For every English action, there must be an equal and opposite Irish reaction— for soccer, Gaelic football; for hockey, hurling; for trousers, a kilt. Thus was born 'the ingenious device of national parallelism' castigated in a recent book by Seán de Fréine as a failure of the Irish mind to clear itself of imposed English categories: 'It was felt that the Irish could not claim as theirs anything that was characteristic of England; on the other hand, not to have it could betoken inferiority.' So, if certain Irish antidotes did not previously exist, they had to be invented—Gaelic football being a classic case of instant archaeology, but definitely not a game known to Cuchulain. So, a new use was found for the Irish language as a kind of green spray-paint, useful in concealing the embarrassing similarity of Irish parliaments as well as Irish post-boxes to their English models, even after the institution of the Free State. It became all the more necessary to call the native parliament the *Dáil* in order to conceal its depressing similarity to

the despised Westminster model. One cannot avoid the suspicion that the new men, having no clear sense of selfhood, were seeking unconsciously to win the approval of those English authorities whom they had just ejected. If Yeats could sanitize a racist slur, then the politicians could spray-paint a parliament. A new word was needed, a Gaelic word like *Dáil*, because for years the nationalists had been pouring scorn on parliamentary processes. The parliament of Clan Thomas had been ruled by churls and called *Parlaimint*—as if the botched version of the true English word were a sign to aristocratic Gaelic bards that the new men of the 1650s could never achieve anything more than a pitiful parody of English ways. But the new men insured against such mockery by changing the word to *Dáil*, a more ancient and revered conception.

The Periphery and Centre in Irish Culture

From the pages of James Joyce, a picture of those new men—and they were, of course, men—emerges. The infant state would be ruled by a combination of peasant proprietors and an emergent administrative middle class in the cities, itself composed largely of first- or second-generation immigrants from rural areas.

SHEEP ON CARLISLE BRIDGE, 1873. Dublin has always been a capital dominated by the values and mores of the rural periphery. A 1972 survey found that almost 50% of political activists in the constituency of Dublin South-Central had cut their teeth in rural politics, importing its brokerist and clientelist traditions into the city. This helped to prevent the emergence of a left-right ideological politics of a kind to be found in comparable British cities.

The interests of both groups were often the same, as Joyce acidly noted in *Ulysses*, which describes Dublin newspaper controversies on such subjects as how to eradicate foot-and-mouth disease in cattle. Dublin in 1904, the year in which *Ulysses* was set, was already a rapidly expanding conurbation dominated by persons and values imported from the countryside. Sheep and cows were still commonly herded to the docks through the major thoroughfares of a city which Joyce liked to dub 'the centre of paralysis'.

His own first story was published in *The Irish Homestead*, a farmers' journal, and he was so ashamed of appearing in the 'pig's paper' that he employed the pseudonym 'Stephen Daedalus'. The editor, in commissioning the story, had appealed for something 'simple, rural, livemaking', which would not shock its readers. The short story was itself a ruralist form, which sprang up wherever folk anecdotes were challenged by the onset of print technology and a written literary tradition. It was ideally suited to capturing what Frank O'Connor would later call 'the lonely voice', the speech of those outsiders and individuals of an unmade society, the 'O's' and the 'Macs' of the emergent rural bourgeoisie. O'Connor, along with his fellow-Corkonian Sean O'Faolain, became one of its distinguished Irish practitioners in a tradition initiated by George Moore's *The Untilled Field* (a significant title, if ever there was one) and maintained by such later figures as Mary Lavin, Benedict Kiely, and John MacGahern. But the form was less effective in rendering the complex gradations and layers of city life.

Readers of the stories in Joyce's *Dubliners* have, accordingly, noted the way in which the collection trembles repeatedly on the brink of the novel form, with many internal links between stories and a character of increasing maturity at the centre of each. Yeats presciently remarked that they contained the promise of a novelist of a new kind. Feeling unrewarded by any sense of difficulties overcome, Joyce subsequently abandoned the short story as a formal oppression, but not before he had recorded the attempts by various characters to escape—as he duly would—the centre of paralysis. What makes *Dubliners* virtually unique in the history of urban writing is the fact that, in each story, movement out of the city is described as liberating, in contrast, for example, to the writings of Balzac, whose typical ploy is to depict a boy from the provinces achieving mature selfhood as he looks, with ultimate satisfaction, over the rooftops of Paris. Joyce found himself reversing that classic trajectory, because for him Dublin was not yet a fully metropolitan city. So he fled it to ply his art in places that were.

Ulysses is, of course, the classic account of the paralysis of Dublin and

JAMES JOYCE photographed by Gisèle Freund in 1938. Joyce abandoned Patrick Pearse's classes on finding that his youthful teacher seemed unable to praise the Irish language without denigrating English, and lived in self-imposed exile, mostly in France. Yet Joyce himself was a scathing critic of the 'brutish empire' which, he claimed, produced 'beer, beef, bibles, bulldogs, buggery, battleships and bishops'. His works, though often anti-Irish in a very Irish way, were conscious contributions to what he called 'the moral history of my country'. The hero of *A Portrait of the Artist as a Young Man* wishes 'to forge in the smithy of my soul the uncreated conscience of my race'.

O'CASEY'S ENGLISH EXILE was never easy. Lacking access to a regular company of actors who might test his ideas in performance, he made his later plays heavily abstract and symbolic. A satire on English romantic misconceptions of Ireland, *Purple Dust*—seen here in a 1953 rehearsal under the eye of Sam Wanamaker, Eithne Dunn, and the author—was hardly calculated to appeal to English jingoists during World War Two. Support for Irish neutrality brought unpopularity, and a rebuke from George Orwell.

Dubliners. Its central chapter describes a city whose traffic has been becalmed and frozen, as in a sepia tint; and its most famous interior monologues recount the experience of men and women defeated by an unsympathetic environment and seeking consolation in an inner world of fantasy. As such, it is celebrated as the definitive text of experimental modern literature, but it is also a very Irish book dominated by short oral anecdotes. If *Dubliners* was a collection of stories trying to be a novel, then *Ulysses* is a novel which can never quite abandon its tendency to disintegrate into a series of separate short stories. The same might also be said of those other experimental novels of twentieth-century Irish writing —Flann O'Brien's *At Swim-Two-Birds*, Máirtín Ó Cadhain's *Cré na Cille* (Graveyard Clay), and Samuel Beckett's trilogy.

All of which indicates the prevalence of ruralist forms even in the most technically daring or politically radical Irish writing. Seán O'Casey's plays are a further case in point. His drama of the Easter Rising, *The Plough and the Stars*, caused rioting at the Abbey Theatre on its first production in 1926. The protestors—mostly relations and comrades of the 1916 rebels—were angered by the appearance of a Citizen Army flag alongside a prostitute in a pub, and by the author's refusal to mythologize the rebel leaders. But the play proved immensely popular with the emergent middle class of civil servants, teachers, and administrators—those rural people who had come to Dublin to shape the new state. They found in the inner-city poor what landless Irish peasants had once been to the Anglo-Irish Ascendancy—literary material. They sentimentalized the victims of their own ruralist politics as lovable urban leprechauns, prone to the same chaotic mispronunciation of words as those stage-Irish peasants who had evoked British laughter in the nineteenth century. They were delighted by the eloquence of O'Casey's characters, whose rolling alliterative speeches owed more to the rhythms of Synge's rural dramas than to the terse locutions of actual inner-city dialect.

What charmed these audiences—although they probably didn't know it—was

FIFTY YEARS AFTER BLOOMSDAY, 16 June 1954. John Ryan, critic and editor of *Envoy* magazine; Anthony Cronin, radical journalist and poet; Brian O'Nolan (alias Flann O'Brien, alias Myles na gCopaleen), novelist and *Irish Times* columnist; poet and essayist Patrick Kavanagh; and Tom Joyce, cousin of James. By the 1980s, Bloomsday was *the* major literary festival of Ireland, with conventions of international writers, re-enactments of the novel *Ulysses* by city personalities, and (in 1982) a non-stop thirty-six-hour radio dramatization of the entire book.

the tacit confirmation of their own cultural hegemony, implicit in the struggle of Dublin artists to render urban life in ruralist forms. One generation later, in the 1950s, the poet Patrick Kavanagh would convert Baggot Street and its nearby canal into 'my Pembrokeshire', rediscovering in inner Dublin the pastoral landscapes he had abandoned in his youth. And *that* version of Ireland proved far more attractive to poetry-readers among the New Dubliners than had Kavanagh's savage indictment of rural torpor in *The Great Hunger* (1942), a long poem which chronicled the miseries of bachelordom on a poverty-stricken Monaghan farm. The programmatic conversion of Baggot Street into pastoral proved palatable to those politicians and architects who were intent on effecting parallel transformations themselves. Like Kavanagh, such New Dubliners in their earlier years tended to deride the rhythms of an urban life which they never entirely mastered; and, correspondingly, in their later years, to sentimentalize the rhythms of a rural life which they had not completely abandoned in their own minds.

The Great Hunger is a magnificent exception to that rule and a thoroughly deglamorized account of the brutalities (and intermittent benedictions) of life among the rural poor. It is a kind of anti-travelogue and anti-pastoral, which opens by rejecting Yeats's beloved image of *soil*. 'Clay is the word', insists Kavanagh, 'and clay is the flesh.' For such bluntness, the poet was visited by the Irish police and the poem itself seized.

This was one of the more ludicrous chapters in the history of modern Irish censorship of books and films, initiated in the 1920s and still practised, in much modified form, on such contemporary works as Alex Comfort's *The Joy of Sex*. Books by many of the foremost Irish and overseas authors—from Edna O'Brien to Scott Fitzgerald—were banned from Irish shops and stalls, once a concerned citizen had lodged a convincing complaint with the censorship board. 'Convincing' could mean proof that the offending book was indecent, obscene, or simply advocated 'unnatural' forms of birth control or abortion. Joyce's *Ulysses*— for some strange reason, perhaps its legendary obscurity—was virtually the only classic of modernism not to suffer this fate. Even the classic texts of Gaelic literature came under scrutiny, and an English translation of *The Midnight Court* was banned at a time when the far more ribald original Gaelic version was still on sale for sixpence in the government's own bookshop. All of which seemed to confirm J. M. Synge's contention that an artist would be permitted many freedoms in Irish which might not be deemed appropriate in genteel, post-Victorian English.

Hearing of the new censorship, Joyce in Paris was appalled. In the Dublin of his youth, he told a visitor, 'there was a kind of desperate freedom which comes from a lack of responsibility, for the English were in governance then, so everyone said what he liked'. Now, there was actually less freedom in a so-called Free

JUNO REHEARSED AT THE ABBEY, 1952. After the 1930s, with Yeats dead and O'Casey in self-imposed exile, the Abbey theatre went into a long decline. A series of kitchen-comedies left it 'the best-fed theatre company in Europe', according to Brendan Behan, but his own plays, like the early works of Beckett, were staged in the tiny Pike theatre by Alan Simpson. The Abbey became a dramatic museum, living off the glories of its past; and only in the 1960s did that gloom lift, with the explosive talents of Tom Murphy and Brian Friel.

State. Many intellectuals and artists, such as George Russell ('Æ'), Stephen MacKenna, and Thomas MacGreevy, preferred to leave Ireland rather than endure such indignity; and the foremost of these was the young Samuel Beckett, who told his bemused family in September 1939 that he preferred to live in a France at war than an Ireland at peace. Indignantly critical of those poets who based their art on Gaelic or Yeatsian traditions, he accused them of 'a flight from self-awareness'. He was equally hard on himself, abandoning the rather stylized wit and wordplay of his early novel *Murphy* (1938)—memorably described by Dylan Thomas as a blend of 'Sodom and Begorrah'—for the astringencies of

BECKETT TRAMPS. Dented bowler hats and shabby suits replicate Charlie Chaplin's portrayal of the decline of the bourgeois gent into shabby-genteel poverty and robotic mechanism. Such figures, along with broken boots, dustbins, blasted trees, and sandheaps were fitting emblems of the reduced post-war Beckettian world, which became as recognizable as a Dickensian illustration or a Brontëesque landscape. This photograph records the first UK production of *Waiting for Godot* at the Arts Theatre, London, in 1955, featuring Peter Bull, Timothy Bateson, Paul Daneman, and Peter Woodthorpe.

French, the second language in which he wrote most of his carefully crafted subsequent work.

Beckett's essential character, the Tramp, was a representative of the now rootless Anglo-Irish middle class, neither English nor Irish, but caught wandering in a no man's land between two cultures. This wanderer figure had already been shaped impressively in the plays of Synge and Yeats—though his ultimate roots were, of course, in the *spalpeen* poets cast out on to the road in seventeenth-century Ireland. 'You should have been a poet', says one of the tramps in *Waiting for Godot*. The other, pointing to his own rags in the manner of an Aogán Ó

Rathaille, replies: 'I was once. Isn't it obvious?' The locales of Beckett's world remained recognizably Irish too, as did his continuing love-affair with Hibernian skies and landscapes—a classic strategy of the Irish Protestant imagination which, discomfited by its own history, sought to impatriate itself through a heightened sense of geography.

A similar attempt at impatriation, by invocation of the Connacht graves in which his ancestors lie buried, marks the poetry of Louis MacNeice, one of the many striking 'northern voices' raised in modern Irish writing. However, even as a boy he felt 'banned forever from the candles of the Irish poor' and, at the same time, resentful of the life-denying forms of clerical Protestantism all around him:

> My father made the walls resound;
> He wore his collar the wrong way round.

Like other northern Protestant intellectuals, from C. S. Lewis to Helen Waddell, MacNeice steered scrupulously clear of the sectarian nature of local politics and, eventually, of Ireland itself, opting instead for a career in England. Yet, the kind of poetry which he wrote—wry, urbane, classical—constitutes a viable tradition on which contemporary Belfast artists like Michael Longley and Derek Mahon can draw.

The recent revival of the arts in the north has coincided with an upsurge in political turbulence in ways which might recall the coincidence of the 'Irish revival' with the period of nationalist upheaval at the turn of the last century. Yet this latest artistic renaissance, like the Civil Rights movement among the Roman Catholic minority in the north, may owe more to the education acts of the 1940s than to any more immediately political cause—for these acts sent, in due time, a wholly new kind of student to university in the 1960s. Most of the poetry and prose written in the north, as in the south, is personal rather than political in nature; and even those artists who address the world of politics write oftenest about the struggle to remain an artist under such pressures. The refusal of the most noted of them, Seamus Heaney, to take a political side is manifest in the ironically titled poem *Exposure*, which asserts that its author is neither internee nor informer, but a thoughtful wood-kerne escaped from the massacre. *Exposure* was written, in fact, in County Wicklow, where the poet and his family lived for a time, having left Belfast as a consequence of threats from loyalist paramilitaries. Such tact is understandable, and has been learned, in part, from Yeats's own meditations during another kind of civil war. Those writers who have addressed the northern crisis in a more direct manner have usually been less politically convincing. Novels like Bernard MacLaverty's *Cal* or Benedict Kiely's *Nothing Happens in Carmincross*, though hugely popular overseas and with the Irish middle class, manage to suggest that violence is rooted less in

social conditions than in the pathology of the person; and those who have addressed the social conditions—like Thomas Kinsella's protest against the murder
of thirteen civilians in Derry in 1972, *Butcher's Dozen*—have often found that in
becoming 'political' they virtually cease to be poets. John Montague's sequence
The Rough Field is a brave, and largely successful, negotiation of this minefield,
blending the history and geography of his native Tyrone in a magnanimous and
lyrical way. By invoking all traditions, this poem—like Heaney's later *Station
Island*—allows all the voices in a complex crisis to win some kind of hearing.

By far the most sustained meditation on the Troubles may be found in Seamus
Heaney's fourth collection *North*. In the preserved bodies of victims of a fertility-
cult dug up from a Jutland bog, the poet finds a correlative for the suffering of
contemporary targets of violence in Ireland. An ancient adulteress found with
a cauled black cap and halter round her head becomes an analogue for the
contemporary Catholic girl tarred and feathered by the IRA for fraternizing
with British soldiers; and the voracious earth-mother who swallows her victims
becomes a version of mother Ireland or Cathleen ni Houlihan devouring her
children in endless sacrificial rites. In the ancient Danish myth, Heaney reads
the contemporary Irish matter-of-fact.

This is, of course, anticipated in the method of Joyce's *Ulysses*, which saw the
wanderings of Homer's Odysseus re-enacted unknowingly by a Dublin ad-
canvasser. And that, in itself, suggests that contemporary Irish poetry is, as often
as not, written under the sign of Joyce rather than Yeats. As are contemporary
Irish plays. The mingling of the mythical and mundane is not just a theme, but a
worry, to playwright Brian Friel. His best-known work *Translations* dramatizes,
with admirable subtlety, the current reservations about 'Irish eloquence', as the
hedge-schoolmaster Hugh explains his native culture to a visiting Englishman in
the 1830s: 'Indeed, Lieutenant. A rich language. A rich literature. You'll find,
Sir, that certain cultures expend on their vocabularies and syntax acquisitive
energies and ostentations entirely lacking in their material lives. I suppose you
could call us a spiritual people.' He says that 'a syntax opulent with tomorrows'
is 'our response to mud-cabins and a diet of potatoes'. The crucial fact of this
exchange is Friel's preceding stage-direction, to the effect that Hugh 'as the
scene progresses . . . is deliberately parodying himself', as he explains just why
the Englishman finds the area and its people so attractive. Hugh culminates the
encounter with a Shavian warning about the danger of lapsing entirely into

TRANSLATIONS. The play is written in English, but the audience is to imagine its speakers using mostly
Irish, as they painfully witness the placenames of their townland being Anglicized by the new ordnance
surveyors. Though set in the 1830s, *Translations* is a covert exploration of the attempt by post-Whitaker
Ireland to convert tradition into modernity without betrayal. The Field Day Theatre Company of
Derry, founded in 1980, has since issued pamphlets and an anthology of literature, in a similar attempt
to forge 'a fifth province of the mind' in which all Irish forces could meet.

mythical dreams: 'it can happen that a civilisation can be imprisoned in a linguistic contour that no longer matches the landscape of fact' because 'words are not immortal'. At the close of the play, he retreats, like Shaw's Keegan, into a purely visionary world, but not before his critique of the English Celtophile updates the depiction of Shaw's Broadbent.

Friel's play, though set in the nineteenth century, is a clear account of the disruptions of modernity and the gapped nature of modern Irish tradition. It isn't hard, for example, to read it as a veiled account of the clash between consumerism and traditionalism in Friel's own Ireland, or even as a version of the clash between Gaelic and English cultures in today's Ulster, where even to speak in Irish to a policeman may be deemed tantamount to a revolutionary act. Yet, when Friel did directly tackle northern politics in *The Freedom of the City*, he produced a vastly inferior play.

The appointment of this playwright to the Seanad (Senate) of the Republic in 1987 was not just a recognition of his artistic achievement, but a signal from Taoiseach Charles Haughey that the old antagonism between artist and politician had died. Ever since the 1960s, the censorship of books and films had been gradually relaxed. Instead, tax-exemptions for artists and, eventually, guaranteed minimal incomes for a projected 150 members of a government-sponsored cultural élite (known as Aosdána) indicated that a *new rapprochement* had been achieved.

This may provide an even deeper reason why contemporary Irish writers tend to fight shy of politics and to locate most of their investigations in the pathology of the individual. They don't wish to bite the political hand that feeds—or might feed—them. In theory, members of Aosdána are free to write what they wish; but, in practice, their work has been a lot less critical of politicians and of social injustice than that of their predecessors, such as Brendan Behan or Austin Clarke. Major political controversies, like the hunger strikes of the early 1980s, or the torture of innocent suspects in Irish and British gaols, or the divorce and abortion referenda of the mid-80s, have passed without finding their laureate. It is hard to imagine a Yeats or an O'Casey failing to be inspired by such challenging material.

While it is salutary that the arts have an honoured place under an enlightened Taoiseach, there is a danger that the Aos (band or group) will not live up to both Gaelic meanings of its name and become truly *dána* in the sense of 'daring' as well as merely 'artistic'. The writers of the revivalist generation believed that it was the artist's duty to insult, as well as occasionally to flatter, his fellow-countrymen; and Yeats spoke for many when he said that a man of real genius is never like a country's idea of itself. But modern Irish artists seem all too like the more conventional bards of Classical Ireland—all too willing to reflect rather than to interrogate current state policy. Within the past generation, there has been a massive change. Not long ago, artists and intellectuals were oppressed by the Irish people; but now, there is a distinct possibility that the Irish people are oppressed—in the sense of misrepresented or ignored—by the intellectuals.

'The Truth and Fiction of an Empty Isle'

Despite all this, the subversive potential of truly great art always remains as an implicit challenge to complacent leaders. They, in turn, have sought to censor or shout down those works written by men and women too integral to be bought. The banning of *The Midnight Court* is one example of the selectiveness of Irish revivalists. The persecution of Synge and O'Casey for reopening traditions of liberated Gaelic womanhood is another. However, the most insidious form of mental tyranny is neither censorship nor suppression, but the sanitizing and misrepresentation of classic texts which goes by the name of education. For example, the very texts which were used in Free State classrooms to purvey the image of a stoic, ahistorical peasant—the autobiographies of the Blasket Islanders—fairly vibrate with hidden class tensions. Their authors report a common experience—to leave the island and set foot on the mainland was to experience once again the fall of man, from a kind of anarchist commune to a world of social tensions and snobbish differences.

In *Fiche Blian ag Fás* (Twenty Years a-Growing), Muiris Ó Súilleabháin recounted how the islanders felt like inner exiles once they set foot on the Kerry mainland. Asked in Dingle the derisive question, 'An Éireannach thú?' (Are you an Irishman?), the migrant boy replies, 'Ní hea, ach Blascaodach' (No, I'm a Blasketman). The islands had bred an egalitarian tribe, who shared a common poverty and a common danger, which left them free of any class feeling. This is even clearer from the pages of *An tOileánach* (The Islandman) by an older inhabitant, Tomás Ó Criomhthain. He recalls his bafflement and outrage at the divisions of wealth and labour which he encountered on *his* first expedition to Dingle. There, on the quayside, were labourers in rags, supervised by a smug, well-dressed gaffer: 'Chonnac daoine uaisle ina seasamh ann agus slabhraí timpeall a mbuilg, daoine bochta agus gan a leath-cheart d'éadach orthu' (I saw noble persons standing there, and ornamental belts around their waists, and poor people without half their share of clothing on them). It is easy to see why socialist authors, from Peadar O'Donnell to George Thomson, have chosen island life as a theme; and also why Máirtín Ó Cadhain, the one indisputably great writer to emerge from the mainland Gaeltachtaí, should have devoted so much of his masterpiece *Cré na Cille* to anatomizing the internal snobberies between those corpses buried in the fifteen-shilling plots and those whose graves cost a whole guinea.

For radicals of all kinds, the western island seemed like an ideal commune, a

repository of what Gaelic Ireland once was and might become again. To John Millington Synge, the women of Aran, dressed in flaming red petticoats seemed untouched by the drab, ladylike Victorian gentility of their counterparts on the Galway mainland. Aran wives reminded him, rather, of the New Women of New York and Paris; and it was this fierce independence of spirit which he re-created in the Pegeen Mikes and Nora Burkes of his plays. In doing this, Synge was consciously reverting to a liberationist eighteenth-century Gaelic tradition manifest in the poetry of men like Art Mac Cubhthaigh and Brian Merriman.

Another attractive feature of the islands, to Synge, was the absence of any social division by class or by labour. This, he found, left each person with a versatile and refined character, and the temperament of an artist, whose work changed with the seasons. Synge acidly noted how the introduction of a police force was slowly leading to a loss of innocence on the islands; and he remarked on the fact that, despite this modernization, the islanders persisted in their age-old belief that imprisonment had no corrective effect on criminals. Even in the case of a murderer, they believed that remorse for such a deed was punishment in itself, 'and can see no reason why he should be dragged away and killed by law'.

Another Dublin writer, Brendan Behan, rediscovered for the next generation

BRENDAN BEHAN, a writer of extraordinary talent, died in his forties without achieving his full potential. Having spent his early years in prison for IRA activities, he first wrote haunting poems in Irish, attempting thus to fuse his cultural and political nationalism. Material success came only with his English-language plays, *The Quare Fellow* and *The Hostage*; and his rambunctious autobiography *Borstal Boy* made him a *succès de scandale* on chat-shows produced by Britain's 'angry young men' of the early 1960s.

many of these themes among the Blasket islanders. His play about Dublin prison life *The Quare Fellow* contains a young Blasketman who, alone among the prisoners, questions the right of any society to inflict capital punishment. And, sure enough, when the prison governor advertises for a native hangman (who must, by civil service law, be an Irish speaker), there are no suitable applicants. It must have seemed brutally symbolic to a republican like Behan that the official hangman of the Irish Free State was a regularly imported Englishman. The islander in *The Quare Fellow* argues that he is in gaol to do penance for the sins of the wealthy and powerful. He clashes with a Dublin *Gaeilgeoir* (Irish-speaker) who has simply used the Irish language to further his own career, in a Free State which has not managed to abolish prisons, but has merely changed the badges in the warders' caps. All the old class-prejudice, imported from England, has not been repudiated in the new state, but is now voiced in bad Irish by Dublin-based *Gaeilgeoirí*. So Behan turns with relief from the wearers of the *Fáinne* (a ring-shaped badge, sported by Irish speakers, which he wickedly dubbed the Erse-hole) to the authentic Gaelic anarchists of the Blaskets. For him, too, the mainland has been infected with the strange virus of private property and punitive institutions. The grim prediction of Friedrich Engels in 1856 has come to pass: 'Despite all their nationalist fanaticism, the fellows feel that they are no longer at home in their own country.' Only a few scattered western islands offered liberation not just from class tensions, but from the very idea of the state as such.

Utopian Literature: Ireland as Nowhere

Something of that freedom is glimpsed in *Allagar na hInise* (Island Smalltalk) by Tomás Ó Criomhthain. He tells of how Blasket islanders, gathered round a fire for Easter 1916, are suddenly bemused by the unexpected news that a republic has been declared in Dublin. 'Abair an focal *republic* i nGaoluinn', says one, 'Say the word *republic* in Irish'. They all rack their brains but can find no term. 'Agus is beag a chuir a soláthar imní, ach oiread, oraibh' adds the laconic Tomás: 'and it's little its attainment worried you either'.

Theirs is a republic which has been scrutinized and investigated by most post-'independence' Irish writers, from Kavanagh to Kinsella, from Ó Cadhain to Behan. It is the republic of all those who happened to be born in a place called

STUDY TOWARD AN IMAGE OF SAMUEL BECKETT, 1965, by Louis le Brocquy. Sensing that words could never rival the camera or tape-recorder in the rendition of surface realities, Irish writers opted to enter the human head. Yeats spoke of poetry as the mind's 'quarrel with itself'; Joyce rendered the stream of consciousness in *Ulysses*; but Beckett, in his trilogy, attempted verbal equivalents for the preconscious. Louis le Brocquy's head, which might be that of an ancient Celtic warrior, records this intrepid attempt.

Edward McGuire

Ireland, but who felt neither allowed nor impelled to take part—some, because they were forced to emigrate and live as aliens in another land, others because they felt sentenced to a kind of internal exile in their own. It is a republic without a name, a place which does not yet exist, except perhaps in the Utopian imaginations of Irish artists, who are continually criticizing the blemished island whence they came and, by this very action, implying the existence of an ideal Ireland into which they might one day come.

It may well be, however, that the very idea of 'Ireland'—like the now deserted Great Blasket which went on sale for a million dollars in the *Wall Street Journal* in 1987—is a kind of fiction, which the mere islanders themselves are finding it harder and harder to sustain. But it is a necessary fiction, and tens of millions of people on our planet turn annually to that fiction for an explanation of their innermost being. All nations are, in Benedict Anderson's phrase, an invented or imagined community, and the Irish have shown more relish for that fiction than most. In particular, they have asked their writers to chart its progress for them. On the other hand, the Irish have also shown a marked aversion to the idea of the state, which levies taxes and asks for other sacrifices—and so have their contemporary writers. The problem is that the ideal nation can only achieve concrete form through the medium of the state, whose apparatus, ever since the colonial phase of their experience, many of them have learned to hate or fear. A true republic—a happy embodiment of the idea of the nation in a state—is something that all Irish people, and not just Ó Criomhthain's Blasket Islanders, have yet to know.

SEAMUS HEANEY, 1974, by Edward McGuire. The leading contemporary Irish poet, he divides his time between Harvard University and his home in Dublin. His early work recorded the violent lyricism of life on a Derry farm. Thereafter, he addressed the political violence endemic to the Northern state, finding a parallel experience in the ancient sacrificial rites of Jutland, whose victims' bodies were rediscovered in this century perfectly preserved in Danish bogs.

FURTHER READING

1. PREHISTORIC AND EARLY CHRISTIAN IRELAND

GENERAL SURVEYS

T. G. E. Powell, *The Celts*, Ancient Peoples and Places 6 (London, 1958), a sober and well-illustrated introduction to the Celtic background.

Máire and Liam de Paor, *Early Christian Ireland*, Ancient Peoples and Places 8 (London, 1958), a well-illustrated and judicious general survey.

Eoin MacNeill, *Celtic Ireland* (Dublin, 1921; 2nd edn., Dublin, 1981), fundamental studies by the founding father of early Irish history.

Gearóid Mac Niocaill, *Ireland before the Vikings* (Dublin, 1972), a general history to AD 800, with particular stress on politics.

Donnchadh Ó Corráin, *Ireland before the Normans* (Dublin, 1972), a thematic treatment of AD 800 to *c*.1166.

Francis John Byrne, *Irish Kings and High-Kings* (London, 1973, repr. 1987), a study of kingship which ranges widely over literature and institutions.

ARCHAEOLOGY AND ART

Françoise Henry, *Irish Art* (3 vols., London, 1965–70).

—— *Irish High Crosses* (Dublin, 1964), a brief but authoritative survey.

—— *The Book of Kells with a Study of the Manuscript* (London, 1974), a masterly study of the manuscript and its history, splendidly illustrated.

—— and Geneviève Marsh-Micheli, *Studies in Early Christian and Medieval Irish Art*, i–iii (London, 1985).

Michael Ryan (ed.), *Ireland and Insular Art, A.D. 500–1200* (Dublin, 1987), the last word by the experts on many of the central problems of Irish art history and its relations with Anglo-Saxon and late Roman art.

A. T. Lucas, *Treasures of Ireland: Irish Pagan and Early Christian Art* (Dublin, 1973), splendidly illustrated.

Harold G. Leask, *Irish Churches and Monastic Buildings* (3 vols., Dundalk, 1955–60, repr. 1977–8), the standard study of medieval Irish church architecture.

E. R. Norman and J. K. S. St Joseph, *The Early Development of Irish Society: The Evidence of Aerial Photography* (Cambridge, 1969), a fascinating collection of early archaeological sites and landscapes (the commentary is poorish).

Terence Reeves-Smyth and Fred Hammond, *Landscape Archaeology in Ireland*, British Archaeological Reports, British Series 116 (Oxford, 1983), a valuable collection of essays on the early and medieval Irish landscape.

CHRISTIANITY AND EARLY MEDIEVAL CULTURE

The fundamental work is James F. Kenney, *The Sources for the Early History of Ireland: Ecclesiastical* (New York, 1929, repr. New York and Dublin 1966).

Kathleen Hughes, *The Church in Early Irish Society* (London, 1966), the best general survey from conversion to the twelfth century.

Collections of essays:

There are four large and very important collections of essays on early Irish Christianity, its culture, and its influence on Europe:

Dorothy Whitelock, Rosamond McKitterick, and David Dumville (eds.), *Ireland in Early Medieval Europe* (Cambridge, 1982).

Heinz Löwe (ed.), *Die Iren und Europa im früheren Mittelalter* (Stuttgart, 1982).

Próinséas Ní Chatháin and Michael Richter (eds.), *Ireland and Europe: The Early Church* (Stuttgart, 1984).

Próinséas Ní Chatháin and Michael Richter (eds.), *Ireland and Christendom: The Bible and the Missions* (Stuttgart, 1987).

ST PATRICK

Works: Ludwig Bieler (ed.), *The Works of St Patrick*, Ancient Christian Writers 17 (London, 1953), containing the 'Confession' and 'Letter to Coroticus'. See also: R. P. C. Hanson and C. Blanc, *Confession et Lettre à Coroticus*, Sources Chrétiennes 249 (Paris, 1978).

Studies: D. A. Binchy, 'St Patrick and his Biographers: Ancient and Modern', in *Studia Hibernica* 2 (1962), 7–123.

R. P. C. Hanson, *St Patrick: His Origins and Career* (Oxford, 1968).

Charles Thomas, *Christianity in Roman Britain to AD 500* (London, 1981), admirably filling in the British background to Irish Christianity.

LITERATURE

Gerard Murphy, *The Ossianic Lore and Romantic Tales of Medieval Ireland* (Dublin: Cultural Relations Committee, 1955) and *Saga and myth in ancient Ireland* (Dublin: Cultural Relations Committee, 1961), though dated, are still useful.

Myles Dillon (ed.), *Irish Sagas* (Dublin, 1959, repr. Cork, 1970), useful general lectures on the narrative literature.

Brian Ó Cuív (ed.), *Seven Centuries of Irish Learning 1000–1700* (Dublin, 1961), dealing with the literature of the eleventh and twelfth centuries.

James Carney (ed.), *Early Irish Poetry* (Cork, 1965), a highly readable introduction to poetry in Latin and the vernacular.

There are three excellent anthologies of vernacular poetry, text, and translation:

Gerard Murphy, *Early Irish Lyrics* (Oxford, 1956, rev. repr. 1962, 1970).

James Carney, *Medieval Irish Lyrics* (Dublin, 1967).

David Greene and Frank O'Connor, *A Golden Treasury of Irish Poetry, A.D. 600 to 1200* (London, 1967).

FROM VIKING TO NORMAN

P. G. Foote and D. M. Wilson, *The Viking Achievement* (London, 1970, rev. edn. 1979), an excellent introduction to Viking life and culture.

Peter Sawyer, *Kings and Vikings: Scandinavia and Europe AD 700–1100* (London, 1982), an excellent and accurate survey, placing Ireland in the general context of the European experience.

Brian Ó Cuív (ed.), *The Impact of the Scandinavian on the Celtic-speaking Peoples: Proceedings of the International Celtic Congress . . . Dublin 1959* (Dublin, 1962, repr. 1975), eight specialist studies (some now dated).

Étienne Rynne (ed.), *North Munster Studies* (Limerick, 1967), containing important studies of Viking raiding and the rise of Dál Cais.

A. J. Goedheer, *Irish and Norse Tradition about the Battle of Clontarf* (Haarlem, 1938), dealing with the impact of the Vikings on Irish literature.

R. H. M. Dolley, *The Hiberno-Norse Coins in the British Museum* (London, 1966), the authoritative treatment of this area.

T. W. Moody (ed.), *Nationality and the pursuit of national independence* (Belfast, 1978), contains material on the kings of the tenth, eleventh, and twelfth centuries.

A. Cosgrove (ed.), *A New History of Ireland*, ii: *Medieval Ireland, 1169-1534* (Oxford, 1987), treating in detail of Dermot MacMurrough and the events leading up to the Norman invasion.

THE TWELFTH-CENTURY REFORM OF THE CHURCH

A. Gwynn, *The Twelfth Century Reform* (Dublin, 1968), a succinct survey.

H. J. Lawlor, *St Bernard of Clairvaux's Life of St Malachy of Armagh* (London, 1920), conveying (with a wealth of annotation) the views of one of the greatest of the reformers.

John Watt, *The Church and the Two Nations in Medieval Ireland* (Cambridge, 1970), placing the reform in the longer perspective of later medieval Irish history.

2. THE NORMAN INVASION AND THE GAELIC RECOVERY

GENERAL GUIDES AND SURVEYS

P. W. A. Asplin, *Medieval Ireland c.1170-1495: A Bibliography of Secondary Works* (Dublin, Royal Irish Academy, 1971).

A. Cosgrove (ed.), *A New History of Ireland*, ii: *Medieval Ireland, 1169-1534* (Oxford, 1987), particularly valuable for its wide range of economic and cultural studies.

G. H. Orpen, *Ireland under the Normans* (Oxford, 1911, 1920; repr. 1968), the most detailed narrative of events to 1333, centred on the lordships rather than the royal administration. Still invaluable.

E. Curtis, *A History of Medieval Ireland* (6th edn., London, 1957).

R. Frame, *Colonial Ireland 1169-1369* (Dublin, 1981).

J. F. Lydon, *Ireland in the Later Middle Ages* (Dublin, 1973).

A. Cosgrove, *Late Medieval Ireland 1370-1534* (Dublin, 1981).

K. W. Nicholls, *Gaelic and Gaelicised Ireland in the Later Middle Ages* (Dublin, 1972), description of society and institutions followed by a rapid survey of individual Gaelic lordships.

Steven G. Ellis, *Tudor Ireland: Crown, Community and the Conflict of Cultures 1470-1603* (London, 1985).

J. F. Lydon (ed.), *England and Ireland in the Later Middle Ages* (Dublin, 1981), essays presented to A. J. Otway-Ruthven.

J. A. Watt, J. B. Morrall, and F. X. Martin (eds.), *Medieval Studies presented to Aubrey Gwynn, S.J.* (Dublin, 1961). Half the essays are on a wide range of medieval Irish topics.

CONQUEST, GOVERNMENT, AND ADMINISTRATION

F. X. Martin, *No Hero in the House: Diarmait MacMurchada and the Coming of the Normans to Ireland* (Dublin, 1975).

J. J. O'Meara (ed.), *Gerald of Wales: The History and Topography of Ireland* (Harmondsworth, 1982), English translation with original manuscript illustrations.

A. B. Scott and F. X. Martin (eds.), *Expugnatio Hibernica: The Conquest of Ireland, by Giraldus Cambrensis* (Dublin, 1978), text, translation, and notes.

J. F. Lydon, *The Lordship of Ireland in the Middle Ages* (Dublin, 1972), a work of interpretation rather than narrative.

A. J. Otway-Ruthven, *A History of Medieval Ireland* (2nd edn., London, 1980), a magisterial work centred on the royal administration.

H. G. Richardson and G. O. Sayles, *The Administration of Ireland 1172–1377* (Dublin, 1963), chronological lists of office-holders, with commentary.

J. F. Lydon (ed.), *The English in Medieval Ireland* ([Dublin] Royal Irish Academy, 1984), essays on the colonial identity.

G. J. Hand, *English law in Ireland 1290–1324* (Cambridge, 1967).

H. G. Richardson and G. O. Sayles (eds.), *Parliaments and Councils of Medieval Ireland*, i (Dublin, 1947), samples of the relevant documents with commentary.

J. F. Lydon, 'The Bruce Invasion of Ireland', in *Historical Studies*, 4 (1963), ed. G. A. Hayes-McCoy, 111–25.

R. Frame, *English Lordship in Ireland 1318–1361* (Oxford, 1982), includes detailed discussion of the extent and consequences of absentee landownership.

E. Curtis, *Richard II in Ireland 1394–5; and Submissions of the Irish Chiefs* (Oxford, 1927), edition and translation with commentary of letters and submissions from the Irish chiefs.

J. F. Lydon, 'Richard II's Expeditions to Ireland', in *Journal of the Royal Society of Antiquaries of Ireland*, 93 (1963), 135–49.

H. G. Richardson and G. O. Sayles, *The Irish Parliament in the Middle Ages* (Philadelphia and Oxford, 1952), a constitutional history.

C. A. Empey and K. Simms, 'The Ordinances of the White Earl and the Problem of Coign in the Later Middle Ages', in *Proceedings of the Royal Irish Academy*, 75 C (1975), 161–87.

K. Simms, *From Kings to Warlords: The Changing Political Structure of Gaelic Ireland in the Later Middle Ages* (Woodbridge, 1987; Studies in Celtic History 7, gen. ed. D. Dumville).

Steven G. Ellis, *Reform and Revival: English Government in Ireland 1470–1534* (Woodbridge, 1986, RHS Studies in History no. 47), uses new documentary evidence for English policy towards Ireland in this period.

RELIGION

R. N. Hadcock and A. Gwynn, *Medieval Religious Houses: Ireland* (London, 1970), an indispensable guide to all recorded foundations, now reprinted.

C. [Conway], *The Story of Mellifont* (Dublin, 1958), throws light on the general history of medieval Irish Cistercians.

John A. Watt, *The Church and the Two Nations in Medieval Ireland* (Cambridge, 1970), a detailed study, which ends in the mid-fourteenth century.

G. J. Hand, *The Church in the English Lordship 1216–1307* (Dublin, 1968); A. Gwynn, *Anglo-Irish Church Life: Fourteenth and Fifteenth Centuries* (Dublin, 1968); and C. Mooney, *The Church in Gaelic Ireland: Thirteenth to Fifteenth Centuries* (Dublin, 1969): fascicles 3, 4, and 5 in Patrick J. Corish (ed.), *A History of Irish Catholicism* (Dublin, 1967–72).

John Watt, *The Church in Medieval Ireland* (Dublin, 1972), a very clear survey.

ART, ARCHITECTURE, LITERATURE

R. A. Stalley, 'The Long Middle Ages', in *The Irish World*, ed. B. de Breffny (London, 1977), a sketch of the art and architecture of both Gaelic and Anglo-Norman Ireland.

J. Hunt, *Irish Medieval Figure Sculpture 1200–1600* (2 vols., Dublin and London, 1974).

R. A. Stalley, *Architecture and Sculpture in Ireland 1150–1350* (Dublin and New York, 1971).

Brian Ó Cuív (ed.), *Seven Centuries of Irish Learning 1000–1700* (Dublin, 1961), essays by Celticists on the various branches of bardic lore.

A. O'Sullivan and P. Ó Riain (eds.), *Poems on Marcher Lords* (London, 1987), five poems to three barons, a chief, and an archbishop in late-fifteenth-century Tipperary.

ARCHAEOLOGY

T. B. Barry, *The Archaeology of Medieval Ireland* (London and New York, 1987), the first general survey for this period.

T. E. McNeill, *Anglo-Norman Ulster: The History and Archaeology of an Irish Barony 1177–1400* (Edinburgh, 1980).

TRADE AND SETTLEMENT

T. O'Neill, *Merchants and Mariners in Medieval Ireland* (Dublin, 1987), a lively anecdotal account of trade and shipping, with contemporary illustrations.

A. Simms, 'Continuity and Change: Settlement and Society in Medieval Ireland *c.*500–1500', in *The Shaping of Ireland: The Geographical Perspective*, ed. W. Nolan (Cork and Dublin, 1986), 44–65, with abundant references to more detailed studies.

C. A. Empey, 'Conquest and Settlement: Patterns of Anglo-Norman Settlement in North Munster and South Leinster', in *Irish Economic and Social History*, 13 (1986), 5–31, based on the Butler lordship.

A. J. Otway-Ruthven, 'The Character of Norman Settlement in Ireland', in *Historical Studies*, 5 (1965), ed. J. L. McCracken, 75–84.

H. B. Clarke and A. Simms (eds.), *The Comparative History of Urban Origins in Non-Roman Europe*, ii ([Oxford] BAR International Series 255, ii, 1985), an Irish-based study with a number of relevant articles.

3. EARLY MODERN IRELAND

GENERAL WORKS

Steven G. Ellis, *Tudor Ireland: Crown, Community and the Conflict of Cultures 1470–1603* (London, 1985), a comprehensive survey of events to about 1570, with excellent chapters on administrative matters and the promotion of religious reform.

R. W. Dudley Edwards and Mary O'Dowd (eds.), *Sources for Early Modern Irish History, 1534–1641* (Cambridge, 1985), the best short guide to the archival sources, with valuable accounts of how the principal manuscript collections came into being.

Ciaran Brady and Raymond Gillespie (eds.), *Natives and Newcomers: The Making of Irish Colonial Society, 1534–1641* (Dublin, 1986), challenging essays.

T. W. Moody, F. X. Martin, F. J. Byrne (eds.), *A New History of Ireland*, iii: *Early Modern Ireland, 1534–1691* (Oxford, 1976), the essential reference book, with comprehensive bibliography down to the date of publication.

Nicholas Canny, *From Reformation to Restoration: Ireland 1534–1660* (Dublin, 1987).

David Dickson, *New Foundations: Ireland 1660–1800* (Dublin, 1987).

Patrick J. Corish, *The Catholic Community in the Seventeenth and Eighteenth Centuries* (Dublin, 1981).

The last three volumes, from the Helicon History of Ireland, provide recent brief summaries.

GOVERNMENT AND ADMINISTRATION

Steven G. Ellis, *Reform and Revival: English Government in Ireland, 1470–1534* (Woodbridge, 1986), an exhaustive study of English administration in Ireland at the close of the medieval period, asserting the challenging conclusion that the English interest in Ireland was strengthened during the years of the Kildare ascendancy.

Brendan Bradshaw, *The Irish Constitutional Revolution of the Sixteenth Century* (Cambridge, 1979), an essential study of the Old English strategy for promoting reform.

Ciaran Brady, 'Conservative Subversives: The Community of the Pale and the Dublin Administration, 1556–86', in P. J. Corish (ed.), *Radicals, Rebels and Establishments: Historical Studies XV* (Belfast, 1985), 11–33, an important article which provides a plausible explanation of the rift between the community of the Pale and the English government in Dublin.

Hans Pawlisch, *Sir John Davies and the Conquest of Ireland: A Study in Legal Imperialism* (Cambridge, 1983), a close study of the use made of the common and civil law to promote social change in Ireland.

Bernadette Cunningham, 'The Composition of Connacht in the Lordships of Clanricard and Thomond, 1577–1642', in *Irish Historical Studies*, 24 (1984), 1–14, an essential study of the operation of provincial presidencies in Ireland.

T. C. Barnard, *Cromwellian Ireland: English Government and Reform in Ireland 1649–60* (Oxford, 1975), analysing the Cromwellian effort to erect a new society in Ireland.

James I. McGuire, 'Why was Ormond Dismissed in 1669?', in *Irish Historical Studies*, 18 (1973), 295–312, perceptive on the politics of Restoration Ireland.

LANDOWNING, SETTLEMENT, AND COLONIZATION

Nicholas Canny, *The Elizabethan Conquest of Ireland: A Pattern Established 1565–76* (Hassocks, 1976), focusing on the originality of Sir Henry Sidney's governorship of Ireland and its implications for the future.

—— 'Identity Formation in Ireland: The Emergence of the Anglo-Irish', in Nicholas Canny and Anthony Pagden (eds.), *Colonial Identity in the Atlantic World 1500–1800* (Princeton, 1987), 159–212, an effort to trace a continuous thread of motivation behind the involvement of English settlers in Ireland.

Michael MacCarthy Morrogh, *The Munster Plantation 1580–1641* (Oxford, 1985), the most satisfactory study of one of the major plantations in Irish history.

Terence Ranger, 'Richard Boyle and the Making of an Irish Fortune', in *Irish Historical Studies*, 10 (1957), 257–97, an original and enduring study of how wealth could be amassed through official corruption.

Michael Perceval-Maxwell, *The Scottish Migration to Ulster in the reign of James I* (London, 1973), still the most reliable on the size and source of that migration.

Raymond Gillespie, *Colonial Ulster: The Settlement of East Ulster 1600–41* (Cork, 1985), the best study of the British background of a migrant group to Ireland, with a description of their settlement in Antrim and Down.

Philip Robinson, *The Plantation of Ulster: British Settlement in an Irish Landscape, 1600–1670* (Dublin, 1984), a geographer's view which stresses continuity as well as change.

R. J. Hunter, 'Ulster Plantation Towns, 1609–41', in David Harkness and Mary O'Dowd (eds.), *The Town in Ireland* (Belfast, 1981), 55–80, an essential account.

T. C. Barnard, 'Planters and Policies in Cromwellian Ireland', *Past and Present*, 61 (1973), 31–69, a breezy and convincing account of Henry Cromwell's intervention in Ireland.

Karl Bottigheimer, *English Money and Irish Land: The 'Adventurers' in the Cromwellian Settlement of Ireland* (Oxford, 1971).

Karl Bottigheimer, 'The Restoration Land Settlement in Ireland: A Structural View', in *Irish Historical Studies*, 18 (1972), 1–21, an essential article on an important episode.

Nicholas Canny, *Kingdom and Colony: Ireland in the Atlantic World, 1560–1800* (Baltimore, Md., 1988), dealing with social consequences of English migration into Ireland.

RELIGION

Brendan Bradshaw, *The Dissolution of the Religious Orders in Ireland under Henry VIII* (Cambridge, 1974).

Alan Ford, *The Protestant Reformation in Ireland 1590–1641* (Frankfurt-on-Main, 1985), a comprehensive description of the training and recruitment of a Protestant clergy for Ireland with a less convincing interpretation of their motivation.

D. F. Cregan, 'The Social and Cultural Background of a Counter-reformation Episcopate, 1618–66', in Art Cosgrove and Donal McCartney (eds.), *Studies in Irish History Presented to R. Dudley Edwards* (Dublin, 1979).

Maureen Wall, *The Penal Laws* (Dublin, 1961), an analysis of the motivation behind the enactment of legislation against Catholics.

S. J. Connolly, 'Religion and History', in *Irish Economic and Social History*, 10 (1983), 66–80, a critical appraisal of the historiography of the penal laws.

INTELLECTUAL HISTORY

Ciaran Brady, 'Spenser's Irish Crisis: Humanism and Experience in the 1590s', in *Past and Present*, 111 (May, 1986), 16–49, a stimulating attempt to account for the bleakness of Spenser's views on social reform in Ireland.

David B. Quinn, *The Elizabethans and the Irish* (Ithaca, New York, 1966), a novel analysis of English perceptions of Gaelic society and how they underwent change through the sixteenth century.

Colm Lennon, *Richard Stanihurst: The Dubliner 1542–1618* (Dublin, 1981), a sympathetic portrait of an Old English intellectual.

Nicholas Canny, *The Upstart Earl: A Study of the Social and Mental World of Richard Boyle, First Earl of Cork 1566–1643* (Cambridge, 1982), an analysis of the private life of the best-documented English settler in Ireland, attempting to assess his typicality.

K. T. Hoppen, *The Common Scientist in the Seventeenth Century: A Study of the Dublin Philosophical Society 1683–1708* (London, 1970), the most important work on the intellectual life of the Irish Protestant community.

J. G. Simms, *William Molyneux of Dublin 1656–98* (Dublin, 1982), an exemplary critical study of a major intellectual figure.

THE NINE YEARS' WAR

G. A. Hayes McCoy, *Irish Battles* (London, 1969), giving an extensive coverage of the main engagements.

Frederick M. Jones, *Mountjoy, 1563–1606: The Last Elizabethan Deputy* (London, 1958).

J. J. Silke, *Kinsale: The Spanish Intervention in Ireland at the End of the Elizabethan Wars* (Liverpool, 1970), a close analysis of the battle with an excellent chapter on the European background.

Micheline Kerney Walsh, *Destruction by Peace: Hugh O'Neill after Kinsale* (Armagh, 1986), a comprehensive if rather uncritical account of O'Neill's career immediately preceding and after his exile from Ireland, with supporting documentation.

THE CONFEDERATE WARS AND THEIR BACKGROUND

Aidan Clarke, *The Old English in Ireland 1625–42* (London, 1966), enduring and influential.

—— 'The Genesis of the Ulster Rising of 1641', in Peter Roebuck (ed.), *Plantation to Partition: Essays in Ulster History in Honour of J. L. McCracken* (Belfast, 1981), 29–45.

Terence Ranger, 'Strafford in Ireland: A Revaluation', in Trevor Aston (ed.), *Crisis in Europe 1560–1660* (London, 1965), 285–308.

Hugh Kearney, *Strafford in Ireland 1633–41: A Study in Absolutism* (Manchester, 1959), the only comprehensive work on the endeavours of an English ruler in seventeenth-century Ireland.

David Stevenson, *Scottish Covenanters and Irish Confederates: Scottish–Irish Relations in the*

Mid-Seventeenth Century (Belfast, 1981), difficult but essential, and containing a totally convincing study of the battle of Benburb.

Jerrold Casway, *Owen Roe O'Neill and the Struggle for Catholic Ireland* (Philadelphia, 1984), comprehensive if uncritical.

THE JACOBITE PERIOD

J. G. Simms, *Jacobite Ireland 1685-91* (London, 1969), a careful and full account of both military and political events.

—— *The Williamite Confiscation in Ireland 1690-1703* (London, 1956).

T. Bartlett and D. W. Hayton (eds.), *Penal Era and Golden Age: Essays in Irish History 1690-1800* (Belfast, 1979), the best representation of modern scholarship on the late seventeenth and eighteenth centuries.

SOCIAL AND ECONOMIC HISTORY

K. W. Nicholls, *Gaelic and Gaelicized Ireland in the Later Middle Ages* (Dublin, 1972), still the most perceptive account of Gaelic institutional life and the impact of Gaelic customs upon previously Anglo-Norman areas.

L. M. Cullen, *An Economic History of Ireland since 1660* (London, 1972), the essential introduction.

—— *The Emergence of Modern Ireland 1600-1900* (London, 1981), indispensable on social conditions.

Maurice Craig, *Dublin 1660-1860: A Social and Architectural History* (London, 1952).

4. ASCENDANCY AND UNION

GENERAL SURVEYS

D. Dickson, *New Foundations: Ireland 1660-1800* (Dublin, 1987), much the best general treatment of the eighteenth century.

G. Ó Tuathaigh, *Ireland before the Famine 1798-1848* (Dublin, 1972).

R. F. Foster, *Modern Ireland 1600-1972* (London, 1988).

L. M. Cullen, *The Emergence of Modern Ireland 1600-1900* (London, 1981), useful for a particularly idiosyncratic and enlightening view of eighteenth-century society.

—— *An Economic History of Ireland since 1600* (London, 1972).

A. T. Q. Stewart, *The Narrow Ground: Aspects of Ulster 1609-1969* (London, 1977), a bleak view with some highly perceptive insights.

David Miller, *Queen's Rebels: Ulster Loyalism in Historical Perspective* (Dublin, 1978).

D. G. Boyce, *Nationalism in Ireland* (London, 1982), excellent on the whole period.

Oliver MacDonagh, *States of Mind: A Study of Anglo-Irish Conflict 1780-1980* (London, 1983), particularly good on the early nineteenth century.

EIGHTEENTH-CENTURY SOCIETY

Arthur Young, *A Tour of Ireland 1770-79*, ed. A. W. Hutton (2 vols., London, 1892), made to bear too much weight as the basis of untenable generalizations, but still an unrivalled guide.

C. L. and R. E. Ward (eds.), *The Letters of Charles O'Conor of Belanagare* (2 vols., Ann Arbor, 1980), a unique reflection of the world of the intellectual Catholic gentry.

T. Bartlett and D. Hayton (eds.), *Penal Era and Golden Age: Essays in Irish History 1690-1800* (Belfast, 1979), a vital collection.

T. W. Moody and W. E. Vaughan (eds.), *A New History of Ireland*, iv, *Eighteenth-century Ireland, 1691-1800* (Oxford, 1986) is already dated, but selectively useful.

A. P. W. Malcomson, 'Absenteeism in Eighteenth-century Ireland', *Irish Economic and Social History*, 1 (1974), an article which fills a wide frame of reference.

Maurice Craig, *Dublin 1660–1860: A Social and Architectural History* (London, 1952).

Patrick J. Corish, *The Catholic Community in the Seventeenth and Eighteenth Centuries* (Dublin, 1981).

D. N. Doyle, *Ireland, Irishmen and Revolutionary America 1760–1820* (Dublin, 1981).

The study of Catholic leaseholding in Kerry referred to in this chapter is by Gerard Lyne in the *Journal of the Kerry Archaeological and Historical Society*, nos. 10–12 (1977–9).

EIGHTEENTH-CENTURY POLITICS

R. B. McDowell, *Irish Public Opinion 1750–1800* (London, 1944).

A. P. W. Malcomson, *John Foster: The Politics of the Anglo-Irish Ascendancy* (Oxford, 1978), a consummate exploration of political mentality.

E. M. Johnston, *Great Britain and Ireland 1760–1800* (Edinburgh, 1963).

G. C. Bolton, *The Passing of the Irish Act of Union* (Oxford, 1966).

Marianne Elliott, *Partners in Revolution: The United Irishmen and France* (London, 1982), a pioneering work of great importance.

Tom Dunne, *Wolfe Tone: Colonial Outsider* (Cork, 1981), an incisive and original pamphlet.

Thomas Pakenham, *The Year of Liberty* (London, 1969), a narrative account of 1798, beautifully written.

EARLY NINETEENTH-CENTURY SOCIETY AND ECONOMY

S. Clark and J. Donnelly, jun., *Irish Peasants: Violence and Political Unrest 1780–1914* (Manchester, 1983).

C. H. E. Philpin (ed.), *Nationalism and Popular Protest in Ireland* (Cambridge, 1987). Both this and the preceding collection of essays, stressing agrarian violence, have much of relevance to the eighteenth and twentieth centuries as well.

Mary Daly, *Social and Economic History of Ireland since 1800* (Dublin, 1981), a valuable introduction.

T. W. Freeman, *Pre-Famine Ireland: A Study in Historical Geography* (Manchester, 1957), a useful starting-point in any attempt to depoliticize the study of the Irish economy.

K. H. Connell, *Irish Peasant Society* (Oxford, 1968), an accepted classic, but a rather impressionistic one.

C. Ó Gráda, *Ireland before and after the Famine: Explorations in Economic History, 1800–1925* (Manchester, 1988).

—— and J. Mokyr, 'New Developments in Irish Population History, 1700–1850', *Economic History Review*, 37, no. 4 (Nov. 1984).

M. Beames, *Peasants and Power: The Whiteboy Movements and their Control in Pre-Famine Ireland* (Brighton, 1983).

J. Donnelly, jun., *The Land and the People of Nineteenth-Century Cork: The Rural Economy and the Land Question* (London, 1975).

E. R. R. Green, *The Lagan Valley 1800–1850* (London, 1949).

R. D. Edwards and T. D. Williams, *The Great Famine* (London, 1956).

David Thomson and Moyra McGusty (eds.), *The Irish Journals of Elizabeth Smith 1840–1850* (Oxford, 1980), a remarkable reflection of life on a small Wicklow estate throughout the Famine.

THE RISE OF CATHOLIC DEMOCRACY

S. J. Connolly, *Priests and People in Pre-Famine Ireland 1780–1845* (Dublin, 1982).

Fergus O'Ferrall, *Catholic Emancipation: Daniel O'Connell and the Birth of Irish Democracy* (Dublin, 1985), the fullest treatment of the subject.

K. B. Nowlan and M. R. O'Connell (eds.), *Daniel O'Connell: Portrait of a Radical* (Belfast, 1984).

H. Senior, *Orangeism in Ireland and Britain, 1795-1836* (London, 1960).

D. Kerr, *Peel, Priests and Politics: Sir Robert Peel's Administration and the Roman Catholic Church in Ireland 1841-46* (Oxford, 1982).

E. Larkin, *The Historical Dimensions of Irish Catholicism* (New York, 1981), containing a highly influential essay on the so-called 'Devotional Revolution' in nineteenth-century Ireland, with some afterthoughts.

K. T. Hoppen, *Elections, Politics and Society in Ireland 1832-1885* (Oxford, 1984), an exploration of the political bedrock of nineteenth-century Ireland and a profile of activity outside the high points of nationalist emotion.

R. V. Comerford, *The Fenians in Context: Irish Politics and Society 1848-82* (Dublin, 1985), an iconoclastic work full of surprises.

CULTURAL THEMES

Jeanne Sheehy, *The Rediscovery of Ireland's Past: The Celtic Revival 1830-1930* (London, 1980).

Norman Vance, 'Celts, Carthaginians and Constitutions: Anglo-Irish Literary Relations, 1780-1820', *Irish Historical Studies*, 22 (1981), 216-38.

D. H. Akenson, *The Irish Education Experiment: The National System of Education in the Nineteenth Century* (London, 1970).

J. H. Andrews, *A Paper Landscape: The Ordnance Survey in Nineteenth-century Ireland* (Oxford, 1975), which maps a territory wider than its title.

5. IRELAND SINCE 1870

GENERAL SURVEYS

F. S. L. Lyons, *Ireland since the Famine* (London, 1971).

M. E. Collins, *An Outline of Modern Irish History 1850-1966* (Dublin, new edn. 1985).

Joseph Lee, *The Modernisation of Irish Society 1848-1918* (Dublin, 1973), more speculative and lively than the two above, but slight and perhaps misleading.

Patrick Buckland, *A History of Northern Ireland* (Dublin, 1981).

David Harkness, *Northern Ireland since 1920* (Dublin, 1983).

Ronan Fanning, *Independent Ireland* (Dublin, 1983), the only one of these surveys to combine original research with a clearly developed theme.

DOCUMENTARY COLLECTIONS

Patrick Buckland, *Irish Unionism 1885-1923: A Documentary History* (Belfast, 1973), invaluable within its limited field, though no fully satisfactory compendium of modern historical documents is yet available.

A. C. Hepburn, *The Conflict of Nationality in Modern Ireland* (London, 1980), very brief documentary gobbets addressing many aspects of unionism as well as nationalism from the 1790s, sometimes overburdened with introductions.

Arthur Mitchell and Pádraig Ó Snodaigh (eds.), *Irish Political Documents 1916-1949* (Dublin, 1985), with a higher ratio of extract to commentary, but concentrating excessively upon southern separatism.

THE ANGLO-IRISH RELATIONSHIP

Nicholas Mansergh, *The Irish Question 1840–1921* (London, new edn., 1965), a many-faceted discourse.

Oliver MacDonagh, *Ireland: The Union and its Aftermath* (London, new edn., 1977) and *States of Mind: A Study of Anglo-Irish Conflict 1780–1980* (London, 1983), meticulously constructed synthetic studies.

Charles Townshend, *Political Violence in Ireland: Government and Resistance since 1848* (Oxford, 1983), a sustained exploration of continuities in the misgovernment of Ireland.

Eunan O'Halpin, *The Decline of the Union: British Government in Ireland 1892–1920* (Dublin, 1987), delving a little below the familiar surface of 'high' politics by examining the performance of successive Dublin Castle executives. Otherwise, analysis of Anglo-Irish relationships is largely confined to monographs analysing the genesis of government policy in particular administrations.

Philip Orr, *The Road to the Somme: Men of the Ulster Division tell their Story* (Belfast, 1987), an interesting and handsome account—though Ireland's massive involvement in the First World War remains largely unchronicled. Nor is there any reliable and systematic synthesis of either the War of Independence or the Civil War, an omission which must flabbergast those unattuned to the significant silences of Irish historiography.

Robert Fisk, *In Time of War: Ireland, Ulster and the Price of Neutrality 1939–45* (London, 1983), an examination at perhaps inordinate length.

John Darby, *Conflict in Northern Ireland: The Development of a Polarised Community* (Dublin, 1976), perhaps the most useful of many introductions to the current northern troubles and their diverse interpretations.

IRISH NATIONALISM

Tom Garvin, *The Evolution of Irish Nationalist Politics* (Dublin, 1981), avoiding tunnel vision without succumbing terminally to the political scientist's twin sins of excessive systematization and meagre documentation. Otherwise, the innumerable surveys of Irish nationalism are generally flawed by their failure to set nationalist movements and ideas in broader political and social contexts.

—— *Nationalist Revolutionaries in Ireland 1858–1928* (Oxford, 1987), complementing his earlier focus on organization by quirkily exploring nationalist mentalities.

Conor Cruise O'Brien, *Parnell and his Party 1880–90* (Oxford, 1957).

F. S. L. Lyons, *The Irish Parliamentary Party 1890–1910* (London, 1951), like Cruise O'Brien's, a lucid if slightly dated monograph (there is no coherent history of parliamentary nationalism).

Leon Ó Broin, *Revolutionary Underground: The Story of the Irish Republican Brotherhood* (Dublin, 1976).

Tim Pat Coogan, *The I.R.A.* (London, 1971). Both this and the preceding book provide useful and entertaining insights, in default of any scholarly history of militant republicanism.

Joseph M. Curran, *The Birth of the Irish Free State 1921–23* (Alabama, 1980), dealing effectively with the political background to the constitutional 'settlement' of 1921–2.

Michael Laffan, *The Partition of Ireland 1911–1925* (Dublin, 1983), a useful booklet (incredibly, there is no searching analysis of the modern Orange Order, Ulster unionist party, or structure of Protestant populism).

David Fitzpatrick, *Politics and Irish Life 1913–1921* (Dublin, 1977), dealing with 'provincial experience of war and revolution' in a microcosmic study of Co. Clare.

CULTURAL THEMES

F. S. L. Lyons, *Culture and Anarchy in Ireland 1890–1939* (Oxford, 1979), containing some thought-provoking passages on a largely ignored subject.

Jeanne Sheehy, *The Rediscovery of Ireland's Past: The Celtic Revival 1830-1930* (London, 1980), an attractive impression of one aspect of Ireland's hybrid culture.

J. H. Whyte, *Church and State in Modern Ireland 1923-1979* (Dublin, new edn., 1980), a balanced if unadventurous portrayal of the political role of Catholicism in the southern state.

Terence Brown, *Ireland: A Social and Cultural History 1922-79* (London, 1981).

David W. Miller, *Church, State and Nation in Ireland 1898-1921* (Dublin, 1973), a painstaking analysis of the hierarchy's earlier political interventions (though reliable broader surveys of the social and political roles of the various churches remain to be written).

Malcolm Brown, *The Politics of Irish Literature from Thomas Davis to W. B. Yeats* (Dublin, 1972), a study of the interaction between culture and its political or social contexts which, like most others, is virtually restricted to Anglo-Irish literature.

LAND AND LABOUR HISTORY

Samuel Clark, *Social Origins of the Land War* (Princeton, 1979), a rather schematic study concentrating upon the half-century before 1879 and virtually ignoring the rapidly changing structures of conflict after 1882.

Paul Bew, *Land and the National Question in Ireland 1858-82* (Dublin, 1978) and *Conflict and Conciliation in Ireland 1890-1910: Parnellites and Radical Agrarians* (Oxford, 1987), categorizing the diverse political responses to rural conflict without elucidating the origins of that conflict.

W. E. Vaughan, *Landlords and Tenants in Ireland* (Dublin, 1984), a booklet examining recent interpretations of 'the land question'.

James S. Donnelly, *Landlord and Tenant in Nineteenth-century Ireland* (Dublin, 1973), providing interesting documentary and pictorial illustration.

Arthur Mitchell, *Labour in Irish Politics 1890-1930* (Dublin, 1974), a sound survey of the urban labour movement in its overstudied political aspect, though there is no complementary study of industrial combination and collective action.

Henry Patterson, *Class Conflict and Sectarianism: The Protestant Working Class and the Belfast Labour Movement 1868-1920* (Belfast, 1980), a provocative if uneven essay in a scantily researched area.

Conrad M. Arensberg, *The Irish Countryman: An Anthropological Study* (London, 1937), offering an elegant model of rural harmony and social control in Clare, to which historians as well as sociologists have remained excessively indebted, in the absence of historical studies dealing with theatres of conflict and combination such as families and fraternities.

ECONOMIC HISTORY

Mary Daly, *Social and Economic History of Ireland since 1800* (Dublin, 1981), a straightforward introduction.

Liam Kennedy and Philip Ollerenshaw (eds.), *An Economic History of Ulster 1820-1940* (Manchester, 1985).

James Meenan, *The Irish Economy since 1922* (Liverpool, 1970), another synoptic study, which despite its title excludes Northern Ireland.

David Johnson, *The Interwar Economy in Ireland* (Dublin, 1985).

EMIGRATION

David Fitzpatrick, *Irish Emigration 1801-1921* (Dublin, 1984), a brief exploration of the functions and profile of emigration.

Robert E. Kennedy, *The Irish: Emigration, Marriage and Fertility* (London, 1973), a more thorough if controversial treatment.

Arnold Schrier, *Ireland and the American Emigration 1850-1900* (Minneapolis, 1958), an interesting appraisal of emigrant mentality.

Kerby A. Miller, *Emigrants and Exiles: Ireland and the Irish Exodus to North America* (New York, 1985), a massive commentary upon emigrant letters and diaries; despite technical flaws, works like this give heart to other historians and pleasure to all those whose interest in history arises from the urge to hear authentic voices of the past.

6. IRISH LITERATURE AND IRISH HISTORY

GENERAL SURVEYS AND BACKGROUND

Douglas Hyde, *A Literary History of Ireland* (London, 1899), a massive tome whose scholarly methods are outdated now, but whose charm remains.

Frank O'Connor, *The Backward Look* (London, 1967), vivid and cogent lectures tracing the story of Irish literature and arguing for the continuity of Gaelic and Anglo-Irish traditions.

Vivian Mercier, *The Irish Comic Tradition* (Oxford, 1962), a wonderfully amusing treatment enhanced by wide reading in psychology and anthropology; its greatest value may lie in its effortless synthesis of Gaelic and Anglo-Irish traditions.

Des Maxwell, *A Critical History of Modern Irish Drama* (Cambridge, 1985), a concise and balanced account of major and minor figures.

Hugh Kenner, *A Colder Eye: The Modern Irish Writers* (New York, 1983), a helpful book by virtue of lively narrative and deft analysis of language, despite its condescension to its Irish subjects.

Terence Brown, *Ireland: A Social and Cultural History 1922-79* (London, 1981), clear coverage of the changes in religion, education, and culture, usefully synthesizing much research while drawing on many journals and magazines. Though weak on Irish-language topics, its humanist perspective makes it a vital updating of O'Faolain's *The Irish* (see below).

GAELIC LITERATURE

Myles Dillon, *Irish Sagas* (Cork, 1968), the definitive essays on the subject.

Proinsias Mac Cana, *Celtic Mythology* (London, 1970), a devoted and entertaining book, learned and shrewd.

Aodh de Blacam, *Gaelic Literature Surveyed*, with an afterword by Eoghan Ó Hanluain (Kennikat, 1970), a readable if old-fashioned account written over half a century ago; the afterword brings it up to date.

Brian Ó Cuív (ed.), *Seven Centuries of Irish Learning 1000-1700* (Dublin, 1961), reputable, informative essays—especially the one on the *amour courtois* tradition in Irish poetry.

Daniel Corkery, *The Hidden Ireland* (Dublin, 1924), a warmly vivid portrait of eighteenth-century Gaelic culture, marred by over-simplification of the class structure.

Sean Ó Tuama, *Filí faoi Sceimhle* (Dublin, 1979), a rigorous appraisal of two of the last major Gaelic poets, Ó Rathaille and Ó Ríordáin, offering clear commentary on the Ireland-as-woman motif.

LITERATURE, HISTORY, AND POLITICS

James Carney, *Studies in Irish Literature and History* (Dublin, 1955), spanning the centuries in its coverage, which is subtle and erudite.

Sean O'Faolain, *The Irish* (London, 1948), provocative and elegant analyses of Irish character as revealed in literature, religion, and political history.

Malcolm Brown, *The Politics of Irish Literature from Thomas Davis to W. B. Yeats* (Dublin, 1972), a lucid and detailed account of nineteenth-century political background to Irish-revival authors, especially Yeats and Joyce.

Sean Ó Tuama (ed.), *The Gaelic League Idea* (Cork, 1972), essays in Irish and English on history, politics, and prospects of Gaelic League activity.

F. S. L. Lyons, *Culture and Anarchy in Ireland 1890–1939* (Oxford, 1979), an elegant commentary on cultural politics, but seriously neglecting the economic factor in explaining conflict in the north of Ireland.

William Irwin Thompson, *The Imagination of an Insurrection: Dublin 1916* (London, 1967), a fascinating if flawed psychological study of the poets, rebels, and texts thrown up by the Rising, with some rigorous early chapters on the nineteenth-century background.

Conor Cruise O'Brien, 'Passion and Cunning: An Essay on the Politics of W. B. Yeats', in A. N. Jeffares and K. G. W. Cross (eds.), *In Excited Reverie: A Centenary Tribute to William Butler Yeats 1865–1939* (London, 1965), cleverly tracing fluctuations in the poet's thought and arguing that he was, in later years, a Fascist.

Elizabeth Cullingford, *Yeats, Ireland and Fascism* (London, 1981), attempting to rebut the thesis that the poet was a Fascist by arguing that he was a nationalist of the school of John O'Leary.

Declan Kiberd, *Anglo-Irish Attitudes* (Derry, 1984), studying the treatment of Anglo-Irish relations by artists from Wilde and Shaw to O'Casey and Behan, with subsequent analysis of the influence of literary stereotypes on the texts of historians.

Dominic Manganiello, *Joyce's Politics* (London, 1980), thoroughly documenting the writer's views and involvements, drawing valuably on Italian newspapers and on Joyce's readings in anarchism.

Richard J. Loftus, *Nationalism in Modern Anglo-Irish Poetry* (Madison, Wisconsin, 1964), a thorough analysis of the major poets of this century.

Conor Cruise O'Brien, *States of Ireland* (London, 1972), an avowedly personal analysis of the conflict in the north of Ireland. Its earlier chapters are full of brilliant insights into, for example, the sources of the *Playboy* riots.

Hubert Butler, *Escape from the Anthill* (Mullingar, 1984), elegant and humane essays reflecting the fortunes of Irish Protestantism.

THE LITERARY REVIVAL

W. J. McCormack, *Ascendancy and Tradition in Anglo-Irish Literary History from 1789 to 1939* (Oxford, 1985), offering new, if sometimes turgidly expressed, insights into nineteenth-century culture and glossing key texts such as Yeats's *Purgatory* in chronicling the Anglo-Irish decline.

David Lloyd, *Nationalism and Minor Literature: James Clarence Mangan and the Emergence of Irish Cultural Nationalism* (London, 1987), an innovative study of a neglected literary genius and a significant contribution to the theory of minor literature.

Philip Edwards, *Threshold of a Nation* (London, 1979), a daring and successful attempt to align the English and Irish Renaissances, demonstrating Yeats's reinvention of a 'Celtic' Shakespeare.

Seamus Deane, *Celtic Revivals* (London, 1985), brilliant analyses of Burke, Yeats, Joyce, Beckett, and O'Casey. The treatment of current authors (Heaney, Mahon, Friel, etc.) is more debatable.

CONTEMPORARY CRITICISM AND CULTURAL DEBATE

Tom Paulin, *Ireland and the English Question* (Newcastle, 1984), useful appraisals of the politics of Irish writing, with peerless commentary on the mental landscapes of Protestant Unionism.

Edna Longley, *Poetry in the Wars* (Newcastle, 1986), attempting to locate Irish war poetry against its British counterpart. Impressive close readings are marred only by vituperative attacks on Dublin literary critics.

Richard Kearney, *Transitions* (Dublin, 1987), provocative essays on Irish cultural debates by a synthesizing philosophical intellect, brought to bear on literature, cinema, and the visual arts.

25

REGIONAL STUDIES

J. W. Foster, *Forces and Themes in Ulster Fiction* (Dublin, 1974), an illuminating and sometimes witty perspective on a previously 'hidden' Ireland.

Fintan O'Toole, *Going West: The Country and the City in Irish Writing* (Dublin, 1988), a radical reassessment of urban–rural tensions.

MEMOIRS

Anthony Cronin, *Dead as Doornails* (Dublin, 1976), a stylish memoir of literary Dublin in the 1950s, combining witty anecdote with penetrating analyses of the intellectual scene.

CHRONOLOGY

AD 77–84	Agricola, Roman governor of Britain, considers the conquest of Ireland
c.130–80	Ptolemy's account of Ireland
367	Major attack on Britain by the Irish, Picts, and Saxons
431	Palladius sent as bishop to the Irish believing in Christ by Pope Celestine I
433/4	Prosper of Aquitaine attributes the conversion of Ireland to Pope Celestine I
c.550–650	The flowering of monasticism in Ireland
563	Foundation of Iona by Columba
575	Convention of Druim Ceat
c.590	Columbanus begins his mission to the Continent
597	Death of Columba
615	Death of Columbanus at Bobbio
c.650–750	Writing of Irish canon and vernacular law in progress
663	Death of Guaire Aidni, Uí Fiachrach king of Connacht
c.670–700	Tírechán and Muirchú produce hagiographical works on St Patrick
697	Synod of Birr and the proclamation of the 'Law of the Innocents'
c.700	The eastern Eóganacht become dominant in Munster
c.700	Writing of *Críth Gablach* (a law tract on status)
704	Death of Adomnán, ninth abbot of Iona
721–42	Cathal mac Finguine king of Munster
c.725	Uí Briúin dynasty dominant in Connacht
734	Abdication of Flaithbertach mac Loingsig. Cenél Conaill now excluded from Uí Néill overkingship
743	Clann Cholmáin first take the overkingship of the Uí Néill
c.750	Completion of *Collectio canonum Hibernensis*
c.750–850	Armagh comes under Uí Néill control
793	Vikings raid Lindisfarne
	Artrí mac Cathail ordained king of Munster
795	Viking raids on Iona, Rathlin, Inishmurray, and Inishbofin
802	Iona burned by the Vikings
c.800	The Uí Néill dominate north Leinster
804	Áed Oirnide of the Uí Néill ordained overking of the Uí Néill by the abbot of Armagh
806	Sixty-eight members of the Iona community killed by the Vikings
807	Construction of the monastery of Kells is begun
820–47	Feidlimid mac Crimthainn king of Munster
836	Viking raids penetrate deep inland
837	Large Viking fleets appear on the Boyne and the Liffey
840–1	A Viking fleet overwinters on Lough Neagh
841–2	A Viking fleet overwinters in Dublin
842	First reported Viking–Irish alliance
845	Forannán, abbot of Armagh, captured by the Vikings

846–62	Reign of Mael Sechnaill I, powerful overking of the Uí Néill
866	Áed Finnliath clears the northern coastline of Viking bases
914	A great Viking fleet arrives in Waterford and the beginning of the second period of raids
919	Niall Glúndub, overking of the Uí Néill, killed in the battle of Dublin
c.950	Close of the second period of Viking raids
956–80	Domnall ua Néill overking of the Uí Néill
980	Mael Sechnaill II becomes overking of the Uí Néill
975–1014	Brian Boru king of Munster, and latterly of Ireland
997	Brian Boru and Mael Sechnaill II divide Ireland between them
999	Brian Boru defeats the Leinstermen and the Ostmen at the battle of Glenn Máma. Sitric Silkenbeard, king of Dublin, submits to him
1002–14	Brian Boru reigns as king of Ireland
1014	Battle of Clontarf. Death of Brian Boru
1022	Death of Mael Sechnaill II, overking of the Uí Néill
1086–1119	Muirchertach O'Brien king of Munster and claimant to the kingship of Ireland (1093–1114)
1101	Synod of Cashel. Muirchertach O'Brien grants Cashel to the church as the seat of a metropolitan
1106–56	Turlough O'Connor king of Connacht and claimant to the 'high-kingship' of Ireland
1111	Synod of Ráth Breasail. Ireland divided into territorial dioceses under two metropolitans
1134	Consecration of Cormac's Chapel at Cashel
1142	Foundation of the first Cistercian house in Ireland (at Mellifont)
1152	Synod of Kells-Mellifont. A national church organization with four metropolitans, under the primacy of Armagh
1166	Death of Muirchertach Mac Lochlainn, 'high-king' of Ireland
	Dermot MacMurrough, king of Leinster, driven overseas. Seeks help of Henry II and recruits Cambro-Norman knights
1169	Arrival of FitzStephen, FitzGerald, and others. Wexford taken, Dermot restored to kingship of Leinster
1170	Marriage of Strongbow to Dermot's daughter Aoife. Siege and capture of Dublin. Invasion of Meath
1171	Death of Dermot. Strongbow lord of Leinster. Arrival of Henry II
	Submission of Irish bishops and most Irish kings
1172	Second Synod of Cashel. Grant of Meath to Hugh de Lacy. Henry leaves
1175	Treaty of Windsor between Henry II and Rory O'Connor, high-king of Ireland, who agrees to rule unoccupied territory as a vassal
1176	Death of Strongbow
1177	Conquest of Ulaid by John de Courcy. Council of Oxford: Prince John made lord of Ireland, speculative grants of kingdoms of Cork and Limerick to Norman vassals
1185	Prince John's first visit to Ireland. Occupation of lands in Limerick begun by Theobald Walter, William de Burgh, and Philip of Worcester
c.1200	Start of Classical Irish period in literature, lasting until 1600
1210	King John's second visit to Ireland. Confiscation of the earldom of Ulster and honor of Limerick. Submission of Irish kings
1235	Final conquest of Connacht by Richard de Burgh. Five 'King's Cantreds' reserved for O'Connor

1257	Death of Maurice FitzGerald; his lordship of Sligo ravaged by Godfrey O'Donnell, king of Tír Conaill. Normans in Thomond defeated by Conor O'Brien and his son, Tadhg
1258	Meeting at Caol-Uisce on the Erne between Aodh son of O'Connor, Tadhg son of O'Brien, and Brian O'Neill, self-styled 'King of the kings of Ireland'
1260	Battle of Down: defeat and death of Brian O'Neill
1261	Battle of Callan: John fitz Thomas of Desmond and his heir defeated and killed by Finghin MacCarthy, himself slain later that year
1263	Earldom of Ulster, long vacant, bestowed on Walter de Burgh, lord of Connacht
1276	Hereditary lordship of all Thomond granted to Thomas de Clare
1292	Custody of rents, homages, and services of all Crown tenants English and Irish in the Decies and Desmond granted to Thomas fitz Maurice of Desmond
1315	Invasion of Ireland by Edward Bruce. His proclamation as 'King of Ireland'
1316	Battle of Athenry; rebellious Irish chiefs of Connacht defeated and killed
1318	Battle of Dysert O'Dea: Richard de Clare defeated and killed by O'Brien. Battle of Faughart: Edward Bruce defeated and killed
1333	Murder of William de Burgh, earl of Ulster. Crown loses control of Anglo-Norman Connacht and the Irish chiefs in Ulster
1361	Arrival of English expedition under Prince Lionel of Clarence, earl of Ulster, to stem decline of colony
1366	Parliament at Kilkenny before Prince Lionel codifies the defensive legislation of the previous fifty years, prohibiting *inter alia* the adoption of the Irish language by the colonists
1394–5	King Richard II's first expedition to Ireland. Defeat of Leinster Irish under Art MacMurrough, and submission of nearly all Irish and rebel English chiefs
1398	Death of Roger Mortimer in war against Leinster Irish
1399	King Richard II's second expedition to Ireland, with inconclusive results
1414–47	Prolonged struggle between the factions of James Butler, fourth earl of Ormond, and John Talbot, earl of Shrewsbury, for control of royal government in Ireland
1449–50	Richard duke of York in Ireland as king's lieutenant. Submission of many Irish chiefs and English rebels
1459–60	Duke of York's second visit to Ireland. Parliament meeting at Drogheda upholds his authority against Henry VI and an English Act of Attainder
1467–8	Edward IV appoints Tiptoft, earl of Worcester, Lord Deputy in place of Thomas FitzGerald, earl of Desmond, subsequently executed for treason. Munster rebels
1478–9	Anglo-Irish opposition frustrates Edward IV's attempt to appoint Lord Grey as Deputy in place of Gerald Mór FitzGerald, eighth earl of Kildare
1487	Earl of Kildare has Lambert Simnel crowned as Edward VI in Christchurch cathedral, Dublin
1494	In the wake of Anglo-Irish support for Perkin Warbeck, Henry VII dismisses Kildare (1492) and sends Sir Edward Poynings as Lord Deputy. 'Poynings' Law' makes all past legislation of the English parliament applicable to Ireland, and requires the king's approval for all future summons of the Anglo-Irish parliament and contents of its legislation
1496	Kildare reappointed
1504	Battle of Knocktoe: by defeating Burke of Clanricard, O'Brien, and the Irish of Ormond, Kildare completes his dominance of Ireland, Irish and Anglo-Irish
1509	Accession of Henry VIII

1513	Death of Gerald FitzGerald, eighth earl of Kildare and Lord Deputy of Ireland, succeeded by his son Gerald the ninth earl, who also becomes Lord Deputy of Ireland
1520	Thomas Howard, earl of Surrey, appointed as Lord-Lieutenant of Ireland instead of Kildare
1522	Piers Butler, eighth earl of Ormond, appointed Lord Deputy of Ireland
1524	Royal commission resolves differences between Ormond and Kildare and restores Kildare to the office of Lord Deputy
1529	Appointment of Sir William Skeffington as royal commissioner
1533/4	Lord Deputy Kildare summoned to court and leaves his son Lord Offaly (Silken Thomas) as vice-deputy
1534	Kildare placed in tower where he dies; outbreak of rebellion led by Lord Offaly
1534–6	Continuing revolt in Ireland; fall of Maynooth Castle, arrest of Lord Offaly (by now tenth earl of Kildare), and he and his five uncles brought to England
1536–7	Meeting of the Irish Reformation Parliament; execution of Kildare and his five uncles at Tyburn
1540	Sir Anthony St Leger appointed as governor of Ireland
1541–3	Meeting of parliament which declares Henry VIII to be king of Ireland; launching of 'surrender and re-grant' programme
1547	Death of Henry VIII; accession of Edward VI
1548–53	Inauguration of garrison policy to surround the Pale with fortified positions; pursued by successive governors Sir Edward Bellingham, Sir Anthony St Leger, and Sir James Croft
1553	Death of Edward VI; accession of Mary I
1556–64	Thomas Radcliffe, earl of Sussex, serves as governor in Ireland
1557–8	Establishment of a military 'plantation' in Laois-Offaly; murder of Matthew O'Neill, baron of Dungannon; launching of a military campaign in Ulster to uphold 'surrender and re-grant' arrangements
1558	Death of Mary I; accession of Elizabeth I
1560	Meeting of the second Irish Reformation Parliament which approves the Elizabethan church settlement for Ireland
1561–4	Sussex pursues intermittent military campaigns against Shane O'Neill and encounters opposition to financial exactions from within the English Pale
1565–71	Sir Henry Sidney serves for his first period as governor of Ireland
1566–7	Sidney launches military campaign in Ulster which produces the killing of Shane O'Neill; he attempts to restore government authority in Munster by arresting the earl of Desmond
1569–71	Meeting of parliament in Dublin which declares the entire lordship of Tyrone forfeited to the Crown; appointment of first provincial presidents in Connacht and in Munster; launching of private colonization ventures in Munster and in Ulster; outburst of local revolts in Munster, in Leinster, and in Connacht against government policy
1570	Elizabeth declared excommunicated by the papacy
1571–5	Sir William FitzWilliam serves for his first period as governor of Ireland
1572	Sir John Perrott and Sir Edward Fitton regain authority as presidents respectively of Munster and Connacht by bringing rebels to surrender
1573–4	Private colonization ventures in Ulster continue even without the consent of FitzWilliam
1575	Sir James Fitz Maurice FitzGerald departs from Ireland to seek Catholic support in Continental Europe for continued opposition to the government

1575–8	Sir Henry Sidney serves for second period as governor of Ireland
1576	Sidney launches an apparently conciliatory policy and brings private colonization to a close. The earl of Essex, the last of the private colonizers, dies in Dublin
1577	The government attempts to increase its revenue from Ireland by the imposition of a land tax and encounters strident opposition from the Pale community
1578	Sidney surrenders his position as governor and leaves Ireland in the belief that his government has been undermined by lawyers in the Pale
1579	James Fitz Maurice FitzGerald accompanied by the English Jesuit Nicholas Sanders returns to Ireland with a Catholic expeditionary force and they establish themselves near Dingle, Co. Kerry. Sir John of Desmond, brother to the earl of Desmond, murders Henry Davells, an English official, and Desmond is forced by his subordinates to make common cause with the rebellion
1580	The rebellion in Munster is joined by a second revolt in Leinster led by James Eustace, Viscount Baltinglass, and Feagh Mac Hugh O'Byrne and supported by discontented Palesmen who profess themselves free from allegiance to a Catholic monarch. Arthur Lord Grey de Wilton is appointed governor to deal with the dual revolt and has his army defeated at Glenmalure in Wicklow but ousts the Continental force from Smerwick
1580–98	Edmund Spenser in Munster
1582–3	Systematic suppression of rebel forces in Leinster and Munster culminating in the killing of the earl of Desmond
1584–8	Sir John Perrott serves as governor of Ireland
1584	Provincial councils reconstituted in Munster and Connacht
1585	Meeting of parliament in Dublin which proceeds with the attainder of Desmond and his supporters, and the confiscation of their property. A commission in England devises a scheme for the distribution of the confiscated Munster property and the establishment of a plantation. The president of Connacht devises the Composition of Connacht; and Hugh O'Neill, baron of Dungannon, created earl of Tyrone
1585–7	Grantees of Munster Plantation lands assume possession of their properties; Perrott experiences increasing difficulty in dealing with his English Protestant officials who consider him excessively lenient in his treatment of Catholic recusants
1586	Eochaidh Ó hEodhusa appointed *file* to Maguire of Fermanagh
1588–94	Sir William FitzWilliam serves as governor for the second time
1588	The Spanish Armada defeated
1589–90	Sir Richard Bingham, president of Connacht, seeks by force to extend the authority of the government into northern Connacht and the southern reaches of Ulster
1591	Hugh O'Neill elopes with Mabel Bagenal, sister to Henry Bagenal, the senior English official serving in Ulster; Fitzwilliam seeks to impose a Composition on the McMahon lordship
1592	Red Hugh O'Donnell seeks to expel all English officials from the lordship of Tyrconnell, and he and Hugh Maguire oppose the imposition of Composition arrangements on their respective territories
1593–4	Opposition to government intervention in Ulster intensifies but Tyrone remains loyal even though his brothers have engaged in rebellion
1595	Death of Turlough O'Neill provides Tyrone with the opportunity to assume the Gaelic title of O'Neill. Tyrone then also enters into rebellion and with Red Hugh O'Donnell opens negotiations for support from Spain

1596	Edmund Spenser completes *A View of the Present State of Ireland*
1596-7	Ulster rebellion intensifies and is imitated by dissatisfied lords in Leinster and Connacht
1598	Major defeat of government forces in Ulster at the Yellow Ford; rebellion extends into Munster and the plantation is overthrown
1599	Robert Devereux, earl of Essex, appointed to suppress the rebellion. Dissipates his energies and agrees on truce with Tyrone
1600	Appointment of Charles Blount, Baron Mountjoy, as governor, and intensification of the government effort to suppress the Ulster revolt
1601	Arrival of Spanish military support at Kinsale where it is joined by a rebel army from Ulster. Decisive victory for the government forces at Kinsale
1602	Order restored to Munster by George Carew, president of that province, as Mountjoy continues to penetrate the province of Ulster
1603	Death of Elizabeth; accession of James VI and I and surrender of Tyrone to Mountjoy; towns seek formal acceptance of Catholic worship
1605	Sir Arthur Chichester appointed as governor; proclamation declaring all persons in Ireland to be free subjects of the king; proclamation expelling Jesuits and seminary priests from Ireland; pressure on Dublin merchant community to conform in religion
1606	Foundation of St Anthony's Franciscan College, Louvain; government efforts to dismember Ulster lordships through judicial investigation
1607	Government investigation of Ulster lordships intensifies; the earls of Tyrone, Tyrconnell, and others abandon the country and are proclaimed traitors
1608	Revolt of Sir Cahir O'Doherty; government decision to plant six Ulster counties
1609-10	Government proceeds with scheme for the plantation of the six Ulster counties and grantees begin to arrive
1610-30	Geoffrey Keating working on *Foras Feasa ar Éirinn*
1610	*Desiderius* by Flaithrí Ó Maolchonaire
1611	Publication of Bonaventura Ó hEodhasa, *An Teagasg Críosdaidhe* (Antwerp)
1612	Publication of Sir John Davies, *A Discovery of the True Causes Why Ireland was never entirely subdued*
1613-15	Meeting of Irish parliament, which endorses the plantation scheme in Ulster, and provides for increased representation of the settler population in future parliaments. Meeting of Convocation of the state church which adopts 104 articles of faith
1616	Death in Rome of Hugh O'Neill, earl of Tyrone
1621	Plantation scheme revealed for settlement of portion of the Irish midlands
1622	Comprehensive survey of the Irish church and government and of all plantations established in Ireland
1625	Death of James I; succession of Charles I
1626	Charles I offers 'Graces' to his Irish subjects in return for subsidies. This provides for the tacit toleration of Catholicism in Ireland, thus vexing his Protestant subjects
1628	Charles I formally issues the Graces; undertakers in the Ulster plantation permitted to retain 'natives' as tenants
1629	Government temporarily in control of Viscount Loftus and the earl of Cork, who attempt suppression of Catholic worship in Dublin
1632-6	Compilation of *Annála Ríoghachta Éireann* (Annals of the Four Masters)
1633-41	Thomas, Viscount Wentworth (created earl of Strafford 1640) serves as governor in Ireland

1634-5	Irish parliament convened and Wentworth reveals his intention to proceed with a plantation of Connacht and to disregard the Graces
1635	Wentworth takes measures to establish Crown title to the province of Connacht
1637	Wentworth takes measures to consolidate and maintain discipline over the state church in Ireland
1639	Scots Covenanters oppose the extension of an episcopal form of church government to Scotland, and Wentworth seeks to have Scots settlers in Ulster swear their allegiance to the king
1640	Wentworth (now earl of Strafford) convenes Irish parliament, which resists him once he has left the country, remonstrating against his rule
1641	Strafford tried, convicted, and executed in England on a charge of treason; outbreak of rising in Ulster; Ireland lapses into political chaos
1642	English parliament seeks for the suppression of the Irish rising through the 'Adventurers Act'; Scots Covenanter army under Robert Monro lands in Ulster (April); Owen Roe O'Neill arrives from the Spanish Netherlands to form an Ulster Catholic army (July); civil war between king and parliament commences in England; Catholic Confederacy assembles at Kilkenny
1643	Overtures proceed between the Confederacy and the king
1644-5	Ireland remains in chaos while Archbishop Rinuccini arrives from the Papacy to provide direction to the rising
1646	Forces of Owen Roe O'Neill defeat those of Monro at Benburb, Co. Tyrone (June) but fail to capitalize on the victory; Rinuccini attempts to prevent the Confederate Catholics from coming to terms with a Protestant monarch; publication of Sir John Temple's *The Irish Rebellion*
1647	Forces of parliament dominant in English civil war; Dublin conceded by Ormond to a parliamentary force
1649	Execution of Charles I; arrival of Cromwell in Ireland and sieges of Drogheda and Wexford (Sept.-Oct.); death of Owen Roe O'Neill (Nov.)
*c.*1650	*Parlaimint Chlainne Tomáis* (Parliament of Clan Thomas) completed; *An Síogaí Rómhánach* (The Roman Fairy)
1650-2	Continuation of Cromwellian conquest of Ireland
1653	Surveys commence for Cromwellian plantation
1654-5	Cromwellian plantation implemented
1658	Death of Oliver Cromwell
1660	Restoration of Charles II; declares he will uphold the Cromwellian conquest and restore property to 'innocent papists'
1661	Reconstitution of an episcopal state church in Ireland; commission investigates Irish land ownership
1662	Duke of Ormond appointed governor of Ireland; commission hears claims for Irish lands
1663	Closure of court of claims for Irish lands, its business unfinished
1665	'Act of Explanation' obliging Cromwellian grantees to surrender one-third of their lands to provide for 'innocents' who had been dispossessed
1670	Synod of Catholic bishops meets in Dublin
1678	Titus Oates plot in England; moves against Catholic public worship in Ireland
1681	Execution of Oliver Plunkett, Catholic archbishop of Armagh
1684	Establishment of the Dublin Philosophical Society by William Molyneux
1685	Death of Charles II; accession of James II
1687	Richard Talbot, earl of Tyrconnell, appointed Lord Deputy of Ireland and sets about replacing Protestant officials with Catholics

1688	Birth of a son to wife of James II (June); 'invitation' to Prince William of Orange and his wife Mary (daughter to James II) to accept the throne of England; flight of James II to France (Dec.)
1689	William III and Mary II enthroned as joint monarchs; James II arrives at Kinsale from France (Mar.); siege of Derry underway and relief provided by Williamite forces (July). Catholic 'parliament' underway in Dublin
1690	William III arrives near Carrickfergus; defeats forces of James at the Boyne (July); James flees to France and William takes Dublin. Sieges of Athlone and Limerick fail but Williamite courts in Dublin commence hearings against those who fought against William III
1691	Athlone taken by Williamite forces; Jacobite army defeated at Aughrim (July); Galway and Limerick taken (Sept.). Irish officers permitted to go to France. Treaty of Limerick signed (Oct.)
1695	Acts restricting rights of Catholics in education, arms-bearing, and horse-owning; Catholic clergy banished
1698	Death of Daíbhí Ó Bruadair
1699	Acts restricting Irish woollen exports
1703	*Parlaimint na mBan* (Parliament of Women)
1704	Legislation restricting rights of Catholics in landholding and public offices (by means of 'tests')
1710	*Stair Éamuinn Uí Chléire*
1713	Jonathan Swift becomes dean of St Patrick's
1719	Toleration Act for Protestant Dissenters
1720	'Sixth of George I': Declaratory Act giving Westminster parliament the right to legislate for Ireland
1724	William Wood granted patent to mint copper halfpence for Ireland, provoking Swift's *Drapier's Letters*
1726	*Gulliver's Travels*, by Jonathan Swift
1728	Act removing franchise from Catholics Death of Aogán Ó Rathaille
1731	Founding of Charter Schools
1738	Death of Turlough Carolan
1750	'Dublin Society' (later Royal Dublin Society) founded
1758	Wide Streets Commission appointed to oversee development of Dublin
1762–72	Viceroyalty of Townshend
1768	Octennial Act limiting duration of Irish parliaments
1772	Relief Act allows Catholics to lease bogland
1778	Relief Act allows Catholics leasehold and inheritance rights
1780	Colonial trade opened to Irish goods, following Volunteers' campaign
*c.*1780	*Cúirt an Mheán Oíche* (The Midnight Court), by Brian Merriman
1782	Volunteers call for legislative independence at Dungannon convention (Feb.); Rockingham government in Britain brings to power an administration favourable to Irish claims; Relief Acts allow Catholics to own freeholds outside parliamentary boroughs and gives access to educational rights (May–July); repeal of 'Sixth of George I' and amendment of Poynings' Law (June). Catholic colleges reopened, using English language
1784	Death of Eoghan Rua Ó Súilleabháin
1789	*Reliques of Irish Poetry*, by Charlotte Brooke
1791	Wolfe Tone's *Argument on behalf of the Catholics of Ireland* (Aug.); foundation of society of United Irishmen in Belfast and—later—Dublin (Oct.)

1792	Relief Act admits Catholics to the practice of the law. Belfast Harp Festival
1793	Volunteers suppressed and arms movements restricted (Feb.-Mar.); Relief Act admits Catholics to parliamentary franchise (Apr.); Irish Militia established (Apr.)
1794	Dublin United Irishmen suppressed
1795	Earl Fitzwilliam arrives as Lord-Lieutenant (Jan.) and dismissed (Feb.); Catholic seminary established at Maynooth (June); Orange Order founded (Sept.)
1796	Insurrection Act (Mar.) and suspension of habeas corpus (Oct.); French invasion force in Bantry Bay (Dec.)
1798	Martial law imposed (Mar.); rebellion in Wexford (May); Humbert lands in Killala (Aug.); Tone arrested and dies (Nov.)
1800	Act of Union. *Castle Rackrent*, by Maria Edgeworth
1803	Robert Emmet's rising
1822	Irish Constabulary Act (setting up county police forces and a salaried magistracy)
1823	Catholic Association founded
1824	Free Trade in manufactured articles established between Britain and Ireland
1825	Catholic Emancipation bill rejected by House of Lords
1826	Waterford electors reject Beresford family's nominee
1828	Daniel O'Connell elected for Clare
1829	Catholic Emancipation Act permits Catholics to sit in parliament; forty-shilling freeholders disenfranchised
1831	Introduction of 'national' system of elementary education
1832	Irish Tithe Composition Act
1833	Irish Church Temporalities Act
1835	'Lichfield House Compact' between O'Connell, Whigs, and radicals
1838	Foundation of Father Mathew's Temperance movement
1840	Foundation of Repeal Association (Apr.); Irish Municipal Reform Act (Aug.)
1842	*The Nation* founded
1843	Repeal meeting at Clontarf prohibited and cancelled
1845	Maynooth endowment spectacularly increased (June); potato blight first noticed (Sept.)
1846	Repeal of Corn Laws (June); Russell and new Whig government decide not to intervene in Irish grain market (Aug.)
1847	Foundation of Irish Confederation
1848	Abortive rising at Ballingarry
1849	Encumbered Estates Act, facilitating sale of land
1850	Irish Reform Act trebles county electorate and reduces borough electorate
1856	'Phoenix Society' (a precursor of the Fenian movement) founded at Skibbereen
1858	Irish Republican Brotherhood established in Dublin
1859	'Fenian Brotherhood', a sister organization, established in USA
1860	Publication of William Carleton's *Collected Works* (*Traits and Stories of the Irish Peasantry*, 1830)
1866	Archbishop Paul Cullen becomes the first Irish cardinal
1867	Attempted Fenian rising
1869	Disestablishment of the Church of Ireland by W. E. Gladstone
1870	Gladstone's first Land Act, recognizing tenant right (Aug.); foundation of Home Government Association by Isaac Butt (Sept.)
1873	Home Rule League founded
1877	Parnell elected president of Home Rule Confederation of Great Britain
1878	Fenian 'New Departure' initiated by Davitt and Devoy

1878–80	Standish O'Grady's *History of Ireland: Heroic Period*
1879	Irish National Land League founded
1880	Parnell elected chairman of Irish Parliamentary Party
1881	Ladies' Land League founded; Land Act introduces judicial fixing of rents (scope extended 1882, 1887), and 'No Rent Manifesto' issued by imprisoned nationalist leaders
1882	Irish National League replaces proscribed Land League; chief secretary and under-secretary assassinated by Invincibles in Phoenix Park
1884	Franchise extended by 'Mud Cabin Act'; Gaelic Athletic Association founded
1885	Irish Loyal and Patriotic Union founded (1891: Irish Unionist Alliance)
1886	Catholic hierarchy endorses Home Rule after Gladstone's 'conversion'; Government of Ireland bill defeated in Commons; 'Plan of Campaign' initiated and proscribed
1889	O'Shea names Parnell as co-respondent in divorce petition
1890	Gladstone's threat to resign if Parnell remains leader, followed by hierarchy's denunciation of Parnell and his repudiation by his party (Dec.)
1891	Anti-Parnellite Irish National Federation formed, followed by Parnell's death; land purchase extended and Congested Districts Board founded
1893	Gaelic League founded; second Government of Ireland bill defeated in Lords. *The Celtic Twilight*, by W. B. Yeats
1894	Foundation of Irish Agricultural Organization Society and Irish Trades Union Congress
1895	*The Importance of Being Earnest*, by Oscar Wilde
1896	Women qualified as poor law electors
1898	United Irish League founded; Local Government (Ireland) Act applies parliamentary franchise to local elections, extending vote to some women
1899	Department of Agriculture and Technical Instruction for Ireland established
1900	Redmond elected chairman of Irish Parliamentary Party and United Irish League
1900	First publication by Irish Texts Society: *Poems* of Keating
1902	Land Conference representing nationalists and landlords, followed (1903) by Wyndham's Land Purchase Act. *Cathleen ni Houlihan*, by W. B. Yeats
1903	Formation of Griffith's National Council and Sloan's Independent Orange Order. *Poets and Dreamers*, by Lady Gregory
1904	Irish Reform Association founded to promote 'devolution'. *John Bull's Other Island*, by G. B. Shaw
1905	Formation of Ulster Unionist Council and Irish Industrial Development Association; reorganization, under Redmondite Board of Erin, of Ancient Order of Hibernians
1907	Dockers' strike and riots in Belfast; Irish Councils bill dropped. Rioting at opening week of *The Playboy of the Western World*, by J. M. Synge
1908	Foundation of Irish Transport and General Workers' Union and Griffith's Sinn Féin; Acts for Old Age Pensions and Irish Universities
1909	First compulsory powers of land purchase enacted
1910	O'Brien's All-for-Ireland League founded
1911	National Insurance introduced; Lords' veto on major legislation abolished
1912	Asquith's introduction of third Government of Ireland bill; Catholic workers expelled from Belfast shipyards; Ulster Covenants signed on 'Ulster Day' (28 Sept.). *Parlaimint Chlainne Tomáis* reissued
1913	Successive formation of Ulster Volunteer Force, Irish Citizens' Army, and Irish (National) Volunteers; Dublin strikes and lock-out

1914   Illegal importation of arms by Ulster Volunteers (Apr.) and Irish Volunteers (July, Aug.); collapse of Buckingham Palace conference just before outbreak of European war; Redmond's futile attempts to reconstitute Irish Volunteers as home defence force (Aug.) and Irish Division (Sept.), followed by creation of 36th (Ulster) Division formed from Ulster Volunteers, enactment and suspension of Home Rule (Sept.); split in Irish Volunteers, and first plans for rising

1915   Irish Republican Brotherhood reorganized and Military Council formed (Dec.)

1916   Irish Republic proclaimed in Dublin (24 Apr.), followed by martial law, rebel surrender (29 Apr.), imprisonments, and fifteen executions; Battle of Somme, shattering Ulster Division; Lloyd George's futile attempt to implement Home Rule with exclusion of six counties. 'Easter 1916' written by W. B. Yeats; privately circulated; published 1920

1917   Ineffectual Irish Convention; reorganization of Sinn Féin and Irish Volunteers (Oct.).

1918   Headquarters staff formed for Irish Volunteers; hierarchy's opposition to extension to Ireland of conscription linked to Sinn Féin and nationalist opposition (Apr.); arrest of republican leaders in 'German Plot'; republican success at general election (Dec.), allowing formation of Dáil Éireann the following month

1919   De Valera's attempt to get recognition of Irish claim by Peace Conference, followed by his eighteen-month tour of USA

1920   Better Government of Ireland Act introduces partition between two Home Rule states; riots in Derry and Belfast, revival of Ulster Volunteers, and expulsion of Catholic shipyard workers followed by Republican 'Belfast Boycott'; reorganization of police, suspension of judicial process and habeas corpus, followed by partial martial law; sporadic violence and ambushes, culminating in Dublin's 'Bloody Sunday' (Nov.) and burning of central Cork (Dec.)

1921   Craig's victory in first elections in Northern Ireland (NI); truce between republicans and Crown forces, followed by meetings of Lloyd George and de Valera, peace conference, and Anglo-Irish 'Treaty' (6 Dec.)

1922   Treaty narrowly approved by Dáil and formation of provisional government under Collins (Jan.); convention of anti-Treaty Irish Republican Army, their occupation of Dublin buildings, and failure of peace negotiations; 'Special Powers' given to NI police (Apr.) to quell sectarian conflict; 'Pact' election followed by arrest of anti-Treaty leaders and outbreak of civil war (June); National Army given emergency powers, reinforced after murder of Collins; 'Irregulars' excommunicated by hierarchy; summary executions of 77 republicans; Irish Free State inaugurated and Northern Ireland excluded from it (Dec.). *Ulysses*, by James Joyce

1923   Irregulars ordered to cease hostilities and dump arms (Apr., May); Cosgrave's Cumann na nGaedheal founded; Free State admitted to League of Nations; remaining tenanted land vested in Land Commission (as in NI, 1925)

1924   National Army reorganization, cut-back, and mutiny

1925   Northern nationalists enter NI Commons; Boundary Commission collapses and partition confirmed by tripartite agreement

1926   De Valera leaves Sinn Féin and founds Fianna Fáil; 'Balfour Declaration' at Imperial conference proclaims Commonwealth co-partnership. Rioting at opening of *The Plough and the Stars*, by Seán O'Casey

1927   O'Higgins assassinated; Fianna Fáil enters Dáil

1929	Proportional representation abolished in NI parliamentary elections (as in local elections, 1922); censorship of publications centralized in IFS. *An tOileánach* (The Islandman) by Tomás Ó Criomhthain
1930	Irish Labour Party separates from Trades Union Congress
1931	Banning of IRA in IFS; autonomy of Free State extended by Statute of Westminster
1932	De Valera replaces Cosgrave as president of Executive Council; 'tariff war' provoked by his withholding land annuities from British Exchequer; Belfast riots demanding more outdoor relief from Poor Law guardians (abolished in IFS, 1923)
1933	Blueshirts (National Guard) formed from Army Comrades' Association, and proscribed; United Ireland Party (Fine Gael) formed under Blueshirt leader O'Duffy; oath of fidelity and right of appeal to privy council abolished
1934	O'Duffy's resignation allows Cosgrave's reinstatement as Fine Gael leader
1935	Importation to IFS and sale of contraceptives banned; Belfast disturbances
1936	IFS Senate abolished; IRA proscribed by de Valera; Governor-General eliminated under Constitution (Amendment No. 27) Act; link with Crown further weakened by External Relations Act
1937	Constitution of Éire replaces IFS constitution of 1922
1938	Agreement between de Valera and Chamberlain to end tariff dispute and return 'Treaty ports' to Éire; UK guarantee to subsidize NI social welfare payments to British levels
1939	IRA bombing campaign in Britain, and raid on Magazine Fort in Phoenix Park; Éire's declaration of neutrality implemented after outbreak of war (Sept.). Death of Yeats
1940	Deaths of IRA hunger-strikers in Éire; joint Anglo-Irish military consultations; covert imposition of economic sanctions by UK against Éire
1941	Worst German air-raids in Belfast and Dublin. Death of Joyce
1942	*The Great Hunger*, by Patrick Kavanagh
1944	Split in Irish Labour Party (healed 1950); American attempt to have Axis legations in Dublin closed
1945	Congress of Irish Unions formed after split in Trades Union Congress
1946	NI National Insurance aligned with British system
1947	Universal secondary schooling enacted in NI
1948	National Health Service introduced in NI; Irish Republic enacted (inaugurated Apr. 1949) after Costello's repeal of External Relations Act
1949	Ireland Act, giving UK's assurance to NI that partition would be perpetuated. *Cré na Cille*, by Máirtín Ó Cadhain
1951	Minister for Health resigns after hierarchy's campaign against Mother and Child Scheme (similar scheme put through by de Valera, 1953)
1952	*Waiting for Godot*, by Samuel Beckett
1954	IRA attacks in Armagh; *The Quare Fellow*, by Brendan Behan
1955	Republic admitted to United Nations Organization
1956–62	Border campaign by IRA
1958	First programme for Economic Expansion in Republic (others in 1963–4, 1969)
1959	Split healed with formation of Irish Congress of Trade Unions
1961	Republic's unsuccessful application to join European Economic Community (repeated 1967)
1963	Hillery's plan for universal secondary education in Republic

1964	First meetings of Lemass and O'Neill raise vain hopes of reconciliation; McAteer's Nationalist Party becomes official opposition at Stormont
1966	Anglo-Irish Free Trade agreement
1967	Northern Ireland Civil Rights Association founded
1968	Clash in Derry between CRA and police; O'Neill's programme for eliminating anti-Catholic discrimination in local government, housing, and franchise
1969	People's Democracy march from Belfast to Derry (Jan.); first in series of Belfast explosions (Mar.) and deaths in 'Troubles' (July); army drafted to NI after Protestant 'siege' of Bogside (Derry) following Apprentice Boys' parade (Aug.); reform of central and local franchise in NI (Dec.)
1970	Provisional Sinn Féin formed after split, reflecting similar split in IRA; initially multi-sectarian Ulster Defence Regiment replaces B Specials (formed 1920); Social Democratic and Labour Party formed from moderate nationalist groups
1971	Internment reintroduced; Paisley's Democratic Unionist Party founded
1972	'Direct Rule' imposed after episodes such as Derry's 'Bloody Sunday' (Jan.) in which soldiers killed thirteen CRA marchers, and bombing of Aldershot barracks; eleven killed in 'Bloody Friday' explosions caused by Belfast IRA (July); 'special position' of Catholic church expunged from Republic's constitution
1973	Republic and UK (including NI) enter EEC; proportional representation restored for NI local elections; Northern Ireland Assembly created, power-sharing executive agreed, and tripartite Sunningdale conference held
1974	Unionists leave Assembly (Jan.), general strike organized by Ulster Workers' Council (May), and direct rule reimposed (May); multiple killings in Dublin explosions (May) and Guildford and Birmingham pub bombings (Nov., Dec.)
1975	Northern Ireland Convention convened; NI internment suspended (abolished 1980)
1976	Convention collapses; British ambassador in Dublin killed; Republic's Emergency Powers Bill referred to Supreme Court by President, who subsequently resigned after ministerial denunciation. *North*, by Seamus Heaney
1978	Twelve killed by Provisionals' fire-bombs in Down restaurant
1979	Earl Mountbatten and relations killed in Co. Sligo and eight soldiers killed at Warrenpoint (Down), in August; relaxation of Republic's ban of contraceptives
1980	Founding of Aosdána. Brian Friel's *Translations* performed by Field Day Company, Derry.
1981	Death of Republican hunger-strikers followed by collapse of Provisionals' strategy of 'H-block' protests
1982	Multiple killings of soldiers at Knightsbridge (July) and Ballykelly, Co. Londonderry (Dec.)
1983	Futile All-Ireland Forum; referendum approves constitutional ban on abortion in Republic
1985	Anglo-Irish Agreement at Hillsborough, generating bitter Protestant protest
1986	Referendum confirms Republic's constitutional ban on divorce
1987	Eleven killed before Enniskillen service for Remembrance Sunday

ACKNOWLEDGEMENTS

The editor and publishers wish to thank the following who have kindly given permission to reproduce illustrations on the pages indicated. They are especially grateful to Brelda Baum and Leni McCullagh of RTE Illustrations Library for their help in researching pictures and for permission to reproduce those on pages 239 (Independent Newspapers), 244 (The Cashman Collection), 255 (The Cashman Collection).

Aerofilms 65 top; Revd Wm. P. Allen, Christian Brothers O'Connell School, Dublin 203; Ashmolean Museum, Oxford 105; J. Bamburg 61; the Marquess of Bath, Longleat House, Warminster, Wiltshire 132; Biblioteca Apostolica Vaticana 2 (MS Urb. Gr. 82 f. 63v–64); Bibliotheek van de Rijksuniversiteit, Ghent 107; Bodleian Library, Oxford 47 (MS Rawl B503 f. 32v), 101 left (MS Laud Misc 610 f. 9r), 101 right (MS Rawl B514 f. iii); British Library 53 (MS 13 B viii f. 26), 56, 87 (MS Harl 1319), 112, 130–1, 134–5, 144, 145, 154, 281; Trustees of the British Museum 150, 179 right, 306; Cambridge University Collection, copyright reserved 23, 46; the Syndics of Cambridge University Library 69 (J. T. Gilbert, *Facsimiles of the National Manuscripts of Ireland*, part III, plate XXXVII); His Grace the Archbishop of Canterbury, copyright reserved to the Church Commissioners and the Courtauld Institute of Art 176; His Grace the Archbishop of Canterbury and the Trustees of Lambeth Palace Library 97 top; Central Bank of Ireland 321; Civic Museum, Dublin 322; Cork Public Museum 236 bottom; Dr Maurice Craig 67, 166; Crawford Municipal Art Gallery, Cork 277; Crown Copyright, the Controller of HMSO/Department of the Environment, Northern Ireland 18; David H. Davison 71, 78, 81, 95, 97 bottom, 102; Dillon Antiques 179 left; Hugh Doran 173; the Drapers' Company 141 bottom; Dublin Corporation 62; the Dublin Institute for Advanced Studies 7 right; G. A. Duncan 264, 268, 269, 327, 335; Bríghid uí Éigeartaigh 334; Trustees of the Right Hon Olive, Countess Fitzwilliam's Chattels Settlement by permission of Lady Juliet de Chair 142; Gisèle Freund/the John Hillelson Agency 323; Christopher Gaisford St Lawrence 296; Genealogical Office, Dublin 138, 146; Hulton Picture Library 185, 197, 208, 221, 222, 227, 247, 251, 272, 324; the Illustrated London News Picture Library 192–3, 214; Trustees of the Imperial War Museum, London 249; Independent Newspapers, Dublin 244; the Irish Architectural Archive, Dublin 200 (William Garner, National Heritage Inventory Collection); Irish Press, Dublin 37; The Irish Times 325; Irish Tourist Board 116, 169, 175, 278; Jarrold and Sons 136 bottom left; D. Newman Johnson 65 bottom; Andrew Kavanagh and National Museum of Ireland 92; Leeds City Art Galleries 178; Raymond Mander and Joe Mitchenson Theatre Collection 284, 328; Mansell Collection 171, 188, 204, 218; George Morrison 258, 300; George Mott 77, 142, 143; Museum of Fine Arts, Boston 15; National Gallery of Ireland 164, 191, 205, 209, 276, 298, 311; National Library of Ireland 109, 119, 122, 129, 136 bottom right, 152–3, 157, 195 both, 196, 210, 219, 262, 282, 293, 318 right; National Museum of Ireland 11, 14, 39 left, 41, 42, 44, 49, 50, 51, 84, 217; National Portrait Gallery, London 123 right, 147, 308, 318 left; National Trust, Co. Down 162; North Down Borough Council, Bangor 140 top; Popperfoto 315; Private Collection 123 (left), 194, 202; Public Record Office of Northern Ireland 207, 232, 270; Commissioners of Public Works in Ireland 7 left, 29, 36, 43, 45, 52, 72, 99, 100, 137; Deputy of Keeper of Records, Belfast, and Ministry of Agriculture 140 bottom; Reform Club 187; Mrs Reichmann 314 (Ashmolean Museum, Oxford) 317 (the Hugh Lane Municipal Gallery of Modern Art, Dublin); Professor Alistair Rowan 136 top; Royal Irish Academy 90; St Patrick's College, Drumcondra 206; Roger Stalley 64; State Historical Society of Wisconsin 319; the Tate Gallery, London 126; Board of Trinity College, Dublin 16, 20, 32, 39 right, 47, 141 top, 182, 242, 279; Rod Tuach 330; Ulster Folk and Transport Museum 230; the Ulster Museum 198–9, 236 top, 266–7; Ulster Television 133; Board of Trustees of the Victoria and Albert Museum 312; A. P. Watt Ltd. on behalf of Anne Yeats and Michael B. Yeats/National Gallery of Ireland 309; A. P. Watt Ltd. on behalf of Anne Yeats and Michael B. Yeats/The Syndics of Cambridge University Library 288 (Jack Yeats, *Life in the West of Ireland*, 1912); A. P. Watt Ltd. on behalf of Anne Yeats and Michael B. Yeats/Windsor Castle, Royal Library © 1988 Her Majesty the Queen 289.

INDEX

PAGE numbers in italics refer to black and white illustrations or maps and their captions. Colour plates (which are unpaginated) are located by reference to the nearest page of text and are indicated by **bold**. Multiple references on a page are indicated by a figure in parentheses after the page number.

Gaelic names beginning with O are listed before anglicized forms beginning with O'. Otherwise, Gaelic forms are given in parentheses after the anglicized name. Dates, given primarily for identification, are normally of birth and death, but occasionally refer to tenure of office.